The Call of Africa
The Reformed Church in America Mission in the Sub-Sahara, 1948–1998

by
Morrell F. Swart

The Historical Series of the Reformed Church in America

No. 29

The Call of Africa
The Reformed Church in America Mission in the Sub-Sahara,
1948–1998

by
Morrell F. Swart

Wm. B. Eerdmans Publishing Co.
Grand Rapids, Michigan

ISBN 0-8028-4615-7

Body text set in Adobe New Caledonia
Chapter titles set in Adobe Garamond

To three godly men:
Bob, Jack, and Dick

The Historical Series of the Reformed Church in America

This series has been inaugurated by the General Synod of the Reformed Church in America, acting through its Commission on History, for the purpose of encouraging historical research and providing a medium wherein this knowledge may be shared with the academic community and with the members of the denomination in order that a knowledge of the past may contribute to right action in the present.

General Editor

The Rev. Donald J. Bruggink, Ph.D.
Western Theological Seminary

Contents

Illustrations

MAPS

x

Editor's Preface

The Call of Africa stands in the honored tradition of *Pioneers in the Arab World* by Dorothy Van Ess, *Sharifa* by Cornelia Dalenberg, and *Grace in the Gulf* by Jeanette Boersma. All were written by those who have given their lives in missionary service. While none claimed to be professional historians or missiologists, all spent their entire adult careers in the service of Christ in foreign lands.

The Historical Series of the Reformed Church in America is proud to include *The Call of Africa* in its series, because it, like its predecessors, records the history and experience of missions in the words of those who were there. It is the story of missions through the eyes of those who committed their lives to the spread of the gospel.

In *The Call of Africa*, we have the story of missions told through the eyes of a wife and mother who experienced the joys of birth and the tragedy of death in sub-Saharan Africa. It is a compelling, personal account of lives committed to spreading the good news of Christ's saving power.

The Historical Commission is grateful to Morrell F. Swart, her daughter, Gayle S. Smith, and all those who have contributed to the publication of this volume.

Donald J. Bruggink
General Editor

Foreword

As the final years of our life in Africa moved relentlessly to their conclusion, a salutary idea was born: I would attempt to write the story of the Reformed Church in America's first fifty years in mission in sub-Saharan Africa. Our sadness in leaving that much-loved continent would be mitigated by reliving that half-century as we recorded something of the experiences of all our RCA mission personnel in that land. It would also be a fitting gift to our church in gratitude for its many years of nurturing, unwavering support.

Correspondence on this project began in April 1990 when I received a letter from Dr. Donald Bruggink:

> Warren Henseler has informed me that you are writing a book... As editor of the Historical Series of the Reformed Church in America I am very interested in your manuscript. At the last meeting of the Commission on History I was charged to start investigating the possibilities of volumes on our work in both Africa and Japan...
>
> Warren suggested, and I think it an excellent idea, if you are willing, that we be in correspondence about the book as it develops...

With the hope that you will consider the Historical Series for the publication of your volume, I remain....

So the salutary idea was also an inspired one. We have moved along in the process with joy and excitement, eager that this work be a worthy gift to the church—but even more that throughout these pages the name of the Lord be exalted, and that the ultimate focus of the story be upon the mighty works of God and his faithfulness to his promises and to his people. If the reader senses clearly that God has been, and is today, the guiding hand, the enabling power, the master strategist, and the source of all grace, joy, peace, and love that are personified here, we will consider this book to have fulfilled its purpose.

Morrell F. Swart
Canon City, Colorado

Acknowledgments

Harambee in Swahili means "pulling together to make something happen."
Bringing this book into being was a *harambee* effort because everyone
mentioned on these pages has had a significant part in telling the story.

My fellow missionaries responded graciously and generously to my
requests for material, offering everything from bare facts to colorful events
from their careers.

My family has been consistently enthusiastic about this seven-year work.
My mother and sister and our children had saved countless letters that we
had written to them over the years. They were a rich source of memory-
jogging information.

When my powers of recollection failed, my husband Bob was a valuable
consultant. He also gladly wrote up some events in which I had not been
involved. And he read and critiqued the content of the rough manuscript.

Our daughter, Gayle Swart Smith, a teacher in Springfield, Massachusetts,
came to my aid at a critical moment—when Dr. Donald J. Bruggink, general
editor of the RCA Historical Series, suggested that I put the manuscript on
disks.

It was one thing to graduate from the African bush, where my manual
typewriter had served me well, to the culture of computers. But it was quite
another to go beyond elementary typing and printing to a more in-depth
probe of word-processing technology. Gayle heard my distress signal and

assured me that she could, and would, put the footnoted manuscript on floppy disks.

The permissions I received from publishers and authors to quote from their books have provided another dimension of authenticity to the account. The *Church Herald* permitted me to quote lavishly from many articles about the RCA's mission in Africa.

Nor could this work have progressed without Dr. Bruggink, who with patience, care, and kindliness guided and encouraged me through the labyrinthine ways of incipient authorship.

To all of these—as well as the Historical Commission, the copy editor, Terry De Young, and Russell L. Gasero for their respective roles in bringing the manuscript to excellence, and to Eerdmans Publishing Company for seeing it through the publishing process—I express my deep gratitude.

Prologue

When I was four years old, my parents, Robert and Wilda Webber, built a new house on Van Riper Avenue in Flushing, Long Island, New York. Van Riper Avenue was only three blocks long, an unpaved, insignificant street on the growing edge of town. But that location played a major role in the direction my life would take.

Eight years later, when I had completed sixth grade, living on Van Riper Avenue meant I could not move with my elementary school classmates into seventh grade; I had to go to a different school.

And I didn't want to! But little did I know the direction my life would take because I lived on Van Riper Avenue. School district boundaries sent me to the same school my mother had attended and put me in touch with a superb teacher named Charlotte Weihe.

Parsing sentences became a game in her grammar classes. Appreciation for music reached new heights under her direction. But in addition to her vocational excellence, I experienced another side of Charlotte Weihe—she, too, was a member of the Reformed Church in America. Her home was in nearby College Point, and she became a family friend.

One summer Charlotte took me to an interdenominational missionary conference at Northfield, Massachusetts. So spiritually impressive was this initial experience at Northfield that I saved my meager allowance week after week in order to return for several successive summers.

1

As a member of the RCA's Camp Eendracht, I met many of our church's missionaries: Edna Beekman, Helen Zander, Jean Walvoord,

Ida Scudder, Tena Holkeboer, and others. Each one in some way left an imprint on my life. Collectively, the quiet influence of their obvious joy in serving Christ overseas compelled me to consider a similar commitment.

When I was a high school senior, Charlotte Weihe planted in my mind the idea of attending Hope College in Holland, Michigan. I'd never heard of the place, but intuitively, as if a prophet had spoken, I knew that it was Hope College for me in 1938.

So it was, that with a $100 grant from a friend and a $100 scholarship from the Women's Board of Domestic Missions—added to what my parents could provide—I was endowed richly and was able to start my college career.

"Morrell is going west!" Grandmother Webber exclaimed.

It wasn't long before Bob Swart appeared on the westward horizon, and I discovered that God's purposes were taking shape—and his mysterious ways are not always past finding out!

Through quite different channels, Bob made the same discovery. He remembers that God spoke to him through his Christian home, which he describes this way:

> I had a father and mother who knew the Lord and served him faithfully in the small rural community of DeMotte, Indiana. The church was the focus of our lives. Attending services twice every Sunday was taken for granted. Perfect attendance in Sunday school was an aim worth striving for. Dad served on the consistory for many years; Mother was consistently active in the various programs of the church.
>
> We had a large home. Because my parents were gracious hosts, most of the visiting preachers and missionaries were our guests. Each of these people—among them, John Van Ess, Tena Holkeboer, Barney Luben, Bernard Rottschaefer—were used of God to plant seeds in my adolescent mind.
>
> My own ambition was to take over Dad's general store whose annual calendar, distributed community-wide, boasted the motto,

"Most Everything."

But Dad, a largely self-educated man, had other ideas for me, borne out of an experience in his boyhood. Whenever I talked about running the store someday, he would tell me this little story:

"When I was still a young boy, your grandfather took me to Holland, Michigan, to see Hope College. We walked around the campus once, and then he asked me, 'Do you want to go to college?'

"'No!' I said emphatically. There was no further discussion. But when I grew to adulthood, I realized my mistake. At least I went back and finished high school after dropping out for a few years.

"Now I want my children to have a college education. Period!"

So there would be no "running the store" for this son. But for what purpose would I go to college?

We lived next door to the town's only doctor. His office and all that was in it fascinated me. He sometimes let me accompany him on his calls around the countryside in his Maxwell touring car. The people respected him and really needed him. This aspect of being a doctor intrigued me, too. Did God want me to pursue a medical career?

But God actually spoke through another man.

A dynamic and able pastor, the Rev. Theodore Schaap, was called to our church. We became friends and I sought his counsel about my future. He urged me to consider the ministry.

"A doctor can help people temporarily," he would say. "But a pastor can help people for eternity."

This was persuasive talk. I began to lean away from medicine and toward a pastoral calling.

Following in the footsteps of several cousins, my freshman year was spent at Wheaton College. At first I was lonely and homesick.

How many times I wished I could jump on the Interurban and go home to work in the store!

I treasured the frequent letters from Dad written at the store on meat wrapping paper. He understood how I felt, but he encouraged me to stick it out—and things in time did improve.

The next year my younger sister and I both went to Hope College. And after some months, in God's wonderful and inscrutable way, my sister's best friend, Morrell Webber, became mine. Together we heard more clearly the missionary call.

This was fortified during the years at Western Theological Seminary when missionaries came as guests to speak to students and talk personally with them about missions. My summer assignment to do American Indian work in Mescalero, New Mexico, was another milestone in our search for God's will.

The seeds sown years earlier were sprouting and about to bear fruit.

After a five-year courtship, Bob and I were married in June 1944 at my home church in Flushing. Bob had just graduated from seminary and had accepted a call to become the pastor of the Grace Reformed Church in Fond du Lac, Wisconsin.

We were on our way together into the days and years ahead, curious what God's intentions were for the long term. While it seemed almost certain we would be sent overseas eventually, for the time being that didn't matter. Grace Church needed a pastor, God had called us to fill that need, and in the heady confidence of youth we "had the world by the tail." We planned to add experience to our resume as we learned what it meant to be his servants on the home front.

It was enough for us.

And it was enough for almost two years. Valerie Vern joined our family in 1945. Her sweetness and beauty added to the joy of our marriage. Our days were peaceful; our hearts content.

The year before we were married, I attended Biblical Seminary in New York on East 49th Street. Great courses, great teachers, great student body—among them a young Mennonite woman whose single-hearted purpose was to go to Africa as a missionary.

The very thought made me shudder. How thankful I was that the Reformed Church had no mission work in Africa; there was no danger of being sent there!

"I'll go to China, Lord, or Japan, or India, or Arabia, but I'm so glad I'll not have to set foot on the soil of the mysterious Dark Continent. Whatever its charms, I am blind to them; whatever hand beckons, I'll turn my back.

"I'll go where you want me to go, dear Lord—but of course it won't be to Africa, because you know, Lord, our church doesn't...."

And then the unthinkable happened.

In the mid-1940s, the small, conservative, Philadelphia-based United Presbyterian Church and the Reformed Church began talks on merging. As part of the wooing process, the United Presbyterians invited the Reformed Church to join them in their long history of mission work in what was then the Anglo-Egyptian Sudan—in Africa!

On September 11, 1946, the Rev. Dr. Glenn Reed, secretary of the Board of Foreign Missions of the United Presbyterian Church, forwarded to the RCA Board of Foreign Missions the following recommendation:

> That the Board of Foreign Missions of the Reformed Church in America be invited to appoint missionaries to the South Sudan with the understanding that...its first group of appointees will participate in missionary work among the Anuaks....[1]

Dr. Don McClure, already a veteran of nearly twenty years as a missionary in Sudan, who in recent years had opened work among the Anuak tribe, made a profound impression as he traveled to RCA churches, colleges, seminaries, and the Board of Foreign Missions. As a result, although the merger of the two church bodies never took place, the United Presbyterian invitation to become involved with it in Sudan was endorsed enthusiastically and accepted.

The Board of Foreign Missions published a pamphlet, "Our New Field—Africa":

> The Board of Foreign Missions, after careful study and full consultation with the General Synod, has decided to open a new field in Africa, among the primitive peoples of the South Sudan. Here whole tribes and areas are completely without the gospel.
>
> Since 1903 another denomination, the United Presbyterian, has been working in the Anglo-Egyptian Sudan, among the tribes near the borders of Egypt and Ethiopia. Centering attention upon one tribe, certain of the missionaries have given themselves intensively to that one group, reducing their language to writing, opening schools, providing a medical ministry, preparing the ground patiently and

[1] Dr. Glenn Reed, copy of a report, September 11, 1946. Joint Archives of Holland, Hope College.

persistently for the eventual establishment of an independent, indigenous Christian church.

It is this type of comprehensive approach which the Rev. Donald McClure and his colleagues have been employing with the Anuak tribe in the South Sudan and it is this kind of inclusive program which the Reformed Church hopes to carry on among another tribe still to be designated, possibly the Murle.

The Reformed Church traditionally has cooperated with other groups on the mission fields; it has never sought to perpetuate its own organization or institutions but has helped to build a church rooted in the land and suited to the culture of the people.

That is its plan again in this instance. No new machinery is to be created or elaborate buildings erected. The main emphasis will be on the contribution of personnel, consecrated, trained missionary recruits. They will be named and trained by our church but serve in the Sudan Mission already at work.

Evangelists will be needed, teachers, doctors, specialists in Christian education, child welfare, agriculture, and the like, so that an all-round ministry may be offered—an introduction to that abundant life in Christ Jesus.

Naturally the Reformed Church is eager to know about this new field which it is entering, what the people are like, their language and religion, and the conditions which our missionaries will face.

Sudan is under the dominion of Egypt and Great Britain, the latter having the controlling voice. The official language of the South Sudan used to be Arabic but now is English. The tribal peoples, however, all have their own spoken tongues....The government is training Sudanese as government clerks and army officers, raising up African leaders to serve their own people. Happily, the government holds a most favorable attitude toward Protestant missions....

The [southern] Sudanese are animists, believing in spirits all about them, some of them good spirits but most of them evil ones, whom one must constantly guard against and propitiate. The missionaries will have to start "from scratch." They will need to join the great company of missionaries before them in other parts of the world who have lived among primitive peoples, given them a written language, and then laboriously translated the Bible into the tongue of the people.

It was ten years before the United Presbyterians baptized their first convert. Now there are well established congregations, made up of clean-living, God-fearing, consecrated Christian folk. It is our hope to bring some other tribe in Sudan similar opportunities. The evangelization of a whole tribe—that is our aim, and then another and yet another tribe.

The first missionary to go to our new Africa field has been appointed. She is Miss Wilma Kats of Nebraska, a graduate of Central College, now teaching in Denver. Other candidates for missionary service in Africa will be appointed later in 1946.

The field is waiting.

The first missionary has been appointed.

The church is eager to go forward.

Prayers, gifts, lives will be needed if we are indeed to "go in and possess the land."[2]

Back in Wisconsin, I still had no qualms. The negotiations were taking place half a continent away in New York and seemed no threat to our tranquillity. Besides, I was beginning to wonder if God had something quite different in mind for us.

Bob had received a call to return to our American Indian Mission at Mescalero, New Mexico. He had thoroughly enjoyed his summer there following his middle year in seminary. He had even wanted to take me there for our honeymoon. Surely he would accept.

But, inexplicably, he declined.

Sometime later, a second call came from Mescalero. Again his reply was in the negative.

When the third call came urgently through the mail, I thought that this surely must be the very voice of God, and I mentally began preparing myself to move from Wisconsin to New Mexico.

But so steadfast was my husband's resolve, so certain was he that God would soon open the way for us to move in quite another direction, to serve him in another land, that the third summons received the same answer as the others: a gracious "No, this is not God's will for us now."

Then I began to realize how serious a matter this was—the matter of being sensitive to the will of God in order to discern his plans and purposes. Bob was several steps ahead of me in this area; I had a lot of catching up to do.

[2] Board of Foreign Missions, RCA, 1946. Joint Archives of Holland, Hope College.

It was February 1946.

We had a delightful guest at the parsonage one weekend. The Rev. Barnerd Luben, a Board of Foreign Missions staff member, had come from New York—no small distance in those days. Barney was a smiling, cheerful person with whom we felt at ease immediately. We had anticipated his coming. He would be speaking at church on Sunday morning.

And I suppose he did—I'm sure he was well received—but I have no recollection of it.

The one only thing I remember about that weekend visit is a stunning question. It pierced my ears and seared my soul like a bolt from heaven.

Very casually, Barney had asked, "How would you like to go to Africa?"

No preliminaries. No gradual easing into the subject. Just the straightforward question, asked gently, with a smile.

Yet the whole house seemed to echo and reverberate with the sound. The words began to sound less like a quiet probe from a board secretary and more like a thundering command from the Lord: "Thou shalt GO!"

I wished with all my heart that the question had never been uttered, and that Barney had never come. I was not feeling so "at ease" with him now. I was filled with dread, all the more because I couldn't imagine taking our lovely little daughter to Africa.

Oh, how ignorant I was. How fearful. How lacking in the quiet spirit of waiting upon the Lord for his direction.

Bob had no such reaction. He was already committed to going anywhere.

I had told the Lord the same thing when I was fifteen years old. It was at one of the missionary conferences at Northfield. In a moment of joyful, abandoned worship, I had said to God, "I am yours. I want to serve you. I'll go anywhere for you."

Now was I saying, "Yes, Lord, anywhere but Africa"? All evidence pointed that way. Where was that lavish abandon and fearless commitment of ten years before?

After some time, however, the patient, forbearing, almost imperceptible work of the Spirit began within me.

Had I told the Lord at one time that I'd go anywhere for him? Did anywhere include Africa, or didn't it?

Well—I guess—yes, Lord.

Could I say to the Lord, "Anywhere BUT Africa"?

No.

Does having a child nullify a previous commitment?

No.

Could I not step out in faith for my child as well as for myself and my husband?

Yes, oh yes, Lord!

At the end of six months, I was able to make a recommitment to him: anywhere, Lord, even Africa, if that's where you want us to go.

In 1947 Valerie's sister, Gayle Elizabeth, was born, and the Lord gave me perfect peace about taking two beautiful little girls across the seas.

We were commissioned that fall at American Reformed Church in DeMotte, Indiana, with the pastor, the Rev. Tunis Miersma, and the pastor of First Reformed Church, the Rev. Fred Dolfin, presiding. Dr. George Mennenga, one of Bob's professors at Western Theological Seminary and a member of the Board of Foreign Missions, conducted the commissioning service.

By the time we set sail in January 1948, together with Don and Lyda McClure, their three children, and Wilma Kats, all fears were gone. The days of preparation had further whetted our anticipation for whatever lay ahead, and as the old Italian troopship Saturnia churned its way out into New York harbor that winter day, leaving loved ones farther behind, we experienced as we never had before the realization that our sole reliance was in our heavenly Father, into whose strong hands we had trustingly placed ours.

Many people had come to the pier to see us off, among them, members of the Department of Women's Work. The minutes of their next meeting included this report:

> Just this past week on Friday, Rev. and Mrs. Robert Swart and their two babies, and also Wilma Kats, left for Alexandria on the first stage of their journey to the Anglo-Egyptian Sudan in Africa. Their ship, the Saturnia, was supposed to sail at noon on Friday. Then the time of departure was changed to midnight. Finally the ship actually sailed on Saturday at noon, although we did not know that until Saturday afternoon. When we left the ship at 12:45 at night, we were told that it would sail at about four o'clock that morning.
>
> I wish that all of you might have been at the pier that night. What an inspiring sight it was! There were the Swarts with their darling babies, the older one being held by Grandpa Webber and the

younger one by a family friend, Rev. Frederick Bosch. The Swarts were completely surrounded by relatives and friends. Mrs. Swart's mother and dad were there, as well as her sister, her grandmother, and others from her family. Mr. Swart's folks had not been able to make the trip from DeMotte, Indiana.

Mr. and Mrs. Kats had come from Holland, Nebraska, with Wilma to see her off. It was their first trip East and it was an experience that they say they will never forget....

There were twenty-one people at the boat from the First Holland Church of Passaic, New Jersey, which is one of Wilma's supporting churches. They had brought her a gorgeous bouquet of flowers and a large box containing gifts, one package to be opened each day of Wilma's journey. After bidding farewell to her, they had a prayer service led by their pastor, Rev. [Elton] Eenigenburg, and they sang a hymn together. Rev. and Mrs. Schermer of the Wortendyk Church were also there. They had entertained Wilma and her parents during the latters' stay in the East. The Hospitality Committee owes them a debt of gratitude for all they did to make Wilma's last days in this country before sailing so pleasant.

We visited the McClures in their stateroom. Their children, ages 12, 9, and 8, were all sound asleep as we visited together. Mrs. McClure was looking forward to their family being together during their trip to Egypt since they soon are to be separated. The children will stay in school in Egypt, 2,200 miles from the McClures' final destination. This is just one of the sacrifices these pioneer missionaries are called upon to make.

We visited the Swarts in their stateroom after their babies were settled. Mrs. Swart had managed in a short time to get things organized in their small quarters. They had fifteen pieces of baggage. Anyone who has ever taken care of a baby can imagine just what it would mean to care for a baby four and a half months old and another not yet three years old in such small quarters. Fortunately, their stateroom was at the end of the passageway and there was some extra space in the passageway for their luggage. It made one stop to think in rather a serious way on seeing a large case marked "Medicine," because that case reminded us of the fact that these babies were being taken to a place 150 miles from the nearest doctor. Just one more sacrifice that these young people are making!

One of the high spots of an evening which seems to be full of inspiring moments, was the privilege I had of introducing the Swarts, Wilma Kats, and the McClures to two fine young people of our church, Lee Crandall and Katherine Bosch. As you all probably know, these young folks are also planning to go out as missionaries, Katherine following in the footsteps of her parents, Dr. and Mrs. Taeke Bosch. They are to be married in two weeks. After finishing their work at Biblical Seminary and other preparatory work needed, they hope to go out to one of our mission fields....

Mrs. Eloise Bosch (sister-in-law of Katherine Bosch) was also there that evening to bid farewell to her school friend, Mrs. Swart. It was rather touching to see these friends bid farewell to each other. They wondered when they would see each other again. Inasmuch as the Bosches will be in China in a few years, there seemed little likelihood that their furloughs would come together for a long time to come.

This report would not be complete without saying a word about the parents of these young missionaries. I was very much impressed by their fine Christian spirit and their attitude. There were two groups of parents, coming from different parts of the country and from different walks of life, one set of parents being city folks and the other being from the country. But they were alike in their Christian faith. They seemed to be happy that they were able to give their children to Christ on the mission field. I will not forget their faces for a long time. Their sacrificial love cannot help making one feel inspired.

And so these pioneer missionaries have set sail on the new venture of the Reformed Church. May I urge you all to pray that they may have a safe journey and that they may be richly blessed as they launch out on this great undertaking for Christ and his kingdom.[3]

[3] Minutes of the Department of Women's Work, RCA, January 13, 1948. Joint Archives of Holland, Hope College.

Seasickness laid us low the very first day. How that ship rolled! As Bob and I lay in our bunks feeling the vessel lean to one side, then slowly right itself, only to tilt in the other direction, we watched Valerie through slitted eyes, running up the hill of our "stateroom" and then down.

"See, Mommy, Daddy! I go up, I go down! Whee!"

And Gayle—she slept well, merely being "rocked in the cradle of the deep."

Don McClure prepared her formula and washed her diapers until we acquired our sea legs, thus introducing us to the reassuring and precious fact that, in leaving home, we had gained other kinfolk, the mission family, who would always be there for mutual support and encouragement.

Once the *mal de mer* was over, sailing the ocean blue became delightful. It was a thrill to pass through the Straits of Gibraltar and to know that to our right lay the continent so long dreaded, but now, strangely appealing. There were stops at Genoa, Naples, Piraeus, and Haifa—and there the delight in travel temporarily ended: the McClure children and Valerie came down with measles!

Lyda and all the children and I were banished immediately to the sick bay, a room in the stern of the ship right over the propeller. Aside from the vibrations and noise, and having to be separated from the others, we were comfortable and adequately cared for.

Lyda's calm spirit ministered to mine. The children improved.

Word had been sent ahead to the American Presbyterian Mission in Alexandria, Egypt, about the McClure-Swart situation, so it was no surprise to them that we were held back from disembarking until all the other passengers had left the ship. They were also aware that we were under orders to be placed in quarantine at the mission for ten days before we could proceed to Sudan.

Lyda McClure remembers the reaction of the Egyptian Department of Health officials: "Your disease is nothing; we have a cholera epidemic!"

But we were quarantined anyway, and we spent those ten days as guests of gracious Presbyterian missionaries, the Rev. and Mrs. Charles Russell, who had lived in Egypt for many years.

Here we were, in Africa, but hardly the Africa we had envisioned. Rather, we found ourselves in a huge, bustling city in the Arab north. Looking down from the windows of the great, gray apartment building which housed the mission personnel, we were fascinated as we watched the milling crowds of Egyptians in their "costumes" which were, of course, their everyday wearing apparel: the women in their head-to-toe black *abas*, and the men in their flowing white *jellabiyahs* and coiled turbans. A few of the men were decked out in what appeared to me to be ordinary Western pajamas.

Were some of the people down there on the city streets Christians? Probably. There was a strong Coptic Church in Egypt as well as an emerging Evangelical Church. But the majority, by far, were Muslims. As I continued to watch them, so many walking on the sidewalks, so many driving on the crowded blacktop street, I wondered if any of those particular ones had heard the good news. "Isa," the prophet, they would know about. But "Isa," Son of God and Savior? And if they had heard, had any accepted him? Had they rejected him?

My heart yearned over them with a newly awakened concern for the followers of Mohammed.

The ten days passed swiftly. Our missionary hosts seemed very old to us. But they were so gracious and patient as we gathered around their big dining room table three times a day.

The only meals I recall were the breakfasts when we discovered the goodness of *bulgur* porridge (coarse crushed wheat) sweetened with equally coarse sugar crystals and enriched with *gamoosa* (water buffalo) milk. It was delectable!

When the quarantine was lifted, we were soon on our way by train and Nile riverboat the length of Egypt. We were amazed at the desert with its

A felucca *on the Nile*

vast expanses of sandy wastes and dunes, but also with its rocks and boulders and its many high *jebels* or hills. People lived in small isolated communities along the upper reaches of the Egyptian Nile. Sometimes only one or two flat-roofed adobe dwellings were in sight.

Ours wasn't the only craft on the river. We marveled as we watched the single-masted *feluccas* tacking from bank to bank, manned by Egyptians who were masters at sailing these ages-old river vessels, regardless of the direction of the wind. They really knew their great river, from the impassable cataracts in the south to the delta that spreads out north of Cairo—the Nile that dates back in history to the time of Moses and the pharaohs, the Nile that is the lifeblood, so to speak, of this ancient country.

At Assiut in Upper Egypt, the three McClure children stayed behind to attend boarding school for the first time. Margaret was 12 years old, Don Jr. was 9, and Polly was 8.

We were amazed at their parents' outwardly casual acceptance of this facet of missionary life. Don made a statement at the time that I have never forgotten: "It is a spiritual experience to trust your children entirely to the Lord." He and Lyda were living out this philosophy on a high plane of faith, and we tucked this gem of truth into our hearts for future reference, thankful that we wouldn't have to face this kind of separation for what then seemed many long years.

The last part of our journey to our initial destination, Khartoum, was by train through the seemingly endless desolate desert of the northern Anglo-Egyptian Sudan. We stopped along the way at every tiny depot with its cluster of round, pointed-roof buildings. Men, women, and children gathered outside beneath the train windows to see who was on board, to hear the news, and to stare unabashedly at the foreigners. Some were hawkers with a few strange fruits or breads to sell.

"How do these people cope," we wondered, "posted way out here in these barren wastelands?"

Surely the train was a link for them to family and friends in Atbara, Khartoum, or Omdurman. As the train clickety-clacked through the sandy wilderness, sending out clouds of sooty smoke, we drew ever closer to the towns of the northern Sudan, and our excitement rose. We were almost surfeited with newness, and the end was not yet.

However, we were traveling in the country that would become our home; we were breathing Sudani air; we were observing some of its landscapes and its people.

We thought we would live in this land for a lifetime. We had no idea that it would be for only fifteen years.

I
From Khartoum to Akobo

Under the headline "First News from Africa," this item was printed in a paper put out by the Department of Women's Work in early 1948. I had written to them from Khartoum:

> We are here—not at Akobo, but after having taken this long to get this far, it does seem as if we've almost reached home. Bob is attending the annual meeting of the mission association held on the mission compound. I would be there, too, if our baby Gayle had not become ill. She is improving but is still very weak from the infection and fever. Otherwise, all is well with us.
>
> We found our journey fascinating in spite of seasickness and the measles. The trip up the Nile by steamer from Shellal to Wadi Halfa was particularly interesting. We expect to proceed southward March 13.
>
> The McClures learned this week that their home needs considerable repair, that their vegetable garden is no more, and several of Don's cows have died. So the children and I may stay in Malakal while the rest go on to remedy the situation. Wilma is well and is enjoying it all, too.
>
> It hardly seems possible that all that is happening here in our lives now is a result of a momentous decision made on the greatest

15

day of our lives in July 1946. We are very happy—and only because we are doing the perfect will of our Lord Jesus Christ. We are so sure of that.[1]

Khartoum was impressive.

This capital of the Anglo-Egyptian Sudan, located at the confluence of the Blue and White Nile Rivers, was a beautiful desert town. It boasted wide, palm-lined boulevards, fine hotels, office buildings, shops, and markets with every kind of merchandise.

Greeks and Armenians ran the more sophisticated businesses, while the Arab merchants managed a thriving trade in the *suqs* and kiosks, dealing in fresh produce, brass, ivory, gold, locally made furniture and cloth, spices, and herbs.

The governor-general's palace, the home at that time of Sir James Robertson, stood in all its grandeur amid palms and bougainvillea, while in other parts of the city, fine statues of Lord Kitchener on his horse and General "Chinese" Gordon on his camel were proud, and at the same time painful, reminders of the British conquest of Sudan in the late nineteenth century.

History, and apparent prosperity, abounded. In the early morning hours and in the cool of the late afternoon and evening, the streets thronged with people.

"But where do all these people live?" we wondered. "We haven't seen any dwellings."

"They live behind all those walls that line the streets," we were told.

Each home was surrounded by a high wall for complete privacy. The American Presbyterian Mission headquarters and guest house were located on a dusty street near the shopping area. It also was surrounded by a wall.

When we arrived that hot February day, the guest quarters were all occupied because the annual association meeting was in progress. Missionaries from the South Sudan as well as the North had gathered for this event, and there was no room in that inn for the new arrivals.

But it had been arranged that Wilma Kats stay with missionary teachers at the Girls' School in Khartoum North, and reservations had been made for

---

[1] Department of Women's Work, RCA, 1948. Joint Archives of Holland, Hope College.

the McClures and Swarts at the Victoria Hotel—not one of the "fine" hotels, despite its regal name. But it was comfortable and clean, and not too far from the mission. Its courtyard was flamboyant with bougainvillea blooms. We basked in this exotic setting.

Only a few details stand out as I look back to that month-long sojourn in Khartoum:

• The fried eggs at the hotel swam in grease, but the toast was delicious. It was served with real British marmalade, dark and bitter, and to this day we prefer it to the sweet American variety.

• Seven-month-old Gayle became seriously ill with bacillary dysentery. But thanks to good medical care and the recently discovered sulfas, she was soon on the mend and bounced back quickly to her usual healthy self.

• Valerie learned a few words in Arabic. She particularly liked the sound of *minfudlik*, meaning "please." Proficiency in saying this word changed her pronunciation of two names: Mohammed became "Minhammad" and McClure became "MinClure." How we laughed!

• Being there for the association meeting made it possible for us to meet several of those missionaries who would be our colleagues in the South. This was helpful. They were all so friendly and welcoming, and we found ourselves more eager than ever to move on to our destination in Upper Nile Province.

• When the meeting was over, we were all able to leave the hotel and take up residence at the mission headquarters. That was a step up, though the Arab music blaring from the coffee house across the street was, to our unaccustomed ears, raucous and unpleasant, and we wished they would turn down the volume.

• The McClures took us to one of the *suqs* in nearby Omdurman to see about furniture for our yet-to-be-built home at Akobo Post. We ordered wooden chairs with woven rope seats and backs, and cushions for comfort, and dressers and *dulabs* (clothes closets) for our bedrooms. When these items were made, they would be transported by Nile steamer to the province capital, Malakal, and then by province steamer up the Sobat and Pibor Rivers to Akobo.

At last all the business affairs were completed. We were now legal residents of the Anglo-Egyptian Sudan. Our work permits were in hand. Our shopping was done.

Our first purchase: pith helmets

Bob was costumed in Sudan-style khaki shorts, and we both sported what was a "must" in those days: pith helmets for protection against the equatorial sun. (A few years earlier, we would have been advised also to buy woolen tummy bands and spinal pads for further protection. The efficacy of such instruments of torture must have been disproved—or else there had been a quiet rebellion!)

Our ocean freight arrived in Khartoum by train from Port Sudan. All our worldly goods came, as well as the little green Jeep and its trailer, a gift from First Reformed and American Reformed Churches in DeMotte, Indiana. Weeks before, this vehicle had been delivered at the docks in New York City, where all the wheels had been removed and the whole outfit squeezed unceremoniously into sizable crates for the long sea journey to Sudan's only port on the Red Sea.

Now it was in Khartoum. The McClures' similarly crated station wagon had arrived on the same train. These boxes, like oversized Christmas presents, were "unwrapped" by scores of coolies, each one as eager as we were to see the contents, and each aspiring to outdo the other with marvelous gesticulations in impressing the foreigner with his strength and expertise. What a cacophony of loud, unintelligible sounds surrounded us! It was bewildering, but we were thankful for the assistance.

Unfortunately their help wasn't always first-rate. For example, the wheel nuts, which had been cut with a left-hand thread, were forced onto bolts by turning them to the right, needing more than one oath in the name of their prophet to get them on. But the task finally was accomplished, and as we drove away there were cheers, not only because the job was done, but also for the generous remuneration that had been given.

The time had now come to prepare for the long, rough journey to the South. Food, water, tents, fuel, tools—everything needed to maintain the vehicles and the travelers had to be on board.

The children and I stayed behind in Khartoum, to follow a week later by plane. Bob recalls the adventure of this first overland trek through sparsely inhabited territory:

> As we started out, we had no road maps, just lots of word-of-mouth advice to guide us southward. But we also knew that we would be in the hands of the Lord all the way.
>
> Don and Lyda McClure in their shiny new Ford station wagon, and Wilma Kats and I in the shiny green Jeep pulling its overloaded trailer, made up our caravan.
>
> The first days brought us through many Arab villages. The Sudanese are hospitable people, and we were always warmly welcomed. Their tea shops were refreshing rest stops as we enjoyed sweet, hot tea or strong, bitter coffee along with new and interesting breads and Marie biscuits from England.
>
> But soon these spots became fewer and fewer. The road petered out, and ahead of us were mere tracks in the desert with clumps of scraggly trees or jagged bare hills in the distance to lead us on the way.
>
> Then we were really on our own. If we were thirsty, we'd make our own tea, using a kerosene primus stove. Occasionally we'd see a sheep herder or a small settlement. But there were a few days when we saw no one. Don, however, having lived in Sudan for many years, knew how to cope in such vast and sparse environments. So he was undaunted. We followed his lead.

Farther south it was exciting when we began to see wild animals and strange birds, more trees and streams, and vistas of grass stretching as far as the eye could see. And then the tall, very tall, people of the South began to appear with their herds. They had made their dry season cattle camps with small grass shelters in which to sleep. We smelled for the first time the fragrance of dung fires. Those fires smoldered all night to keep the mosquitoes away.

The herders—taller, blacker people than I'd ever seen before— would cover their bodies with the gray ashes from the dung fires for their own personal mosquito repellent. Thus bedecked, they looked like creatures from another planet.

Now it was warm milk, rather than tea, that was offered to us. But again, the refreshment was given with grace and generosity. The gourds, filled with foaming milk fresh from the cow, were proffered with both hands, a customary sign of wholehearted hospitality.

After a week of many new sights and smells, countless bumps and tooth-rattling jars—and a growing admiration for the abilities of the Jeep—we entered Malakal, the capital of Upper Nile Province. We were driving once again on macadam streets—busy, small-town thoroughfares not only for vehicles of a variety of unfamiliar makes and vintages, but also for the citizenry and tribal folk who wandered in from nearby settlements.

As we drove into town, we had the impression that the Southerners were just as friendly as we'd found the Northerners to be, just as proud of their culture and way of life, and just as curious about us. I'm sure they wondered, "Who are these people from far away? Why have they come here?"

They would soon discover that we had come to join others in proclaiming the good news of Jesus Christ.

It hadn't been easy seeing Bob and the others start off for, what was to us, the Great Unknown. But I did understand. It would have been a doubly difficult journey with the children. Since we had a room at the mission guest house, we were among friends and were well cared for. Our reservations for flying to Malakal were in hand already. So, by focusing on that date, my high spirits returned, and the time passed pleasantly.

For the children and me, it was no gradual approach to the southern region as it had been for Bob and his fellow travelers. In less than two hours, we were whisked from Khartoum to Malakal; from an Arab city surrounded by desert to a sub-Saharan African town built on cottonsoil with savanna on every side. The only feature they shared was the Nile.

But upon landing, my eyes searched for only one person—and Bob was there, of course. What a glad reunion for us all! We drove immediately to the mission compound where we were further welcomed by all those living there, and particularly by the hosts at the guest house, the Rev. Matt and Ruby Gilliland. We felt part of the family right away.

The mission was a colorful place, bright with bougainvillea and fragrant with the creamy blooms of frangipani. Some of the yards were bordered by low crown-of-thorn bushes with their tiny green leaves and brilliant red flowers.

And Malakal itself was an attractive town. Everywhere there were flowering shrubs and trees, and along the streets down toward the Nile were the great spreading banyans that send down extra shoots from their branches. These take root in the ground and become secondary trunks.

Along the river were the grand homes of the British officials. We had only a passing acquaintance with these dwellings. We became much more familiar with the Greek shops in town which were operated by their owners, Limnios and Stavros.

Since their stocks were not plentiful when we first arrived, we were advised by our more experienced friends to order our canned goods from a wholesale house in New York. This we did for some years. However, such staples as flour, sugar, salt, rice, tea, and coffee were readily available at the Greek shops. These supplies generally were transported to our mission station commercially—in the dry season by truck and during the rains by paddle-wheel steamer.

By far the most intriguing aspect of the Malakal scene were the Africans themselves, the Sudanese of the South. With the exception of a few traders, we had left the Arabs hundreds of miles to the north among their mosques and minarets. Not having traveled overland, it was here that I had my first encounter with people who were really black, and many of them extraordinarily tall and lean.

It was obvious, even to us newcomers, that there were members of several different tribal groups in town. We were told that a Shulla (sometimes known as Shilluk) man could be recognized by the raised beads of scar tissue in a row from temple to temple just above his eyebrows. Nuers were distinguished by six thin, straight lines of scars, also from temple to temple, across their foreheads. Dinkas had similar markings.

Many men and women wore decorative plugs protruding from holes in their lower lips, some of bone, others of wood or woven wire. These could signify membership in a particular age-set. Earrings and necklaces of beads and seeds—sometimes even safety pins or keys—adorned the women.

The most common mode of dress—and this was true of both men and women—was a length of *demoriya*, or unbleached muslin, draped under the left arm and drawn together in a knot over the right shoulder. Simple, modest, cool.

But Nuer men usually were not so clothed. A proud people, they gloried in themselves just as God had made them. Somehow a black body didn't seem quite so naked as a white one. Nevertheless, it was a while before I could accept this state of affairs casually!

Now that we were in Malakal, we had only one more lap to go in order to reach Akobo Post where the Anuak people lived. One more lap, we thought. As it turned out, we actually had two laps ahead of us because Valerie came down with dysentery and we had to delay our departure. It seemed best to move only as far as Doleib Hill in Shulla country where we stayed with the mission doctor and his family, Dr. and Mrs. Albert Roode, and their sons Peter, John, and baby Philip.

How grateful we were for Al's and Ruth's unstinting hospitality, and for Al's expertise in caring for Valerie. She was a very sick little girl.

The week at "The Hill," about an hour's drive from Malakal, was also a helpful period of orientation for us—a giant step toward realizing something of what life would be like in the even more remote bush. The Roodes' house was mud-walled, thatch-roofed, and had a concrete floor. We learned about coping with, and appreciating, the small household lizards that are harmless and help keep the insect population in check. One variety of lizard was active in the daytime; others came out at night. We were warned to be on the lookout for scorpions and snakes.

All the drinking water, which came from the river, had to be filtered through twenty-gallon clay *zeers*, then boiled, cooled, and poured into long-necked clay *goolas* for further cooling. With two families to serve, the *goolas* had a hard time keeping pace with our thirst; most of our drinks were lukewarm.

During this blessed delay at Doleib Hill, we were impressed again at how the mission family functioned, and how quickly and solidly close ties were forged. The RCA and the UPC had merged in mission in the Anglo-Egyptian Sudan.

Don McClure had gone ahead to Akobo in the Jeep; Lyda and Wilma had stayed behind with us. We were so grateful. Finally, after about a week, we were ready to roll again. Valerie was well, having gained strength rapidly once the bug was vanquished. So late one afternoon we started out in the McClures' station wagon. The rear section had been arranged so that the children could sleep. We would be traveling all night—the coolest time to drive across the flat savanna. We would leave the Nile far behind as we made our way eastward through the Sobat River country where the Dinka and Nuer live, and over to the Pibor River, where we would find Akobo Post and the Anuak tribe.

The children slept well. But there was no sleep for the adults. This was so exciting! In just a few hours we'd be THERE, and we certainly didn't want to miss any of the sights along the way.

Sights, after dark? Yes, eyes! Thousands of them, illumined by our car lights. We have no idea how many eyes we saw that night as the station wagon bumped along on the cottonsoil track. Countless! Our lights picked out herd after herd of various kinds of antelope. It was like seeing cities of tiny lights here and there in the inky black of an African moonless night. A lone hyena loped across the road. Nightjars, resting on the warm track, flew up vertically in front of us. It was a night to remember.

As day dawned, we were approaching Akobo Post.

"There's the windcharger!" Lyda exclaimed.

We could barely make it out as it towered slenderly in the distance. But Lyda knew the landscape and was familiar with the horizon. She was so happy to be getting back after an absence of two years.

We passed through Akobo's government center where the British district commissioner lived, with the police lines and the Arab merchant shops in their appointed locations. Then we were on the mile-long straight stretch to the mission, *neem* trees bordering the way. Coming closer we could see the thatched peaks of the McClure house nestled in more *neem* and eucalyptus trees.

Don, along with scores of coal-black Anuaks wearing the traditional *demoriya* garb or khaki shorts, were waiting to greet us all.

It was April 5, 1948. We had come home.

II
The First Year

For several weeks, we all lived together in the McClures' glorified African home.

Don and Lyda had opened work at Akobo Post a few years earlier, having been missionaries first in North Sudan and then at Doleib Hill in the South. So when we arrived, we were not surprised to see a school compound, a once-cultivated garden area, and an irrigation system, as well as the McClure dwelling.

This house was based on a unique floor plan shaped roughly like a short-shafted anchor. Four round rooms, or *tukls*, located at the extremities of the design, were joined together by screened verandas. And the whole was roofed over with rough pole trusses and covered with thatch. The thick walls were of dried mud, or adobe. Reed mats made a suitable, sweepable carpet for the floors and gave off a pleasing fragrance as well.

Outlined in the front by lantana hedges, the house faced the Pibor River, which is low between steep banks and out of view during the dry season but highly visible and flowing swiftly during the rains. Lyda's expertise with plants and flowers made the path from the front door to the river a riot of color and beauty, with a back drop of bougainvillea on both sides. That black cotton-soil could produce bountifully with a Green Thumb on the job.

The lawn—how pretty it was—did not need mowing. *Lubia*, planted sparsely during the rainy season, soon spread to become a thick ground cover. That kind of green carpet over the otherwise baking hot black soil made the whole yard cooler. Another lantana hedge bordered the lawn on the river side.

The vegetable garden area had lain fallow during the two years the McClures were away, but there was one surviving crop: a kind of spinach that grew and spread close to the ground. And nearby were several papaya trees with green fruit hanging under the canopy of leaves at the top.

Spinach and papaya. These were our two dinner vegetables for many weeks, served on alternate days. The spinach, of a rather slimy consistency, was good-tasting. The papaya was peeled, seeded, diced, placed in a baking dish with molasses, and then popped into the oven and baked until tender. Different, tolerably good, and a quite ingenious recipe!

The irrigation system was to us a wonder to behold, a marvel of inventiveness, and made growing produce all year long possible. The machine was called a *shaddoof* and was used commonly in Egypt.

At the river's edge, a shaft perhaps twenty feet long pivoted on a short crossbar between two upright poles planted firmly at the river's edge. A heavy pack of mud weighted down the back end of the shaft. A rope was tied to the other end, and a bucket was fastened to the dangling rope.

In order to operate the *shaddoof*, one had to grasp the hanging bucket and pull it down to the water to fill it. This action raised the weighted end. When the bucket was full, the operator, with the help of that heavy mud pack, raised it to a point where it could be emptied into the brick-lined irrigation ditch. It's an ancient, tedious procedure, but it gets the job done. Fruit trees, garden vegetables, lantana hedges, and lawns were all watered in this manner.

It was among all this fascinating newness that we spent our first days at Akobo Post.

Language study began almost immediately. Every morning at about nine o'clock, a sleepy neighbor named Jok Deng came to the house. Wilma, Bob, and I sat around the dining room table with our informant, who knew a fair amount of English, and we would ask him how to say common words and phrases. Thus we learned some of the basics of the Anuak language. (A brief course taken at the Summer Institute of Linguistics at Norman, Oklahoma, during the summer of 1947 was a help in getting started.) Then, at eleven o'clock, Don brought in three of the older school boys for comparative pronunciation of the wonderful new words. (Have you ever said a word beginning with the *ng* sound?)

After our lesson we went to the riverbank to try out our newly acquired language skills on the children who always gathered when we went outside to enjoy early evening coolness. When we began to hear familiar words in Anuak conversations, we knew we were making some progress.

Many of the Anuaks were close neighbors. Their villages were strung up and down the river, usually not far from the bank, providing easy access to water. When a family's daily supply of water had to be carried in a large gourd or a five-gallon tin on a woman's head, one chose to live as near to the river as possible.

Anuak homes, or *tukls*, were built neatly with round mud walls protected by thick, conical, thatched roofs. There were no windows. A low doorway gave entrance into the dark interior. Walls and floors, including the outer yard, were *mawned* smooth with mud plaster. The courtyard, usually surrounded by a cornstalk privacy fence, was swept each day with a cornstalk broom.

These outward aspects of Anuak life were easy to observe. But we were ignorant largely in those early days of what was going on in the villages around us, from the simplest conversations of children to the mysterious pagan rituals of witch doctors. We had a long way to go, and we knew that we'd have to persevere if we truly wanted to become friends with these gentle people, to get to know them on even the most basic terms.

In those first months, our letters home were full of detail. We wanted our families to "see" all the strange sights and to enjoy our new life with us:

> The thatcher is putting new grass on the roof of the McClure house. He makes a hole up into the thatch with his wooden paddle, stuffs a small bundle of new grass into the hole, and paddles it up and in until it is smooth. A repaired roof resembles a leopard skin with the colors reversed: the old grass is weathered and gray; the new is a golden brown. There are whole villages of leopard-skin-roofed *tukls* this time of year....
>
> Two Anuak women came one afternoon this week. They brought a half-gourd filled with corn flour which they had ground themselves. They wanted a little cloth in exchange. Lyda told them kindly that her supply of cloth had not yet come. But they left the flour anyway, and we had muffins that evening made from their gift....
>
> The Anuak women cook this corn flour (we would call it cornmeal) with water and eat it as a porridge without benefit of milk, sugar,

or salt. It is their principal food. Fish is also an important item in their diet. The men fish with spears; it's surprising how many they catch....

Every two weeks or so, Don and Bob go out in the Jeep to bring home a fresh supply of meat. Wild game abounds; they are seldom gone for more than an hour or two. When they return with a couple of oribi, a reedbuck, a waterbuck, or even a great eland, the work of dressing the animals begins right away, The Anuaks are glad to help, for there is always plenty to share. Nothing is ever wasted; the Anuaks relish not only the prime cuts but also the parts we find less appealing....

The rains are on the way. We have had a couple of mild thunderstorms and there are often clouds in the sky. They say the rainy season is by far the nicer. While there is more humidity, there is also much more coolness, and the land is more beautiful, too. Now it is all brown and dried up except for the vegetation on the mission grounds....

The roof was patched, but still needs more done on it, as there were several leaks during the rain we had last evening. Of course, as Don says, many places that leak in the first hard rain, do not do so again because the grass swells. But he's going to put the roofer to work again....

Lyda recently discovered, in the bathroom, a meter-long snake in the process of devouring a bat. The snake was dispatched in short order. ... And one night I saw my first scorpion about two feet from where I stood in my bare feet giving Gayle a drink of water. Scorpions seek shelter in the house during the rains. So we are really on our guard, especially when the shadows begin to fall. They seldom appear in the daytime....

This week, Lyda and Wilma have been caring for a little mite of skin and bones who must be nearly two months old. Her mother has been sick for some time. Don has been treating her and she is improving, but she still cannot feed her child. The baby seemed to eat well at first from one of our Vitaflo bottles. Something seems to be wrong now. It is hard to tell what, with such a pitiful little thing of four and a half pounds. Missionary life is many-sided....

Bob and Wilma are now in charge of the clinic before breakfast every morning. They assisted Don at first and learned from his medical knowledge, which is really amazing considering the fact that he's not a doctor....

Don and Bob take turns leading the Sunday evening services here at the house. One evening there were twenty-five present representing eight languages: Anuak, Murle, Shulla, Nuer, Zandi, Arabic, English, and Dutch. (Don counted Wilma as the Dutchman!) But all understood English....

Bob, with Jok Deng interpreting for him, preached at the church service this morning. He did very well, I thought, in presenting his message for the understanding of the people....

April and May passed and the rains tentatively began. The cracked, black, cement-hard cotton-soil tracks soon became clay quagmires, to be closed for several months, forcing all travel to be done by boat.

Fed by tributaries and streams pouring from the foothills of neighboring Ethiopia, the Pibor River rose from a low, muddy watercourse, sluggish almost to the point of stagnation. As the current increased, small grassy clumps, having broken off from great sudd islands upstream, floated in the swelling flood past the mission, en route to the Sobat and then the Nile.

As the water rose, it became clearer. In the Nuer language, "pibor" means "white water." So doubtless this river was named during flood time, and the inhabitants along its banks were reminded, even when the river was at its lowest and muddiest, that there would come a day when it would become white and clear again.

It was nearing the time now when the McClure children would be coming home from school. They would travel the same route that we had taken: by train and Nile steamer to Malakal. Don and Lyda were preparing to meet them.

Though the rains had begun and the river was rising, it was still early enough in the season to attempt, without too much risk, the trip overland to Malakal in the station wagon. Before they left, we assured Don and Lyda that we would move to the house available to us up near the police post before they returned with the children.

"We feel ready to be on our own now," we said. "Thank you for the many weeks you so graciously put up with us in your home, and for giving us such a good start in our life at Akobo."

"Well, with the river coming up, the first province steamer of the season should arrive anytime," Don replied, "and it should have your freight on board. So you'll have your things to start housekeeping up at the post. Stay here as long as you need to, of course, but we'll appreciate having room for the children when we return. We're glad you've joined us here at Akobo. We should be back in about two weeks."

And soon they were off. We felt like babes in the bush! Bob was in charge now. Through an interpreter, he led morning prayers for the mission workers and supervised their labors. The all-important language study continued.

Wilma and I shared household responsibilities. The little ones claimed a lot of attention, and kept us busy and laughing and marveling at the wonderful works of God.

One morning an Anuak worker called us.

"Come! Listen!" he exclaimed excitedly.

We all dashed outside toward the river, letting the screen door bang shut behind us. We listened. At first we didn't hear a thing except the river flowing, the soughing of a light wind through the *neem* and eucalyptus trees, a rooster crowing, the scream of a fish eagle.

We continued listening. And then our ears began to sense something else: just a faint, rhythmic pulse way off in the distance, a sound one could almost feel, rather than hear—a kind of muffled throbbing. But as it drew nearer, we could hear the splashing of paddle wheels. Then we knew without a doubt that a province steamer was approaching. The steamer would be bringing not only our freight from the United States and the furniture we had ordered in Omdurman, but also supplies for the mission, the Arab shops, the police lines, government offices, and the district commissioner's household. What excitement for the whole community!

At last we could see the crow's nest of the steamer as it made its way upriver. It was moving ever so slowly, turning in one direction and then another as the skilled *rais* (ra'ees) navigated his vessel, negotiating the river bends between its narrow banks. (The *raises* never liked navigating the Pibor. They declared that it was no river at all because its channels were just too confined to be worthy of such a designation.)

After some minutes, the whole steamer was visible. It was the Nakheila. A rather ungainly conglomerate, the main section housed the power plant that activated the paddle wheels and pushed the vessel forward. Tethered in front was a two-story living barge for passengers, complete with sleeping quarters and a screened sitting area. On either side was a flat barge for freight. No wonder the navigators had difficulty on the serpentine Pibor River!

Province steamer on the Pibor River

Soon the Nakheila was chugging and churning past the mission, cheered on by waving hands and shouts from the riverbank as it continued on its way upriver to the police post where it would tie up and the unloading would begin.

It was June 21, 1948—a very happy day. We needed no other celebration for our fourth wedding anniversary.

All our household goods had indeed come on the steamer, and we moved without further delay into the red brick house waiting for us about a mile up the road. Known as the government rest house, it had been built some years before to accommodate visiting government officials. The house at this time, however, was hardly ever used, so the district commissioner had offered it to Don McClure as temporary housing for new missionaries. We were thankful.

We appreciated the high ceilings, the cool tile floors, and the screened veranda along the front where we set up our beds. How good it was to be able to make this place our home for a few months until our own house was built. But I missed being at the mission, in the center of things—where the action was. Bob left every day right after breakfast to carry out his several responsibilities at the school and clinic. The little girls were sweet and entertaining and we kept one another company, but the mornings dragged. How our spirits lifted when Bob came home for lunch.

In the afternoon Jok came for language lessons. If we thought Jok was sleepy during our morning sessions at McClures' house, he was more so later in the day. And worse, we ourselves responded in like manner to the languid afternoon heat. But we all kept at it, and each day Bob and I managed to learn some new facet of this African tongue.

Besides being lonely, and too timid and somewhat fearful about getting out on my own into that little community of police families, government people, and Arab merchants, I found it difficult to employ "houseboys." Everyone had servants, usually three: one to cook, one to clean, and one to wash and iron clothes. To be a servant was an honorable and much sought-after position.

We settled for two houseboys, named Omot and Oshul. It took a major adjustment for me to give orders or even have them around, dependent on me for daily employment. The day would come, however, when my schedule would be all askew if even one of them didn't show up for whatever reason. The "dependent" issue would completely reverse itself.

The home of the British district commissioner (D.C.) was not far from the rest house. Captain Richard E. Lyth was the D.C. for all of Pibor District, which included both Akobo Post and Pibor Post ninety miles south in Murle country. The D.C. and his wife, Nora, with their children, spent time in both places. But Akobo, being the more accessible, was their principal dwelling place.

During our first weeks at Akobo, the Lyths were living at Pibor, and in July they were due to go home to England for three months. So we scarcely met them in the brief interim they were at Akobo. We had heard through the McClures that Dick and Nora were fine Christians who, contrary to Foreign Office policy, witnessed for Christ and established a church wherever they served.

We had no idea at this time that the Lyths would play a very large part in our lives during the next few years.

We had not been settled in our rest house home many days when the McClures returned with their children. All of us were thankful with Don and Lyda that Margaret, Donnie, and Polly were home from school for the long holiday. It made us all more light-hearted with a great feeling of family completeness.

About this same time, we had word that Harvey and Lavina Hoekstra and their two little boys would be arriving by steamer in early August. We all greeted that news with joyful and lively anticipation. We began preparing for their coming. Providing a suitable residence for them became top priority—and God, in his wisdom, had already met this need.

A mile downriver from the mission, in an area called Pakang, was a house that had been put up by another mission agency during the McClures' two-year absence. This had caused some consternation because, according to comity policy, no more than one mission group could work in any defined region. This was clearly American Mission territory—and finally that matter was resolved with a financial settlement.

So the house was there, never having been occupied, but it would need further work to make it habitable for a family with small children. In the meantime the Swarts would move over at the rest house to make room for our new coworkers, with five-year-old Dennis and four-month-old Jimmy.

The Hoekstras left the United States July 2, 1948, on the freighter Excambion, bound for Port Said, Egypt. Sixteen days later, they arrived at the port, and Africa lost no time in giving the newcomers a series of dubious welcomes.

In order to disembark, they had to descend a stairway precariously located on the ship's hull, and let themselves down into a dinghy that took them to shore in Port Said. In Cairo they lived through a frightening Israeli bomb attack on the city. In Khartoum they were warmly welcomed by missionaries and a sizzling early morning temperature of 111 degrees, followed a few days later by what the old-timers termed a small *haboob*, or dust storm. It was significant enough, however, to make a big impression on Harvey and Lavina, especially the next morning when they picked up a very dusty Jimmy from an equally dusty bassinet.

These experiences made the Hoekstras wonder if they'd misread their summons to Africa. But their luggage, including the priceless trunkful of baby food, had made the journey intact, and the seven-day steamer trip on the Tamai from Malakal to Akobo was idyllic. So by the time they reached their destination one dark evening, they knew they'd been on the right track all the way.

Our RCA contingent in the Anglo-Egyptian Sudan now numbered five adults.

Lyda McClure, with an Aladdin lamp and a bevy of school boys, was there on the riverbank to greet the new arrivals. In no time, their luggage was whisked off the steamer, and soon the Hoekstra family was seated about the McClures' dining table enjoying a sumptuous meal served on candlewick dinnerware and topped off with cherry pie.

Candlewick? Cherry pie? Out in the middle of nowhere? Surprises fairly emanated from the McClure household—lovely touches that eased the orientation of more than one novice to life in the bush.

As soon as we knew they had come, Bob drove to the mission in the Jeep to welcome the Hoekstras and transport them to our home. Space was limited, and the accommodations were hardly luxurious. But they graciously accepted the makeshift arrangements, enduring with patience the rigors of sleeping on Army cots, using the clothes closet Bob had fabricated from our refrigerator box as if it were a fine wardrobe, and philosophically bearing with the fact that complete privacy, for the time being, was an unattainable luxury.

Somewhat more difficult to endure was a new aroma. It was guava season. The harvest was plentiful and our food safe was full of this tropical fruit. The pungent fragrance filled the whole house; there was no getting away from it.

Harvey, suffering from an ailment common to newcomers, was nauseated by this unmitigated assault on his olfactory senses, and he thought he'd never, ever, be able to eat a guava—though time proved him wrong.

(Decades later I marvel that we did not, in mercy, remove the offensive fruit, give it away, or bury it! I suppose for the sake of the rest of us, and the fact that fresh food of any kind was at a premium, we heartlessly kept the precious produce and prayed that Harvey would live to forgive, if not to forget.)

After breakfast every morning, Bob and Harvey drove away down the road toward the mission. Lavina and I felt somewhat bereft each time. But there was never a dearth of tasks to keep us busy as we cared for the household and the children—and we knew that "the work" must go on.

Most pressing at the moment, of course, was getting the Pakang house ready for occupancy. The structure of mud, wattle, and thatch was sound enough. It had weathered, though, and needed further repair and refurbishing.

In about three weeks, all was ready. Moving day came. Small and humble though the building was, it must have seemed like a palace to the Hoekstras as they set up their furniture and made themselves comfortable in what was to be their home for the next few years.

At first Harvey and Lavina felt as we had when we moved from the mission to the rest house; they seemed to be way out on the fringe of things, far from the hub of activity. But it wasn't long before they realized that they were in an ideal location for their primary assignment: language learning. They were living close to several Anuak villages and were at a distance from other English speakers.

So, even though it had been a trespass of sorts, the other mission group had done the American Mission a great favor by building on that particular site—and certainly God had allowed them to go ahead, knowing that the whole matter would be resolved for the good of his kingdom and the spreading of his Word. For Bible translation was the ultimate commission for the Hoekstras, and it was at Pakang that they were able to lay a strong foundation for language acquisition.

Life at Pakang was never dull or forgettable. Years later Dennis Hoekstra didn't have to delve too deeply into his memory to recall some early adventures:

> As a small boy, living in the grass-thatched, mud-walled house at Pakang, I remember having monkeys, ostriches, gazelles, and other pets that were given to me by my Anuak playmates. Snakes and scorpions are also vivid in my memory, but not as pets! As children, we were warned by everyone to treat each snake as a poisonous one, and each scorpion as one that could inflict a deadly sting.
>
> While lying in bed one afternoon, I watched a cobra slither its way up into the thatch above my bed. Our houseboy came and killed it.
>
> A standard piece of equipment at night was a flashlight always kept under the pillow on each bed. We used it to shine on the floor should we have to get up in the dark, to make sure there were no scorpions or snakes in our path. During the rains we really needed to be on the lookout for scorpions.
>
> A few hundred feet from the front of our house was the Pibor River, low at that time of the dry season, its waters a muddy gray. But for all its murkiness, this river provided hours of entertainment. We swam, or we fished, either with a line or with harpoons. Fish were thick as the water receded. We could even catch fish by going out in the outboard; it wasn't uncommon to have one or two jump right into the boat!

During the rainy season when the river was high, the Pibor would become a dangerous place. We knew better than to go swimming then because crocodiles would swim up the river from the Sobat looking for fresh feeding grounds. Frequently, the Anuaks would come to Dad and plead, "Odolo, come to the river! Bring your gun! Shoot the crocodile that wants to eat our goats when they come to the river's edge to drink."

One day Dad and another missionary killed and skinned a fifteen foot croc that had made meals of several people over the years. Steel bracelets in its stomach were mute testimony to that fact.[1]

The rains descended that season—wonderful, wonderful rains that cooled off the countryside and made everything green, but also caused problems. The flat roof of the rest house leaked seriously across the length of every crossbeam. Each time the rain poured down—and that was daily—we had to muster every receptacle big enough to catch the countless, constant drips. Wash tubs, cooking pots, basins—all were commandeered to contain the little waterfalls that otherwise would have spread like a small tide throughout the house.

Rains made the road—in one direction to the police post and in the other to the mission—completely impassable. Motorboats, and one's own two feet, were the only means of transport for some months.

However, it was good to see the land transformed by lush growth and to know that there would be abundant pasture for the Anuaks' cattle, plenty of heaven's irrigation for their corn crops this season.

At planting time it was decided that we would stake out our house and then plan our initial landscaping, for the building of our house would start in October at the close of the rains. So new starts from the McClures' lantana hedge were set in the ground, and the irrigation ditch was extended should it be needed between storms. Someday we would put in bougainvillea and hibiscus bushes, more lantana near the house, and *lubia* for the lawn. But these would have to wait until there was no danger of their being trampled by builders and roofers.

In November 1948, I recorded a happy event:

> "In the burning of the noontide heat" on 18 October, a Christian mission home was dedicated at Akobo. The service was held at the

[1] Dennis Hoekstra, "Raised in Africa," June 30, 1992. Joint Archives of Holland, Hope College.

site where the house will stand. Together, Anuak workers, school boys, teachers, and mission families, in prayer and song committed the dwelling to be used for the Lord. It was a simple impressive moment, another witness to the purpose of our being here.

Trenches have now been dug and are in readiness for the laying of the red brick foundation walls. The brick will extend up as far as the window ledges. The remainder will be made of adobe, with a grass roof to top it off....

In the background, yet conspicuous in any mission scene, is the testimony of the Christian home as an ideal in family relationships. The family is the basic nucleus of Christian life, and while personal evangelism is the keynote of missionary endeavor, it is also imperative that the establishment of whole Christian families be an ultimate objective.

Thus we rejoice greatly in the building of a home which will be ours while we serve at Akobo.

Ours? It has been dedicated to the Lord. His it is, and his it shall be![2]

As soon as the last bundle of grass was paddled into the thick thatch, and the cement floors were set and dry, we moved in. It was early April 1949. The Monarch wood stove was hooked up to the chimney; water pipes ran from a fifty-gallon steel drum into the kitchen and shower room. We set up chairs in the sitting veranda, tables and chairs and dish cupboards in the dining veranda, and beds in the sleeping veranda. The *dulab* and mahogany dresser were placed in our dressing room, and Bob's desk and bookshelves went into his office. All canned goods and other food staples were stowed in the pantry. Twenty-gallon *zeers* were ready for filtering river water, and goolas were in place on their special table to cool the filtered, boiled water.

Waves of contentment almost overwhelmed me as I lay in bed the first night in our new home. Valerie was asleep in her bed beside us, Gayle on the other side in her crib. The night air was cool as the breeze wafted over us through the veranda screens. Next door, a hundred yards downriver, was the McClure residence. Just upriver, work was beginning on the house for

---

[2] Morrell W. Swart, "The Witness of a Christian Home," Department of Women's Work, RCA, 1948. Joint Archives of Holland, Hope College.

Wilma. The Hoekstras were a mile downriver, but we had moved a mile nearer to them, too. The sense of community was strong.

All was well. Again I experienced the euphoria of well-being, because we had come home.

One of my first household jobs was to make curtains for the screened windows. Thanks to Wilma Kats, material was available.

Wilma by this time had begun to lead weekly women's meetings. She taught them the basic truths of Scripture, sharing with them the love of Christ. As an incentive to encourage them to come each week, Wilma would give out feed sack cloth to those who had come regularly for a stipulated number of meetings.

Feed sacks in those days were colorful, and many of them were designed in attractive prints. One feed sack, cut in half, was just right for a window. Because Wilma had a generous supply, she let us have what we needed.

My old second-hand Singer treadle machine was put to good use, and soon there were pretty accents of color in each room. (I also made play clothes for the children out of feed sacks, and Bob proudly wore feed sack shirts—a vogue introduced by Wilma. Since these were the days before loud shirts were even dreamed of, this new style caused quite a stir!)

Feed sack curtains were decorative but hardly adequate for keeping out the rain of heavy, tropical downpours. Canvas curtains had to be stitched up and then installed on the outside of each window, and also on all of the twenty-foot long, screened-in verandas. The Singer, however, was equal to the task, and well before the rains returned, all the canvas curtains were in place. Stapled firmly at the top to the wood frames that secured the screens, and with a dowel of suitable weight in the "tunnel" sewed at the bottom of each canvas, the curtain could be dropped from the inside by means of ropes on small pulleys. And when the rain was over and the canvas had dried, it could be raised in a neat roll out of the way above the screens and under the protective eaves of thatch.

It was an ingenious arrangement that had probably been worked out originally either by British colonialists or by early missionaries. I never thought to ask.

It was a year since we had arrived at Akobo Post—a long year of orientation to life in a strange land, among people we didn't understand, either in speech or in culture. Language study was a slow, exacting discipline that demanded much but seemed at times to result in so little. We had gained some insights into the art of living in close association with our fellow missionaries—and learned a lot about ourselves in those relationships. We knew we still had a long way to go. The first year was truly one of adjustment and growth, as well as triumph in the Lord.

At one point during the lonely time at the government rest house, we would have welcomed any legitimate excuse to return to the United States and take up life again in what was still to us a normal situation. But praise be to God, we were mired in the cotton-soil clay at Akobo, and he dealt with us in his firm, loving way. By his grace, we came through that dark period, satisfied that this was indeed the place in all the world where we were supposed to be, and that there would be no turning back. The years that stretched out before us would be lived a day at a time, hour by hour, and his grace, strength, and peace—his very presence—would be ours in abundant supply.

So our initial commitment was reaffirmed. Never again would we experience even the slightest degree of doubt about our calling. Our eyes and our hearts were fixed on a career in Africa under the lordship of Jesus Christ.

III
God Gives the Increase

Having kept house at Akobo for a year, I was quite adept at things domestic, even in managing the houseboys.

The Monarch stove reigned, as its name suggests, in white enameled splendor in the kitchen. It was by far the most elegant piece of furniture in the house. Baking day was the greatest challenge, but once the fire was going and the oven reached the proper temperature, it could turn out four crusty loaves, golden brown and delectable. Or maybe we'd bake just two loaves and use the rest of the dough for sticky, sweet cinnamon rolls.

Another important item was our kerosene refrigerator, an eight-cubic-foot Servel. It had a good-sized freezing unit across the top where we could store several pounds of meat and still have space for ice cubes and ice cream as well. Kerosene was readily available, a good supply being brought in annually by steamer. We were thankful to have this means of preserving food in a climate where foodstuffs spoiled so quickly.

Near the refrigerator was a screened food safe, or *nemoliya*. Its four legs stood in tins half-filled with water. In the safe we would store the less perishable fresh fruits and vegetables that could be ravaged by hordes of ants and flies. The screened sides and water kept out the pests.

We also learned to be prepared for darkness because near the equator there is almost no twilight. Well before sundown, we would see that the

39

wicks of our lamps were trimmed, bases adequately filled with kerosene, and glass chimneys sparkling clean.

We used three different kinds of lamps: the hurricane lantern, which we set inside the back entry to light a possible visitor's path to the door, or to carry along if it was necessary to walk to a neighbor's house after dark; the Aladdin lamp, which was the most pleasant to read by because it was bright, relatively cool, and quiet; and the pressure lamp, which gave the brightest light but also generated a lot of heat. Any of these lamps, particularly in the rainy season, attracted clouds of insects, so our evenings often were short!

In due time the station enjoyed the luxury of a generator, providing us with electric lights for three or four hours each evening. But we kept the old standbys handy because the newfangled machine wasn't always reliable.

By the time we moved into our house at the mission, Dr. and Mrs. Albert Roode and family had been in residence at Akobo for three months. They had moved from Doleib Hill in December 1948, Ruth having traveled ahead with Peter, John, and baby Philip on the Nakheila as far as Nasir to await the arrival of Al and all their furniture on the next steamer. Nasir was one of the old established outposts on the Sobat River in Nuer country, and was a welcome stopping-off place on the long river journey from Malakal and nearby Doleib Hill up to Akobo.

The day of Al's departure on the SS *Metemma* came a week or so later. Ruth and the boys came on board at Nasir as planned, and all reached Akobo on December 13. "It was exciting to see the compound as we approached and to dock at the riverbank right in front of the mission with all of you folks there waving," Al said.

Since the McClures were on vacation at the time, the Roode family settled into the McClure house and stored their furniture at the rest house.

We had a memorable Christmas celebration that year with the Roodes, Hoekstras, Swarts, and Wilma Kats all gathered around a festive dining table. It was the second Christmas in Sudan for Al and Ruth, but for the rest of us it was the first. We marveled at how filled with joy we could be without the usual props of cold and snow, gaily decorated homes and stores, church services and programs brimming over with Advent music and worship, and generations of families gathered together in customary observance of the day. While our hearts longed for the familiar, we found in this limited fellowship in a remote corner of Sudan the resources to rejoice wholeheartedly in the birth of our Savior. It was the beginning of new traditions in celebrating Christmas in Africa.

We were not the only ones who celebrated at Akobo. The Anuak Christians were well aware that Christmas had come. The birth of Jesus had taken place under conditions as modest as Anuak dwellings. Surely they felt a kinship with him on that basis, and surely Christ could identify with the humble circumstances of the Anuak way of life. So, high and lifted up though our Lord is, he is at home among the lowly, and even the least of us can celebrate and be at ease in his presence. He is, indeed, the Savior of us all! So, in that spirit, we all gathered together for a joyful service of worship and praise that morning. It was a special day indeed as Christians and pagans alike sensed festivity in the air. We considered ourselves to be so favored in being a part of that community on the banks of the Pibor River.

We were all thankful that a doctor had joined our team. While Don McClure had valiantly carried on basic medical work with a Merck manual, common sense, and much prayer—assisted for a while by Bob and Wilma— it was right that he be relieved of that responsibility. Al Roode took over with capable zest. Though it took a little time for the Anuaks to trust this newcomer as they had Don, they eventually understood that a real *hakim* had come to minister to them, and they were grateful for his professional skills and his compassionate interest in their health problems.

While doctors all over the world are busy, none is busier than the bush doctor located hundreds of miles from any other medical help. Under less than ideal conditions, and with less equipment than most would consider the barest essentials, Dr. Roode had an effective ministry at Akobo. He was especially adept at making accurate diagnoses of exotic symptoms, and many a person was healed, many a life saved, because of this intuitive gift.

As soon as we moved from the rest house to our newly completed house at the mission, the Roodes settled into our former dwelling and were happy to have a home of their own, surrounded by all the furniture and whatnot they had brought from Doleib Hill.

By this time, I knew that our third child was on the way. The Hoekstras' third son, David Jonathan, was born in May 1949 and had the distinction of being the first mission child to be born at Akobo.

June brought the McClure children home again for the summer, and as always the weeks flew. To offset the daily round of continued language study, school, clinic, and women's programs, Saturday afternoons were set aside for relaxation in the form of tea and volleyball. All the mission staff and the district commissioner and his family gathered after the heat of the day.

Tea was served either at our house or at the McClures'. Then, fortified for exercise, we lobbed the volleyball with might and main, sometimes so mightily that it flew high over the net and down the bank right into the Pibor River, with "old" intrepid Don McClure in hot pursuit. (In our late twenties, we were amazed at Don's agility. He was forty-three!)

August came, which meant the time was drawing near for the children to return to school—not only the McClure children this time, but also Peter Roode. Both families would be leaving for a few weeks, but Dr. Al didn't feel right about leaving us without any medical help. Yet with our baby not due until mid-October, we urged him to go. In fact, we said, "If it will make you feel any better, we'll make arrangements to fly in September to the American Mission hospital in Dembi Dollo, Ethiopia, and await the birth there in cooler country."

At that time it would mean traveling an extremely circuitous route: by outboard motorboat to Malakal, plane to Khartoum, an international flight to Addis Ababa, and Ethiopian Airlines to Dembi Dollo. But we were ready for the adventure and eager to see the beautiful Ethiopian countryside.

It pleased us when Al and Ruth acquiesced, leaving on August 13 for a few weeks of vacation before taking Peter on to school in Egypt. Word was sent to Dr. John Cremer at Dembi Dollo to expect us around the middle of September.

Ten days later, on August 23, we heard the approach of a province steamer—its pulsating sound now familiar but no less exciting. We welcomed the supplies, but even more the mail, because the previous postal delivery had been a month to six weeks before.

Sometimes the steamer brought unexpected guests; on this occasion its two surprise travelers were Dr. Ronald Trudinger and Talmage Wilson. Dr. Trudinger was from Australia originally. He had come to Sudan many years before as a medical missionary with the Sudan United Mission. For the previous twenty years, however, rather than practicing medicine, he had worked almost exclusively on translating the Bible into the Dinka language. He had become a member of the American Presbyterian Mission, based at Abwong, located between Doleib Hill and Nasir, but on the other side of the Sobat River. Tal Wilson had come out to Sudan as a short-termer to assist Dr. Trudinger in any way he could.

These two men had hopped on the steamer just for the ride, taking advantage of a fine opportunity to visit the relatively new mission post upstream on the Pibor. Though the McClures were planning to leave in a few days with their children, they gladly welcomed these guests into their home.

The steamer, in the meantime, continued on to the government post to unload and take on freight, such as cattle hides, to take back to Malakal. A steamer's stay in that port usually was four days, diverting tribal attention from mission activities to all the hustle and bustle up at the government post.

When August 25 dawned, we had no notion that the day would bring anything other than the normal schedule of events. I showered in the morning and prepared for the day, but soon I suspected that something else was about to happen. Stirrings within me made me realize that this baby was probably not going to wait until October, or even until September, to put in an appearance. The birth was imminent—and oh, how thankful we were that Dr. Trudinger was there! With Lyda McClure assisting him, he helped me deliver our third daughter at about noon. She came seven weeks early, weighing in at three and a half pounds, but all was well.

The next day, at our insistence, Don and Lyda started off to take their children back to school. A day later the steamer paddle-wheeled away with Dr. Trudinger and Tal Wilson on board.

It was no happenstance that the steamer had come that week, or that the doctor and his young friend had decided on the spur of the moment to wend their way up the winding rivers to spend a few days with old and new friends at Akobo. With no doctor there, God knew that one would be needed, both for the parents' peace of mind and perhaps for the survival of the prematurely born infant. We praise God to this day and thrill in thanksgiving for his provision at that momentous time in the life of our family.

Meryl Cathen, whom we call Merry, survived without benefit of incubator or any other equipment considered essential for preemies. Surely it was the power of God's Spirit within her that gave her daily breath.

A few days later we were surprised when another steamer was seen making its slow way toward Akobo. This one, however, was not an ordinary province steamer; it was the Lady Baker, the medical steamer. The Upper Nile Province medical officer was making a routine, scheduled safari to the outposts on several rivers and their tributaries.

We were pleased to see Dr. Bloss whom we had met previously in Malakal. I don't recall if he had heard of Merry's birth, but he certainly was informed upon his arrival. He came right to the house. Giving one keen diagnostic look at my eyes, he declared, "You have hepatitis; your eyes are jaundiced. That's what caused this premature birth."

So the mystery of Merry's early advent was explained. Fortunately, mine was a light case, and the baby was doing well. We praised God for sending yet another doctor with timely assistance and welcome advice—and for the precious gift of another daughter.

Before we knew it, October was upon us. If our original plans had materialized, we still would have been living in a high state of expectancy among the cool hills of western Ethiopia. But here we were, at home in Akobo, delighting in our three little girls, and living out our ordinary daily schedules, not dreaming that something else of an extraordinary nature was about to happen—something that had to do not so much with birth as with rebirth.

The mission at Akobo had been in a spiritual rut, missionaries and Anuaks alike. Nothing was happening. Soul-winning seemed at a standstill; the Anuaks gave little outward sign of response to the preaching and teaching of the Word. Our vision was becoming blurred.

Nor was there any evidence of potential spiritual leadership among the Anuak Christians, or of initiative and compulsion in spreading the gospel among their own people. Scores of villagers who were seen regularly at church services still had not openly confessed Jesus Christ as their Savior and Lord. Indeed, there were some living in the immediate vicinity who had never even begun to search for the Truth.

We had long been praying for revival, and our concern mounted as the months rolled by. Petitions became more and more earnest.

Then, during the third week in October, the answer came. The Spirit of God moved powerfully among us, clearing our vision, sweeping aside all that had been blocking his way—and the radiance of his glory shone through. The joy and thrill were almost more than we could bear, and we were continually filled with praise to God.

On October 26 Don McClure sent the following cablegram to the Board of Foreign Missions of the United Presbyterian Church: "Rejoice! God's Spirit working wonders; more than one hundred confessed in three days; still coming; pray without ceasing." This message was relayed in turn to the RCA's Board of Foreign Missions.

God brought this about in a most unexpected manner. Missionaries themselves were not instrumental in effecting the spiritual awakening;

rather, God had prepared a man from outside the mission ranks for this moment.

Our district commissioner, Captain Richard Lyth, and his family had returned recently to Akobo after spending a holiday in the area in Uganda where revival in the church had been going on for some twenty years. The Lyths were devout Christians already, but God had more and deeper truths to teach them; he took them another step into understanding what life in Christ was all about. It was their sharing with us this vital spiritual experience that proved to be the spark that set the Christians of Akobo aflame for Jesus Christ.

Using themes of "brokenness" and "walking in the light," Dick Lyth, in a Sunday morning service, quietly gave an account of what he had learned and experienced in fellowship with the *balokole*, the revived Ugandan church. In brokenness of spirit, this government official, having already confessed his sins before God, confessed also before us all: missionaries, colleagues, employees, African students and teachers alike. The Holy Spirit was powerfully present.

As a result, and in subsequent meetings, many other confessions followed.

"Sir, may I speak?" teacher Ojulo almost shouted. "Today I became angry with my mother-in-law because she took our sick baby to the witch doctor. The baby died, and I told her in anger that she had been the cause of his death. I drank beer because I was so angry. But when I reached home, I went into the house and threw myself face downward on the floor, ashamed and repentant for trying to drown my sorrow and anger in drink."

Okwor, a fourth-year student, made this startling confession: "In 1943 I helped kill a man with my spear. I was only a little boy then, and the people in my village said they would keep it quiet. This is the first time it has been told. If I knew who that man was, I would go and tell his family, too."

A blind man from a nearby village said, "I can't see women, but I always want them. I can't see beer, but I always want it. But that is finished now because I believe in Jesus and he will help me."

The mission foreman, Okac, was able to put aside his pride and in humility admit: "We were angry at the mission for cutting our wages. But the Lord has opened my eyes. I see now that we were not doing the work as we should. We were cheating the mission."

These are but samples of the many little talks that poured out of newly Christ-filled hearts. When the question of questions was put to the students, the teachers and about a dozen boys rose without hesitation to make a declaration of their faith in Jesus Christ as their Savior. Eventually, all in the room—a hundred and more—were on their feet, announcing to all new life in Christ.

Furthermore the students themselves started a campaign to win for Christ all the people in the villages between the mission and the Arab shops. Every day they went out witnessing with newfound power. And what was thought to be impossible actually happened: the leader of these villages, known for his drinking, gambling, and other vices, declared his readiness to confess publicly his belief in Jesus.

The swift, positive impact of the power of the Holy Spirit in the lives of the Anuaks was an almost incredible fact. But the story didn't end there. The missionaries themselves, as a group, experienced spiritual cleansing such as we had never known before.

We had met together for our usual Thursday evening prayer meeting, but God made it an unusual one. He took hold of each one of us and broke us, taking away our pride. Together we talked over things, confessing petty misunderstandings, jealousies, desire for authority—all these sins that stood in the way of being effective in our work and witness.

Even as the Anuaks had opened their hearts so spontaneously and poured out their burdens, so had we, and our hearts became clean and filled with the love of Christ. We were blessed beyond measure. Then, as never before, we were able to serve God because we had come into newness of life in Christ—over and above our assurance of salvation—and could share fully in the joyful experience of rebirth along with our Anuak friends.[1]

When the spiritual renewal began, Bob Swart and Harvey Hoekstra were off on an exciting assignment, commissioned to locate a site for the opening of new work among the Anuaks on the Ethiopian side of the border. They left Akobo on a province steamer bound for Gambela, taking camping gear and a motorboat to use for exploration once the steamer had reached its destination.

Gambela, situated on the Baro River deep inside Ethiopia, was a mile-square enclave under British rule by a special agreement with the Ethiopian government. It was a staging area for commerce serving western Ethiopia. Steamers from Sudan brought in goods such as cloth and aluminum pots,

---

[1] Mrs. J. Robert Swart, "Miracles of Grace at Akobo Mission" (not strictly quoted). Reprinted from the *Church Herald*, December 2, 1949: 8, 9.

and returned with a cargo of coffee, beeswax, and other Ethiopian exports. It was a mutually beneficial arrangement.

To reach Gambela, the paddle wheeler splashed its way down the Pibor to the junction of the Sobat and Baro rivers in Nuer country. Then, turning eastward up the Baro, it soon crossed the border. An uninhabited no man's land gave way after some hours to Anuak territory. The travelers surveyed the scene on both sides of the Baro as they moved along, alert to various kinds of terrain.

The first Anuak villages they saw were located at some distance from the river because that area was a marsh. But farther on the land became considerably higher and hilly. At one point, when the steamer rounded a bend, they spied a large Anuak village perched on a sizable hillock right on a curve of the river. They filed that site, as well as a few others, in their minds for future reference.

The steamer eventually arrived at Gambela where it tied up for a few days. Bob and Harvey were invited to be the guests of the British commander of the enclave, Captain Dibble, who regaled them with stories of the locale as well as with a breakfast of pork and beans and corn on the cob.

But the two men had work to do while the steamer was in port. So, taking leave of their host, they launched the motorboat, loaded with enough gear and food for several days, and took off downriver to explore more carefully the potential mission sites. As they followed the meandering river through Anuak country, every turn had a surprise. Each sandbar was heavily populated with huge crocodiles and river birds: ibis, egrets, ducks, geese, and Goliath heron. Often they saw various kinds of antelope grazing undisturbed, or perhaps a herd of zebra.

Taking into consideration factors such as proximity to Anuak villages, a tract large enough to accommodate several buildings, and stability of the riverbank, Bob and Harvey concluded that the area near the village on the hillock would be an ideal site for future mission work.

The men returned to Gambela in time to catch the steamer ride back to Sudan. They rode as far as the mouth of the Gilo River, a tributary of the Pibor, disembarking there in order to seek out yet another segment of the Anuak tribe.

There was no bank at this spot for the steamer to tie up to, so the captain was not able to stop. Lowering the boat and then the motor over the side of the barge was hazardous because of the current and the steamer's spreading wake. Once that was accomplished, they still had to pull away without swamping the small craft in the churning waters of the continuously turning paddle wheels. It was no mean feat! Their success testified to the skill and alertness of the men, the stability of the boat, and the mercy of God.

The Gilo was hardly a river. It was filled with grass, had little if any current, and the land on either side was marsh. Villages were located miles back from the channel. The only Anuaks the men saw were fishermen in their dugout canoes.

It didn't seem feasible to explore further, so they turned the motorboat toward the Pibor River and headed for home. They reached Akobo just in time for that life-changing prayer meeting. Bob wrote at the end of his report: "Little did we know that we would come home to an experience of spiritual blessing that God had planned for all of us in the Anuak work."

On December 4, as revival continued, Harvey Hoekstra wrote an account of the power of the Spirit in one man's life.

> We are experiencing a real moving of the Holy Spirit [at Akobo]. Let those who no longer believe in the supernatural gospel of a living Christ and the power of the Holy Spirit come and behold what wonders are being wrought here.... Really, it is something tremendous as life after life is touched and changed....
>
> Let me tell you [about Dilok]. He had first come to our home very sick with dysentery....I started him, in our doctor's absence, on a course of pills which God blessed. He returned each day for his medicine.[2]

During those months, Dilok would listen to portions of Scripture that Harvey and his informants were working on. For example, he heard over and over again the reading of Mark 15–16 as the men struggled to get the Truth translated into just the right Anuak idiom. And during that time, Harvey ...

> ...had the joy of teaching him the wonderful fact that God had sent his beloved Son to shed his blood on Calvary and to be his sacrifice. He heard this message gladly and accepted it with all his heart and believed. Soon he was begging to be baptized....

2 Harvey T. Hoekstra, "The Reawakening at Akobo Mission." Reprinted from the *Church Herald*, January 20, 1950: 5.

But in his village stood a tall shrine, built of a bamboo pole with corn ears tied on it, and a small gourd. Beneath this shrine were the bones of more than ten sheep which he had sacrificed during the past two years in an effort to find satisfaction and health, and that his barren wife might have a child. In his house were the superstitious fetishes and sticks and articles of his religion....

What would become of all this now that he was a believer? I spoke to him about it. He considered carefully and said he wanted to remove them all and be baptized and become an evangelist to his people. This went on for several weeks.

Finally one morning [during the revival experience], he asked in earnest to have a service that week. We missionaries prayerfully considered his request and spoke to him at length. It was evident to us that here was a soul who had truly been born again.

The service was arranged. First we sang and had prayer in his village called Wangdwar. Then Dilok arose, stood beside his shrine, and told how he had been lost and deceived, but now he had found satisfaction and health through Christ.

While speaking, he rapped the shrine with his knuckles, and the corn ears and fetishes rattled prophetically...of the shaking of the kingdom of the devil in Anuak land....

Then he pulled the shrine up, dug up the bones, chopped everything up, and burned it in front of his people, while many looked on with fear and trembling. Never before had they seen anything like this in their villages.

Dilok then knelt and I had the joy of baptizing my first Anuak convert with the words: *"Dilok, pi akith bat wii, ni nyodhi yini dhan Jidhath. Man atia, atia ki nyen Wuo, ki nyen Jidhath Krayth ma ni War Jwok, ki Ywey Atar."* [Dilok, I put water on your head to show that you are a person of Jesus. This which I do, I do in the name of the Father, the name of Jesus Christ who is the Son of God, and the Holy Spirit.]

I wish you might have been there to see the expression of radiant joy on his face.

Then we missionaries and the baptized believers met in a circle of fellowship and partook of communion. We used native bread and tomato juice for the elements, and each of us drank from a small gourd with which Dr. McClure served us.

Truly we were one…and while our intellectual perception differed, we knew that the Anuaks experienced that feasting upon the Bread of Life as truly and with as great a blessing as we.

Afterward Don McClure said to me, "Harvey, I have never experienced a service quite like it to this day."[3]

Within days after Dilok's baptism, the number of RCA missionaries at Akobo increased by three: we welcomed with joy Lee and Kitty Crandall (whom we had met on the deck of the Saturnia in 1948 two weeks before their wedding) and Lillian Huisken. Lee came as an agriculturist; Kitty and Lillian both were trained, experienced nurses.

In a letter written in early 1950, Kitty records her first impressions:

We approached Akobo in bright moonlight at 1 a.m. on December 2, 1949, inching along the Pibor River on a steamer. An African moon gives off so much light that we were able to see all the countryside.…First, the Hoekstra house came in sight, then some Anuak villages, the school compound, the unfinished Chapel of Hope, and finally the McClure and Swart homes. The boat stopped directly in front of [the mission] and we soon took our first steps in Anuak country.…

Next thing we knew, we were wonderfully surprised to find ourselves seated in an African-type home with American trimmings, eating [Lyda McClure's] cherry pie a la mode. Then we had prayer together, thanking God for bringing us all the way in safety and in good health, and asking him to make us worthy ambassadors for him to these people. After a few hours of sleep, we rose early to move our things into the Swart home where we are now living.

It didn't take us long to feel the new spirit in Akobo, both in the lives of the Anuaks and the missionaries. The Anuaks gave us a warm reception. One man, at a large gathering, exhorted his people to listen to our message, for God had sent us many miles from home to help them learn the only true way of life.

3 Ibid.

The earnestness with which these people speak of, pray about, and listen to the Word of God, and the enthusiasm with which they sing their hymns would tell anyone that the Spirit of God was moving within them. We found ourselves loving each one, despite the apparent differences between us. Christ unites us. We have visited several of the surrounding villages and find many people eager and receptive to the gospel.[4]

The "unfinished Chapel of Hope" is a story in itself.

Hope College in Holland, Michigan, is one of three liberal arts colleges closely related to the Reformed Church in America. For many years, a Mission Emphasis Week was scheduled into Hope's fall program. A particular project was chosen; daily informational and inspirational services were held; and at the close of the week, an offering for the project was taken.

It was 1947. The RCA was about to send its first missionaries to the AngloEgyptian Sudan to work side by side with missionaries of the United Presbyterian Church. One of the speakers during that year's Mission Emphasis Week was Dr. Don McClure—and the project, as a result of his earnest, persuasive message, was a chapel for Akobo.

The chapel was built on the school compound, but it took a while. Thousands of burned bricks were ordered from entrepreneurial Arab merchants at various locations downriver—merchants who knew good clay when they saw it. The finished product was then loaded on barges and transported by steamer to Akobo. Grass had to be gathered and bundled for the thatched roof. The construction itself, which had to be done between rainy seasons, was accomplished during the dry season of 1949–1950. In honor of the Hope students who made it possible, this place of worship was called the Chapel of Hope.

When representatives from the RCA Board of Foreign Missions came in the fall of 1950, the chapel was dedicated. Dr. Luman Shafer and the Rev. Barnerd Luben came for the event—the same Barney Luben who had asked us four years earlier, "How would you like to go to Africa?"

He recorded the story:

> Only a few degrees from the equator, far up the tributaries of the Nile on the bank of the Pibor River, is Akobo. Here in the heart of

[4] Kitty Crandall, "First Impressions of Akobo," Board of Foreign Missions, RCA, n.d. Joint Archives of Holland, Hope College.

Africa...is where our missionaries...with their United Presbyterian colleagues, witness to the truth of the gospel. It was here that Dr. Shafer and I were privileged to spend Sunday, the first day of October.

The first gathering of the day was an especially happy one for us who are graduates of Hope College. This was the worship service and dedication of the Chapel of Hope, the gift of the students of Hope College. It's a sturdily constructed building, straw-thatched to blend with the native scene.

Some one hundred fifty Anuaks were there, about one-third of them Christian. Ten non-Christians trekked in from neighboring villages. Three or four tall Nuer men, keepers of the mission cattle, sat with the congregation on the floor. Spears were parked outside the door. Children sat with their mothers.

Bob Swart led the congregational singing. How these folks can sing! And how wonderful it was to hear these songs of Zion on a sabbath morning in a place where but a few short years ago only the songs of the pagans were heard in their dances. Bob is employing his musical gifts in a wonderful way in teaching these people to sing their way to victory.

Harvey Hoekstra preached the sermon. It was gratifying indeed to see this gifted linguist, after so short a time in Sudan, hold these people in rapt attention as he spoke to them in their own tongue on the meaning of worship and the place of the church. It was evident that the policy of setting aside one member of the station for special and intensive language work was paying dividends.

Don McClure, dean of the station, then asked the elders to stand in front of the congregation for the dedication ceremony....One interesting feature was the way the converted witch doctor, though not an elected elder, joined the elders. After all, in view of past leadership, wasn't he an elder, too?

Deputation "Luman and Luben" spoke briefly....then the Christians all walked to a nearby village for the baptism of a sick woman....As she was seated on the ground in front of her hut, the woman made her confession and vows, and the Holy Sacrament was administered. It was a beautiful sight to see Wilma Kats seated beside her, holding her hand during the simple but impressive service.

In the afternoon was the baptismal service in the river near the chapel. There were ten adults and a boy. One woman had a fever and so was sprinkled [as she stood] on the bank; the others were immersed.

As Bob and Don and Harvey stood in the river, I confess it was with some concern that I watched. That river is infested with crocodiles....But in the impressiveness and deep emotion of the occasion, one forgot even this, and praised God for his wonderful grace in redeeming these people.

A stirring incident occurred when a man and his wife were to be baptized. All fetishes and charms must be surrendered when confession of faith is made. This man's faith, however, had not been strong, and he had concealed his pagan relics.

But now came the time for his baptism, and with him came the sacred gourd and all the other things. Before he stepped into the water, he smashed the gourd and threw everything into the [flowing river]. The congregation pelted the objects with missiles and sank them. The man had now made a clean break and was baptized.

From the river to the chapel, the congregation marched singing....Don led in a communion service. We partook of native bread made of grain sorghum and sipped tomato juice from a gourd. As Don spoke on the meaning of the sacrament, the communicants reverently and quietly partook. When we had sung a hymn, we went to our homes.

That evening the missionary force met for a hymn sing and to hear Dr. Shafer [give a report]. As he was speaking, we could hear the steady, rhythmic beat of a drum half a mile away. It was not the beat of an African drum for a tribal dance. It was the throb of Islam in the South Sudan. The Arab merchants were holding a meeting at which many Anuaks and Nuers were present, chanting...to the beat of the drum.

On our Sabbath in Sudan, we saw the Cross and the Crescent strive for the heart of Africa. God speed his church and send his Spirit that Christ may win.[5]

---

[5] Barnerd M. Luben, "One Day in the Sudan." Reprinted from the *Church Herald*, January 19, 1951: 9, 23.

After a Sunday morning service at the Chapel of Hope

The Chapel of Hope stood for many years among the Anuaks, a symbol of hope and new life. Because of countless gatherings within those walls, beneath the cool thatch, many hundreds of Anuaks heard the "good tidings of great joy which shall be to all people" and became followers of their newfound Savior.

These gatherings were always informal, the men sitting on one side of the floor space and the women with the children on the other. They loved to sing song after song, clapping in rhythm. At each service, opportunity was given for confession of faith in Christ and for testimonies to his saving power. The Anuaks were not at all hesitant about sharing what Christ meant to them.

The preacher for the day was chosen by a group of seven men who served as a church council. Attendance averaged about one hundred twenty adults (about eighty baptized Christians) plus the boys from the school when it was in session. Those were good numbers, except for the sad realization that there were scores of people within easy walking distance of the chapel, all of whom had been exposed to the old, old story that was still so new to them, who sat complacently in their villages with apparently no desire to hear more. It hardly comforted us to be reminded that such is the condition of people all over the world.

But tell the neighbors that there would be pictures and the news would spread like wildfire from village to village. On the darkest night, when mosquitoes were thick and there was perhaps a hint of a storm in the air, whole villages would walk miles and the chapel would be packed.

These picture services, centered around a few selected slides of the life of Christ, were begun to counteract the increasing popularity and irresistibility of the Muslim drum. At the first meeting, we were thankful when we no longer could hear the drumbeat because of the singing of the Anuaks.

The use of visual aids—slides and flannelgraph in particular—proved to be of tremendous value in fixing a truth in seeking minds. A picture of the crucifixion was especially significant to them. Some said, "Before, we just heard that Jesus died on a cross for us, but now it has really come into our hearts."

The school compound on which the Chapel of Hope was built was always a beehive of activity. In its twelve years of existence, the school had come a long way, as Wilma Kats indicated in a 1950 article about the mission school at Akobo.

Mission work at Akobo began in 1938 when Don and Lyda McClure moved there from Doleib Hill. The McClures lost no time in opening a school, and though they lived at Akobo only three out of the next ten years, the school has had a continuous history. For six of those years, the school was taught by an Anuak who had been educated at Nasir in Nuer country. He was a born teacher as well as a fine Christian. His sudden death was a real blow to the school and to his people.

Now, in 1950, the school has four grades with five teachers. During the past two years, the enrollment has hovered around one hundred thirty. About eighty of these boys are in boarding school; the others come in daily from the nearby villages.

Approximately half of the boarders come from an area about one hundred miles from Akobo. They walk all the way. Each school term, when they return from vacation, they bring new boys with them. Because the school year begins in May just before the heavy rains, the paths are still dry, and walking is not difficult. However, school closes again in November just after the rains, and sometimes the boys have to swim across rivers and wade through swampy pools in order to reach their villages.

Fortunately, in walking to and from school, they are not encumbered as we are with baggage. Most of the boys arrive at Akobo with no other clothing than a loincloth. They carry no food, for they are fed in the homes along the way wherever they spend the night.

When school begins, each student is given a yard and a half of unbleached muslin which he wears draped under the right arm, with two corners knotted on the left shoulder. He is given soap once a week to keep this garment clean. When it needs mending, he is given a needle and thread.

The schoolboy spends his day in the classroom, in the school garden, and on the playground. The day gets off to a good start with six o'clock prayers, followed by physical exercises or marching drills.

In the classroom he is taught reading, writing, arithmetic, and most important of all the way of salvation from the Word of God. With the exception of the English reading and writing lessons, the teaching in the first three grades is done in the Anuak tongue. But in the fourth grade, all teaching is in English. In this way, the students will be better prepared for further education at schools where all the teaching is done in English.

The boys are required to work in the school gardens where they grow their own food: beans, *durra* (sorghum or milo), corn, and pumpkins. Once a week, a bull is slaughtered to provide meat. Day pupils receive one meal a day at the school; boarders have the customary two meals a day.

Each boy must pay a small fee when he comes to school, the equivalent of about fifty cents per term. If they don't have the money, they are given special work to do so they can earn it.

The school has played an important part in the evangelistic program of the mission. This has been especially true in the recent spiritual awakening at Akobo. The schoolboys and teachers have been going from village to village giving the gospel message. They learn Christian ways in the chapel meetings and in daily study. Then they are encouraged and given opportunity to take what they have learned and share it with their people.

Sad to report, there is no formal girls' education here at Akobo to date. All that has been done so far has been the daily Bible meetings with the women and children in nearby villages. These have not been without gratifying results, but it is not adequate. I have been thrilled to be able to conduct these daily meetings. However, I am looking forward to the coming school year when I hope to devote my entire energy to educating young girls. The aim will be to raise up fine Christian wives and mothers who can pass on to their villages the blessings of a Christian home.

There are many problems involved in this matter of girls' education. The life of a little Anuak girl is a busy one. Her mother has taught her how to pound grain using the mortar and pestle, and also the fine art of carrying water on her head from the river. She is expected to care for the younger children.

Could an Anuak girl find time to go to school regularly? Would her parents give permission? Would it be wise to remove her even that much from her village life? Would she be willing to go back to it again when she had completed her training?

And about the curriculum: what should the girls be taught? They need training in home and family life so that they may take their place gracefully in the culture pattern.

Plans for the coming year are not complete, though we have made some decisions. For the time being, we shall not have a boarding school. My proposal is to have them come to school for not more than three hours each day. The greater part of that time will be spent teaching them the Bible and preparing them for reading it in their own language.

The remainder of the session will be used in teaching them simple sewing and mending, and ways to make home and personal life more healthful and pleasant.

The task will not be an easy one. It will require much prayer as well as guidance from the hand and heart of our great Teacher, Jesus Christ.[6]

As Wilma had hoped, the next year saw her dream realized. A day school for girls was opened at Akobo with an enrollment of eighteen, not including the baby sisters who had to be carried along each day. Most of these students came from homes where at least one of the parents was a Christian. They ranged in age from about five to fifteen years.

Since the government had no part in its financial support, the school was not subject to government regulations. So Wilma was able to set her own curriculum. It was a simple one: Bible study, reading, writing, handwork, and crafts.

The consensus among Anuak men at that time—even among the most enlightened—was that they would not want to have an educated wife. In fact, one of the finest Christian fathers refused to allow his daughter, who was approaching marriageable age, to attend the school.

It was earnestly hoped that this attitude would change, and that educated men would seek to have educated, Christian wives for joyful fellowship in reading the Word and growing together in Christ as they developed Christian Anuak families.

The "ladies' house" was built just upriver from the Swarts' place. This was Wilma's home. It was also the home of Joan Yilek and Lillian Huisken. Joan was a United Presbyterian missionary who devoted herself entirely to women's evangelism.

Lillian received her call to become a missionary when she was serving as an Army nurse in England during World War II. Commissioned by the RCA in October 1949, she traveled to Sudan, arriving at Akobo, on December 2 with Lee and Kitty Crandall. Responsibility was soon on her shoulders.

With Dr. Roode's furlough imminent in 1950, Lillian applied herself intensely to language study. As she could, she assisted the doctor at the clinic, picking up at the same time a smattering of medical vocabulary.

---

[6] Wilma Kats, "Going to School in Africa," Board of Foreign Missions, RCA, 1950. Joint Archives of Holland, Hope College.

So, when the day came for the Roode family to leave, though she was still trying to get her ears tuned to the strange-sounding words and groping her way through the maze of Anuak grammar and sentence structure, Lillian was able to cope quite well, with the help of an interpreter. In those early days, the clinic was open for about two hours every morning.

Before treatment was given, except in the case of emergency, patients were instructed briefly from a passage of Scripture and prayer was offered that those who were ill would be healed by the touch of the Great Physician's hand.

Then the ulcers were dressed and the diseased eyes treated. Medicine was given out for malaria, dysentery, and leprosy.

Lillian did some medical work out in the villages, also. She and her language teacher would go out to visit those who were too ill to walk to the clinic. Her visits always included a time of sharing from the Word as well as prayer for blessing on the medicines and for the healing of the patient. Lillian regarded this means of service to be a great privilege.

Two years later, with considerably more knowledge of language and tropical medicine behind her, Lillian told about some of her experiences:

"Madam, we have here a dead baby."

At the kitchen door stood Oko, one of our sincere Christian teachers. With him was his wife who is not a believer. Their faces showed deep concern.

The baby was suffering from an intestinal disorder which was not difficult to diagnose, and after a few days of treatment, he was again back to health.

Before they came to the door, and while Oko was busy teaching at the school, his mother and his wife had taken the child to the witch doctor after having already received medicine at the mission clinic. Oko later said, "Now we have two doctors. I thank God because my baby is well, but my wife thanks the witch doctor. It is very hard when a man is a Christian and his wife is not; they cannot be one."

It is not surprising that at first the Anuaks think of the "white man's medicine" as another form of magic when a shot of penicillin brings such dramatic changes in some of their ailments. Many patients come to the clinic wanting only a "shot of magic." Having experienced the quick results of the drug, they think it must be good for every disease, and they become impatient with repeated dosages or dressings—any prolonged treatment.

Medical work, however, does present many opportunities for showing the love of Christ and telling the Good News. In one village, there was a woman who had been consistently unfriendly, refusing to join those who sat around to hear the gospel. Then she became very ill with pneumonia. After treatment, she recovered. Since then she has been friendly and warm in her welcome, and willingly sits with the others to listen.

Although our work is among Anuaks, members of the Nuer tribe who also live in the vicinity make up a good percentage of the patient load. In the dry season, some have walked from as far away as sixty miles, sometimes carrying sick children. Even Murles who live in the Pibor area, ninety miles away, have come for treatment. Besides the usual dysenteries, malaria, and upper respiratory problems, we also treat yaws, venereal disease, tuberculosis, and a few cases of leprosy. There are also numerous baffling skin diseases which are typical of the tropics.

At the beginning of the rains this year, there were several cases of polio. Unlike the epidemics in the United States, polio seems to be endemic among these people; it's always there, but in a milder form. Certainly some immunity has been built up over the generations. Smallpox, too, is quite common, but again, usually not so severe—though in Murle country last year many people died of this illness.

Because they don't know about germs and bacteria, their lifestyle often contributes to the unnecessary spread of disease. Families sleep together in close proximity, and eat from one gourd in sickness and in health.

At a village where a schoolboy lay dying with polio, several mothers with their children were squatting immediately outside the door of the hut. When I urged them to take their babies to their own village, their response was cold and indifferent: "Can a woman take her child away from a village where another is sick? Does she not care for the sick child, or does she love her own much better?"

The dying boy's baby cousin had been sleeping with him in the same hut every night. When the boy died and was buried, each related child had to throw a handful of dirt on the grave as a dismissal of the evil spirit, lest he, too, should become ill.

Superstition is not easy to overcome, even among those who claim to trust Jesus Christ. Abongo is a Christian, but for the first three weeks of her newborn baby's life, she would not take him beyond the cornstalk enclosure of their village for fear that someone might cast an evil eye on the child and he would be cursed in some way.

But there are a few who, in times of temptation and trial, really do look to God with childlike faith. Apio is one of these.[7]

Wilma Kats takes up the story here:

Apio is not very tall. Her name tells me she is the first one of twins. Her skin is coal-black. When she and her sister Anuaks come up from a bath in the river, their bodies shine like polished ebony in the noonday sun....

Apio has a husband and five sons. Her husband, Agwenyang, looks much older than she....Perhaps he was older when he married Apio because he didn't have any sisters, and it took him many years to gather together a bride price that an Anuak man must pay for a wife: ten cows, twenty goats, fifty spears, and three strings of marriage beads called *demoi* [or *dimui*]. Some of these things are almost unobtainable unless the man has a sister who is being married, in which case, items of that bride price are being paid to the family. It often takes a lifetime to finish paying for a wife.

I once asked Apio, "Wouldn't you have preferred having some daughters, rather than all sons?"

She just smiled and said, "Isn't that the talk of God?"

"The talk of God" is a familiar phrase. To an Anuak, everything is the talk of God. He goes fishing. If he returns empty-handed, it's because "God refused him." A baby falls into the fire and is badly burned. It's the talk of God. The sacrifices of the witch doctor fail to restore a wife burning up with fever. She dies.

"What about that?" you ask.

7 Lillian Huisken, R.N., "In the Name of the Great Physician." Reprinted from the *Church Herald*, February 13, 1953: 5.

He shrugs his shoulder and replies, "Isn't it the talk of God?"

But when Apio says the phrase, it is more than just an idiom of the Anuak language—more than just an expression of a fatalistic approach to life and death. Because Apio knows Jesus.

Both Apio and her husband are baptized Christians. I saw her the day she stepped down into the river to receive "the sign of Jesus" on her head. She had heard about Jesus at the women's meetings. It was there she learned to pray. We refer to her as "the praying woman."

If she is pounding grain when I call on her in her village, she puts down the heavy pestle and sits beside me. We visit for a short time; then she says, "Let us pray." And Apio prays.

Should she hear that one of the missionaries is in bed with a fever, she lays aside her work and goes to visit the sick one. She doesn't stay long, nor does she say much, but before she leaves, she says, "Let us pray." And Apio prays.

Sometimes Apio brings her youngest son to our house for us to admire. She gives us a few minutes with the baby, all the while smiling with pride—and again she says, "Let us pray."

One night Apio came to the house with that baby burning with fever, his little body stiffened with convulsions. Our nurse, Lillian Huisken, administered medicine. We prayed. Apio prayed. The fever burned on. More medicine, more prayer. The convulsions continued to grip the child.

All the next day there was no change. After another sleepless night, the baby seemed to be dying in the throes of another terrible seizure.

Then Apio cried out, in the agony of her mother heart, a prayer that God heard and understood, because he, too, had had a dying Son:

"What are we doing? Why are we trying so hard? Does not my baby belong to God? Didn't he give him to me? Did I create him inside of me? Wasn't it God who made him? Then can't God have him if he wants him?"

God's answer came; the baby rallied and lived.

Apio knows Jesus. She has her ups and downs in the Christian life
as we all do. But she loves her Lord and believes in him alone.[8]

Missionaries can learn so much from those to whom they have been sent
to minister. They often find themselves on the receiving end of ministry. For
many years, Apio, in her simple, steadfast faith, was an encourager, as well
as a minister, to the missionaries at Akobo.

---

[8] Wilma Kats, "Apio, Anuak Praying Woman." Reprinted from the *Church Herald*,
February 13, 1953: 8.

IV
Our Expanding Mission

The mission program at Akobo gradually was attaining full stature. Evangelism was a many-pronged endeavor. Schools for both boys and girls were flourishing. The clinic was meeting a tremendous need in the community. Ministry among women was nicely underway. Successes as well as setbacks were part of the continuing story.

Some months after the Crandalls' arrival, when the rains began, Lee began experimenting with a few agricultural projects—but not without hazards. Melons grew well on the banks of the river, but the Anuaks were too eager; because the fruit disappeared long before it was ripe, Lee had to post a guard day and night so the melons could mature.

He encouraged a few of the Christians to grow fruit trees—papayas, guavas, citrus, mangoes—but soon they gave up bothering to water and nurture the trees. "We know our people," they said. "They'll steal all the fruit."

The Anuaks were satisfied to continue their monotonous, though nutritious, diet of *durra*, a crop high in protein. An occasional fish rounded out their meals.

An effort to upgrade the local poultry ended in disaster. Lee brought in a dozen large eggs along with a hatchery in which to incubate them. The eggs hatched. The chicks, carefully tended and kept in a fenced area, were half-grown when a cobra slithered in somehow and devoured them all. The next morning, imprisoned by his own voracious appetite, the snake was still there, the twelve bulges along his length a silent testimony to his crime.

(Is it any wonder that Lee went to seminary during his first furlough and returned simply to do evangelism?)

But the mission garden prospered under Lee's expertise. By this time we had a gasoline pump for irrigation. It floated on pontoons near the river's edge. With this more efficient means of watering the garden, we enjoyed all kinds of fruits and vegetables, including tomatoes, beans, beets, carrots, peppers, citrus fruits, bananas, papayas, and mangoes.

Lee also supervised the management of the mission herd that gave each family a few quarts of fresh milk every day. If we were careful, and determined, we could collect enough cream for an occasional treat of ice cream or butter.

We were grateful for our "aggie's" ministry among us; fresh foods allowed us a measure of good health that might not have been ours otherwise.

Another great blessing, which sent missionary spirits soaring and opened up many more possibilities for carrying out the Great Commission, was a gift from God right out of the blue: wings.

In November 1950, Bob and I, our three children, and Lillian Huisken started off from Akobo in the mission boat, the first lap of a journey that would take us to Khartoum for a brief vacation. Because the boat's engine was temperamental, we drifted most of the way to Nasir. After three days there, a steamer, coming from Gambela, stopped at Nasir and agreed to tow us to Malakal. By the time we reached that town, we had been en route for nine days. A Nile steamer and a train took us the rest of the way to our destination.

While we were enjoying the amenities of Khartoum, the Missionary Aviation Fellowship (MAF), having passed certain tests and obtained necessary permits, cleared with the Sudan government and was ready to fly. Upon our return to Malakal some days later, so were we.

On the appointed day, we departed in the five-passenger DeHaviland Rapide. Below we could see the river snaking its way in deep U-curves through the desolate savanna. Instead of the winding path we had traveled

The first MAF plane in Sudan: the DeHaviland Rapide

a few weeks before, the plane in one and a half hours took us straight to Akobo without swerving.

MAF is a Christian organization whose main purpose is to facilitate the spread of the gospel, especially in areas where transportation is a problem. In 1950, the missionaries stationed at Akobo spent a total of 366 days traveling. Had MAF been available, the same distances could have been covered in thirty-six hours.[1]

MAF services were invaluable for medical emergencies, survey flights, and taking missionary personnel into distant or otherwise inaccessible country. The dedication and reliability of MAF personnel—at that time, Steve Stevens and Stuart King—were exemplary. They became a vital, indispensable arm of many mission strategies. Africans themselves realized their worth and prayed for them. The Anuaks would say: "God, we know it is your power that keeps that sky-boat up in the air; it has no strength in itself."[2]

[1] Robert Swart, "God Gave Us Wings" (not strictly quoted). Reprinted from the *Church Herald*, March 23, 1951: 4.
[2] Ibid.

To the mission children, Steve and Stuart were heroes; their favorite pretend game was flying an airplane.

Before knowing where its plane would be based, MAF established headquarters at Akobo. This was possible because Bob had supervised the building of another house on the compound. The Hoekstras had moved into their new home from Pakang, and soon after left for the States on their first furlough. The Stevens family moved in and Stuart lived with us for a time.

In the meantime, the Crandalls had gone to Tanta, Egypt, for the birth of their first child. Alan was born on January 5, 1951. Upon their return to Akobo, they moved in with the Stevens family.

On March 31 someone in the house lit an Aladdin lamp, and when everyone's back was turned the flame crept up the chimney—and found the grass roof. In a matter of seconds, the whole thatch was ablaze. The parents could no nothing but grab their children and escape. We praised God that no one was injured—or even singed—but the trauma remained for some time.

The other households took in the two families. As word of the fire spread through the mission by radio, cartons of clothing and household items began arriving. It wasn't long before our friends were well equipped once again.

As soon as the bricks cooled, Bob started clearing away the rubble and rebuilding on what was left of the foundation.

Our fourth child was due the month after the fire. On April 20 there were signs that this little one wasn't going to wait any longer. So MAF flew to Nasir and returned with Dr. Mary Smith. With Kitty Crandall and Lillian Huisken also in attendance, Dr. Mary delivered Chloe Jeanne during the wee hours of the twenty-first. Our cup of joy was running over.

Paul and Laurel Arnold, with their three small youngsters, joined our ranks that same year in October. Paul was to be the headmaster of the Akobo school.

When they arrived in Khartoum, there was a letter from the Crandalls urging them to fly from there all the way to Akobo so that Paul could see the school while it was still in session. It would close on November 10.

The MAF Rapide could take only three hundred pounds of baggage, so besides doing some quick shopping during their two days in the capital city, they had to decide what to take and what to leave for the steamer. It was a three and a half hour Rapide flight from Khartoum to Malakal, and another one and a half hours to Akobo.

Laurel wrote about their arrival:

> Oh, what a hilarious time! We tumbled out of the plane and
> everyone gasped and laughed. They could hardly believe it was us.
> We'd made the quickest time to the field so far....We were loaded
> into Crandalls' Jeep truck and carted back to the station where the
> wives and children met us with more hilarity. Finally we
> remembered we were hungry and Morrie Swart opened some cans
> and fed us. Folks broke out cots, beds, sheets, blankets, a bureau,
> and set us up in Crandalls' house, the same one that burned last
> March.
>
> The first night we were here, we had a station meeting. Lee and
> Kitty have applied for a special furlough in December. Swarts are
> due for furlough in the summer, as well as Wilma Kats. The Roodes
> may have to leave Akobo if [permission comes through to open new
> work at Pibor Post].[3]

Don and Lyda McClure had, during the previous year, moved to Ethiopia,
the mission having been granted by the government a two-mile strip along
the Baro River for a station among the Anuaks there—the same site that Bob
and Harvey had recommended. Don named the area *Pokwo* which means
"village of life." Joan Yilek would soon be joining Don and Lyda at Pokwo.

> ...which leaves Paul and me and Lillian Huisken here to hold the
> fort next year. We were a bit jolted at first, but we're quite used to
> the idea now of having school responsibility in May 1952. It gives
> us six months of solid language study.
>
> The men are getting the house at Pakang ready for us—color-
> washing the walls, repairing screens, etc. It was Hoekstras' old
> house....We'll have a good chance to study language there; it's too
> easy to use English here [at the mission]....
>
> The day we moved...the Christians gave us a welcoming dance.
> The men brought the big school drum and set it under a tree, also
> a smaller one. Small boys held them; the men took turns beating
> them. One man led the singing....He led off the first line in a high

---

[3] Laurel Arnold, from letters written home, 1951–1952. Joint Archives of Holland,
Hope College.

falsetto and the rest would join in. Paul and Lee did a dramatic dance with spears which made everyone hoot with enjoyment. Then Kitty and I tried the forward and back shuffle with the women; there is a sort of slow trot they do, too, and a high jump. We danced with them for a half hour and were exhausted. Yet such dances sometimes last three days and nights, and the Anuaks keep going!4

Christmas that year was memorable for the Arnolds, especially the pageant put on by Wilma's schoolgirls:

Using the kerosene projector for light against the school wall, it was lovely. The girls wore their native garb, with a draped headdress to denote shepherd, or a crown to denote king. They sat on mats. "Mary" was sifting *durra* flour Anuak style when the angel announced the conception. It was their first try, full of giggles and prompting, but on the whole, a lovely thing....Then we went to Swarts' for the climax of our Christmas: two hours of the "Messiah," and chocolate cake and coffee....5

Dr. Al and Ruth Roode had returned from furlough just a few weeks before the Arnolds arrived. They brought with them someone new for us to meet. Their sons Peter, John (Joe), and Philip now had a little sister named Janet.

How long the Roode family would be at Akobo was a question. Negotiations with the British government were underway to establish a mission presence ninety miles south at Pibor Post among the Murle people. The Roodes were slated to spearhead that new venture; the Swarts would join them following their stateside leave.

The Hoekstra family had left Akobo for their furlough some days before the fire. They returned early in 1952, thus allaying any apprehension the Arnolds may have had about "holding the fort."

To have the doctor in residence again and to have the linguist-translator back at his post once more, was a real boon to the ongoing, comprehensive agenda of the mission: that of meeting the tribal needs of body, mind, and spirit. We praised God for his safekeeping of both families in all their travels. They had been the first of our number to go and return.

4 Ibid.
5 Ibid.

As months became years, the sense of urgency in getting out the Word increased. Islam was relentlessly moving southward. Nationalism and independence were in the very air we breathed. It was uncertain how much longer missions in Sudan would enjoy the benevolent presence and approbation of the British government.

As soon as new missionaries could put words and sentences together, they would go out into the villages to practice what they had learned and also to give the Good News of Christ. On Sundays they would go farther afield with translated Bible stories and Christian songs of joy. Occasionally longer treks were made to the far reaches of the tribe. There were always Anuaks who wanted to hear.

The importance of hearing cannot be overestimated. However, to ensure a strong church, greater maturity in faith, and spiritual perception, hearing eventually must be coupled with an ability to read the Word.

So that the Anuaks could become readers as soon as possible, Harvey Hoekstra's specific and sole assignment was to provide, in the Anuak tongue, reading primers and other suitable materials for intensive literacy programs— and to translate the Bible. Though Harvey has confessed that he often felt guilty sitting in his office doing the work he loved while other colleagues worked in the hot sun, no one begrudged him his assigned task. Don encouraged him to "stick with it. Nothing is more important." All of us agreed wholeheartedly.

> To this task we set ourselves prayerfully, seeking that wisdom which is from above, and setting our heart and mind to it with long hours of undivided attention. Progress sometimes seems slow and spasmodic....Nevertheless, sufficient data has been accumulated so that the language is reasonably written....We rejoice in the completing of a first reading primer with illustrative charts, and a second reader. These will be used primarily among the adult Christians who are now learning to read. Two Bible story books with about thirty-five stories with applications have already been distributed among the teachers and students....
>
> Our goal is that every believer should be a Bible-reading Christian. Church history teaches us so clearly that wherever the Bible has been translated into the language of the people, the believers have been strong and firm for Christ.

It was a happy day at Akobo when the Gospel of Mark was completed. Two Anuaks seemed by chance to be at the door when we had finished the last verse. I went out and we sat down. I read chapters fifteen and sixteen to them. I wish you might have seen the eager expressions on their faces as they listened intently to the message of the crucifixion and the resurrection of Christ. I shall never forget that day. Today, one of those men is baptized.... More than fifty persons were baptized on Christmas Sunday. Now most of these folks are learning to read. Will these believers revert back to the superstitious customs of their fathers? We are convinced that it will not be so because, having learned to read, they will be grounded in the faith.[6]

At once exhausting and exhilarating, the task of translating the whole New Testament took Harvey thirteen years. The completed work, published by the American Bible Society, would arrive at a crucial moment of the Christian missionary endeavor in the South Sudan, in the early history of the Anuak church.

Our first son was born in 1952. Because the births of Merry and Chloe in our home at Akobo had been such pleasant experiences, I wanted so much to stay there until after this child's arrival in July. But the dovetailing of furlough schedules and the hope of being able to push south into Murle country toward the end of the year overruled my desire. Indeed, it was God himself who overruled. We left Akobo in March.

Because of my "delicate condition," we made the extravagant decision to fly from Malakal to Khartoum and on to London. Once in London, we waited nine days for a ship from Southampton to New York. I spent those nine days in a London hospital, while Bob and the four little girls suffered from claustrophobia in one room of a lodging house during England's coldest March in over eighty years.

We were home with my parents on Long Island for two weeks when, on April 22, I had to go to the hospital again—where I stayed until May 16 when John Robert Jr., was born by cesarean section. The problem was a placenta praevia, but God made everything work together for our good. Humanly speaking, neither Jack nor his mother would have survived had we remained

---

[6] Harvey Hoekstra, "The Splendor of the Word," a brochure published by the Board of Foreign Missions, 1950. Joint Archives of Holland, Hope College.

at Akobo. To me, this story illustrates the wisdom of saying in any circumstance, "Not my will, O Lord, but yours be done," and then submitting to his sovereignty. Our Father in heaven does know best!

So we sent out the glad word that God had blessed us with a son. But during that year at home we received the heartbreaking news that one of our families in Sudan had lost a little son. Laurel Arnold had felt relieved to be taking her children away from polio epidemics in the New York area. What she didn't know was that poliomyelitis was endemic among the tribespeople; although a few died of it, it never reached epidemic proportions. Measles was a much more deadly disease in Africa.

Chris Arnold was stricken in the lumbar region and died in a matter of days. What a blow to the whole mission family. The parents were devastated. Paul wrote a letter that began with the incredulous words, "Chris is dead." Laurel walked and walked by herself in the rain, and the Anuak women would say to her, "Go home, Nyiray." They were afraid she might take her own life as grieving Anuak mothers sometimes did.

Decades later, Laurel wrote: "[Chris's grave] is a bit of us that will always be in Sudan....The pain will always be in our hearts as long as we live, but it doesn't take away the thankfulness for God's victory, for Al Roode's agonizing and care, the love of those around us."

For many years it had been the desire of the American Presbyterian Mission to take the gospel to the Murle tribe whose territory was farther up the Pibor River. Bob Swart and Al Roode made several survey trips in Murle country around Pibor Post and even as far south and east as the Boma Plateau near the Ethiopian border. This was a dream not only of the mission, but also of our district commissioner. But it was another matter to convince even the friendly British officials at the provincial level that this would be a good move.

With the possibility of independence for the Anglo-Egyptian Sudan looming nearer, it was essential to obtain permission while Sudan was still a British colony; it was doubtful that it would ever be granted by any future Muslim regime. But Governor Long of Upper Nile Province refused. He said in essence, "You Americans start a mission station in a new place [Akobo], and then you want to open still other work before the first one is completed. Stay where you are."

But to "stay where you are" was not God's plan; for some years, he had been preparing for this moment, as revealed in three vignettes:

About 1940, the Rev. Dr. Glenn Reed, a United Presbyterian missionary then working at Doleib Hill, was concerned for the Murles. He took a steamer as far as Akobo and then walked the rest of the way to Pibor Post. Upon his return to Doleib Hill and then to Malakal, he went to see the incumbent governor. He asked for authorization for the mission to open a station in the Pibor Post area, and permission was granted. The governor sent a request to the central government in Khartoum, and it was approved. But during the war years, this was not acted upon.

Happily, the Rev. J. Lowrie Anderson, who was general secretary of the American Presbyterian Mission at the time of Long's governorship, recalled Glenn Reed's trek of ten years before. He knew that the consent papers must be somewhere in government files.

So, with his memory jogged, Lowrie Anderson went back to Governor Long to present his case. Sure enough, there in the records was the forgotten permit. The governor relented, gave his permission, and sent to Khartoum for approval. A few months after we had left for furlough, all papers were cleared, and in September 1952 Dr. Roode and his family moved from Akobo to Pibor Post.

During World War II, a young British army officer was stationed with his troops on the Boma Plateau to keep the Italians in Ethiopia from entering Sudan. Since there was little activity at this segment of the border, the officer spent much of his time studying the Murle language. He learned it well enough to compile a dictionary and a grammar that were published by the government in Khartoum. This young officer, Captain Richard E. Lyth, in a few years would be assigned as the district commissioner for all of Pibor District, which included both Akobo and Pibor Posts.

While he was still stationed on the Boma Plateau, God used Dick Lyth in another amazing way. Lado Lukurngoli was born an Anuak. When Lado was a small child, the Murles raided the Anuaks and took him, among others, back to Murle country as a slave. So Lado grew up as a Murle who for years apparently had no contact with his Anuak roots.

One night after he had become a young man, Lado was awakened by a light in his hut, and he heard a voice calling his name and saying, "You must find the true God and then tell your people about him." Though Lado knew that this was no trifling matter, he was slow to begin his quest. But when he could no longer ignore that call, he started out on a journey that took him, as if a star were guiding him, to Dick Lyth, the only man in the world who knew his language, and who also could tell him about Jesus Christ. Upon hearing about the Savior, Lado knew immediately that his search was over.

Dick later said that Lado did not need to be converted in the usual sense; he was already a believer who drank in every word of instruction as a man dying of thirst seeks for water. Older though he was, this new Christian went to school for four years at Akobo where Don McClure eventually baptized him.

And Lado, the Anuak, became the first evangelist to the Murle, the very people who had enslaved him. He worked alongside Al Roode during the early months at the new mission post, and he continued in his roles as evangelist, interpreter, and friend of us all, following our return from furlough in early 1953, when we joined the Roode family in Murle country at Pibor Post.[7]

---

[7] Albert G. Roode, "History of the Murle Church," an unpublished document, n.d. Joint Archives of Holland, Hope College

V
The Move to Pibor

The nine-month furlough ended and on January 16, 1953, we and our five children were on our eager way back to Sudan on the *SS Franconia*. Lambert (Bud) and Kate Ekster and their three children traveled with us. Bud would fill the need for a second mission builder as new work opened up in the South Sudan. (United Presbyterian Ted Pollock had been the sole mission builder for several years.)

Our route took us via Liverpool, England, to Port Sudan on the Red Sea. Satisfying as furlough had been, we had that "at last" feeling as soon as we disembarked and set foot on Sudanese soil. We had lost our hearts to this country. The South beckoned, and we were champing at the bit to get there.

On our way through Khartoum, we met LaVerne and Lorraine Sikkema, who had arrived the previous September on a Dutch freighter. They were staying in the North for some months to study Arabic, which recently had become a requirement.

The Sikkemas' interest in the Anglo-Egyptian Sudan was sparked in the fall of 1947 when they, along with hundreds of other Hope College students, heard Dr. Don McClure speak during Mission Emphasis Week.

Verne and Lorraine had already declared their inclination toward becoming missionaries when Ruth Ransom, from the New York office, had come to the college seeking recruits. But Don's impassioned appeal stirred them to further action, and they set their sights on Sudan.

75

Verne grew up on a farm near Morrison, Illinois, and following graduation from Hope College he took advanced training in agriculture at Cornell University in Ithaca, New York, to prepare for a rural ministry in Sudan.

The Crandall family had left Akobo for the States by the time Verne, Lorraine, and baby Linda Faith (born July 11, 1953, in Tanta, Egypt) arrived to carry on their assignment among the Anuaks. Sometime later they were joined by agriculturist Charles (Chuck) Jordan and his family, United Presbyterians from Nasir. Together Verne and Chuck followed Lee Crandall as the "ag team," and for several years they worked together on various projects and training programs.

Those in the first training program included not only Anuaks, but also Nuers who were gradually moving in to the Akobo environs, as well as several Shullas. It was hoped that learning better methods in many areas of agriculture would substantially raise their standard of living.

After prayer and Bible study in the early morning, the practical work, under Verne's and Chuck's supervision, was done before the heat of the day. Classes of a more academic nature, such as the three Rs, were scheduled for late afternoon.

One of their practical experiments had to do with *durra*, the Anuaks' staple crop. Chuck had brought seventy seed varieties of this grain from Texas A&M. Not all of them did well, but the experimental plot generated a lot of interest in the community.

Verne, practically raised on a John Deere tractor, was keen to introduce mechanical farming to the Anuaks, knowing that, if done properly, it would produce a far greater yield. For several years, the gray Ford tractor and other machinery, including a grain drill, disk, rotary grass cutter, and an ensilage cutter, became part of the Akobo landscape.

Another encouragement for the people was the provision of a grain storage bin. The annual hunger season occurred because of poor storage methods, the pestilential rat population, and the Anuaks' need for cash during the year. Just after harvest, when *durra* was plentiful, they would sell kilos and kilos of this precious commodity to Arab merchants at a low price. Then, a few months later, when the Anuak supplies ran out, they sold the grain back to them at highly inflated prices. Tribal folks were at the mercy of these northern traders.

Besides working to improve crops and storage, attempts were made to upgrade breeding stock of local cattle. A young Jersey bull, imported from

Egypt, died of rinderpest after two years in the South. But some cattle, purchased from another mission area, fared better. And milk production increased when the cows were fed ensilage stored in a pit silo. But constant apathy and reluctance to change made it all uphill work. About the pit silo people said, "It won't work!" About the new varieties of grain women would complain, "It's so much harder to pound into flour," or "It just doesn't taste right."

After the British left in 1954, another barrier to improvement arose: the success of a cash crop of melons grown by a Nuer Christian named Philip. But his lucrative business roused the ire of the Arab merchants who complained to northern officials. Philip was called in. They asked him why he had taken a Christian name, and where he had obtained the melon seeds. They put a ceiling price on his produce and decreed that he could no longer sell them at the government post. So this entrepreneur's market was gone; his profits, of course, shrank to nothing. The new government officials and local Arabs also singled out for harassment some of the Christian elders and young leaders who had the advantage of several acres of tractor-plowed fields at their disposal.

Pressure against the mission and the Christians was building and we all began to wonder what the future would hold.

If we had the "at last" feeling when we set foot on Sudanese soil way up north, it was "home at last" when we reached Akobo and were welcomed by mission colleagues, our Anuak friends, and the wonderful fragrance of the dungfires.

Bud Ekster, in recalling the trip overland to Akobo, remembers his initiation to dungfires:

> ...we took off for Akobo in late afternoon. Bob and I were riding on top of the Jerk [an old mission truck] and we passed through a village. They had their dungfires going and the air was heavy with smoke.
>
> Bob turned to me and said, "Do you smell that, Bud?" And he had an expression on his face as though he were smelling Chanel No. 5. "That's the Sudan!"

But Akobo would be our home no longer. As much as we loved our first place of residence in Africa, Pibor Post was now our ultimate destination, and we were eager to be on our way. The Roode family had preceded us by several months.

While the children and I remained as guests of Wilma Kats and Lillian Huisken at Akobo, Bob went on ahead to see the lay of the land and to encourage Al and Ruth personally that others soon would be sharing the rigors and intriguing responsibilities of opening new work.

How favored we were to have the wholehearted backing, even the aiding and abetting, of our district commissioner. Not only had Dick Lyth assisted Al Roode in locating a tract of land suitable for a mission station, but he and his wife, Nora, also offered us the use of their house at Pibor Post while ours was being built.

So after six weeks, the whole Swart family was able to move ninety miles south of Akobo to a place that would be our home for the next ten years.

The American Presbyterian Mission at Pibor was about a mile upstream from the government post. The land there was about thirty feet above river level, the highest in the area. Unlike Akobo, which was surrounded by starkly beautiful savanna country, that section of the Pibor River was fairly thickly forested with great tamarind trees and another thorny variety which was called *heglig*. We would always be grateful for the shade those native trees afforded us.

The Roodes' first shelter was rectangular, made of grass tied to a stick frame, not unlike the Murle homes which resembled old-fashioned haystacks flattened at the top. Our permanent houses, however, were designed like those at Akobo, but were built somewhat more substantially.

Thirteen miles away was a rocky outcrop that rose conspicuously a few hundred feet out of the otherwise flat countryside. We often went to "The Mountain" for picnics, climbing to the top so we could look out over the vast panoramic plains on all sides. That outcrop supplied us with rock for the walls of both our dwellings. With floors made of small, smooth, cement squares, and the roof of thatch, we were again comfortably housed and sheltered from the tropical heat.

As always in a new tribal area, language study demanded much of our time during those early months. We found Dick Lyth's grammar and dictionary to be of tremendous value, and together with an informant, we made encouraging progress in learning the Murle tongue.

Even as Jesus went about preaching and healing, the combination of evangelism and medicine has usually insured a welcome entree into a previously unreached field. So it proved to be among the Murles.

Early on, Dr. Roode discovered that there were several cases of leprosy in the vicinity. In order that these patients could come and stay for prolonged treatment, he had a designated piece of land cleared where they could put up "cattle camp" housing for themselves. The patients received their daily treatment month after month, and through Lado's ministry, they were introduced to the Savior who loved them and had great compassion for suffering mankind.

One of the first Murles to declare herself to be a believer was Ngachor, a frail little woman who had been ravaged by leprosy for many years. She had hardly any remaining toes. Her fingers were wasting away, her face was covered with nodules, and there wasn't much left of her nose. But Ngachor had a sweet spirit, and she truly loved the Lord.

Ngachor's special gift was songmaking, and over the years she taught many original, indigenous hymns to her people. In her high, pleasing voice, she led Christians and seekers in singing:

Iya Ngerti Joo tama [Came the Son of God from heaven]

Itona rii Joi, Ngerin [God sent his Son]

Iya Yesu, anyaket zooz o tama [Came Jesus, he brought the talk of heaven]

Kagaya Jok, adingding laadun. [We know God, esteemed forever.]

Ngachor was baptized on Christmas in 1953.

Among those baptized with Ngachor was a man named Nyati. He and two other young men, Omato and Lamong, had been under Bob Swart's instruction for some weeks.

This was not the first time that Nyati had heard the good news. A few years before, this man had worked at the government post at Pibor as a water boy—twice a day filling five-gallon kerosene tins with water from the river and hanging them on a kind of yoke across a donkey's back. Nyati then led the donkey as he carried water to all the government dwellings.

Unfortunately, one of the donkeys became rabid and bit Nyati in the face. The district commissioner, Dick Lyth, sent him to the clinic at Akobo for treatment. Dr. Roode, who was still at Akobo at that time, gave Nyati the necessary injections for the prescribed twenty-one days. And for twenty-one days, this Murle heard the gospel message. Following treatment, he returned home to Pibor.

Some months after the Roodes and Swarts had established the mission at Pibor, a man appeared at our door declaring that he wanted to become a Christian. It was the former water boy, Nyati.

A follower of Jesus Christ, Nyati also became a devoted and intrepid evangelist among his people. While Lado continued in his more mission-based ministry, Nyati walked tirelessly from village to village spreading the good news of God's Son.

During these initial years of our missionary experience, we were well aware that the saga of colonialism in Africa was fast drawing to a close. We saw it happening before our very eyes, not only in growing tensions as nationalism increased in the Sudanese consciousness, but also in the actual turnover of power.

In January 1954, the Anglo-Egyptian Sudan became the self-governing Republic of Sudan. Sayyid Ismail al Azhari was Sudan's first prime minister. A few months after his election to this office, he made an official visit to Malakal, the capital of Upper Nile Province and the location of our mission headquarters.

Dr. J. Lowrie Anderson, the mission's general secretary, wrote an account of that visit:

> Our little town of Malakal has had a distinguished visitor—no less than Sayyid Ismail al Azhari.... Since his elevation to the premiership, he has been kept busy in Khartoum making plans to replace the British in the government with qualified Sudanese. Within the month most of the British, who have ruled Sudan for fifty-five years, will be gone....
>
> Independence is heady wine. The people of Malakal were thrilled to welcome to our town the man who represented their newfound freedom. Shops in the downtown area blossomed with new flags, and rows of colored lights were strung in several places where he was to have important meetings....
>
> At last the great day came.
>
> In the early morning, Shilluks [Shullas] began to pour in from the neighboring villages dressed in their finest toggery—feathers,

paint, beads, and colored cloth. They also carried shields and spears, for there was to be a big dance....

Just an hour before the prime minister was scheduled to arrive, a bicyclist arrived at our door with invitations to all members of the American Mission to greet him at the airport....After hasty consultation and quick revision of our day's plans, we started out....It seemed that half of Malakal was going out to meet the plane....The other half was lining the three-mile stretch between the town center and the airport. Everybody was in a gala mood.

When we reached the airport, we presented our tickets to the perspiring policemen who were able to make a path through the crowd...It was 1 p.m. and the runway reflected the heat of the African sun.

There were about two hundred of us who formed the welcoming committee. At last someone signaled that the plane was sighted. A long, slim Dakota descended in a swift glide and taxied to the stand where hundreds stood waiting to show their respect.

The British governor, the new Sudanese governor, and a guard of honor marched over to the plane. The door opened and a short, stout man came out and stood briefly at the top of the steps. After greeting the high officials, he walked briskly to the waiting committee. This was the signal for the crowd to burst into cheers and clapping....One special section broke into a chant: *"Yahya Ismail! Wahid al Nil!"* (Long live Ismail! Great son of the Nile!)....

When I sat next to him at the supper party, I had an opportunity to ask him questions. He spoke warmly of his friendship for America and the Americans....

The problems which his government faces are staggering....Many people in the South Sudan, the home of the blacks, resent the fact that the leadership and the good jobs are mostly in the hands of the northern Arabs. Some are demanding home rule within the new independent state.

Another basic problem undoubtedly is poverty. The prime minister mentioned in his speeches his interest in the experimental work being done near Malakal in growing rice and sugar and new varieties of grass for fodder.

He promised that his government would greatly increase the work being done to improve the cattle of the South Sudan. He promised more pump schemes and more schools. Both are badly needed, but the problem of finding men with technical training is already acute, and there is a great dearth of teachers.

The prime minister did not speak of the work of missions, nor of what they have already done for the people. He did not mention the tensions that can build up as both Islam and Christianity present their claims to the pagan South.

The new government has given assurance that full religious liberty will be the rule. [But] even now, many Christians are afraid of discrimination because of their religion. Let us pray it may not come; let us also pray that if it comes, they may continue strong in their witness to their Lord.

Said an Englishman who knows Azhari: "I know he is a good man. He is sincere and will work wholeheartedly for what he believes is the good of his country!"[1]

One evening in June 1954, we sat with Dick and Nora Lyth outside on their lawn at Pibor Post. It was the last prayer meeting we would have together. The Lyths shortly would be leaving Sudan. Our hearts were heavy, even as we sang hymns of praise—and heavier still when the last "Amen" was said.

Karrar Ahmed Karrar was to be our new district commissioner. He seemed friendly and pleasant enough. But we knew that the government-mission relationship never could be the same again.

At the end of that July, the Swart family flew to Addis Ababa, Ethiopia. The years had passed relentlessly, and the heart-wrenching time had come for Valerie and Gayle to enter boarding school. They were enrolled at Bingham Academy, the Sudan Interior Mission's school for missionary children located just outside of Addis Ababa.

While we were there in Ethiopia's capital city, our second son was born at the Seventh Day Adventist *Fil Wuha* Hospital. We named him Richard

---

[1] J. Lowrie Anderson, "The Prime Minister Visits Malakal." Reprinted from the *Church Herald*, December 13, 1954: 5, 21.

for that good friend who had so recently gone home to England. The arrival of this son made our family, and our joy, complete.

Early in 1955, Bob expressed for us all our initial mood of optimism concerning the turnover to Sudanese rule:

We were at Boma Post [in southeastern Murle territory]—at the end of the road. "We" were an Arab merchant, two Murle men, a young Surma girl with a clay saucer as big as a lid from a pound can of Crisco in her stretched lower lip, a northern Sudanese in government medical service, a school boy who could speak English, and I. We were listening on the merchant's radio to the opening of the first full parliament of the new Sudan. The process toward final self-determination had begun....

That was a year ago. Now the last British official has left our province. What does the future seem to hold?

Fears of curtailment of the work of Christian missions in this Muslim land have vanished. Statements by the new Sudanese governor of the province, supported by our own district commissioner, have assured us freedom of religion...freedom to preach the gospel as long as we stay out of politics.

A sincere desire to have a good and just government is evidenced by the caliber of men sent to this province [which is] one of the least developed, one where Christian missions is very active, and one which is politically a hot potato owing to the tensions between the pagan/Christian blacks and the more sophisticated Muslim Arabs.

The top position of governor has been filled by a man with every personal qualification for his office, as well as education and government service both in Sudan and abroad. The district commissioner...is equally well-equipped for his position and already has evidenced a keen desire to serve the people of his district with good government. The rights of the tribespeople are being protected, and development...is going ahead with the enthusiasm of a young and new regime.

True, this is but the beginning, but this generation is building on good foundations laid by the British. Time alone will tell if the present goals are really reached, but the future looks bright from our vantage point....2

Official Independence Day was celebrated on January 1, 1956—marked by jubilation in the North and hope mingled with apprehension in the South. The general feeling among southerners was that their position had not really changed; British masters had merely been replaced by their Arab counterparts.

But black Africans by nature live largely in the present. So they accepted philosophically each day as it came and for some years went about the normal activities of tribal life.

Mission groups, too, carried on their many-faceted witness unhindered. We were encouraged.

Lado needed a house nearer the mission. He and his wife, Ariet, could have built one; that ordinarily would have been expected. But another plan was afoot.

The Crandall family had returned to Akobo in 1953 following an extended furlough, bringing with them Alan's baby brother, Gary, and a new title for Lee. Having graduated from New Brunswick Theological Seminary in New Jersey, he was now the Rev. Charles Lee Crandall, and his primary emphasis in mission had changed from agriculture to working directly with the church.

Besides training two young Anuaks, Ojulo and Othow, as lay evangelists, Lee encouraged the church body in its faith and growth, and along with Bob Swart laid the groundwork for putting practical Christianity to work across tribal lines.

Cross-cultural can refer to entering another country, but it also can mean going into a neighboring tribe's territory where language, customs, and mores are entirely unlike those of contiguous groups, and where attitudes

2 Robert and Morrell Swart, "Vignettes from the Sudan." Reprinted from the *Church Herald*, March 11, 1955: 13.

of superiority and hatred exist. Many times at Akobo an Anuak called our attention to a Murle walking along the path, probably bound for the clinic, sneering in contempt: "See! There goes an Ajiba!"—using the Anuaks' derogatory name for the Murle people.

So it was no small triumph of the Spirit when a group of eight Anuak Christians responded with enthusiasm to the heretofore unheard of idea of building a house for an evangelist in another tribal area. Their reaction was: "Lado is our brother. Let's go and help him build his house. It will take us only a few days; it would take him over a month."

Olero, a leading Anuak elder, largely was responsible for getting the project rolling and making arrangements for travel and food.

Following an abortive attempt to get through to Pibor because of rain and the impossible cottonsoil mud, they started out on the by now dry, rough track, and after four hours arrived at their destination where they were warmly welcomed by the Murle Christians. It was a Thursday.

Because all necessary materials already had been gathered, and the site for the house had been cleared partially, the Anuak volunteers lost no time in getting to work. That very day they measured the area and dug the circular foundation ditch. On Friday the wall poles were placed upright and tied, and the ditch was filled in. The circular, pointed roof frame was made on Saturday, lifted up on to the wall, and tied in place. On Monday the roof was thatched.

On Tuesday Lee drove off to the accompaniment of eight happy Anuak men jubilantly singing praise to the Lord.

It had been a singularly joyful event for all. Besides helping Lado erect his house, Anuaks and Murles had worshiped together each day, led by evangelists Ojulo and Lado—and had feasted together on the roasted meat of five antelopes that Bob and Lee had provided. It was a time of celebration as a practical demonstration of "domestic missions" testified to the Murle community what Christ does in a person's heart.

At one service, Olero remarked, "See, Anuaks and Murles can worship together!"

And as the group from Akobo was leaving, an Anuak articulated the spirit with which the men had worked: "We haven't helped build a house just for you, Lado, but a house for God. Walk with him and he will continue to bless you and your people through his Son."[3]

---

3 Crandall and Swart, "The Tribal Barriers Are Breaking." Reprinted from the *Church Herald*, July 29, 1955: 4, 5.

The evangelist Lado teaching in a Murle village

One Sunday Bob and Lado went out to the village of Dura to find Chief Lutillim seated tailor-fashion in front of an old man who was a *dari*, or witch doctor. A handful of marble-size stones had been placed on the chief's sweater that was spread upon the ground between them. The *dari* picked up the stones, shook them in his cupped hands, and threw them back on the sweater. After studying them he gave several to the chief, who rubbed them on his stomach.

Lado rebuked the *dari*, in the spirit of Christ, and asked him, "What are you getting from the chief for doing this—a goat? Why do you witch doctors cheat the people? You know you have no real power. Are you God? You just fool the people!"[4]

And Lado went on to give a message of hope and truth in Christ Jesus to these two men and those who had gathered there.

This was the voice of a fellow African, not that of a foreign white man who was considered beyond the powers of the witch doctor. It was the voice of one made strong, as were the first apostles, by the ever-present Holy Spirit.

How thankful we were for this fearless messenger of the true God! Upon such as Lado rested the hope of the Murle church.

4 Swart, "Vignettes from the Sudan." 20

VI
More New Personnel

During the early years of independence, Sudanese visas were issued to fewer missionaries.

The Rev. Paul Hostetter, his wife, Winifred, and their young daughter, Mary Beth, arrived in Khartoum in January 1955. Following the new requirements, they remained in the North in order to acquire a working knowledge of colloquial and classical Arabic. They lived in a comfortable Sudanese house in Omdurman during this period, which led to a happy encounter:

> A slender, ebony lad ambled past us on the hot, dusty street. He was singing softly. With our foreign ears, we listened eagerly to the strange sound. But this tune did not strike us as the weird, tempestuous strains of local music. Startled, we recognized the hymn tune [for] "In Christ There Is No East or West." What a surprise to hear Christian music here in Omdurman...where dance and drum fill the night air with a wearying, relentless beat. What a thrill to realize that in this strange city, so deep within the Muslim world, was a Christian brother!
>
> We turned to tell this...singer of our delight in his hymn, but he was already gone. Still, to us, his unknowing witness was a promise of hope for the days ahead.[1]

1 Paul Hostetter, "The White Curtain and the Black." Reprinted from the *Church Herald*, February 10, 1956: 12.

In October 1955, the Hostetters welcomed into their family a second daughter, Martha Ruth, who was born at the mission hospital in Tanta, Egypt.

The expanding responsibilities of parenthood, however, did not curtail activities of these new missionaries. Paul and Winifred both were excellent students of Arabic. And Paul, not content to be occupied only with language study, also taught history at the Commercial High School, preached on occasion at the Sunday afternoon English service, and conducted a Bible class for southerners.

At the end of a year, the family had hoped to be on their way south to begin the work to which they had been called at Pibor. However, an uprising in the South of the Sudan Defense Force against its northern superiors, together with the signing of the Declaration of Independence in December 1955, closed the door temporarily to new missionary activity in the southern region. We all prayed that the situation would be reversed.

The delay proved beneficial when the extra months in the North enabled further preparation for ministry among the Murle.

John Kireru, a Murle, appeared on the scene, claiming to be a Christian. Since he was without other work, Paul employed him, and for three months they worked together on the Murle language.

The experience proved valuable because it permitted Paul and Winifred to get a headstart learning and analyzing the language, and then translating the Bible so that the Murles would have God's Word in their own tongue.

So, with a significant preliminary knowledge of the Murle language already acquired, the Hostetters were more eager than ever to move when God opened the South again.

They arrived in Malakal in January 1957, in time for the annual mission association meeting—a great way to meet colleagues working in various tribal areas. Some days later, the Hostetters and Swarts were off together for Pibor, driving the nearly four hundred miles overland—a rough, rugged initiation to travel in the southern bush country.

An attractive prefab Arcon house had been put up for our new family not far from our own dwelling. They settled in happily and gave themselves wholeheartedly to life and work among the Murles.

Kireru followed the Hostetters to Pibor. Having worked with Paul in Omdurman, he knew something of what was expected of him, and the study went on apace with the use, initially, of both Arabic and English.

In the first months, Paul was able to make a linguistic analysis of the phonetics of the Murle language. He also prepared a phonemic statement that later was confirmed by a Wycliffe Bible translator. To put his earliest findings to work, and to give practical reason to pursue such research, Paul soon began translating selected verses of Scripture—truths which the Murles could memorize and tuck into their minds and hearts, both to introduce them to their Savior and to build up their faith.

Two primers were written to take incipient readers through the alphabet and into the actual reading experience. This had to be done in Arabic script, according to a decision made at the 1958 association meeting. It was not an easy task because, as Paul noted, "Arabic script is designed for Arabic alone and is not flexible like Roman script." However, he and Harvey Hoekstra were able to create innovations that made it possible to be read in the Murle context.

But Paul's contributions were not all executed at his desk. There was a community beckoning for help, and he responded. He conducted a weekly Bible study at the mission church-under-the-tamarind-tree and once a month spoke at the Sunday morning service.

There was also an intertribal Christian group at the government center whom Paul helped to nurture both in spiritual things and in literacy. At one time, he had fifteen students learning to read in Arabic.

And always, there was Winifred. In both gentleness and strength, she was there faithfully for her husband and daughters, a loving support to her family. Brilliant in her own right and equally dedicated to their calling, she was able to encourage Paul in all his endeavors. As a hostess, whether to colleagues or to Africans, she was gracious and kindly. Her home was her domain; her children were her joy; and, as she once said to me, her husband was her life.

In every respect Winifred was a lady, and as such she was a tremendous asset to our missionary sub-culture in the bush at Pibor.

But Fritz, as she was more familiarly known, was by her own confession as humanly frail as anyone else. She spoke for us all when she wrote:

> The missionary who works in the tropics is spared the effort of going to the ant to consider her ways. The ant, all uninvited, comes to him....There are the little brown ones which so often manage to get at our carefully hoarded sweets before we do. Even the ant-

proof hanging cupboard is not safe from their invasion. From the ceiling, down the thinnest wires, over kerosene-soaked rags, they make their way into sugar, spice, and all that's nice...

Less omnipresent, but almost as troublesome, is the middlesized black ant. The children do not quickly forget its painful sting. The large brown ant and its cousin, the invisible biting sandfly, have an uncanny way of locating their prey in the dark, especially at bedtime....The deadly invasion of the army ant, and the gnawing destruction of the white ant we have yet to experience. But the activities of their relatives, the disease-carrying housefly and the malaria-bearing mosquito, we know only too well.

To the same family belong leaky faucets, painful boils, temperamental houseboys, and sleep-robbing sandstorms—a host of annoyances, big and small, whose unrelenting barrage threatens to undo the missionary.

We don't often tell you about these things, but how we do need prayer for the power to live above them! It is more difficult to live with ourselves on the field. Even those of us who never had trouble with shortness of temper at home, find it surprising us here.

Patience is a virtue we seem to need in increasing quantity. We want you to pray for the work, the church, the lost, but when you have occasion to consider the ant, pray for the missionary, too, will you?[2]

Arlene Schuiteman had been scheduled to sail with the Hostetters on December 30, 1954, but she was delayed for two months because her visa for Sudan had not been granted yet. The transition from British to Sudanese rule was still underway, and visas were becoming more difficult to acquire.

Arlene was born on a farm near Sioux Center, Iowa. In 1943 she began her teaching career, a year in which she was challenged by Dr. Paul Harrison at

[2] Winifred Hostetter, "The Ant Comes." Reprinted from the *Church Herald,* June 28, 1957: 4.

a mission conference in Orange City. But because it was a call for medical personnel in Arabia, she ignored it, and she continued teaching for eight years—until a message preached by her pastor, the Rev. P. A. DeJong, stirred her to take action.

Arlene resigned from teaching and entered the nursing field. She graduated from the Methodist School of Nursing in Sioux City, Iowa, and applied for missionary service. The Board of World Missions, in October 1954, interviewed her and assigned her to work at Nasir in Sudan among the Nuer people.

At the commissioning service her home church was filled—the beginning of overwhelming and unwavering support the congregation lovingly provided during all her years in Africa. In fact, Dr. Barney Luben even spoke with the consistory at one point about the advantages of having other churches share in her support; some of the members felt that they wanted to carry the entire financial burden!

Arlene's parents accompanied her by train to New York City. When the visa finally arrived, she boarded the ship Scythia and traveled for eleven days to London where she picked up a flight on a twin-engine plane to Khartoum. The entire trip cost $427.76.

In early March 1955, she reached the Sudanese capital and felt the first blast of oven-hot air; eight days later she was flown to Malakal. Bob Swart and LaVerne Sikkema traveled in the Swarts' Jeep truck to purchase supplies for Akobo and Pibor and to greet her. It was decided that Arlene should be oriented to other areas of Upper Nile Province before proceeding to Nasir. So when Verne and Bob headed south, she was on board for the long safari across the grasslands and sparse, thorny forests. She was amazed at how the men knew the way, for there seemed to be no roads.

It was Easter Eve when they arrived at Akobo. Kitty Crandall had supper ready for them, including the ever-impressive ice cream, a memorable treat at the end of a hot journey.

Arlene spent that night in the home of Wilma Kats and Lillian Huisken. The next morning she attended the Easter celebration at the Anuak church, singing praises to the beat of drums. Lorraine Sikkema interpreted the Easter message for her.

That afternoon, Bob and Arlene continued on to Pibor. Dr. Mary Smith, now serving at Akobo, and Eleanor Vandevort from Nasir, were there on a short assignment. Arlene remembers that "each morning we all gathered in the living room of the Swarts' home and knelt in prayer. How much we needed the help of our Father in heaven in the awesome task he had called each of us to do. I was also beginning to realize how strong the mission family ties would become."

On April 25, MAF had scheduled a flight to include Pibor and Nasir. So Eleanor and Arlene flew in the Rapide and were soon at their station on the Sobat River in Nuer country.

They landed at the far end of the town where the new Sudanese district commissioner's offices were located. Beyond, lining the river front, were the Arab merchant shops. (Arlene would get to know the merchants' wives well for they practiced female circumcision and needed the help of a midwife during childbirth.) Contiguous to the shops was the mission property. The entire settlement extended for less than a mile.

Arlene lived with Presbyterian missionaries Eleanor Vandevort and Marian Farquhar, who spoke the Nuer language fluently. Eleanor was, in fact, a linguist and was already engaged in Bible translation. Marian was in charge of the girls' school.

The Gordon family, also Presbyterian, were the only other missionaries there. Arlene had been assigned to assist Dr. Bob Gordon in place of the RCA's Amy TeSelle, who had worked at Nasir for one year and then had left for Korea to marry Ben Sheldon.

Arlene described the Nuers as being "very tall and very black and also very slim." A man could often be seen along the river's edge, standing on one leg with the other foot propped against his knee. A spear, held firmly in one hand and with one end fixed solidly on the ground, enabled him to keep his balance, and he could stand in that position, like some giant crane, for an amazingly long time.

The men also spent hours debating their most prized possessions—cattle. Sometimes a group of fifteen or so men, sitting under a shade tree, would bargain at length over a bride price, using small sticks to represent cattle.

While this was going on, women were busy carrying water from the river, grinding *durra* for porridge for the evening meal, cooking, or milking the cows. A large cattle barn was the center of each homestead, and the small huts nearby were for the wives.

It was at Nasir that Arlene planted her roots deeply in Nuerland. Learning language was her highest priority. Two informants came daily to sit at a big homemade table on the veranda to teach her.

As a diversion from the intensive study schedule, Arlene sometimes went to the clinic. Gac Duac, Gac Rik, and Tut Gatkuoth had been trained to assist Dr. Gordon, and they decided her Nuer name would be Bigwa, which means "You will be good." Because her father's name was John, they suffixed John to Bigwa. And since Nuer girls' names have the prefix "nya," her full name became Nyabigwa John. Succeeding Nuers knew her by no other name.

Over the years at Nasir, Nyabigwa encountered people who came to the clinic needing treatment for malaria, meningitis, trachoma, pneumonia, worms, measles, chicken pox, whooping cough, yaws, and dysentery. Patients came with bites from hyenas, crocodiles, and snakes, as well as scorpion stings; with obstructed deliveries and retained placentas. Once a woman came carrying a newborn baby in a reed basket on her head and needed assistance with the baby's undelivered twin!

Once an elderly man named Yuol Bithow was very ill with tuberculosis (TB). Sacrificing many cows to several gods hadn't brought healing. Eventually his educated nephew, Chieng Piny Luak, read the Gospel of John to him and talked about his own experience of being cured from TB at Nasir, and that persuaded Yuol to go for treatment.

While receiving his daily medication, Yuol was exposed further to the living Word of God. Each morning, a few verses of Scripture were read and explained to the patients sitting in the shade of the spreading wild fig tree. Arlene confessed, "I often questioned the effectiveness of this type of ministry since there seldom seemed to be much response. But Yuol was different; he wanted to hear more and more."

Eventually Yuol improved so much that he wanted to return home. He felt compelled to tell his people the good news he'd been hearing. Taking a supply of medicines with him to continue his treatment, he left in a dugout canoe. He was off on a mission of his own.

Chieng Piny, now back in school in Khartoum, was concerned for his uncle, especially for his spiritual condition. As a very young Christian, Chieng Piny knew he would be a victim of pressures from his pagan family and from attacks of Satan. He wrote to Arlene: "I think of Yuol as Daniel in the den of lions."

Word did come that Yuol's faith was remaining strong and that he still observed the Lord's Day with the help of a "calendar" of seven sticks to remind him which day of the week it was.

But later came the report that Yuol had become very ill again. Also, one of his sons had died, three cows had been sacrificed, and a shrine had been replaced in his *kaal* (the village yard). Those at Nasir sensed a responsibility to go to him for both physical and spiritual reasons.

Eleanor Vandevort, Reet (a church elder), and Arlene flew with MAF to Akobo. Yuol's village was still sixty miles away. So, taking the little Willys Jeep that Bob Swart had brought out in 1948, and loading it with all the necessities from food and drink to bedrolls and extra gasoline, they started off. By the time they reached Yuol's village, they found that he'd gone off to cattle camp. There was no road, but the intrepid Jeep and the equally intrepid travelers made it over the rough, bone-rattling terrain. The hood bounced off and had to be tied on with a rope. They lost a plastic battery cap, replacing it with a whittled stick. And the radiator had to be filled with water about every twenty minutes. But they made it!

They found Yuol sitting beside a pool of dirty water, his back resting against the trunk of one lone tree.

Would he want to go to Nasir? Would he be strong enough to make the trip?

"Let's go," he said.

They got back to the road well before dark, a guide having directed them to a slightly smoother route. As they stopped to give the Jeep a drink, some local Nuer men noticed Yuol in the car. They heard one man tell another, "They went to get Yuol, the man who has Jesus for his God."

They reached Akobo by 7 p.m., and the next morning they all flew back to Nasir.

Can you imagine what this meant to old Yuol, sick and weak, who had had only his own two legs or a canoe to take him from one place to another all his life? Arlene said that his heart was filled with gratitude, and all he could say was, "What has God done?"

As her knowledge of the Nuer language increased, Arlene began teaching a class of women on Sunday. She also started health education classes for them. Eleanor encouraged her to put these lessons in writing so that an Old Testament Bible Story booklet was printed, as well as one on Maternal and Child Health, and their use continued for decades.

In February 1957, the Gordons were on furlough, so Dr. Mary Smith was again serving at Nasir. One day Arlene and Dr. Mary went to an Arab home to do a home delivery.

They always get their homes spic-and-span for the occasion. The hard dirt floor was swept clean. An oil cloth covered the homemade table. Clean spreads were on the beds. This is a very special moment for all Arab women—a social event.

Soon tea and cookies were served. I was on the third cookie when things began to happen...and soon the baby was born. The joy cry sounded out, and the husband inquired as to the sex. This time it was "only a girl," so no big deal.

Before I had finished cleaning up the newborn baby, she had been kissed by all present. Dr. Mary stayed to watch the mother for another hour...Before I left, I was offered orangeade and a cup of *gahwa*, very strong coffee. Then I was anointed with cologne which poured down my head onto my shoulders.

From that day, I began to plan to go to the midwifery school in Hyden, Kentucky, on my next furlough so that I'd be able to do deliveries myself.[3]

Arlene's first furlough came in 1959, and Lillian Huisken left her work at Akobo to take Arlene's place at Nasir.

Along with enjoying reunions with family and friends and meeting with supporting churches, Arlene was able to take the courses in midwifery in Kentucky. Just as she was completing this course, her father passed away from a heart attack.

Difficult as it was to leave her family at such a sad time, Arlene left on schedule and arrived back at Nasir in January 1960.

The RCA's Roxanna Sarr was also a nurse. She was commissioned by the General Synod in June 1955.

Following a year of study at Biblical Seminary in New York, she arrived in Omdurman for Arabic study in November 1956. She also studied midwifery at the Omdurman Midwifery School.

---

[3] Arlene Schuiteman, from "Sudan Notes," n.d. Joint Archives of Holland, Hope College.

With these years of preparation behind her, Roxanna, or Rocky as she was known to all her friends was, by mission standards well qualified to be launched into her nursing career in the South Sudan. When permission to go south finally came through, she found herself, in July 1958, on her way to Ler, which was another station among the Nuers but on the west side of the Nile, southwest of Malakal. Her colleagues were the Rev. and Mrs. Robb McLaughlin, Presbyterians, and Dr. and Mrs. Jim West from England, transferred to the American Mission from the Church Missionary Society.

> I was there only two and a half years, though it seemed a very long time somehow, both at the time and even looking back. Not that it was dull or lonely, though it was both at times—but because so much learning was packed amongst the serving, and trying to communicate in Nuer; and, in cultural terms, it demanded so much emotional energy. It was just so different from anything I'd ever experienced.
>
> The Nuer language was difficult for me...but I did learn a hospital vocabulary of sorts. My teacher-informant was Gabriel Yoal who had completed eighth grade. His quiet wisdom and intelligence impressed me a lot, and with a friend's assistance, he was given a place in the Commercial High School in Omdurman. He graduated and went on to hold top government positions.
>
> I feel a certain satisfaction in having been a steppingstone to his success; if I hadn't been there at the time, needing his help in language acquisition, his whole life might have been very different.
>
> I remember that my missionary friends worried about me because there weren't other single women at Ler. But I also remember having a strong loyalty to Ler, the McLaughlins, and the Wests.[4]

Rocky was very well prepared for mission service and was dedicated fully to a career overseas, but it was not in God's long-range plan that Rocky remain at Ler indefinitely, or anywhere, as a single woman. Rocky had met Jerry Nichol during the months of Arabic study in Omdurman. Jerry, who

---

[4] Roxanna (Saar) Nichol, from a letter to the author, April 2, 1992. Joint Archives of Holland, Hope College.

had helped Gabriel Yoal further his education, was a teacher at the Commercial High School.

On December 20, 1960, Rocky Sarr and Jerry Nichol were married at the church in Malakal.

Arlene Schuiteman remembers her trip from Nasir to Malakal to attend the wedding:

> Marian, Eleanor, and I were planning to fly to Malakal, but the pilot became ill. But Verne and Lorraine Sikkema had come to Nasir for the birth of their fourth child. Maybe Verne could take us part way in the mission launch. We knew that if we started out at once, and if a car would meet us half way at a point where the road was open, we could make it in time for the wedding.
>
> We quickly tossed bedrolls and trekking gear onto the launch and were off with Verne at the helm. The launch was a lovely little houseboat. Some people called it "The Thing" because it didn't always behave just right. But I liked it....
>
> We arrived in Malakal an hour before the wedding. Many homegrown poinsettias were used for the floral arrangements. It was a beautiful wedding. We saw Rocky and Jerry off as they boarded the Sudan Airways plane that afternoon.[5]

Rocky changed her support base from the RCA to the United Presbyterian Church and moved to the North Sudan to work beside her husband.

5 Schuiteman, "Sudan Notes," n.d. Archives.

VII
Tensions Mount

Because Don and Lyda McClure, now stationed at the Anuak mission post at Pokwo in Ethiopia, were scheduled for furlough in 1953, the Hoekstras were asked to carry on the work there in their absence. They arrived at that station on the Baro River in April. For twenty-one months, Pokwo was their home.

On December 21 of that year, Carol Joy was born at the mission hospital at Dembi Dollo, Ethiopia. No more wonderful gift could have been given the Hoekstra family that Christmas.

When their assignment at Pokwo came to an end, Lavina and the three younger children flew back to Akobo on the MAF plane, while Harvey and their oldest son Denny traveled on horseback the one hundred forty miles cross-country.

Denny recalls that it was the most memorable trek he had ever made with his father. They slept in villages or along the trail each night. One night they heard lions roaring as they lay in their sleeping bags. And they often had to swim their horses across rivers.

"The aches and pains of being in the saddle for eight days were soon gone," Denny said, "but the memories of that trip will remain forever."

They reached Akobo the day before the annual association meeting which was being held there in February 1955. Every mission house was bulging hospitably at its earthen seams with guests from Malakal, Ler, Doleib Hill, Obel (where there was a boys' school), Abwong, Nasir, and Pibor.

It was during that wonderful, hectic week of meetings and fellowship that the Hoekstras' fifth child was born. With four doctors and several nurses available, as well as numerous "aunts, uncles, and cousins," no baby was welcomed into the world more thoroughly, or with more care, than was Mark Stephen. Nor was any young mother ever congratulated with more solicitude than on February 16, 1955, a banner day!

The Ekster family, who had traveled out to Sudan with us in 1953, spent their first few months at Akobo. Bud was engaged in several building projects, including work on the school, gas store, and barn. At the end of that year, they moved to Pibor to continue the building program there: finishing the hospital, the mission houses, and putting up a workshop. Their abode during those months was a tent. Kate's kitchen was a grass and stick shelter that served its purpose primitively, but adequately.

Unfortunately, Bud's health was less than adequate for the rigors of this kind of life, and in April 1954, he had to fly to Kampala, Uganda, for surgery. This improved his condition enough to permit him, later that year, to do an important stint at Bishop Gwynne Theological College at Mundri in Equatoria Province. Bud was kept busy on a number of fronts: working on the dormitories, houses, and the school itself. He was enthusiastic about the place.

> Our dormitories are small, individual units; the chapel and library are contained in a grass-roofed building with plain benches for seats. There are only two study rooms, and the members of the student body, though not large in number, are straining to absorb all they can of knowledge of God's Word and methods of approach to their own people.
>
> [The hopes and aims of Bishop Gwynne Theological College] are as high, or higher, than those of similar institutions on the face of the earth, while the raw material for attaining these goals is only half as well equipped to begin with.
>
> This college is a theological school founded by the Church Missionary Society [CMS] of England.... Our mission was asked to go into a program of cooperation in training students for evangelism and pastoral work. This past term, there were four students from our mission and eight from the CMS.
>
> The spiritual tone of the school is very good. We have found that all CMS missionaries directly concerned with evangelism are

people who live close to God. There are differences in our form of worship....But we find that these things are just on the surface, and underneath, both groups have a deep desire to serve and worship Christ. This is our common ground, and from this the aim is to produce a thriving, spiritual, Christ-centered, indigenous church in the South Sudan.[1]

After this rich experience at Mundri, the Eksters returned to Pibor where they took up residence in the solid, cement block workshop. But after only a few months, it was obvious that Bud's health would not permit the family to stay on indefinitely. In fact it was imperative that they head back to the United States soon.

So in May 1956, we sadly said good-bye to these dear friends, Bud and Kate, and their three children, Sandra, Peter, and Cheryl. My parents would be meeting them when they arrived in New York. Though the Webbers had never met any of the Eksters, I assured them by letter that they'd have no problem in recognizing the family.

"Just be on the lookout for a Lincolnesque man!" I wrote.

And they linked up without any difficulty.

Presbyterians Monte and Mary Parr came to Pibor in 1957 temporarily to complete the building program in which Bud Ekster had been involved.

Near the close of 1954, the Crandall family flew to Nasir to await the birth of their third child.

On one occasion at Nasir, Lee accompanied Dr. Bob Gordon on one of his rounds of Nuer villages. In one village, they found a case that was hardly medical, but their assistance was needed.

A Nuer had excitedly called to them: "A baby leopard is in that *tukl* over there. Come help us get it out!"

Bob and Lee did not hesitate to oblige. While they were trying to coax the kitten out the door, Lee all of a sudden yelled, "Here comes the mother!"

Poor Bob "went through the roof" in fright—and then looked around to find Lee doubled over with laughter. Bob, who was a prankster himself,

[1] Lambert B. Ekster, "Training for Christian Work in the Sudan." Reprinted from the *Church Herald*, February 10, 1956: 12, 23.

surely understood the temptation to which Lee had yielded, and was able to join the hilarity once he had descended and calm was restored.

Lee's and Kitty's daughter, Ann, was born December 19 in the little thatch-roofed guest house at Nasir. On March 6, 1955, she was baptized at Akobo by the first Egyptian missionary sent out from the Evangelical Egyptian Church, the Rev. Swailem Sidhom. Kitty's parents were visiting them at the time. It was a joyful occasion.

Kitty was a busy mother with her three small children, but she found time and strength to assist Wilma Kats in the girls' school, as well as Lillian Huisken in the clinic. She welcomed these opportunities for showing Christ's love in the teaching and healing ministries.

Teacher Omot's wife, Akelo, learned to read under Kitty's tutelage, so they had become good friends. When Akelo became pregnant, she moved, according to Anuak custom, back to her parental village which was about three miles downriver. Kitty would attend the birth when the time came.

The day arrived. Kitty hastily grabbed up a bandage scissors and a pair of shoelaces still in their wrapper.

> We climbed into a dugout canoe and Omot paddled vigorously. We found Akelo squatting just outside her mother's *tukl*, with all the village women gathered around, each one telling her what to do. The village midwife was beside Akelo.
>
> Omot requested that I be permitted to help his wife. As I was making my way through the crowd, the baby presented himself, and the midwife took a foot-long piece of bamboo that had been split down its length. She was about to use it to sever the umbilical cord.
>
> Then I showed Akelo and the midwife the things I had brought. The midwife moved aside. I quickly milked the cord, tied it in two places about one inch apart, and cut the cord with the scissors.
>
> The women were aghast! The job was done so quickly and without the loss of a single drop of blood![2]

The impression that this procedure made on Omot and Akelo was evidenced in the name they chose for their son. They called him Magath which is the Anuak equivalent of the Arabic word for scissors.

[2] Kitty Crandall, from a letter to the author, n.d. Joint Archives of Holland, Hope College.

The church in the South Sudan during the mid-1950s was experiencing a disturbing ebb and flow of growth. As a result of deep concern, Lee Crandall reported:

> There has been a continuous movement of people into the church at all our stations...[but there is also] a constant turnover...: men and women coming into the church with the glow of Christ in their eyes, but in a very short period...drifting away and returning to the old ways. It is heartrending....
>
> We have been restless, dissatisfied, seeking, studying, praying, discussing. Then we held three significant meetings....
>
> At the first meeting early in 1956, six American pastors, one African pastor, three seminary students, and a dozen leading Christians from the churches at Doleib Hill, Nasir, Akobo, and Pibor, came together at Doleib Hill....At that meeting, the basis and background work for our present situation was set: "No other foundation can anyone lay than that which is laid, which is Jesus Christ."
>
> Some weeks later, the Rev. William Anderson [son of our general secretary, Lowrie Anderson], the three seminary students, and I met for three weeks at Abwong with fifty keen Christian young men for an evangelistic conference held in the vernaculars.
>
> Mr. Anderson had made all the arrangements for housing, food, and courses of study. At the last evening devotions, God was given great praise and thanks in a spontaneous testimonial period....
>
> While this conference was in session, Shilluk [Shulla] pastor, La Maloker, and Dr. Lowrie Anderson were in Egypt petitioning the Synod of the Nile of the United Presbyterian Church to disband our relationship to them, allowing us to form a new presbytery. Following favorable action by our African brothers, we met again in April [to form] the Church of Christ in the Upper Nile.
>
> Days were spent discussing and praying about the reasons why so many who came into the church quickly left....We praise the

Lord that he has opened our eyes and bound us together in a plan to remedy this discouraging defection. As we followed our Lord's leading, we concluded:

1. Top quality African church leadership is an utmost necessity....God has been raising up such men according to his promise. The requirements for church elders in I Timothy 3:1ff are the basis of election.

2. A single, definite code of Christian behavior...must be made known to our people, upon which church discipline will be based.

3. The church, from July 1, 1956, will fully support its own ministry, the evangelistic outreach, church buildings and housing, and give partial support to the seminary students, looking to the mission for Bible translation and the training of evangelists and pastors.

We praise God for readying us for these important steps at this crucial time in the total life of Sudan.[3]

As political tensions grew during the late 1950s and the church experienced more restrictions, revival seemed about to break out in Malakal and environs. People like Lee Crandall and Bill Anderson were asked to work with the national Christians in that area. Lee, Bill, and Adwok, a Shulla pastor, became close friends and colleagues. Christian inspirational meetings were held daily, many lasting into the night. On one Sunday, fifty-six adults were baptized.

Authorities were becoming upset. They put a ban on evangelistic meetings held outside the city, suspecting them of being a source of civil disobedience.

One day, when Adwok and Lee were driving outside Malakal, Lee was arrested and placed in custody. He spent three days and nights in jail. Kitty was able to take food to him but was not permitted to hold any conversations. After a hearing, Lee was released, but the Crandall family was given five days to leave the country.

In 1959, ten years after their first arrival, and with scores of national Christians to see them off, Lee and Kitty and their three children flew from the Malakal airport. Adwok, who led the group in prayer before the plane took off, was arrested the next day and imprisoned for many months.

---

3 Lee Crandall, "No Other Foundation." Reprinted from the *Church Herald*, December 21, 1956: 4.

But, like Paul and Peter centuries before, Adwok's lips could not be sealed. He faithfully shared the gospel, and many of his fellow prisoners became followers of Jesus Christ.

As Kitty wrote: "The church is growing. We praise and thank God that we were privileged to have a tiny part in planting the seed of the gospel in Sudan."4

The uprising in the South, which kept the Hostetters from moving on schedule from Omdurman to Pibor, also had its effect on the Sikkema family. They were en route from Ler to Malakal and then on to Akobo following the birth of their second child, Karen Jean, on July 3, 1955. They were able to reach Nasir, but were prevented from proceeding any further upriver for the months of August and September. In fact, all travel throughout the South was curtailed during this tense period.

Restrictions were lifted eventually, however, and Verne and Lorraine, with their two little girls, were able to make it home to Akobo where Verne continued his work in agricultural missions with Chuck Jordan.

But the Sikkemas did return to Nasir on two occasions in the next few years: in 1957 for the birth of their son, Milton Dale, on November 9, and in 1960 for Arloa Beth's arrival on December 23. The missionaries at Nasir, rich in medical, educational, and evangelistic workers, lacked a Mr. Fixit. So, aside from the fact that the Sikkemas were pleasant company, and Verne was good for a score of laughs a day, the Nasirites appreciated his expertise in repairing the windmill, overhauling the water system, working on outboard motors, and any number of other projects that needed mechanical know-how.

So waiting at Nasir for the more or less unpredictable arrival of blessed events was a beneficial time for all.

---

4 Kitty Crandall, from a letter to the author. Archives.

In 1957 it was becoming more evident than ever that Africa was a continent trying to burst out of its great, heaving chrysalis. The term "Darkest Africa" really was no longer applicable.

No one who knows the Africa of today will continue to speak of it romantically as the "Dark Continent." Nationalism, like a grass fire in a gale, is spreading from country to country. Political upheavals are no longer news. Education is the thing!

Just since January 1, 1956 [Sudan's Independence Day], a school has been built right here at Pibor with sixty Murle boys enrolled. Last year there was scarcely a thought of a school. The Sudanese government has a definite timetable to take over all education, including mission schools. Last year, three mission schools were absorbed. Khartoum, the capital, is eager to assume the responsibilities of a twentieth century, enlightened government.[5]

In the midst of all that was going on in that New Day in Sudan, missionaries had to keep focused on their reason for being in that country, realizing that God, in his inscrutable way, was indeed working out his purposes, and that our tenure in that land could be very short. In 1956:

...the Church of Christ in the Upper Nile was formed: an African church, an African moderator, African pastors, and African elders. This is among a people who, some twenty years ago, were settling inter-tribal problems with spears.

A people who once sat in darkness are now walking in the light of the Savior.

In our own tribe, we are rejoicing in new evidences of the work of the Holy Spirit. Three Murle boys, who are attending school at Akobo, have been baptized. The Spirit used the witness of an Anuak Christian to lead them into the fold.

Such is the interest of five people here [at Pibor], that a daily class [taught by Bob Swart] is being held for their instruction, and four have professed their faith in Christ as their Savior and have asked for baptism.

[5] Robert and Morrell Swart, "Dawn in Africa." Reprinted from the *Church Herald*, April 19, 1957: 4.

The darkness of sin is being dispelled; the Truth is astounding people. When the Spirit gives them sudden comprehension, some roll back on the sand floor and laugh for sheer joy.

We are praying that others will soon experience true rebirth and become new creations in Christ. The Holy Spirit is at work and we look with confidence to the day when Christ's church will be firmly established among [the Murle] people.[6]

Under the spreading tamarind tree was a lovely, cool place to meet for church services during the dry season. But no matter how thickly foliaged it was, it couldn't keep out the wetness of tropical downpours. So the grass and stick structure that had been the Eksters' temporary kitchen became our meeting place during the rains.

Early one drenching Sunday morning, Paul Hostetter sloshed over to our house.

"Say, Bob, did you hear the news? The church collapsed!" he exclaimed.

"I'm not surprised," Bob replied. "Those termite-ridden supporting poles have been leaning for some time, and after this storm, the grass roof must have been terribly heavy."

"It's a blessing we weren't having a service at the time. Those cross pieces of the A-beams in the roof are only about a yard from the ground. If there had been a crowd in there, some would surely have been hurt," Paul observed.

"Again the Lord was watching over us," Bob added.[7]

What to do?
The Lord showed us clearly that whatever was done should be no mere missionary project; it should belong to the whole Christian community,

---

[6] Ibid.
[7] Morrell F. Swart, "Building God's House." Reprinted from the *Church Herald*, February 21, 1958: 4.

The new church at Pibor with evangelist Lado

American and Murle alike. He brought this about by leading the Murle Christians to volunteer to build a church.

How we praised God for this response! Every afternoon for several weeks, missionary and Murle worked together, first choosing the site and measuring it out. Next, the supporting poles were placed in the ground and the roof frame constructed. Last of all, the grass walls and roof thatch were tied in place.

On the day the building was dedicated, a seven-foot cross was hung at the altar end of the church. It was painted red (at the Murles' suggestion) to symbolize the shedding of Jesus' blood.

Today in Sunday School for our own children, we studied about Solomon's temple. It was overlaid in gold throughout and fabulously ornamented....The Lord honored the work of men's hands by sending a cloud into the temple.

> We believe earnestly that, though the floor is of sand and the
> walls are of grass, God will honor this simple structure as it is used
> day after day to his glory.[8]

In that humble edifice, in the shadow of that rough-hewn, blood-red cross, songs of praise rose week after week from hearts newly aware of God's love. Lado, Bob, and Paul preached from the Word, further strengthening the little flock in the truth.

Nor did this house of the Lord stand empty during the week. Courses in evangelism were taught. Classes in health maintenance were held, the material translated from lessons Arlene Schuiteman had authored for the Nuers. Sessions in literacy were offered.

Because Paul and Harvey had conspired successfully in creating a readable Murle alphabet using Arabic script, Ruth Roode and I were inspired to collaborate in putting together simple, illustrated primers to encourage literacy among women.

First we had to learn how to write the script acceptably. It was like entering first grade again! Our Roman script-oriented fingers weren't accustomed to writing "backwards," let alone forming the unfamiliar shapes and symbols.

Ruth made good progress, however, and soon she was transscribing my laboriously written sentences into Arabic calligraphy. Informants checked them. Spearhead Press in Malakal printed them. And we were in business.

It was a happy, productive period for us, and Ruth and I believe the reading lessons were a help to some in stretching their minds and lifting their hearts.

In September 1957, we had visitors from the United States: Dr. Barnerd Luben and the Rev. John Buteyn from our Board for the Christian World Mission (formerly called the Board of Foreign Missions). Dr. Glenn Reed from Eritrea, now our field secretary, accompanied them.

What would be their most vivid memory of those days at Pibor? Would it be the evening prayer meeting around the fire out in the village? Or would it be the afternoon meeting that grieved our hearts so much because the

8 Ibid.

questions the Murles asked had to do with wages rather than eternal truths? Would they remember above all the modest church of grass and sticks that the Murles and missionaries built together—with its tree-trunk pulpit and the rough-hewn cross hanging at the front? Would it be their first brush with local color in the motorboat on their way to the mission from the airstrip? Bob had consented to take a Murle woman across the river. To the uninitiated, the odor of an untanned goat-hide skirt combined with rancid butter smeared on the body can be quite overpowering. And when a rank fish is added to the bouquet, the result can amount to an assault on delicate senses. John Buteyn also had to keep ducking that fish's tail.

Would corn-on-the-cob for every meal stand out in their memories? Or the lovely view of the river with the beauty of our trees? Or the fine caps Ruth Roode made for the men chiefly because Barney Luben, in hurrying to catch the plane in New York, had left his hat in his car?

Perhaps they would recall most clearly Lado's answer when John and Barney asked the group, "What are you going to do about witnessing to your people?"

Lado himself had been spreading the good news for many years, but when he spoke, he answered for all the Christians. He said, "We are like a man who has been asleep. He wakes up and sees some food near him. He says to himself, 'Here is some good food, but I must not eat it all myself; I must share it.' We are just beginning to wake up. We see that we have something very good and we know we must share it."

That response lifted our hearts and assured us that indeed God would have his way with the Murles—that he was at work in mighty ways among them. And with leaders like Lado, empowered by the Spirit, the Murle church would prevail through the uncertain and potentially tumultuous years ahead.

Our second furlough was suddenly upon us in 1958.

By this time not only Valerie and Gayle were attending boarding school in Addis Ababa, but also their sister, Merry. At the end of the school year in June, we traveled home, going by way of Brussels, Belgium, to take in the World's Fair.

We carry vivid memories of that trip. On the way to Brussels, we did some sightseeing in Italy. Boarding the train in Milan was an adventure in itself. The crowds traveling were an almost overwhelming flood as we hurried along with the flow. With eight of us needing to board, and the train about to depart, I got on and received the children one by one as Bob hoisted them into the car through a window. What a scramble!

At the fair, besides almost losing three-year-old Dick in the crowds, Bob had his shirt pocket picked of fifty dollars in the Russian building.

We also remember standing in the great round theater in the American building, watching, and feeling a part of the moving, circular panorama of our homeland, from a ride on the Staten Island ferry, across the wheat and corn fields of the Midwest, to the Golden Gate Bridge of San Francisco—all to the tune of "America, the Beautiful." Tears streamed down our faces in appreciation for our country.

Our children did not particularly share this sentiment at that time. To them Africa was home; America was foreign land.

We loved Africa and its people, but the sight of the Stars and Stripes and the sound of America's patriotic songs always would stir us profoundly. We were thankful that we were on our way home to renew old ties and to breathe deeply of the American spirit.

We were visiting at Bob's parental home in DeMotte, Indiana, in August 1958, when a telephone call revealed that Sudan had ordered the Hostetters to leave the country.

Ruth Ransom, of the Board of the Christian World Mission in New York, relayed the stunning news. On that hot August evening, we felt frozen with disbelief.

In an attempt to teach biblical principles to a young Christian who was having a dispute with another Christian, Paul, in a letter, cited 1 Corinthians 6 concerning lawsuits among believers. By some fluke, this written admonition fell into the hands of the local authorities.

"The letter was completely misinterpreted as casting reflection on the courts of the country, and the order for their expulsion followed."[9]

Nearly a year later, Winifred Hostetter described a poignant scene of their last days in Murle country:

> It haunts me still—that last memory of Pibor. As our plane circled the mission station for the last time, Kaaka was standing alone in the

9 Reprinted from the *Church Herald*, October 17, 1958: 11.

center of the workers' village, waving and waving good-bye. How dearly I had learned to love that girl....

She could be as bitter as her name, Kaaka. But sometimes she was so sweet. Just two days before, she had come to the house of her own accord and amused our girls hour after hour while we packed. The government had ordered us to leave Sudan....

We'd had an appointment, Kaaka and I, that Wednesday morning, to fit her with a dress. The tailors in the market knew nothing about Sanfordizing cloth; she was always complaining about the ill-fit of her dresses after washing. Nothing but a dress of mine would do.

It was the morning the plane brought the notice of our immediate expulsion....I was numb with shock, but I could not disappoint her. We went ahead with the fitting, and she carried off my dress in triumph.

It wasn't until later that she learned the awful news, and realized that all the while, my heart had been breaking with grief. Kaaka was deeply moved. During those last few days together, I felt her close to the kingdom.

It was that dress of mine she was wearing as she waved farewell to our plane. I have seen her just like that in my prayers this year, and I will until I hear she has made her peace with God.[10]

Paul and Winifred, with their two little girls, were able to spend six weeks in Khartoum before they left the country. It was time well spent: they had been asked to revise the Arabic language course materials.

One bit of irony: while in Khartoum, they met the governor of Upper Nile Province on the street one day. He personally apologized for the expulsion order. He explained that it had been given by the district commissioner at Pibor over the governor's head.

Out of a need to share with the Reformed Church in America the missionaries' perspective of the expulsion order, Harvey Hoekstra, on behalf of all the Hostetters' colleagues, wrote a letter to the editor of the *Church Herald*.

The church will be shocked to learn that the Hostetters had to leave Sudan because of a government order. The mission has made the

10 Winifred H. Hostetter, "Bittersweet." Reprinted from the *Church Herald*, May 20, 1960: 5.

strongest appeal possible, even as far as to the prime minister. All have been rejected....We wish the church to know that the mission feels that their expulsion is tied up in the political tensions and nationalism of our day.

In the loss of the Hostetters, we feel we have lost one of our finest and strongest missionary families. Our hearts bleed with theirs, and we have wept together at the loss of devoted servants and friends who had so much to contribute toward the salvation of the Murle people, and in the providing of the Scriptures in their own language.

We commend Paul and Winifred to the love and prayers of our churches. May they find victory in the assurance that the Lord is the Lord of history and of our lives, and that he doeth all things well....

To Paul and Winifred we say, the love, the prayers, and the esteem of your colleagues follow you.[11]

Bob Swart had been teaching a course for evangelists. Nyati, one of the students in his class, said after a reading session: "Now I understand the gospel better. Now I know what to tell the people because my heart has seen it. I want to read it all. You must write all of God's Word in our language."[12]

Koko, living in a stick and grass hut and subsisting from a few cows and a poor garden, once told Bob, "I am willing to have a teacher live with me as my son, if he will teach me to read God's Word."[13]

Now that the Hostetters were no longer at Pibor, who would respond to the heart cry of the Murles to have the Word of God in their own language? Whom would the Lord call out to carry on this great task?

---

[11] *Church Herald*, October 17, 1958: 21.
[12] J. Robert Swart, "Books and Ammunition." Reprinted from the *Church Herald*, September 23, 1960: 13.
[13] Ibid.

VIII
Floods

In May 1959, we visited Bob's parents one last time before returning to Africa. His brother and sister and their families were there, too, and we posed for pictures in the living room: children, their spouses, and ten grandchildren all gathered around Dad and Mother Swart. We were a close and loving family.

Soon we were back at Pibor. How good it was to resume fellowship with the Roodes, to hear the familiar greetings of our Murle friends, and to take up residence again under our thatched roof. No matter the scorpions. No matter the necessity of having to boil all our drinking water. No matter the thorns and mosquitoes. We were home.

But in the midst of our homecoming joy, a telegram arrived, telling of Dad Swart's unexpected death on June 23. We were bereft of a dear father and a good friend. The family portrait was now more precious than ever.

Two months later, we felt bereft again when all four of our daughters went off to school in Egypt.

Bingham Academy in Addis Ababa, Ethiopia, was now closed to all mission groups except their own, the Sudan Interior Mission. So our girls were enrolled at Schutz, the American School in Alexandria, Egypt, which was sponsored by the Presbyterian Church.

During the years of World War II, Schutz had been moved to Assiut in Upper Egypt where it operated for several years. It was sometime in the

1950s that it returned to its original location in the bustling port city on the Mediterranean Sea.

If "sacrifice" is an element of the missionary experience, this is it: having to send one's children hundreds of miles away for their education. I don't know how we, or our colleagues, tolerated the long separations year after year. Perhaps it was a matter of partaking of God's grace and finding it sufficient for accepting, if not wholeheartedly endorsing, this inevitable state of affairs. I would not want to have to go through that phase of missionary life again.

Even in bereavement, though, life goes on. We had come back to Pibor in early June to find the Spirit moving among the Murle Christians:

> There is a new consciousness in our young Murle church; the Christians are beginning to feel a responsibility for evangelizing their own people.
>
> Nyati especially seems to be Holy Spirit-impelled to spread the Word of Truth. Carrying with him a few Bible stories and pictures, and a small record player, he goes out for several weeks at a time, walking from village to village. No sooner does he return from one preaching trek than he is impatient to be off on the next. Between treks, however, he remains here for a period of instruction, absorbing Bible teaching with an eagerness that can spring only from true hunger and thirst for the Word of God.
>
> The Murle church includes Christians who are living in far villages, isolated from other believers. Encouraged by an occasional pastoral visit, they are taught and strengthened daily by the Holy Spirit.
>
> One Sunday morning, a woman from Dolnat appeared at the church service. Ngachor, our sister in Christ, afflicted with leprosy, had witnessed to her of God's love, Christ's death, and the new life all can have in him. When this woman arrived at Pibor, she asked another Christian, "Is this talk true?"
>
> The unhesitating reply came: "It is true!"
>
> That morning, she made confession of her faith. Later we learned that she was the wife of one of Dolnat's witch doctors.
>
> Not long ago, we received a letter from Babanen. Babanen is an educated Murle Christian who was a member of parliament until

the coup of November 1958, when the military took over. He is now living in his village about thirty miles away. He sent word that his whole family, twenty-seven strong, including in-laws and nieces and nephews, desired baptism.

Babanen, no longer in the employ of the Sudan government, continues to work faithfully for the kingdom of God.

Our three evangelists—Lado, Nyati, and Bob Swart—are planning a trek to Akelo soon to preach in the many villages in that area, and to baptize Nyikcho and his family. Nyikcho and his wife were here recently and could have been baptized in the church, but they preferred to have the service in the village that it might be a witness to their people.

The follow-up work of such witnessing is a tremendous challenge. It cannot be done effectively when our numbers are so few. But we take heart when we consider what God is doing now through the few who are his own. We look expectantly to him, confident that he will call to himself more and more of those who can be trained and whose one desire is to feed his lambs.[1]

In light of this crying need, it was imperative that a replacement for Paul Hostetter be found. Without the Word in their language, the Christians could not be nourished and established adequately in their faith. We made it a matter of urgent prayer, for we knew that God surely must have someone in the wings ready to fill the gap.

And he did.

The Anuak New Testament was nearing completion. Harvey Hoekstra had been working diligently on this top-priority assignment over the years, whether at Akobo in Sudan or at Pokwo in Ethiopia. Verse by verse, chapter by chapter, the work progressed.

Then he received a letter.

We were still working in Anuak at Akobo when Bob Swart's letter arrived. The Hostetters had been expelled and Bob was asking me to consider coming to Pibor to complete the Anuak translation there and to get going on the Murle, taking up where Paul had left off.

[1] Morrell F. Swart, "Growing Spontaneously." Reprinted from the *Church Herald*, December 4, 1959: 4.

I knew in my heart immediately what God wanted me to do and we made ourselves willingly available if the mission should want to assign us for that task.

What most of you did not know was that I had a plan to pursue a field doctorate from the Kennedy School [of Missions] in Hartford, Connecticut. I had done the required linguistic classroom work to qualify for working on their field degree program with Dr. Bill Welmers as my mentor. My selected subject was "A Study of the Anuak Religion As It Relates to Communicating the Essential Christian Message Among Animistic Peoples."

When the call came to consider Murle translation, the importance of pursuing that faded into insignificance. I never thought of it again.[2]

So the Hoekstras came to Pibor, taking up residence in the former Hostetter home. The Anuak translation was completed there.

Over the years, limited editions of individual gospels and several of the epistles had been printed by the American Bible Society. These proved to be invaluable not only in the teaching ministry of the Anuak church, but also in helping to perfect the final translation.

The entire work was done with the help of Anuak informants. The finished manuscripts, which were typed by Stephen Omot Didumu, totaled more than seven hundred pages.

When the typing was completed, conferences were held in which other missionaries and Anuaks participated. Some Africans walked more than one hundred fifty miles in order to attend. This was vital stuff!

After nearly a year of scheduling conferences, where final proofreading and retyping took place, the manuscripts were sent to the American Bible Society in April 1961.

What thanksgiving when the message came: "Manuscripts arrived safely."[3]

[2] Harvey Hoekstra, from a letter to the author, July 29, 1993. Joint Archives of Holland, Hope College.

[3] Harvey T. Hoekstra, "The New Testament in Anuak." Reprinted from the *Church Herald*, February 2, 1962: 11.

Yet even while the Anuak New Testament was nearing completion, Harvey was also busy at work on the Murle language.

It was a time of urgency. Who knew how much longer any of us would be permitted to work in Sudan? Ever since independence, and in spite of an initial sense of optimism, uncertainty was in the air. The expulsion of the Crandalls, the Bill Andersons, and the Hostetters did nothing to dispel the somewhat oppressive mood.

That meant only one thing: get on with the work "while it is yet day."

But occasionally we took time out to relax, to celebrate special events, or just to make memories.

In June 1960, all the children were home from Schutz. Denny Hoekstra had graduated; this was his last vacation before going to the United States for college. So we three families—the Roodes, Hoekstras, and Swarts—planned a daylong outing. We packed a picnic lunch and started out in two Jeep trucks, heading out farther and farther into the bush, in country watered by the Kangen River, one of the tributaries of the Pibor.

All of a sudden we found ourselves slowed to a crawl because we were completely surrounded by migrating herds of animals: giraffe, zebra, and a variety of gazelles and antelopes. Beside us, a mangy lioness slunk along, surfeited for the time being with fresh meat, but already planning the next kill. A lone hyena, an animal seldom seen in the daytime, loped in ungainly fashion ahead of us.

We were all speechless with wonder. To be in the midst of thousands of animals on the move was more than we could articulately respond to. "Oh! Oh!" seemed the only exclamation we could utter. Eventually my tongue was untied enough to remark, "If there were elephants here, the scene would be complete." And there on the near horizon appeared thirteen elephants moving ponderously in single file. I snapped a picture of them, with a group of white-eared kob in the foreground, and Denny Hoekstra and John Roode off to one side taking in the amazing scene.

It's thrilling to remember that day. We had planned the picnic; God had provided a sumptuous feast.

The white-eared kob produced an annual faunal phenomenon. At the end of the rains, thousands of white-eared kob would make their way through the southern Sudan. When they reached the Pibor River, hundreds of them swam to the other side right at the curve where the mission was located. Once across, the seemingly endless herds bounded through the compound, snapping wire fences in their haste to get out to the wide open plains beyond, and even on to the Baro and Akobo River areas in western Ethiopia. They had come all the way from Uganda on their yearly migration and no barrier could stop them.

Well, hardly any. The Murles took advantage of the kobs' vulnerability in the river, slaughtering many of them for a meat supply that would enrich their meager diets for weeks. Our reaction to this was ambivalent: we were sad for the kob, but glad for the Murles. We enjoyed kob meat, too, on occasion. One unusual incident occurred at the end of a migration when most of the kob had left our area. This particular evening, Dick and I were the only ones at home, and Dick was sound asleep. Some movement outside caught my attention, and when I looked, there, standing in the glow of our yard light, were three kob that seemed to have strayed from the herd. I have no idea what startled them, but suddenly two went bounding off into the dark, while the third dashed for our dining veranda, made a flying leap through the screen, and landed with unaccustomed lack of grace, all four feet splayed awkwardly on the cement floor. Both of us were astonished.

The kob made its way into our shower room. I closed the door—and called Harvey. He brought his gun. None of us had eaten meat for a while, so we were thankful for this unexpected gift, akin to the quails in the wilderness, even to the poor animal's flight through the screen!

Most of our mission stations were in the "remote" category, but we were linked together not only in our common purpose, but also in a more tangible way, by radio-telephone (RT). A designated person in Malakal emceed the network each day at a scheduled hour.

This means of communication kept us all in touch with mission news and prayer needs. We all looked forward to the daily RT conversations. But not all news was good to hear.

In April 1961, Al Roode was out on the plains toward the Boma Plateau with a Sudanese government team that had gone out by truck to investigate the incidence of tapeworm in antelope herds. Bob was in Malakal on business. Harvey Hoekstra was operating the Pibor RT that was located in the Roodes' house. I was listening on our own receiving set.

Lowrie Anderson was speaking from Malakal—with difficulty. What he had to say was incredible: John Roode, our own "Joe" from Pibor, out in the Egyptian desert on a Boy Scout hike on April 22, had died when he fell to the bottom of an ancient well sixty feet deep. Joe, a high school junior would have been seventeen in May.

When Lowrie learned where Al was, he made arrangements with MAF to fly out to the area and drop a note to let him know of his son's death. Plane and truck met later at Boma. The next day, MAF flew Al back to Pibor. After seemingly endless hours of grieving apart, Al and Ruth were united in their sorrow. This in itself afforded some comfort.

The rest of us were dumb with vicarious grief—that this tragedy could have happened to such a fine young man. Six days before his death, Joe had written a letter to his parents:

Dear Mom and Dad,

...I really got myself into a lot of work when I took the job of yearbook photographer....I've spent about twenty hours in that darkroom so far....

We got a few letters from home today. I am sort of stunned with all this news of plans for going home on furlough....Everything that means anything to me is in Sudan. Now in six weeks, I'll be pulling up my stakes in Egypt only to leave everything in Sudan two months later....(It's sort of like dying!)

I'm not saying I don't like what is happening. It's just that everything is so strange. I'm an American in the truest sense and am not disloyal to my country, but I still have ties in Sudan....

To sum it all up, I'm simply changing atmospheres completely and don't know what to expect. To make it harder, I've also lost something that means the most to me—Sudan, its woods, its animals, its customs, and its people.

I know I can take the change, but the thought of losing my life in two months sobers me.

Well, that is about all.

Love,

Joe

This prophetic letter reached Al and Ruth about two weeks after the accident that took Joe's life so precipitously.

The Lord gives; the Lord takes away. A son dies; a son is born. Life and death—the rhythm flows relentlessly.

In June of that same year, the Hoekstras were awaiting the birth of their sixth child. By usual calculations, the birth day was long overdue, and there was some concern on the part of us all.

But on the morning of June 27, we read Oswald Chambers' meditation in his classic devotional, *My Utmost for His Highest.* The theme verse was: "I am with thee to deliver thee, saith the Lord" (Jeremiah 1:8). I dashed over to Hoekstras' house.

"Did you read Chambers this morning?" I asked breathlessly.

"Yes, we did," they replied. "Today must be the day!"

And it was so.

Late that afternoon, Bob and I took all the Roode, Hoekstra, and Swart children out to our special "mountain" for a picnic supper so Lavina could have her baby in relative peace and quiet, with Dr. Roode in attendance. We always enjoyed going out to this rocky outcrop, the source of all our building stone. It was easy to climb, and from the top, one could look out over miles and miles of unrelieved flatness. For those moments, one was king of all that could be surveyed.

We returned home before dark. The children were all asleep when, sometime after nine o'clock, Harvey shouted the news: "It's all over; we have a perfect baby boy!" So we went to the Hoekstras' house to meet Paul Douglas and to congratulate his mom and dad. Carol woke up next morning to learn that she now had five brothers.

That summer, the Roode family went to the States on their scheduled furlough. They didn't realize it at the time, but they had said good-bye to Sudan forever.

Dr. Mary Smith came to Pibor to carry on the medical work.

Sometime during that same year, frail little Ngachor gave birth to a son. She and her husband, Kajach, named their new son John, in memory of John Roode. Through his mother's teaching and example, John Kajach grew up knowing that he had a savior.

As 1961 gave way to 1962, we marveled that, six years after independence, the American Mission was still at work in Sudan. It seemed an appropriate time to take stock of the situation, to outline in general terms where we stood as a mission in relation to the indigenous church:

> The story of the work in Sudan today...is more and more the account of the Church of Christ in the Upper Nile.
>
> To date, the church is composed of eight organized congregations and a score of preaching centers, two of which will become organized churches this year. There are four ordained Sudanese pastors with six more able young men at present in seminary: four at Bishop Gwynne College in Sudan, and two at London Bible College in England. For those full time evangelists able to study in the vernacular only, an apprenticeship training course has been set up.
>
> Numerical gains have not been spectacular other than to give evidence of the presence of real life....The Sudanese church [is becoming] aware of itself as an indigenous body....The thrilling accounts of spontaneous growth of several worshiping groups through the witness of one keen African Christian points to the fact that governments, or missions, cannot stand in the way of the working of the Holy Spirit.
>
> One place, an island in the Sobat River, has literally become a Garden of Eden as the leader of the Christians demonstrates his change of heart in this practical way. Another group, more than a hundred miles from any mission, built its own church building independently and put on it a cross that dominates the village.
>
> With government policy toward the Christian minority in fact being determined at a local level, a churchwide strategy of witness [has to] be varied. In some places, gathering of crowds of more than five people, other than in established churches, is forbidden. In other places, literacy work is not allowed, and in another area, no witness to minors, or even baptism of children without the written signature of the father being registered with the government. For a time, even repair of present church buildings was stopped.
>
> So Paul's admonition to be all things to all men in order to win some is very practical here. In broad terms, new emphasis is being

placed on women's work, church conferences, special weeks of witness in the established churches, and personal lay evangelism.

...Bishop Gwynne College, as the single theological seminary in Sudan, [is] carried on jointly by the Church of England and the American missions. The Southern Evangelical Council is [an agency] where all the churches and the various missions share in consultation and present a united voice to the world. Especially helpful is the [shared] planning by this body in the field of Christian literature and publications.

Being a church of five tribes with five [different] languages in a Muslim land where the lingua franca is yet another language, [presents] a hurdle for united action. The variance between constitutional freedom and actual freedom, of worship and belief is discouraging. The constant battle for the allegiance of men's hearts in a modern world, but in a land only one step from a wheelless society, is unique. The finding and training of leaders who understand both, yet stand with Christ, is a primary concern.

The whole field of literature [in the vernaculars] in an increasingly literate church is hardly more than a thought. The establishment of the Christian home with its teaching of the sanctity of marriage, the realization that it is the foundation of the Christian community, is just dawning in the thinking of a few. Sunday schools, though existent in several of the churches, are without any indigenous study materials to build upon.

This church cannot ask for more missionaries to help. Those [missionaries] now present live constantly under the Damoclean sword of possible expulsion.

[But] training of leadership is a costly task this young church cannot carry alone. Dissemination of the gospel by the printed page is an [undertaking] that can be done only with a lot of help, equipment, supplies, and training that permit quantity and quality which will make a difference.

Our church in America must not repeat history as it was written in Sudan at the time of the death of General "Chinese" (Charles George) Gordon during the siege of Khartoum when those who had the resources and the ability to save arrived too late with too little.[4]

Because the summer of 1962 would be Valerie's last vacation before graduating from high school, it was decided that her trip back home to Pibor should be more adventuresome than the usual hour and a half MAF flight from Malakal. Merry, Chloe, and Jack had already traveled home by plane, but Bob met Valerie and Gayle in Malakal. The journey back would be made in our new nineteen-foot aluminum canoe, an experience that proved to be an adventure.

Their route took them eastward on the Sobat River to Nasir where they spent the first night. On Saturday they continued on the Sobat and then turned south on the Pibor River, expecting to reach Akobo by evening. After a few hours, they came to a junction and decided the main waterway was the fork to the left, a judgment based on steep banks. From that point, their troubles began and multiplied.

Valerie's account includes such details as having to portage the canoe and all their gear around a huge, mile-long block of dense water hyacinth; Dad coming upon a croc lurking in high grass; climbing tall termite mounds to get their bearings; camping in a mosquito-ridden swamp; and just being completely fagged.

On Sunday they learned the disheartening fact from some Nuer villagers that they were not on the Pibor River, but on the *Khor* Makway. Since *khors* are dead-end streets, they turned around.

In the meantime, concern in Malakal, Nasir, Akobo, and Pibor was mounting. On Monday morning, I heard on the RT that search parties, having started out by outboard the day before from both Nasir and Akobo, had met midway between the two stations without having found a clue about the "lost ones." An aerial search was being organized.

Suspecting that such would be the case, Bob and the girls retraced their wearisome, swampy, hyacinth-blocked passage. When darkness fell that

[4] Morrell W. Swart, "Hurdles and Hopes in the Sudan." Reprinted from the *Church Herald*, July 13, 1962: 4.

Sunday evening, they made camp again and slept peacefully until one o'clock. As Val described it:

> Dad woke us up and told us he was going to shoot; he had heard a boat and he wanted to tell them where we were. Those in the boat heard the shot, shone lights, blew whistles, and yelled. Dad yelled back, trying to tell them to come through the swamp. They found their way in.
>
> It was Uncle Harvey Hoekstra [at Akobo for a meeting], Aunt Marian Farquhar, and Uncle Ted Pollock [Presbyterian builder] who had come to our aid. We loaded up and left at two o'clock.
>
> We got back to the river, and with the moon shining brightly overhead and lighting the river a little, we began our seven-hour trip to Akobo.
>
> At 6:40 we stopped. Uncle Harvey got out his little transistor...to see if we could hear Akobo talking to MAF. It was quite a picture with all of us crowded around the radio and Uncle Ted off to one side holding the aerial up in the air with a bamboo pole. We listened to the plans everyone was making for the search. No one knew that we had been found....Uncle Lowrie was encouraging Mom....Akobo folks said they'd contact MAF again at eight o'clock.
>
> We decided somebody ought to go to Akobo and let them know that we'd been found before something really began happening. So Uncle Harvey sped off alone in his boat. He arrived at Akobo just on time. All he said was, "Generator! Turn the radio on!"
>
> Of course, everyone thought that something terrible had happened, and they didn't know we'd been found until they heard Uncle Harvey tell MAF the news on the RT....
>
> Everyone seemed so glad to see us when we got to Akobo at nine o'clock—even the Africans. They had been told about our being lost and were quite concerned.
>
> We changed into dry clothes, had a late breakfast, and then rested. All of us were absolutely beat.[5]

5 Valerie Swart, "A River Adventure," June 1962. Joint Archives of Holland, Hope College.

The river played a role in another drama at Pibor that year. We'd already had a flood in 1961:

> The water rose gradually....It was the cumulative effect of the weather in the Ethiopian mountains that kept filling these rivers of the plains over a period of three months....The sister floods in Kenya Colony, Tanganyika, and Somaliland made international news. Not so, our Upper Nile flood, and we have no way of knowing the extent of suffering caused by it.[6]

[But] the flood of 1961 proved to be but a dress rehearsal for the real thing staged here in 1962. The drama unfolded slowly as the water rose inch by inch, flooding land and gardens; filling the hospital, patient houses, and one of the mission residences to a depth of nearly two feet....People were crowded together on the highest ground in makeshift shelters: grass and stick huts, truck racks with roofs and sides of zinc sheeting with canvas thrown over and tied at strategic spots.

The church was occupied by the medical assistant and his family....The grain store became the temporary dwelling of a TB patient....The government school...had been evacuated to Akobo one hundred miles down river, as were many police, soldiers, and their families. Three province steamers had remained here in case of further evacuation needs.

The water had reached its peak and had started down....Then came the storms. Wind whipped the heavy rain in every direction, flapped the canvases, rattled the zinc, soaked those poor dwellings inside and out, and dampened spirits considerably.

"Mr. Swart! Mr. Swart!"

Why was [a man's voice] coming from the direction of the river on such a night?...Then we heard the clang, clang of the steamer gong, and again,

"Mr. Swart, come here with your boat!"

"Yes, I'm coming! I'm coming!"

---

[6] Morrell W. Swart, "Flood at Pibor." Reprinted from the *Church Herald*, February 9, 1962: 13.

They had come up from the government post for Dr. Mary Smith. A woman "had stopped breathing and her heart had stopped beating." But she was still alive. She had a five-day-old baby. Bob and Mary went down by motorboat.

...It was with real thanksgiving to God that we heard upon their return that the woman was well again. She had fainted, and of course, everyone had been frightened.

Clear skies greeted us in the morning.

Oboich, one of the TB patients, had contracted cerebral malaria. Today he was worse, unconscious, and his young wife wanted to take him home....No amount of pleading would change her mind. In spite of the fact that she knew there was no medicine in the village, her fear of his dying in a strange place had the greater influence on her.

Oboich came from Koko's village....Just that morning a note [had come] from Koko saying that his mother was sick and his little baby had fallen out of a high bed. Please send medicine.

It is, under normal conditions, about a four-hour walk from Koko's village to the mission. It had taken this messenger three days to get to us because of the flood waters. Under these circumstances, it seemed right that we take Oboich home in the motorboat. His wife was in good spirits...she held Oboich propped between her knees.

It took only forty minutes [to reach our destination]. Because of the high water, we could take the boat right up to the village itself. An old woman came wading out to meet the boat....As we came nearer, paddling now, she could see Oboich slumped against his wife, to all appearances lifeless. Using Bob's Murle name, she said, "Torkomiti, this is my boy."

Others joined her about the boat, and then began the haunting death wail of uninhibited fear and grief. It was to no avail that we told them he was still living....

Dr. Mary gave him another anti-malarial injection, and they carried him into a house. The wailing continued....

In the meantime, we waded through water, muck, and ooze...to the cluster of dwellings where Koko's family lived. [As we approached], we could see strips of meat drying, and a ewe with her unborn lamb lying dead in the yard. Vultures sat on the rooftops. It was apparent that the people were living on the meat of their dying herds. [Many] cattle had been driven way back to better grazing land.

Friendly smiles and outstretched hands welcomed us to Koko's village....We were pleased to find Ngachor there (her leprosy now in remission), together with her older son, Oleo, and her small son, John.

We all gathered in the house of Koko's mother. She was sitting back in the darkness by her little fire, leaning against one of the poles that supported the roof, and smoking a long-necked gourd pipe. Her complaints were many and varied; she was given medicine, as were several others. The baby who had fallen...had few scratches but was otherwise pronounced well.

Afterwards we all squatted down to sing and pray. There were believers and unbelievers in the group, but all sang:

Kanatit, kanatit Baatinang [Praise, praise our Father!]

Jok ci abona ter; [God is very good;]

Anyet ageet ngerin [He sent us his Son]

Kelawet ageeta dook [In order to help us all.]

...Then it was time to leave in order to get home before the tropic's sudden sunset. [Oboich's] village was quiet by that time. We left, but our hearts remained there. Our prayers are much for that village and the witness of Koko and Ngachor. A few days later, word came that Oboich was quite himself again.[7]

As time went by, to witness for Christ became more a life-threatening venture, especially for the nationals. But Nyati, our most sincere and devoted Murle evangelist, went tirelessly from village to village, telling the gospel story.

The new district commissioner, Hassan Ngacingol (a Murle who had turned his back on Christianity for expediency's sake), repeatedly forbid Nyati to teach his people. But this dauntless servant of the Lord continued

---

[7] Morrell W. Swart, "In Time of Flood—Retreat or Advance?" Reprinted from the *Church Herald*, December 21, 1962: 20, 21.

to share the good news faithfully even after being arrested and jailed by his turncoat fellow tribesman. He was even threatened with death. Nothing deterred him.

"Nyati was like another Paul, the apostle, for he suffered for his Christ and never renounced him. The compulsion to serve the Lord was always in his heart."[8]

The Hoekstras had left Pibor temporarily to teach at Bishop Gwynne College in Mundri. So, because the Pibor River was occupying our house, we three Swarts moved into theirs until the waters abated—which they did, though ever so gradually.

However, before we were able to return to our own abode, another event occurred that overshadowed floods and all other frustrations: the thread finally had given way; the Damoclean sword fell.

---

[8] Dr. Albert Roode, "History of the Murle Church," an unpublished document, n.d. Joint Archives of Holland, Hope College.

IX
Last Days in Sudan

No general radio-telephone contact was scheduled for Sunday, just MAF's emergency standby. Many of us liked to tune in anyway to glean whatever news there might be. On the last Sunday of October 1962, we gleaned some news we would rather not have heard. Our new general secretary of the mission, Milton Thompson, called both Akobo and Pibor. "I'm afraid I don't have very good news for you folks," Milton said. "The Swarts and the Sikkemas have been given expulsion orders by the Sudan government. You are to be out of the country in six weeks."

The gradual fraying of the silken threads that had held aloft the threatening blade for more than six years, had not fully prepared us to face the inevitable; we were bewildered and incredulous.

Lorraine Sikkema recorded her reaction:

> Verne and I were completely stunned, for this was home! How could we just leave with our small children? It was especially hard because our youngest daughter, Charlotte Mary, had just been born in our Akobo home on September 16.
>
> Later we walked over to the Ladies' House to inquire whether or not they had heard the radio traffic that morning. Lillian Huisken and Wilma Kats were likewise stunned and perturbed by this latest government action...the only good thing we could see was that now

129

we would be reunited with our daughter Linda who had gone at the
end of August to attend boarding school in Egypt for the first time.[1]

At Mundri, the Hoekstras heard the news. According to Harvey:

> I had been to our regular morning chapel. I returned to the house
> for breakfast during the time of the morning mission broadcast. We
> had our Zenith radio, enabling us to listen but not to transmit. That
> morning, when I opened the back door, Lavina, with head close to
> the radio, raised her hand and ordered me to be quiet. She said,
> "Sh, sh! The Swarts and Sikkemas have both been expelled."
>
> I fell silent, stunned by the shock, and put my head next to hers
> to catch every word. Within a week, my teaching career was over
> and we were on our way back to Pibor.[2]

The government gave no reason, other than "your work is finished,"
adding erroneously that we had come to Sudan to engage in educational
work. Schools now had been taken over by the government, so our presence
was no longer essential.

Our hearts were heavy. The future, always uncertain at best, now seemed
utterly blank. After nearly fifteen years in Sudan, the thought of having to
leave this country and her people brought a kind of wrenching grief. Pibor
was home to our children. Five of them were in school in Alexandria. They
had left in August not knowing that they'd never come home to Pibor again.

Did this mean that Valerie would not be able to graduate with her class in
June? Our furlough wasn't due until September. What would we do in the
meantime? Questions whirled in our minds even as we began preparations
for leaving.

We received letters from our school children after they'd heard the news
through other mission friends, particularly the McLaughlins in Malakal who
were able to communicate more readily than we were. All were written on
November 4.

Dear Mom and Dad,

We received word yesterday from Aunt Megs [McLaughlin]
about your having to leave Sudan in six weeks. Sikkemas also. It was

---

[1] Lorraine Sikkema, from an account sent to the author, n.d. Joint Archives of
Holland, Hope College.
[2] Harvey Hoekstra, from a letter to the author, July 29, 1993.

really a blow to us and even now it hardly seems possible....I really had high hopes of getting back [to Pibor] for part of the summer before going to the States. And now all my hopes are shattered. It just doesn't seem possible that we'll never be back at Pibor again—our home, the place we love, the people we love, and just everything that makes up the place. I keep asking, "Why, why, why did this happen to us?" But then I realize that the Lord has a plan for each of our lives and he probably has a reason for this.

This was your life work and to have it suddenly taken out from under you without any warning is really a terrible thing....I certainly will be praying that the church will remain strong...and also that God will comfort you and give you peace....

I would appreciate it if you could say good-bye to all those I knew down there and [tell them] that I will be remembering them in my prayers.

Love to all,
Val

Thou wilt keep him in perfect peace whose mind is stayed on thee.

Dear Mommy, Daddy, and Dick,

The Lord sure has a lot of surprises in one's life. We were dumbfounded when we got the news on Saturday morning....It's really something, this sudden change. We're praying and thinking of you constantly in the decisions that are going to have to be made and know that the Lord will lead you wisely and help you in the tremendous load of work that has fallen on your shoulders. Praise the Lord that you have six weeks instead of two or one....We're looking forward to some word from you and are praying for you continually.

Much love,
Gayle

Dear Mom and Dad,

Yesterday morning we heard the awful news. It sure made all of us here feel sick and it probably was even much worse for you to hear. All the other missionary kids here are wondering when they will be sent out. It sure is going to spoil lots of our summer plans....I wish we could come home and help you get everything packed. It must be hard to know what to take and what to leave. Most of my stuff seems pretty important to me but if we can't take it, OK. Just leave it....

Love you all,
Merry

Dear Mom, Dad, and Dick,

On Saturday we heard about us and the Sikkemas being kicked out. It's terrible....Tim McLaughlin got a letter from his mom and he told Jack and Jack told me, so the news got around. We still haven't gotten a letter from you and I hope we will soon, telling what you are going to do, where you are going, etc. I know God will help you to decide wisely. I'll be praying for you.

I hope I'll be able to see Pibor again sometime. And I hope I'll be able to see Dr. Mary again sometime. And I hope we can go to Ethiopia and be able to be missionaries there. I want to go to Schutz for school and I don't want to live in the States.

Lots and lots of love,
Chloe

By this time, the flood waters had receded and our house was drying out. But we continued living in the Hoekstras' home for a while, and used our dining veranda as a packing room. Steel drums were lined up in the center of the floor. We gradually filled them, choosing carefully the items we would want shipped to the States, should the Lord lead us to return there permanently. These things went into the drums painted with a wide red band....If he called us to serve in another country, we would need all the drums. The furniture would have to stay behind. Much of it was sold to government personnel.

When we heard that the Hoekstras were on their way from Mundri, we moved in with Dr. Mary who was living in the Roodes' house. It was Thanksgiving Day when Harvey and Lavina and their children arrived. What a bittersweet day. We had so much to be thankful for, yet the pall of expulsion brooded over us all. However, we were able to praise God for the years he had given us in Sudan, for the work he had enabled us to accomplish for his name's sake, and we had faith that this turn of affairs must be interpreted as being marching orders from on high. He would surely open other doors for us somewhere.

In early December, the very day before MAF was scheduled to fly us out of Pibor, the Hoekstras received their equally jolting orders; they were granted one week before having to leave the country.

We arranged to stay an extra day to help them as we could. Lavina had a fever, but she kept going and did what had to be done.

The day of departure came. We'd been saying good-bye to our Murle friends for weeks. On that last day, a young Anuak woman came to our door in tears. Now she was married to Owo, who had been trained as a dresser and had been assigned to work alongside Dr. Mary and the medical assistant, Barayona Lami, at the mission clinic at Pibor.

Nyakili was not able to speak. Nor was it easy for me. The only words that came were: "I love you, Nyakili. I'll see you in heaven." That much we were sure about, and we were at peace.

The plane took off. It was painful to look down on all the familiar landmarks—but we were on our way to some new adventure in faith.

In Malakal Lowrie Anderson had prepared a comforting, encouraging farewell service for us. In Khartoum a missionary friend gave us a final word of assurance: "They have expelled you, but they can't expel God!" These ministrations sustained us all the way to Alexandria, Egypt, where we spent the next six weeks with our children at Schutz. The Sikkemas were there, too. After a few days, the Hoekstras also arrived. They brought word that several Presbyterian missionaries by this time had received their orders to leave Sudan. Our hearts plunged once again.

But they also brought news that gave us much reason to rejoice and praise God: Two MAF planes went to Pibor to fly out the Hoekstra family. In the midst of loading the luggage, one of the pilots said to Harvey, "There's a small package here that you may want to open before you leave."

To their unspeakable delight, they found inside the first five beautiful, blue, hard-covered Anuak New Testaments printed by the American Bible Society. With them was a note saying that the balance of the one thousand Anuak New Testaments were with the Bible Society in Khartoum.

Harvey and Lavina remember that it lessened their pain at having to leave when they considered this evidence of the perfect and precise timing of the Lord. An Anuak leader, who happened to be there at the plane that day, said, "You have left us God's best gift. You have given us his Word in our language." Hearing of this singular kindness of the Lord relieved the sadness of us all, and made us realize anew who, after all, was sovereign in this season of banishment.

An early 1963 issue of the *Church Herald* carried a news release from the Committee on Cooperation in the Upper Nile and the Board of World Missions, RCA:

> The Sudanese government has ordered the expulsion of seventeen United Presbyterian and Reformed missionaries...although denominational officials said that authorities gave no reason for this action.
>
> A joint statement by the United Presbyterian Commission on Ecumenical Mission and Relations and the Board of World Missions of the Reformed Church in America said that six of the seventeen have already left the country, and the remaining eleven must quit their posts by January 19....
>
> The Presbyterian-Reformed statement said that the new Missionary Societies Act, which became effective in mid-November, requires mission organizations in Sudan to obtain an annual license which will permit limited and localized forms of activities under the new law. The new regulations limit social contact between Christian clergymen and the people, and also prohibit children from entering into church membership without the legal permission of their parents or their guardians in the presence of an authorized government official. It is noted that these regulations were in general effect before the Missionary Societies Act was formally instituted.
>
> The statement indicated that those expelled have been at their posts for an average of twelve years. All the American missionaries

complied with the new law and made application [for the annual license] with the hope of continuing their service in Sudan.

Sixteen remaining missionaries, scattered among nine stations, are trying to regroup and carry on their programs as best they can. Four medical doctors and two nurses are among the number permitted to stay. But their services may be impaired by the absence of colleagues who shared in much of the maintenance, transportation, and administration.

Similar evictions have already practically eliminated other Christian missions in the adjoining provinces of the South Sudan. It is also noted that the small Church of Christ in the Upper Nile is continuing to conduct worship services for Christians in that area....

It is expected that a decision on the reassignment of [the Sikkemas, Swarts, and Hoekstras] will be made at an early date. The Reformed Church missionaries remaining in Sudan are: Miss Wilma Kats, a teacher, and Miss Lillian Huisken, a nurse, at Akobo; and Miss Arlene Schuiteman, a nurse, working with Dr. and Mrs. Robert Gordon at Nasir.

The seventeen evicted missionaries, the sixteen missionaries remaining in [Upper Nile], and the Christians of the country are commended to the church for intercession and prayer.[3]

With the Swarts and Hoekstras now gone, Dr. Mary was alone at Pibor, a place that was described in later years as "a hundred miles beyond the Great Commission." And with the Sikkemas gone, only Wilma and Lillian were left at Akobo. (The Jordans had moved some time ago to a Nuer area over the border in Ethiopia. The Arnold family was on the field only one term.) So it was decided that Dr. Mary should return to Akobo and make periodic visits to Pibor. This arrangement pleased and relieved us all.

Arlene Schuiteman was still at Nasir with the Gordon family and also Marian Farquhar. Lowrie and Margaret Anderson were the only personnel now at mission headquarters in Malakal. Their burden was heavy.

In my Bible, in the margin beside Psalm 4:1, is a notation: "At Schutz, '62." The verse reads: "Thou has given me room when I was in distress."

3 "Missionaries Expelled From the Sudan." Reprinted from the *Church Herald*, January 4, 1963: 13.

Four large, brand new rooms had been built at the top of one of the Schutz school buildings. They had just been completed when the Swarts, Hoekstras, and Sikkemas were in need of a temporary dwelling place, and they were graciously turned over to us. We were comfortably housed for as long as we needed to stay. To be there with all our children was added balm to our spirits.

The Sikkema family left for the United States on December 20. Verne would be pursuing a new career in missions and was eager to get on with his training. As for the rest of us, the trumpet was not yet sounding a clear call.

However, Dr. Glenn Reed, our area secretary who lived in Asmara, Eritrea, came to Alexandria during our sojourn there. Among other business that brought him to Schutz, he approached us about the possibility of continuing our association with the American Mission by moving to Ethiopia. This suggestion struck a responsive chord. As a result, Bob and Harvey flew to Addis Ababa to assess the situation personally. The challenge loomed large.

But before any decision could be made, it was necessary for the Swarts to hold a family consultation. We needed the children's input. Chloe had already expressed herself in her letter. But how would the rest react, and how was Chloe feeling now? At this juncture, were they perhaps hoping that we would return to the States and live a "normal" family life? Valerie would be entering Hope College in the fall. Would it be the better part of wisdom to become stateside residents again for her sake? The children's thoughts would help to guide us.

Bob chaired the meeting. He gave the pros and cons as we saw them, and encouraged discussion. When it came to the vote, there was not one dissenting voice; Africa was the continent of choice for us all.

So, while the Hoekstra family stayed on in Alexandria for several months, we left for an early furlough at the end of January with the intention of returning in September. Our four youngest children accompanied us. Valerie and Gayle opted to finish out the school year at Schutz and then join us in Holland, Michigan, in June.

In the meantime, Arlene Schuiteman was making plans for a short furlough and had applied for a reentry visa.

At the end of September...

> ...Lowrie Anderson made a special trip to Nasir to tell me that, although three others had received their reentry visas, mine was

not issued. It was decided that I would cancel my furlough plans for a while.... I kept wondering what they had against me, but Lowrie said that I must not try to figure it out because I might never know....

On October 15 a messenger came to our door to deliver a letter. I opened it and found it to be from the Ministry of Interior terminating my stay in Sudan. I was given seven days to leave....

It was hard to say good-bye to Marian and the Gordons. The Nuer women came again and again and just sat there looking as if I had died. It was, as another friend had said, like attending one's own funeral.

I remember visiting with one of our patients. Her husband, John Kuac Ruee, came with her. While I was listening to her, I was watching two of my favorite hoopoe birds pecking away in the grass. Then the husband walked away saying, "I believe God wants me to tell others about Jesus now."

MAF came for me on the appointed day at 4 p.m.... There was a final glimpse of our house from the air, a last glimpse of our clinic with two of the dressers waving in front of the door—and Nasir was out of view. The pilot knew that Lillian and Wilma would be listening on the RT at Akobo; I said my good-byes to them over the air. We landed at Malakal at 5 p.m.

Upon arrival the police checked my whereabouts and noted where I would be staying. They made sure that I would be flying on to Khartoum the next day, which was Sunday. That morning the pastor preached on the text, "I have fought the good fight, I have finished the course, I have kept the faith."

That afternoon I flew to Khartoum. Police were there when I left Malakal and again when I arrived in Khartoum. They followed me to the mission headquarters to note where I would be staying.

Bob Meloy went with me to the Ministry of Interior on Monday morning. We were given an appointment for Wednesday with permission to stay on until then. We asked for an opportunity to review the charges against me....

I was given an appointment with the Minister's Permanent Under Secretary on Wednesday at twelve o'clock. As I committed this affair to the Lord, I thought about the passage in Luke: "You shall be brought before kings and rulers for my sake…" and also Proverbs 16:33: "The lot is cast into the lap, but the decision is wholly of the Lord."

The interview lasted only about five minutes. I was informed that there would be no change in the decision; that no case had been brought against me which could be defended in court; that I was simply required to leave without being given a reason. It was firm and final.

I left Khartoum on October 21…spent some time with the Reeds in Asmara…visited our missionaries in the Persian Gulf…and stopped in Bethlehem. I arrived in New York November 3.

Back in Malakal, Lowrie Anderson questioned a friend who knew about my expulsion and who worked in a government office. He said that the reason I had been singled out was that I had examined and treated a Nuer woman who was being used as a mistress by one of the army officers at Nasir. After treating her, I spent time talking about being careful not to contract venereal disease again if she hoped to have more children. Also, this was not the way of life taught in the Bible. The man was very upset when she refused his attention and used his authority to get me out of the way.

Later, when a black list was posted in one of the Arabic newspapers in Khartoum, my name was among them. The reason for my expulsion was given: "Her activities are aimed at destroying the unity between the North and the South, and she taught that Christianity was the cure for all their ills."[4]

Following a furlough, during which time she studied at the University of Iowa for a bachelor of science degree in nursing, she received a call through the Rev. John Buteyn of the Board of World Missions to consider an assignment in Mettu, Ethiopia.

"It was impossible to return to Sudan," she reflected, "and this place would be just across the border in Ethiopia. It was God's call to me."[5]

---

[4] Arlene Schuiteman, "Sudan Notes," n.d. Joint Archives of Holland, Hope College.
[5] Ibid.

In spite of deteriorating conditions and drastic cuts in personnel, those left behind in Sudan carried on valiantly. Nor was their sense of humor diminished. Just prior to Milton and Peggy Thompson's departure from the country in January 1963, Wilma Kats and Lillian Huisken sent them the following telegram:

SOS COMPLETE BREAKDOWN PUMP GENERATOR JEEP BOAT TRANSMITTER AND US DELAY DEPARTURE BRING TOOLS AND ROOK HAMMER HERE signed AKOBOITES

I can hear Wilma chuckle as they composed the message.

At least Wilma, Lillian, and Dr. Mary had a hammer, and perhaps a few nails, to help hold things together, and an indomitable faith that would sustain them during the few months they would still be permitted to serve at Akobo. Wilma and Lillian were now the only remaining RCA missionaries in Sudan.

The Rev. Norman Tenpas, pastor of First Reformed Church in Oostburg, Wisconsin, sent a letter in 1963 to the *Church Herald*:

...the Rev. and Mrs. Robert Swart came and laid their program of the past and future before the congregation. They explained why and how they were ordered out of Sudan, but hardly had they finished, when Mr. Swart told of flying over hundreds of villages in Ethiopia where the gospel of Christ had never been preached. His enthusiasm for the new opportunity must have reminded many of us of the challenge given by Dr. Don McClure fifteen years ago when our church first organized and sent missionaries to Sudan.

How many of us remember Dr. McClure telling of the plan to put on an intensive, fifteen-year mission drive, trusting that an indigenous Church of Christ would be formed in that time? Could it be that what has happened in the South Sudan is God telling us: "Keep to the original plan. You may have liked to stay longer, but this is an indigenous church in my sight. What is here is as much as was in my churches in the early days of the apostles"?

Could it be that God is telling the church, "Move on to other
fields with the same enthusiasm and zeal with which you started
your past work. Forget what has happened in the past. But pray for
these churches that they may hold fast to the faith that dwells in
them by the power of the Holy Spirit"?[6]

During our seven-month furlough, we received bits of news. One
particularly encouraging word from Lowrie Anderson and Dr. Mary Smith
told of a service that had been held in the little church at the government
post at Pibor one Sunday in August. People from five different tribal groups
were in attendance. Shulla pastor Isaiah Otor baptized six Morus, three
Nuers, four Dinkas, and twenty Murles that day, and more than eighty
persons were served communion.

It was a confirmation of God's faithfulness to his promises. Perhaps
Norman Tenpas was right. The indigenous church had been established,
and God would never fail or forsake his people. It substantiated the fact that,
though missionaries had been expelled, God could not be. He was there in
all his glory and power. And his Son, Jesus Christ, would always be the head
of his church.

---

6 Norman Tenpas in a letter to the editor. Reprinted from the *Church Herald*,
   August 1963.

X
Opening Omo
and Godare

Bob and I were not the first RCA missionaries to enter the country that called itself "the oldest Christian empire in the world." The Hoekstras had preceded us by a few weeks and were there to welcome us when we arrived in Addis Ababa, Ethiopia, in September 1963.

Valerie was now a student at Hope College in Holland, Michigan. Gayle, Merry, and Chloe had returned to the American School (Schutz) in Alexandria, Egypt. Jack and Dick would board at the new Good Shepherd School just outside of Addis Ababa.

Our earthly possessions, so carefully packed in steel drums at Pibor, had arrived ahead of us and were stowed safely in the storeroom on the American Mission compound. We had old friends—Ted Pollock, Robb McLaughlin, Milton Thompson, MAF pilot John Ducker, and Nyati—to thank for expediting the sizable task of transporting these goods by canoe and sundry trucks across rivers and plains and rugged terrain. We were both grateful and heartsick to hear that, at some point during this operation, Peter-like Nyati was arrested for being critical of the government in ousting the missionaries. He was imprisoned and so badly treated that it affected his mind.

(Word came to us later that he had escaped somehow, making his way over the border into Ethiopia. He showed up at Maji where he was apprehended again. Presbyterian missionaries there ministered to him until he was sent back to Sudan. Verne Sikkema saw him at Pibor in May 1973. He reported that Nyati was "still radiant" and that over three hundred believers had been baptized at Pibor the week before his visit. Praise God that the seed sown long ago was bearing fruit.)

That the Swarts, Hoekstras, and other Sudan colleagues had been permitted to enter Ethiopia at all was unquestionably an act of God. And again our friend, Don McClure, was in the forefront of the negotiations with officialdom.

The McClures, after working at Pokwo on the Baro River for ten years, pushed farther into Anuak territory and established a mission outpost on the Gilo River. However, after only two years there, they moved to Addis Ababa.

> Don was asked to assume the office of general secretary of the American Mission....With offices located in Addis Ababa,...he was also to work as the field executive, representing and facilitating missionaries.[1]

> When his missionary colleagues were driven out of Sudan, Don sought permission for many of them to live and work in Ethiopia, but he had great difficulty, because the Sudan government officially asked neighboring nations not to receive them.[2]

> This has been a week of great furor in Addis Ababa [Don wrote to his parents] because the Ethiopian government has also capitulated to Sudan by barring all missionaries expelled by Sudan from coming into Ethiopia to live or even to visit. This week three Sudan Interior Mission missionaries, who were just stopping over, were ordered to leave Ethiopia within twenty-four hours because they had come directly from Sudan. Sudan has sent a list of some three hundred former Sudan missionaries who have been expelled and has asked all neighboring countries not to admit them into their territory. This is the most brazen piece of effrontery I have ever heard.[3]

But through his importunity, the "invincible stubbornness of the true Scot,"[4] and with the affirming power of God to aid him, Don was able to procure visas for all who were destined to move from Sudan into Ethiopia.

[1] Charles Partee, *Adventure in Africa* (Grand Rapids, Michigan: Zondervan Publishing House, 1990) 329.
[2] Ibid. 348.
[3] Ibid.
[4] Ibid. 349.

This was one of Don's most remarkable achievements. For compelling political reasons, Ethiopia had refused to accept Christian missionaries who were exiled by the civil war in the South Sudan, but the government made an exception for Don's old colleagues. In this way, Don was able to relocate experienced African missionaries...thereby increasing his church's missionary personnel in Ethiopia from thirty persons to more than ninety.[5]

The compulsion behind the negotiations stemmed from Don's great burden for the unreached tribes in southwestern Ethiopia.

> In the area for which our church is responsible there are more than thirty different tribes who have never heard the name of Jesus spoken in their language....
>
> After a team of experienced Ethiopian missionaries made an aerial survey of Kaffa and Illubabor provinces, Don proposed in a letter to Haile Selassie that the American Mission was prepared to begin work with the Nuers in Ethiopia; the Masongos [or Mesengos], estimated at between 20,000 and 30,000 people; the Mochas, with 40,000 to 50,000; the Teshenas, estimated at 100,000 people; the Tid-Termas, with approximately 20,000 and once thought to be two tribes; and the Gulebs [or Gelebs], perhaps the least known and most inaccessible of all the tribes of western Ethiopia.
>
> ..."Recently," Don wrote, "I had a conference with Haile Selassie and he gave me permission to start work in ten of these tribes....As he surveyed the unreached areas and untouched tribes on the map, His Imperial Majesty looked almost pathetic. He cannot provide what he desires for his people without our help. The doors are wide open."[6]

And through those doors, swung wide open we believe by royal decree under Higher Orders, filed a significant contingent of Presbyterian and RCA missionaries lately come from Sudan.

But missionaries—to "the oldest Christian empire"?

There are no records to tell us what influence the converted Ethiopian eunuch in the first century had when he returned to the court of Candace.

5 Ibid. 350.
6 Ibid. 376, 377.

But recorded history indicates that Christianity was introduced into Ethiopia during the fourth century. As it developed and spread, this country became a stronghold of the Orthodox, or Monophysite, branch of the Christian church.[7]

Lacking the warmth and zeal of evangelicals, the Ethiopian church tended to stagnate. Its coffers bulged and its people fasted religiously. But it had turned inward and there was little sharing of the gospel. Numerous tribes throughout the country had yet to hear the good news of Jesus Christ.

In the twentieth century, however, many mission agencies found fertile spiritual fields to till and sow in Ethiopia. But more help was needed, and we were among the privileged few who had been called to this great task.

The Hoekstras would go to the Mesengos in the rain forest of Illubabor Province; the Swarts, to the Gelebs on the Omo River in Kaffa Province— that is, after a year of language study in Addis Ababa.

During that year, Swarts and Hoekstras were next-door neighbors in attractive, new houses located within walking distance of the American Mission compound and the indigenous Bethel Church that we attended each Sunday. Although eager to move out to remoter areas, we recognized the value of becoming acquainted with Ethiopia's capital city, and acquiring at least a basic knowledge of the country's official language, Amharic, with its unusual sentence patterns, exploded consonants, and script requiring the skill of an artist to write legibly.

Our boys, as well as the Hoekstra children, came home from Good Shepherd School on weekends, which was a nice break and made the boarding school experience—the "away from home" phase—more palatable for us all (although, their Mennonite dorm parents, Paul and Erma Lehman, were heaven-sent, and all "their boys" remember them with much affection to this day).

The Hoekstras resided in Ethiopia at this time only on a tourist visa. Permanent visas were denied them because Harvey was classified as a linguist on the application forms, and the chairman of the government committee dealing with visas did not want anyone working on vernaculars. So their status in the country was precarious at best. Yet they studied Amharic with the faith that is described in Scripture as assurance that what is hoped for will come to pass.

---

[7] Ethiopian Tourist Organization pamphlet, "Provinces of Ethiopia," n.d. Joint Archives of Holland, Hope College.

Thankful though we were to be in Ethiopia, our hearts were still in Sudan, wondering how Wilma Kats, Lillian Huisken, Dr. Mary Smith, and our other Presbyterian friends were coping. News was sparse.

But on February 27, 1964, as we were listening to the BBC evening news, we were struck dumb to hear that the Sudan government was deporting all the remaining missionaries, some three hundred strong, from the South Sudan. On February 29 I wrote to our daughters:

> Dr. Reed called our mission headquarters from Asmara (Eritrea) this morning to say that all our American missionaries had to leave the South Sudan and they were given no time at all except to pack their suitcases. According to Dr. Reed, all out-station folks were coming into Malakal this morning and all were leaving for Khartoum this afternoon. Oh, how hard it must be for them all! What a sad time!
>
> Dr. Reed also said that...Aunt Wilma, Aunt Lillian, Aunt Marian [Farquhar, colleague of Arlene Schuiteman at Nasir], and Dr. Mary were coming to Addis Ababa on tourist visas. Uncle Don McClure has already seen one of the high government officials who has assured him that His Majesty would certainly welcome all these missionaries into the country. And Uncle Don is working now on getting them in....
>
> Those wonderful words of one of our favorite hymns, "God is working his purpose out," which helped us so much during the months following our expulsion, are still true today, and we can be certain that he has his reasons for allowing this to happen. This is no doubt the beginning of harder times than ever for the Sudanese in the South, and the church will go through terrific testings, we are sure. But that never killed a church; it was generally a means of strengthening. God grant that it may be so in this case....

So it was that, as of the last week in February 1964, the more than sixty-year involvement of the American Mission in the life of the South Sudan came to a close. The last of the RCA and Presbyterian personnel had been forced to leave. Again we commended the Church of Christ in Upper Nile, and the church throughout the southern region, to the faithful hands and heart of God.

Language study continued to consume our days. Every six weeks, a "step" was completed and we suffered through both oral and written exams. Bob and I previously had dealt only in unwritten tribal languages—with neither courses nor tests—but this strenuous and stressful exercise was valuable.

At the end of April, with two "steps" yet to go, the Hoekstras' tourist visa expired, and they had to leave the country while application was made for a permanent visa. We all hoped and prayed that Don McClure would be able to procure one quickly.

One day in late May, Don appeared at our door. He and Bob had a quiet consultation, then met with me in the living room. Don handed me a telegram that gave news of the death of my father. It was most unexpected, and my heart went home to my mother. My own sense of loss was tempered in thankfulness that my father had, only in recent years, returned to the church and had just been elected a deacon—a definite answer to importunate prayer.

So I could rejoice and find comfort in knowing that, as God had wooed him back to himself, he had also called him to his heavenly mansion—and we would meet again.

Late in June, Don, confident that visas were being granted, sent a wire to the Hoekstras in Nairobi, Kenya, to come, and on July 3 we met them at the airport. It was a jubilant reunion. We were all thankful for Don's persistence and for our God who hears prayers and doesn't permit sticky officials to stand in the way of his plans.

After completing Amharic language study in July, we prepared to bring the good news of Christ's love into virgin territory: the lush, vine-entangled forests of the Mesengos, and the semi-desert country of the Gelebs which is bisected by the Omo River.

Survey trips into areas of RCA responsibility were planned carefully. Made by plane and on foot, these surveys enabled the teams to choose the most suitable sites, taking into consideration the terrain itself, proximity to a water source, location relative to tribal settlements—and, most importantly, the consent and blessing of the people themselves on the site selection. This was accomplished.

One item of business remained: the final trip to the Omo River would be made overland, but we had no vehicle. The International Scout that Bob had ordered was on its way by freighter to Massawa, Eritrea's port on the Red Sea.

In November we had word from Dr. Reed in Asmara that the freighter would be reaching Massawa just before Thanksgiving. So we set out with the Presbyterian Pollock family (Ted and Dolly and their children, Ginny and Tom) in their Jeep for that northernmost province—a spectacular trip over Ethiopia's rugged mountains, with hairpin turns and magnificent views—and then down the escarpment to the port city. The Scout had indeed arrived, and it was soon in our possession.

After spending a delightful Thanksgiving day at the Reeds' home, we returned to Addis Ababa by another route that was even more awe-inspiring than the journey northward: grandeur at every turn, jagged peaks, and immense tors with spires like giant steeples.

It was to our souls' benefit to have beheld these awesome panoramas, to tuck away for future remembering when our scenery would be less than grand and our outlook less than enraptured.

Now that we had our vehicle, there was nothing more to delay us in starting out for points southwest. We were again traveling with the Pollocks. Jack and Dick were also with us. Our initial destination was the mission station among the Ghimeera people near Mizan Tafari. Departing Addis Ababa on December 20, we hoped to reach Mizan by Christmas. But, as we wrote to the girls:

> After the first two days, the trip was more nightmare than pleasure. But we were ever aware of the Lord's protecting care of us. Much of the road was hardly worthy of the name. It was probably a good road during the Italian occupation (1936–1941), a continual up-and-down route over more mountain ridges than we could keep track of. Now, after more than twenty years of neglect, the road is full of deep, deep ruts—muddy sloughs that nobody had bothered to drain, even when they were in the midst of a settlement—and rocky ravines that really wracked the cars. Both vehicles were stuck innumerable times, both in muck and also by being hung up in the center on a too-high rock or earthen ridge.
>
> Our trailer fell over on its side once, breaking the hitch. Another time, the Scout tipped over very gently. The boys suffered a few bumps as the baggage shifted, but no one was hurt. At one place, the log bridge across a stream was most unsafe. So the men spent three hours making a way for the cars to get across through the stream....

On the December 23, Ted Pollock, in trying to avoid a terrible mud hole, found himself almost rolling down a mountain side. The Jeep was tilted at a frightening angle. Attempts to get it back on the track were fruitless. So, securing it by means of rope and cable to some trees, we made camp for the night. In the distance we could hear thunder. But it didn't rain.

About 9:30 that evening, we were awakened by a call from a couple of men who had arrived carrying flashlights. We were startled, of course. Dad got up and greeted them. They handed him a note which he read by flashlight. It was written both in English and in Swedish:

"This letter comes from Wosho Coffee Plantation. I will come tomorrow with some boys and try to help you as much [as] I can. With me will I have good tools and also a hand winch with a 30 mm cable. Eat of this food we with these boys are sending you. Do not worry for them. They are very honest boys. Please send with these boys a note how you are. The boys must go back as soon as possible. I hope the night will not be too hard for you. Yours, Nils Gustaf von Rosen."

Needless to say, that note filled us with great joy and made us very aware that God was really with us. Travelers on foot who had seen our plight had taken the word to the plantation....

Nils von Rosen, a most friendly young man, arrived about noon on the next day. He had a little lunch with us, then they all slogged to the site of our "waterloo." They returned to our camp at three o'clock; the Jeep was back on the road.

What a godsend Nils von Rosen was! And he told us that the only pay he wanted was for us to spend Christmas Eve with him and his wife.

We broke camp as quickly as possible and proceeded to the plantation. Britte von Rosen, a beautiful young woman, came out to meet us. She had hot water ready so that we could all take baths, and beds all ready for us in their little guest house.

That evening we had a Christmas Eve smorgasbord. We ate by candlelight. Later Nils asked Dad to read the Christmas story, and then we listened to Christmas music on Dad's tape player. Guess what the music was: the Schutz choir singing Christmas carols!

Next morning we learned that the coffee plantation is on land given to Nils' father, Count Gustaf von Rosen, by Haile Selassie in gratitude for his role in flying for the Red Cross during the Ethio-Italian war a quarter of a century earlier. We understood he was also instrumental in some way saving the emperor's life.

Well, after having tea late in the morning on Christmas Day, we again started on our way. We felt such an outpouring of gratitude and affection for that young couple for having taken us in so wholeheartedly. Britte said that our being with them had been a help, too, so they wouldn't be homesick thinking of their family and friends in Sweden.

We finally arrived at Mizan Tafari on the December 28. We would not reach the Omo River for another three months, but we were on the way.

The Hoekstras, in the meantime, had moved into the Godare area among the Mesengos. No one can tell the story as vividly as Harvey himself:

"Do you think this horse can make it up this bank with me on him?" Lavina called back to me as we crossed one of the rivers on our trek into the Godare. My assurances were obviously ill-founded because the first thing I knew, the old black horse lurched backwards, sitting down in the water, and Lavina was slipping over the tail end into the river.

It was all in a day's journey....We'd spent most of the first day assembling our supplies in manageable sizes and shapes to be distributed among the carriers and pack animals. Then we took a couple of hours loading the mules. They were more frisky than normal from lack of work, and we had our suspicions that they hadn't been sold to us for any good reasons.

This was confirmed when, within less than one minute after starting out, we saw mule heels flying thick and fast and three of them had successfully kicked off their loads. The belly bands slipped, loads hung under the animal rather than on the back, and boxes and bundles were scattered everywhere like debris, with mules knee-deep in our things, staring at us with looks of defiance and triumph....

We had traveled ten miles the first afternoon, and discovered upon arrival at this last outpost of civilization before entering the forest proper, that our promised trails had not yet been started. This involved a delay of a couple of days and meant we would have to ration our food supplies more carefully....

Carriers were always an uncertain quantity (also quality) and we never knew from one area to the next whether we would find new carriers or not. Once seventeen carriers dropped their packs and started back, leaving us stranded with our gear....

We used one hundred fifty carriers in all during the five days [en route]. Local chiefs rounded up their men, women, and children and they all accompanied us to the next local chief, usually about two hours away....

The last morning out, we set up the transmitter and contacted Missionary Aviation Fellowship [MAF]. That same day, less than an hour after we arrived at Godare, MAF with its little plane was overhead. The pilots [dropped] warm blankets, dry clothes, food, and other supplies....

They made two trips that afternoon, and as they sped away, we were again alone, gathering up the dropped bundles with the help of friendly Mesengos who must have wondered what all this might mean....

The rain forest hadn't become so dense for nothing. Even as the plane flew away, huge black clouds had already rolled in, and in a matter of minutes we were engulfed in another tropical storm. That night, as darkness fell, we made our way, soaked, hungry, and weary, to the proposed site which was to become our home. Three bedrolls on the wet ground [three-year-old Paul also made this trek], with a single mosquito net stretched crossways over our heads, was our home for the night. Morning was never more welcome!

Early the next morning, Mesengos began gathering, and a small shack was built before nightfall in a newly cut clearing among the vines and brush....

We recall with a bit of pride, I fear, those first days when for six weeks tree stumps were our chairs; tables and shelves were fashioned from sticks laced together with vines; Lavina baked bread in tin cups; and all meals were cooked over an open fire with pans perched precariously on three stones.[8]

Part of the reason for our delay in proceeding to the Omo had to do with Hoekstras' need for a vehicle. Their Land Rover could be flown on an Ethiopian Airlines DC3 as far as Teppi, the airstrip nearest to the Godare. However, it would take a team of missionaries and Africans to get the Land Rover from Teppi to its destination.

Bob, Ralph Borgeson, and two Christian Ghimeeras headed the expedition. Brush would have to be cut, streams forded, and the vehicle winched up and down steep inclines. This was accomplished in a month's time, taking good chunks out of January and February.

The men returned to Mizan Tafari on February 11, thin, bearded, and weary, but grateful for the experience, for the opportunity to become bushwhackers for fellow missionaries, and for God's mercies along the way.

Now our focus turned again toward the southwesternmost corner of Ethiopia: the land of the Gelebs along the lower Omo River.

On the DC3 that brought Bob and the others back to Mizan were old friends from Michigan, Frank and Gladys Kieft, who had come out for the specific purpose of assisting in the opening of the Godare and Omo mission posts. Since the clearing of the Godare airstrip had not been completed yet, and the overland route in from Teppi would be too hazardous, it was decided that the Kiefts should trek south with us first.

To beat the rains, Frank and Bob made a preliminary trip with the Scout along the treacherous mountain byways to the mission at Maji. They left the vehicle there and flew back to Mizan with MAF to finish preparations for the long haul to the Omo. All essentials would have to accompany us, including camping gear, clothing, food, water, and gas.

---

[8] Harvey Hoekstra, "Hoekstras Journey to Begin Godare River Post," *Ethio-Echo*, Vol. 4, No. 4, Summer 1965: 4, 5. Joint Archives of Holland, Hope College.

On March 13, 1965, the Swarts, Pollocks, and Kiefts flew on a DC3 to Washa Wuha, the Ethiopian Airlines strip south of Maji. There we met Harold and Polly Kurtz and two others who would make up our traveling party. They had come down the mountain in three vehicles: the Scout, the Maji Jeep truck, and the Kurtzes' Jeep.

> We were quite a caravan as we started out from Washa Wuha. Two of the vehicles were pulling trailers besides their own loads. Frank and Emil, a professor at the university who asked to come along to study the bird population in the area, were perched on top of the truck, holding an umbrella for protection from the sun.
>
> The mountains were now behind us, as well as their coolness. The rest of the way was over vast, hot, grassy plains, extremely rough, but at least flat.
>
> We spent four idyllic days at German Wuha [*wuha* in Amharic means water] while some of the men reconnoitered a way through an area of thorn forest ahead. German Wuha, with its spreading trees and clear water—we were loath to leave this oasis and start out through the dusty, arid country before us....
>
> Because of the reconnoitering efforts, and with the help of a guide the last few miles, we made it through the forest without having to cut a road through.
>
> We reported in at the police post at Bumei at three o'clock the afternoon of March 19. The country now had become almost desert with outcroppings of rock which we have discovered since are rich beds of petrified bones and fossils.
>
> Dusk found us at the police post at Kalam, and a few miles from there, we set up camp on the Omo River. It was a beautiful moonlight night, and the moonlit view of that river after the miles of arid wasteland was almost intoxicating. And the fact that we had at last reached our destination was real cause for rejoicing and thanksgiving to the Lord.[9]

Not only was March 19 arrival-at-the-Omo day, it was also Harold Kurtz's birthday. Polly had brought along a cake she baked at Maji. She iced it by

[9] Morrell Swart, "New Post Opens on Omo River," *Ethio-Echo*, Vol. 4, No. 3, Spring 1965: 1, 2. Joint Archives of Holland, Hope College.

moonlight and stuck an oversized candle in the middle of it. We sang the birthday song to a happily surprised Harold, and proceeded to demolish the lovely, sweet confection. Ordinary events become gala occasions out in the bush.

Much was accomplished during the few days our friends could be with us:

A stone foundation for the floor of our tent was laid. The floor was built and the tent pitched on it, with an extra canvas above it for more protection and coolness. A stick framework for a kitchen-dining room next to the tent was erected. An ingenious stone fireplace was made outside for cooking.

A plot of ground was dug for a garden. An airstrip for the MAF plane was cleared of debris, dragged with an old truck frame, and marked with piles of bleached bones which littered the area. Load after load of driftwood was hauled in for firewood, and our first load of freight aboard a chartered DC3 was off-loaded at Kalam and brought to the site.[10]

All too soon, our friends had to leave us to return to their respective mission posts and responsibilities. Ted Pollock would continue to be of tremendous assistance in planning and prefabricating buildings for the several new mission posts that were opening simultaneously. The Kurtzes would be a continuing source of great encouragement to us, particularly after Harold became general secretary of the mission. And the Kiefts now were able to fly with MAF to the Godare to give several weeks of practical support to the Hoekstras.

Frank and Gladys Kieft were among the first of several waves of volunteers who came out to share their strength, talents, and time in valuable, selfless service wherever they were needed.

Frank was a businessman from Michigan and an RCA member. He was a mentor for both Bob Swart and Harvey Hoekstra when they were in seminary. When asked why he came out to Ethiopia, he answered:

I've been behind a desk all my life. But when I talked last September with Dennis, Hoekstras' oldest son…I knew I would love to come and work in these pioneer efforts. I didn't know if I

[10] Ibid.

had the physical strength for the job. And yet, in the four months here, I repaired cars, cleared an airstrip, built a pier in the river, assisted in other buildings, and helped in all the initial work of establishing the Omo River Post. It was a great experience, and my wife and I have enjoyed these weeks of work and fellowship with the Swarts and the Hoekstras.[11]

So began what was known as the IK Project: new posts being opened in Illubabor and Kaffa Provinces. Rather than IK representing merely the names of the provinces, we linked these letters to Christ's invitation to those at his right hand—"Inherit the Kingdom prepared for you"[12]—which was, in our hearts, the watchword for this undertaking. By 1967 four of the seven proposed outreach areas were staffed and in operation: two by Presbyterians, two by RCA personnel.

Each thrust into a new region actually was an invasion—a peaceful one physically, but in the spiritual domain, it was an act of aggression. Conflict between two kingdoms had begun.

The "prince of this world" long had held sway in these pagan strongholds, enthroned complacently in every captive heart. But the name of God's Son was now heard in the realm, and the battle for sovereignty was on. The complacency was gone; the foe must stir himself and make sure that eyes remained blinded, hearts hardened, consciences blunted, fear rampant, truth hidden.

Because he already knew that defeat would be his ultimate end, the enemy contended all the more desperately against that day when his former slaves would stand at the right hand of the King of Kings and hear him say, "Come, O blessed of my Father, inherit the kingdom prepared for you."[13]

According to the promise, there shall be those from every tribe and tongue and nation standing in that great throng.[14]

---

[11] Ibid. 13.
[12] Matthew 25:34, Revised Standard Version.
[13] Ibid.
[14] Morrell Swart, "The IK Project." Reprinted from the *Church Herald*, June 30, 1967: 16.

XI
Early Years—
With MAF's Help

We had lived on the banks of the Omo River only a few months when a letter came from our missionary friend, Tena Holkeboer. It was a letter I so much wanted to answer. But how could it be done? Just a week before, the Lord had called Tena to her heavenly home.

It seemed appropriate then to make our answer an open letter to the Reformed Church via the *Church Herald*. These excerpts from both letters are descriptive of those early days among the Gelebs:

Dear Bob and Morrie,

Your September letter just arrived, and, believe it or not, I'm sitting right down to answer it. I think of you so often, and realize better than most what you have gone through in trying to settle in a pioneer field once more. Even so, I sense that there is much that I cannot imagine, for our work in China and the Philippines has been in such a different setting....

Yes, it is no doubt very different, Tena.

All our surroundings here force our minds backward. Outside of our little compound, which is on land given us by the chief, there is not one symbol of the twentieth century in evidence, nor any of the preceding twenty centuries. The outcroppings of rock in this

Omo River valley are rich in petrified bones and fossils, luring many a scientist bent on new discoveries. The termite hills, some rising ten and twelve feet like chimneys, have a grotesque, prehistoric look. Even the wind blows an ancient breath as it sweeps across these vast plains from Lake Rudolf. Certainly the Geleb way of life is the same as it was thousands of years ago, with clothing of animal skins; crude little huts made of sticks, mats, and skins; gourd utensils, and dung fires.

...My heart goes out to you and your family, and I thank the Lord for the grace and courage he is giving you.

Truly his grace has been sufficient through all these early months, renewed each morning, replenished every hour.

We have lived among the Geleb people for eight months. It has been a period of intense curiosity on their part, and for us, one of orientation which has been, and continues to be, a many-faceted experience.

Our fifteen years in have stood us in good stead....But the tribal personality of the Anuak and the Murle did not prepare us for that of the Geleb, which is raucous and demanding, albeit friendly and good-natured. Their unabashed curiosity has been a tremendous strain on our peace and patience.

Living in tents reduces privacy to a minimum, in spite of catalog advertisements to the contrary, and we have found ourselves moving in the ever-present spotlight of Geleb gazes. It has turned our thoughts often to our Lord who saw the multitudes who crowded in upon him, and for whom he had compassion, for they were as sheep without a shepherd. So it is with these people. But their friendliness has been real cause for encouragement and thanksgiving.

This life in the open has not been without its advantages: we revel daily in the glorious splendor of sunrise and sunset, and nightly our souls are lifted as we consider the brilliant heavens with the constant planets and constellations in their gyrating orbits. This manner of living has given a new dimension to our worship of the great Creator. Each new glory, made more glorious in contrast to the drabness of Geleb life...encourages our spirits to soar again when they are too often prone to wander on more unworthy planes, in the company of these as yet unredeemed.

For what is there in Geleb society to uplift and inspire them? Walk with me to a Geleb village across the airstrip back of our compound. The cluster of huts squat in the barrenness of the desert, not a morsel of shade anywhere except inside the mean dwellings or under the small platforms on stilts on which grain is stored.

In more than one hut, a sick person huddles, made more miserable, but not realizing it, by the flies and filth in which he lives. The ground 'round about is littered with the bones, bleached white by the sun, from many a feast.

During the day, the village is inhabited mostly by women, young girls, and small children. It is only toward evening that the young boys return with the herds of cows, sheep, and goats, having walked many miles for pasture. And the men wander in after a day of

Geleb house and grainstore

talking and sleeping in the shifting shade of some bush or tree near the river.

Life is empty and purposeless for these people. Their horizons extend only as far as their cattle range for forage. Their experiences are confined to the most elemental—and yet they too were made in God's image; in them also is that divine spark; and for them also Christ died. Geleb country was included in that directive which commanded that the gospel be preached to "all the world."

I read a circular letter from the Hoekstras recently, and through it, discovered that you are not on the same station, but a couple of hundred miles apart. Is that correct? Are you entirely on your own? Or do you have fellow workers from the United Presbyterian mission?

Others have wondered about these things, too. The Hoekstras are working among the Mesengo people who live in densely forested, mountainous country about two hundred miles north of us. Their setting is in marked contrast to ours. We are both part of a new thrust of the American Mission in the Illubabor and Kaffa Provinces. One family is to enter each of seven tribes to establish a post for the eventual evangelization of the tribe.

Schools and clinics are also vital parts of this outreach. These are to be conducted by trained Ethiopian teachers and dressers. The work is new, and the challenge is tremendous....

Are you in tribes that have different languages? Or are they all Gelebs so that you both don't have to work at reducing a language to writing? We shall certainly try to be faithful in prayer for you.

Unfortunately the tribal languages of all these posts are entirely different; each language will have to be reduced to writing separately. And it will have to be done in the Amharic script, which isn't nearly as complicated as Chinese, I'm sure. But it will take some doing!

To our unaccustomed ears, the Geleb language is still a confusing jumble of glottal stops and implosive consonants, although we are hearing more frequently some familiar words in the midst of meaningless sounds.

Our first attempts at language study were made with the help of a Geleb boy who knows some Amharic....This was helpful for elementary study, but we soon bogged down through lack of knowledge on both sides.

So we were overjoyed when Hailu, a Geleb young man who knows some English, appeared this summer. He was with us only a few weeks, since he had to return to high school in Addis Ababa. But during that time, he gave us many lessons and left us with much material on reels of tape to which we can listen over and over again to sharpen our ears and increase our understanding. Now we are going through this material with two other informants.

Hailu was also able to tape several Bible stories for us, which are not only useful for our listening, but are also proving to be a means of introducing the fundamental truths of Christianity to the people in the villages.

The response is varied: some are eager, some are fearful, some are disturbed, while some others are indifferent and would rather that the little box that speaks in their language would tell them if the

Hailu with Geleb tribesmen in ceremonial dress

river is going to rise, or if it is going to rain. There is not a race of men anywhere among whom the parable of the soils cannot be applied.

But there is never a lack for an audience; whether in the villages, or along the river in their gardens, people will gather to hear. Yet how much more satisfactory it will be when we are able to speak to them ourselves concerning this life-or-death matter!

...I am glad the children could be with you for the summer months. Was it necessary for them to fly in order to get home?

Yes, when the children come home, they must fly.

When we made the initial trip to the Omo River, we traveled overland. It took many days over incredibly nightmarish mountain roads. And then, once below the escarpment, it took a few more days to cross the trackless, bumpy prairie and to find our way through an all but impenetrable thorn forest. After that, we linked up with a road that made the last forty miles seem like highway travel.

So, since overland travel in this part of the country is so difficult and time-consuming, air travel is the most feasible means of transportation. The Missionary Aviation Fellowship planes serve all these outposts. They bring our children home from school and take them out again. They bring in needed supplies, and, along with our radio-telephone, are virtually our only link with the outside....MAF has come in countless times, and no matter what the occasion, it is always a time of excitement....

...I think you knew that I went back to Southeast Asia this year for a visit, didn't you? It is five years now since I retired, and I was eager to see my friends and former pupils once more before I became too old to make such far journeys. Among the alumnae there are some who are not yet Christian, and I had a great longing to challenge them once more for Jesus Christ. I left home May 4 and returned September 21. I was very weary, but none the worse for wear, I hope.

My thoughts are often with you. God continue to make you an instrument for the bringing in of his kingdom.

> *Ever lovingly,*
> *Tena*

When we received this letter on November 12, we did not know that Dr. Tena Holkeboer, one of RCA's most intrepid missionaries, had taken an even farther journey just the week before. When the news reached us a few days later, the letter, as we read it again, seemed like a message from the very gates of heaven itself.

God grant that ours, like Tena's, may always be a life of obedience to the Lord, ever ready to go in response to his commands, with an unquenchable longing "to challenge them once more for Jesus Christ."[1]

While we had taken a circuitous route, both in time and in travel, to get from Pibor to the Omo River, we actually hadn't come all that far—about two hundred miles separate the Murle from the Geleb.

We had come, however, to a very different world. Gone were the *heglig* and tamarind trees that shaded our grassy, undulating compound on a bend of the Pibor River—the narrow, meandering waterway that the riverboat captains declared was not worthy to be called a river. Gone were the neighboring woods, alive with the cheery notes of the *chilikook*, the strident shrieks of the hammerhead stork—and at night, the rasping grunt of a leopard passing by. No more would we see great fishing parties waist deep in the murky river water: women with their basket cages, men with their spears, moving toward each other, trapping multitudes of fish between them.

That was another time, another era. Now the desert challenged us to love it and its people as much.

---

[1]Morrell Swart, "A Letter to Pioneers." Reprinted from the *Church Herald*, January 21, 1966: 16.

In a 1980 issue of Kenya's newspaper, the *Sunday Nation*, the Geleb tribe was featured as part of a series of articles written by Gavin Bennet following his Round Lake Turkana (formerly Lake Rudolf) Expedition. Bennet describes the Geleb as:

> ...part-desert, part swampy-delta people, warlike by repute, but often indolent by nature.
>
> There are between 15,000 and 30,000 of them depending where you draw the tribal lines and whether you count those who have drifted south into Kenya around Todenyang on the west of Lake Turkana and around Ileret on the east.
>
> To an outsider, their mixed economy seems a balance between cultivation and pastoralism—they neither cultivate enough nor keep enough cattle to survive on one system alone.
>
> The people themselves are adamant that they are pastoralists...who also cultivate. They look down on fishing, and the only food they admit taking from the river is hippo, which they occasionally hunt with spears.
>
> Their society is male-oriented. Only men may own stock. They pass on a few head to their sons, and their progeny become a separate herd.
>
> Women have no right to stock or any other material objects, so are totally dependent on men throughout their lives. Each woman passes from the domination of her father to the domination of a husband.
>
> [However], watching the [Geleb], the women certainly don't behave in a markedly subordinate way. That may be because their husbands have one single favorite pastime—sitting down.[2]

When a person first arrives in Geleb country, he is impressed by the heat, the drabness and desolation of the land, and the extreme primitiveness of the tribe. And one is apt to ask himself, "Why haven't they done something to better their lot during all the centuries of their existence?"

[2] Gavin Bennet, "Tribe That Lost a Name," *Sunday Nation* (Kenya), March 30, 1980:
13. Joint Archives of Holland, Hope College.

But after living among them for a while and observing the pattern or rhythm of their nomadic life in this desert land, one can't help but feel a kind of admiration for the Gelebs for having discovered—not the abundant life, by any means—but certainly a way of life that supports the tribe and all its herds.

The Gelebs have an amazing number of cattle, and they are comparatively well off agriculturally. With the wide and deep Omo River flowing through the center of their territory and flooding every year from the torrential rains in the mountains to the north, acres and acres of grain sorghum (*durra*, or milo) are planted and harvested along its banks as the water recedes. The Gelebs even help supply neighboring tribes where conditions are more difficult, bartering their grain for such necessities as clay pots, hard wood for making walking sticks, or maybe more sheep and goats.

Their low, round houses, framed with sticks and covered with goatskins, can easily be opened up to dry when it does rain; or taken apart, loaded on a donkey's back, and transported to a new village site.

How often, when our tent was buffeted unmercifully by a storm, or the protecting tarpaulin was torn from its frame, we have said, "Hats off to the Gelebs! Their architecture is much more sensible than ours!"

So they have withstood, and emerged an apparently content, cheerful people as a whole, intent only on increasing their herds, their wives, and their children; triumphant over a very hard environment.

Triumphant? Let's look again!

A baby burned because the fire was on the ground.

A woman wasting away from dysentery because of unsanitary tribal habits.

A man dying (literally) from fear because he believes he has been cursed.

Mothers afraid to uncover their babies for fear of the evil eye.

There is no triumph here. For while they have managed to eke out an existence, they have at the same time been helpless, unknowing captives of the "prince of this world" who would keep them bound in the darkness of ignorance and filth and sin. And there can be no change while that ruler holds sway.

But the name of Christ is being heard in the land, and the spiritual battle for dominion over Geleb hearts has begun. "We are powerless against this great multitude....But our eyes are upon thee." And the Lord replied, "Fear not, and be not dismayed at this great multitude, for the battle is not yours, but God's."[3, 4]

From the screened veranda of our tent, we could look out over the Omo, the largest river of western Ethiopia. Our site was located just a few miles north of the delta that feeds Omo's water into Lake Turkana, one of the lakes of the Great Rift. Because of its proximity to the delta here, the river was sizable even during the dry season. Except for a green strip on either side of the river where a few wild fig and *mye'de* trees grew, along with a hardy bush, locally called *aalany*, the flat desert stretched out as far as the eye could see. The heat was merciless. Goathead burrs abounded. The wind blew incessantly, stirring up great clouds of dust that whirled dervishlike across the landscape.

But we had only to lift our eyes to be reassured that all the world had not become a sandy plain. To the south, the horizon was broken by a mountain ridge over the border in Kenya; to the west, a range in Sudan provided dramatic staging for magnificent sunsets. And the rounded Kibbish Hills to the northwest reminded us daily that our friends at the Swedish mission were only fifty miles away.

> Dusty desert, blistering sand,
> Thorny brush in a barren land;
> Withering wind on some wild spree,
> Dust devils dancing in maddened glee.
>
> Whooping hyenas, bleating goats,
> Braying donkeys—such raucous notes!
> Nothing to give a lilt to the day?
> No song sung in sweeter lay?

[3] 2 Chronicles 20: 12, 20, Revised Standard Version
[4] Morrell W. Swart, from the page of an unknown magazine (possibly the *Missionary Monthly*) n.d. Joint Archives of Holland, Hope College.

Hark!—the lark, the crested lark
Out on the desert sand;
And the warbler trills as glory fills
Dawn skies over Omo land.

Watch color change on the mountain range,
The fossil ridge, beige then blue;
And the Kibbish Hills in their scalloped frills
Stand serene in royal hue.

Following rain, earth blooms again—
The desert, a carpet of gold;
And the fragrance is sweet in the tropic heat
As the flowers in sunlight unfold.

And oh, the nights! the luminous lights
Of myriad orbiting spheres;
And the river flows by as the moon rides high—
A river of silver tears.

Amid the starkness, in the darkness,
Bounteous beauties bide;
So, by God's grace, in a Geleb face,
May Christ's beauty one day shine.

—MFS

Camping on the Omo became a way of life rather than a brief vacation away from it all. Because of the mission builder's hectic schedule and our own desire for staff housing and a clinic as soon as possible, the building of proper living quarters for ourselves was put on hold for three years.

But our tent was comfortable; our kitchen-dining shack was adequate; and we could sit outside in the evening and marvel at the brilliance and proximity of the African star-studded sky.

This lifestyle afforded the Gelebs daily entertainment. We had an audience from sunup until sundown, observing and commenting on our strange ways. Nothing like these *ferenjis* (Amharic for foreigners) had ever lived among them before.

We observed them, too.

Girls and women, like the Murle, wore skirts made of goatskins, and many beads and bracelets. Men wore muslin cloth, sometimes even blankets, wrapped around their loins and tucked in at the waist. But hairdos were their most distinctive feature.

Here and there in clayey outcrops on the desert floor were deposits of reddish earth which, when moistened, became pliable. The Geleb men worked this into their hair, creating a smooth plate above the forehead, with a topknot just behind into which was gathered all the hair above the nape. Upon the surface was affixed a small, hard lump of clay into which a few holes had been worked. Then on the occasion of a tribal dance or some other festive event, ostrich feathers often were placed decoratively into the holes where they would remain secure, regardless of the frenzied exercise of mock battles and great leaps into the air. The only instruments for such affairs were the iron ankle rings worn by young girls of marriageable age, which jangled as they jumped up and down in rhythm, or small bells tied by leather thongs to the arms of the young men.

We lived among a colorful people.

After a year had gone by, we began to feel more like friends and neighbors to the Gelebs rather than mere uninvited guests. That was a happy, satisfying change, for truly we had felt like intruders in their land. The chief had indeed given us this small area on which to make our home. But Geleb cows had always grazed down by the river where we planned to have our garden. What about that man's tobacco field? Where would he plant next year? And Geleb men had always slept under that large *mye'de* tree in the heat of the day. Now it was in our front yard.

We had also found ourselves to be under suspicion as the disturbers of the seasons. According to the Gelebs, the Omo River ALWAYS rose in September, flooding its banks to leave a rich layer of silt on their planting areas. When it would begin to recede, they'd start planting their sorghum.

Bob and the Geleb chief, Namuruputh Kalam,
who had given land for the mission

In 1965 the river did not rise at the appointed time. Since we
were the new factor in life on the Omo, we were the logical cause,
and we were blamed relentlessly—until, on October 12, the river
finally fulfilled its annual duty. Then the accusations stopped.

There were probably other dark conjectures about us of which
we were unaware. But by this time, we were quite sure that the
Gelebs who knew us realized that our purpose in coming was to

help them, not to harm them. Nowhere was this more obvious than in our simple medical program.

Under the supervision of visiting medical personnel and in consultations by radio, Bob was able to care for many hurting people. It started during our very first days when they carried in a youngster whose upper thigh was laid wide open from a stick wound. Others came with infected eyes. Since we had with us the essentials for treating such ailments, how could we turn them away? So Bob spent every morning in the shade of the clinic tree ministering in the name of the Great Physician.

One day a man was brought in who had been snatched from the jaws of a crocodile. He had been swimming with his cattle, as they crossed the river, when the reptile attacked him. A fellow swimmer was able to beat him off, and then brought the victim by dugout canoe to the mission. His abdomen and lungs had been punctured. Bob treated the patient with lots of prayer and sulfa powder.

When Dr. Roy Marion flew in with MAF some days later, he examined the man and pronounced his wounds clean and healing well. We all praised God for his power and his mercy. And we began praying more earnestly than ever for someone to come to take over the medical work. Medical student Jim Ceton (who came with his friend Don Sill) was with us for two summers: and nurse Vivien Demarest helped out for several months. (Both were Hope College graduates.) How grateful we were! But where was the person who was both well qualified and also willing to serve for an extended period in this remote area? Surely God was preparing someone to join us. As it was, we had to wait three years for the person of God's choice to come.[5]

We found that no matter how remote our location, we became a focal point on many a traveler's itinerary, especially at Omo River Post.

5 *Ethio-Echo*, Vol. 5, No. 4, Summer 1966: 4. Joint Archives of Holland, Hope College.

An anthropologist from the Hebrew University of Jerusalem came for an in-depth study of, as he described them, one of the last tribes in the world still unspoiled by civilization.

Four Austrians, on a safari around Africa to advertise the wonders of their powerful Czechoslovakian truck, were on the last segment of their journey when they met their waterloo at the Omo River; the little government ferry was unequal to the task of floating the truck to the other side of the river. It began to list and no amount of frantic bailing could save the situation; the huge truck slid off into the river where, together with the hapless ferry, it rests in its muddy bed to this day.

In July 1970, we were honored to have the United States ambassador to Ethiopia, William O. Hall, and his son, Robert, pay us a brief visit.

Another William was our guest in early 1971: the late Prince William of Gloucester, Kensington Palace, London, came to move a boat that had been "docked" at the mission for some time. He thrilled Jack and Dick, who were at home for the Christmas holiday, by taking them out for a ride with the royal flag flying.

Neal Sobania visited us more than once, first as a member of the Peace Corps in Ethiopia and then when he was researching the tribes around Lake Turkana—both on the Omo and later in northern Kenya. Dr. Sobania went on to become a professor at Hope College.

There were tourists and adventurers from every continent. And fellow missionaries and mission board secretaries. And scientists.

One day in September 1966, an unexpected, unknown plane landed on our airstrip. Bob went out to investigate. As he and the visitors walked back to our compound, I could see that one of the men had a shock of white hair. Even at a distance, and even though we had never met, there was something strangely familiar about him.

It was Emperor Haile Selassie, who on a visit to Nairobi, Kenya, that year had met with Dr. Louis S. B. Leakey of Olduvai Gorge fame.

He asked this well-known paleontologist to organize an expedition in Ethiopia to see if he could make some exciting discoveries in his ancient country. Dr. Leakey's arrival at Omo River Post was the first step in fulfilling the emperor's request.

With Dr. Leakey were his son, Richard, and his daughter-in-law, Margaret. They were expecting a delegation from the Ministry of the Interior to meet with them at the mission that very day.

The delegation, however, did not arrive until the following morning. Around the dining table in our humble mat-and-sacking shack, the Leakeys and the Ethiopian officials, speaking in French, hammered out the terms for what was to be known as the Omo Research Expedition. The location of the proposed dig would be the fossil beds about forty miles north of the mission—a windblown, weather-worn, eroded moonscape that fairly beckoned to archaeologists and paleontologists with the promise of rich finds.

Full-scale operations began the next year. Richard Leakey headed up the group from Kenya. There were also an American team from the University of Chicago and a French team from Paris.

Though we had viewed this invasion at first with some apprehension and dismay, these scientists carried on their meticulous work only during the summer months. Their comings and goings became such a part of the rhythm of life on the Omo, and the work they did was so fascinating, that we found ourselves caught up in the excitement of search and discovery. We looked forward to their annual expeditions and frequent stops at the mission.

Limes from the laden lime tree in our citrus orchard provided gallons of limeade for all these visitors. (An attaché from the American embassy dubbed our limeade "Missionary Melotti"—Melotti being a brand of beer manufactured in Ethiopia.) And we were thankful that we could send many work-worn, travel-worn sojourners on their way refreshed in body and, we trust, in spirit.

The year was 1968. Essential building needs had been completed at the new mission posts. And now a house for the Swarts moved up to top priority. We were excited. I remember marking the outline of the house plan in the sand and then walking from room to room, through imaginary doorways, reveling in the about-to-be-realized dream of having a home with solid walls and a roof that wouldn't flap and snap in the wind and concrete floors that could be swept clean.

At about this time, volunteerism was becoming a more viable means of short-term service, and many of us were the beneficiaries of such assistance. Frank and Gladys Kieft had led the way. Scores of others were to follow.

One summer we were glad to have Ron Verwys, who became an RCA pastor, and Philip Roode with us as volunteers. Philip, the son of our Pibor colleagues, Al and Ruth Roode, became a physician like his dad. Others came to build a house for us.

After three years of living in tents, Bob and Morrie Swart of the Omo River Post will soon have a home! Reformed Church in America volunteers Harold Stauble, Frank Timmerman, and Bill Corstange of Kalamazoo, Michigan, and Carlton and Warren Brouwer of Holland, Michigan, were able to see a house for the Swarts rise from a concrete slab in a house-building bee of five weeks, reminiscent of pioneer days in the USA.

Needless to say, a tremendous amount of preparation on Bob's part went on for months before their arrival [laying the cement slab, having bricks made and dried, etc.], and on Ted Pollock's part, of designing and prefabricating the geodesic dome roofs in his workshop at Mizan Tafari, all of which was transported in MAF planes!

The five men first heard of the Swarts' need through the two earlier contingents of RCA volunteers from Michigan who had given a tremendous boost to the building of Godare and Chebera posts. They reported that the families assigned to the posts were having to take time out from language study, visiting among the people, teaching, preaching, counseling, and binding up wounds to carry on building operations.

So each of the five men began to realize that there was a need which he could fill in some special way. For Carl and Warren, mason brothers from Holland, the clinching factor was a slide picture shown during a talk by Swarts' oldest daughter, Valerie, in which piles of pressed earth bricks appeared, just waiting for skilled hands to lay them up into walls. Like the other three, they just couldn't resist the "call."

Much correspondence ensued between the men and RCA's Board of Foreign Missions, the American Mission in Ethiopia, and the Swarts before the volunteers were really on the plane. At considerable personal sacrifice, they had planned to pay the entire cost of the trip out of their own pockets. But their home churches

were so thrilled with the venture, that special offerings and gifts
provided about half the cost of each ticket.

They came to work, and work they did, each one wearing a tool
apron sporting this ad: Own Your Own Omo Dome Home! There
was no overtime pay for the hours after 5 p.m., nor for Saturdays
and holidays—there was no pay at all, save for the satisfaction of
building a mission home in a faraway place.

Not a single job needed to be done which one of the men hadn't
had experience in doing previously. Their only regret was the fact
that a truckers' strike held up the flow of materials and prevented
their bringing the house to full completion. But they did use up all
the building supplies on hand, and the house was very nearly ready
for residence when they had to leave.

Although the men were all Christians of long standing, they went
back to their homes and churches stirred anew to the possibilities
of Christian service everywhere. They were impressed with the
enormity of the task which remained, and were looking forward to
telling their story and advising others to "go and do likewise" for the
experience of a lifetime.[6]

The work that the volunteers accomplished under Ted Pollock's direction
was amazing—and so was the fun and fellowship. When we remember Bill
Corstange, one particular incident always comes to mind. We had been
telling the men how good crocodile meat was; it tasted like fish but was
somewhat firmer. Bill, who was not adventurous where food was concerned,
made the remark, "Well, if you ever serve crocodile meat, don't tell me!"

The men went fishing one afternoon and brought back enough fish for a
fine meal. I thawed strips from small croc tails, cut them up, and Dolly
Pollock and I fried them along with the fish. At suppertime, the platter, piled
high with golden fish and croc fillets, went round and round. How those men
ate! When the meal was over, I casually asked, "Did you all enjoy your
supper?"

"Sure did," they replied with enthusiasm.

"Do you know what you were eating?"

"Fish!"

6 Unknown author, extensive quotes from "Housing Bee on the Omo," *Ethio-Echo*,
Vol. 7, No. 1, 1968: 6. Joint Archives of Holland, Hope College.

"Yes, fish. But there were also pieces of crocodile tail on that platter." Bill looked incredulous.

"And I had three helpings!" was all he could say.

Before we went home that summer for our last yearlong furlough, the Omo dome home was closed in. It was now ready for occupancy. We were glad to move our things from the shack and the tent to the more protective walls of our new house.

A man and his wife were hired to live on the premises in our absence. Akol had come to us with fine recommendations. He was half Geleb, half Turkana (a large tribe in northwestern Kenya). His wife, Nakademo, a full Turkana, was shy and pretty. We sensed that all would be well in their care.

We were eager to be on our way to the United States. Just how eager was reflected in a letter I wrote to our mothers in December 1967:

> It's so terribly hard to be away from the children. I'm afraid I feel very rebellious sometimes. As a matter of fact much of this whole term my heart has been very much divided, and I've wondered many times if it's worth it. As a missionary, I've been a flop. As Bob's wife, I've wanted nothing more than to be by his side. As a mother, if that were my only role, I'd have flown the coop long ago to be with the children. Well, next summer is coming.

Three of our daughters were in the homeland now. Gayle had married Wally Borschel and our first grandchild, Dawn Marie, was just a few months old. So, after attending Chloe's graduation from Good Shepherd School, we with our three younger children were soon airborne. (The Six Day War in June 1967 made it necessary to close the American School in Alexandria, Egypt. Chloe and several of her classmates had transferred to the school in Addis Ababa.)

During this furlough, we acquired two more sons-in-law when Valerie married Newt Powell and Merry married Don Hill. Bob tied both knots, assisted by our good friend, the Rev. Gordon Van Oostenburg. Don's grandfather, the Rev. Michael Veenschoten, a retired missionary to China, also had a role in the Hill ceremony.

Suddenly, half of our children had homes of their own.

Meanwhile, up in the forested home of the Mesengos, the Hoekstras were making good progress. Because an airstrip had been cleared among the huge primeval trees, they no longer had to rely on airdrops for their food supplies; MAF could now land in the clearing.

And thanks to volunteer help—particularly Larry and Betty Zudwig from Kalamazoo, who spent two years at Godare—Harvey, Lavina, and five-year-old Paul had been able to move from their grass and stick shelter into their partially completed dwelling. Houses for their Ethiopian medical dresser and teacher, as well as the clinic building, were nearly finished. And the school structure was well underway.

Raising up water from the Godare River up to the mission was another story:

> The river is seven hundred yards from the compound at its closest point; and it lies two hundred fifty feet below the level of our grounds. By digging a six-foot canal for two hundred yards, we have been able to join two loops of the river together and thereby create a head of seven feet of water. This is enough to operate a hydram which is now putting out a stream of water twenty-four hours a day at no cost beyond that of the installation.
>
> After struggling with barrels and a trailer for nearly two years, you can imagine the rejoicing when that first stream of water came from the end of the long black tubing on a Saturday night at five minutes before midnight. What a dream come true to have water at the top of the hill, and what time and cost it is saving!...
>
> ...But, thanks be to God, there is more to report than just clearing and building. In all of these activities, God is at work. The word spreads that interesting and unusual things are happening where the foreigners live. Daily, scores of people come to watch with amazement as sharp saws fashion logs into boards, and a gray, fine "sand" in bags, mixed with sand and water, becomes so hard that one can't break it with a stone. Frequently the work stops, and for a brief moment the missionary sits in the circle with his new friends and tells them of Jesus.
>
> On Christmas Sunday, more than one hundred Mesengos gathered on the beautiful clearing at the edge of the forest. Two years previous to this, none of them had ever heard the name of

Jesus. But that day, they heard the sweetest story ever told, as they have heard it many times in the intervening months. In addition to casual, spur-of-themoment gatherings, regular worship services are held twice daily on the compound. One of these services is coupled with lessons in spoken Amharic and reading. So far, only a few are interested, but one day, God's miracle will occur....

These first months, hammers and saws and tools seem to have first place. But already, the love of God is being felt by many. The sick and needy receive loving care by an Ethiopian Christian medical dresser. A few weeks ago, the first patient was flown out on an MAF plane for hospitalization.

It was an occasion of great praise and rejoicing when, two weeks later, the young boy returned, healed and well. Some fifty Mesengos and missionaries gathered around the plane and lifted a prayer of thanks and praise to God.

In a few months, the school will open with a trained Amharic-speaking teacher in charge. We are just beginning! It is like "a cloud the size of a man's hand." It is like seed being sown and growing secretly.

God's gracious purpose for the people to whom he has sent us will find fulfillment. One day, in God's time, the lives of many in this forest shall become a doxology of praise to him whose name is above every name. Christian Victor![7]

As has already been noted, MAF played a strategic role in the opening of these new posts. In the interim between Don McClure's interview with the emperor when he said, "I want you to start this work as quickly as possible," and the actual arrival of the first "refugee" missionaries from Sudan, God called MAF to Ethiopia.

---

[7] Harvey Hoekstra, *Ethio-Echo*, Vol. 6, No. 3, 1967: 4, 5, 6. Joint Archives of Holland, Hope College.

God in his never-failing providence has brought the services of the widely used Missionary Aviation Fellowship to western Ethiopia at a time when the new Illubabor-Kaffa project calls for the use of small plane transport. Although the service is under the British wing of MAF, an American pilot with ten years experience in New Guinea will do the flying for the first few years.[8]

That pilot was Bob Hutchins from California. Bob started the ball rolling in Ethiopia for the invaluable support that MAF gave to missions there for many years. More pilots and more planes joined him as the work expanded. Among those who came were three fine pilots from Great Britain, and two from the RCA. One of them was Denny Hoekstra.

Denny was one of the mission children to whom MAF pilots were larger than life—heroes to be imitated and admired.

It was the airplane and its pilots that impacted my life to the point where I thought I wanted to become an MAF pilot and return to the mission field to help with transportation needs.

After college and flight training, I did become a missionary pilot with MAF and worked in Zaire, Kenya, and Ethiopia.

The story could not end without saying that this was very special to me, one of the many blessings the Lord has given to me, to be able to go back to Ethiopia and fly the missionaries I had grown up with in the southern Sudan. This little rascal of a kid was now their pilot.

It was a real thrill for me to see the missionaries now, as an adult, and realize their dedication in Christ's service. I have great respect for these of my mission family.[9]

Verne Sikkema, the other RCA pilot, loved flying. On a regular furlough in 1961, he took flying lessons. And following their expulsion from Sudan in 1962, he took further aviation training at Western Michigan University in Kalamazoo where he acquired not only a commercial pilot's license and an instructor's rating, but also his airframe and engine mechanic's license. Verne's dream was to become an MAF pilot. He and Lorraine went to

[8] *Ethio - Echo*, Vol. 1, No. 4, Spring 1961: 6. Joint Archives of Holland, Hope College.
[9] Dennis Hoekstra, "Raised in Africa," June 30, 1992. Joint Archives of Holland, Hope College.

Ethiopia in faith that this dream would be realized. But that faith was to be tried.

When the Sikkemas arrived in Addis Ababa in September 1965, MAF's roster of pilots was filled. So Verne's first assignment was as the purchaser and shipper for the American Mission. On the side, he was able to apply his flying and teaching skills at the Ethiopian Airlines Pilot Training Center when a shortage of instructors made his services invaluable.

During this period, the three oldest Sikkema children went by bus every day to Good Shepherd School. But after two years, they became boarders when their parents were given a second assignment: to work at the remote and beautiful station of Maji.

Important though the tasks of maintenance and building were to the physical health of a mission station, and in spite of the majestic grandeur of the Maji mountains and the close fellowship with the other missionaries, Verne was restless; this was not what he had returned to Africa to do. Why all those years of flight training, the hundreds of hours of flying time to his credit? Believing that his full potential was not being utilized, he again contacted MAF.

> Our days at Maji were a time of testing, and as the weeks passed with no response from MAF, we became rather discouraged.
>
> Then one morning in July 1968, Alastair MacDonald (program manager for MAF in Ethiopia) came to visit and to tell us that we had been accepted by the MAF folks in England, subject to release by the American Mission. Verne would have to be checked out by [veteran MAF pilot] Gordon Marshall in Kenya, and later would have to receive some special field orientation....
>
> MAF was glad that we knew some Amharic, and thankful that we had had some previous mission experience. It was almost unbelievable, such an answer to prayer after months of silence.
>
> So, on September 4, 1968, we were moved by MAF in a C185 to [the MAF base in] Jimma to become part of that mission family. We stayed an additional year that term to fit in with the MAF schedule of furloughs. This enabled our daughter Linda to finish her high school education in Ethiopia....We were fulfilled and happy there, and the years passed quickly.[10]

---

[10] Lorraine Sikkema, from a report written to the author, n.d. Joint Archives of Holland, Hope College.

But during that long term, both of Lorraine's parents and Verne's mother passed away. Going home in 1971 confirmed the loss; those dear ones just weren't there to greet them. Their "Welcome home!" would come on another day.

Linda was now a student at Northwestern College in Orange City, Iowa. When the Sikkemas returned to Ethiopia in 1972, all their children became boarders at Good Shepherd School. The wrench of frequent family farewells was an unrelieved aspect of the missionary experience.

Nevertheless, they were thankful to be back home in Jimma, Verne picking up again the life of an MAF pilot along with Lorraine, his "radio-active" wife.

> The log books indicate that MAF covers about 250,000 miles over Ethiopia in a year....To enable other missionaries to live in difficult-to-reach places...the planes fly over dense rain forests, across rugged mountains, along winding rivers, and over high plateaus and semi-desert areas....
>
> The wives who "stand by" [at the radio]...often have a busy day, recording faithfully the transmissions of the pilots as they report the time and place of every take-off and landing, and give, in addition, the number of passengers on board and the amount of fuel carried....They also respond to calls from various stations....The weather in an area may deteriorate, with low clouds and rain making visibility "zero." Certainly the pilot should know this....
>
> Emergency flights occasionally change a day's schedule, too....If someone urgently needs the plane that day, the scheduled flights are postponed, or altered to care for the emergency first. These calls are medical in nature....Most patients are taken to Mettu where there is a government hospital staffed by both Ethiopian and American Mission personnel....
>
> On one emergency flight of about forty minutes duration, the plane flew over a good-sized lake. For the helper who was accompanying the patient, this was a new world. He...had never seen such a large body of water before. Soon after crossing, he leaned forward, tapped the pilot on the shoulder, and asked, "Now are we in America?" He was sure he had crossed an ocean!
>
> About 75 percent of the flying done from Jimma is for the American Mission, which has airstrips at twelve of its stations and IK posts, besides four satellite strips....

Building materials make up the bulk of freight carried by the planes. Cement, lumber, roofing, as well as medicines and groceries, school books and Bibles, small cassette recorders and tapes, to say nothing of young chickens and bull calves, all find a place in MAF planes....

It is particularly satisfying to Verne to help his former colleagues in mission, or to participate in a communion service with fellow Christians of the Nuer tribe, some of whom he knew formerly in Sudan. Having had experience in a "bush" station, he is better able to empathize with others living and working in such places....

The objective of MAF is not just to assist missionaries, not just to relieve suffering in the world. But above all, it's to get the gospel of Jesus Christ to the more inaccessible areas, to assist in evangelization, and to encourage church growth....

More and more the glad Word is being spread. How encouraged we are as we hear of Ethiopian men and women, unashamed of the gospel, going out to teach their own people as well as those of neighboring tribes! Then we know that it's all worthwhile: the loading and unloading of the planes, the tired and aching backs, the hours spent in working out efficient schedules—because we realize that the "wings of mercy" which fly across Ethiopia are also bearing "good tidings of great joy which shall be to ALL people."[11]

The editor of Ethio-Echo added this note:

In these days of urgency in mission...MAF personnel and planes are among God's timely tools in the more rapid spread of the gospel. All who benefit from the [MAF] program...can testify to their singularly selfless service. The schedule of church growth would, humanly speaking, be lagging far behind today if it were not for the vision and dedication of MAF to the divine task.[12]

---

[11] Lorraine Sikkema, *Ethio-Echo*, Vol. 9, No. 4, June 1973: 6, 7. Joint Archives of Holland, Hope College.
[12] Editor, *Ethio-Echo*, Vol. 9, No. 4, June 1973: 8. Joint Archives of Holland, Hope College.

XII
An Advanced Dresser Trained at Mettu

Mettu, the capital of Illubabor Province, was in the area where the RCA, in partnership with the Presbyterian Church, was seeking to reach several tribes tucked away in hard-to-reach places in Ethiopia.

When Arlene Schuiteman returned to Africa from the United States on September 25, 1966, her destination was Mettu. Emperor Haile Selassie had requested the American Mission to staff the Mettu hospital and administer the provincial health program. Three missionary doctors and two missionary nurses were assigned to work there with the Ethiopian medical staff.

From the very outset, our goal was to establish a church and train local leaders in both the church and medical work. When we had accomplished that, we would leave.

My responsibility was to educate young Ethiopians as nurses who could work either in the hospital or in small rural clinics in remote places. My students were young men of eighth-grade level who had a grasp of English. In fact, the Ministry of Health required all health classes to be taught in English. Samuel Herumo, a newly graduated Ethiopian registered nurse, was my assistant. He had had no teaching experience, so I became his mentor.

I was very happy in my new role as teacher, nurse, and midwife. Surely my parents' decision that I should take the Normal Training

180

Teachers course in high school was all part of God's plan of preparation for this work he had called me to do now. I sensed how all of my past experience in teaching in the States and working in Sudan had led to this work. And the interim spent at the University of Iowa and the special seminar in curriculum building were all a part of his plan. This was the beginning of a most challenging and happy time for me.[1]

But there was still a question whether this would be a long-term position; there was a possibility that she and her colleague from Nasir days, Marian Farquhar, eventually would work together among the Nuers on the Ethiopian side of the border. At Christmas, both women went down to that area.

We stayed with the Jordans, formerly of Nasir and Akobo, who were already established at a place called Adura. The first night we were there, we discovered a snake in the bathroom, sheep in the garden, and someone called, "Come, there is a person who is dying in a canoe at the mouth of the river!" It was just like old times. We had come home to Nuerland and it was so good.

I would spend each morning working in the clinic. Two of the helpers were men who had worked with me at Nasir. In the afternoons, there was time for long talks with old friends who had fled from their homeland into Ethiopia. I sat on the animal skin laid out for me near the hut's door and listened.

My namesake, little NyaBigwa, was there pounding grain for her mother. She was ten years old now, and a beautiful, obedient little girl.

Pastor Moses Kuac told of his year in prison with heavy chains on his ankles, and of his release. His wife NyaTiac, so young and beautiful, told of her fear-filled experiences. Kuac paused in his story and said, "She suffered more than I—yes, she suffered more than I."

In the evening I walked amongst the cattle tied to their stakes with the dungfires burning, and it was so good to be there.[2]

1 Arlene Schuiteman, "Ethiopia Notes," n.d. Joint Archives of Holland, Hope College.
2 Ibid.

What impressed Arlene most during those two weeks in Nuer country was that, in spite of having become refugees, and having lost most of their possessions, they had not lost their faith.

> They certainly did not understand his ways, but they worshiped him....I felt it deeply, and I wondered if the fragrance which ascended to God's throne from that desolate, forlorn little spot might not be among the sweetest of all prayers of praise.
>
> This first visit with the Nuer at the border was so good. But I began to realize that the work in a remote clinic as the diagnostician was something that I did not really enjoy. It forced me into a doctor's role and I felt inadequate for that.
>
> I began to realize that one of the reasons I was so happy at Mettu now might be because my assignment there was one for which I felt better qualified and prepared. At year's end, the Executive Committee would consider whether I should return to work with the Nuer or stay on at Mettu. In any case, I was to have a year of Amharic study first, beginning in September 1967.
>
> Language learning was not as exciting and enjoyable as teaching nursing had been. It was a good course, but at times I thought I would burst if I heard another word of it....But there is a time for everything, and this was the time to discipline myself to study this language.
>
> Besides learning Amharic, we spent time absorbing the culture of this land and the customs of the people. We were able to visit historical sites. For our holiday, Wilma Kats, Marian Farquhar, and I drove to Asmara in Eritrea. Wilma was already having symptoms of a complication of amoebic dysentery and hepatitis. But on this happy holiday, we did not know that after one year, she would be leaving Africa to be under medical care in the States. I admired Wilma, and it was impossible to understand why such a talented and effective servant was afflicted with such a debilitating disease.[3]

(Following Amharic study, Wilma served briefly among the Anuaks at Pokwo until her illness forced her to return to the United States. The prognosis was poor; she was told she had only two or three years to live. But,

[3] Ibid.

thanks to God and the specialists who cared for her, she was given ten additional years, during which time she lived in Holland, Michigan, and worked as a volunteer at Portable Recording Ministries. The Lord called her home in 1980. Wilma lived valiantly in health and in infirmity. Her life truly belonged to Christ—and many belong to him today because of her faithful witness.)

Arlene was delighted and encouraged one day to receive a letter from John Kuac, who had learned to read in an adult literacy class at Nasir during the final months in Sudan. His wife had received treatment for infertility at the mission clinic. John Kuac wrote:

> Dear NyaBigwa, Peace. I am at Kadesh [Nuer refugee camp in Ethiopia]. I am very happy because you have given me a gift. My wife has given birth. The child lives. We have named her NyaBigwa. I want you to see her with your eyes. May the peace of Jesus Christ be with you. Perhaps you can come at Christmas time. Live in peace. I am John Kuac from Nasir.[4]

According to Arlene, the Holy Spirit used John to bring many of his people to faith in Christ.

In July 1968, Arlene returned to Mettu to take up her work of teaching student nursing again:

> It was hard to put the Amharic language to use since the majority of people spoke Gallinya and I was teaching the students in English. And I continued to use the Nuer language because many Nuer were now finding their way to the Mettu hospital.
>
> A pathetic example was old Deang who was hopelessly blind. He had faith that the white doctor would cause him to see again. As I interpreted for him the doctor's diagnosis that his was not an operable condition, I witnessed this old man's faith crumble. He left Mettu several weeks later, having concluded that this was not a disease which could be cured, so it must be spirit, and he would go home and sacrifice to his gods again.
>
> Many people, including missionary personnel, came seeking medical and surgical care. This meant that we were called upon to entertain many guests.

4 Ibid.

One of my house guests was Sister Mulumbet, the governor's wife. She came for the birth of their eighth child. Later Sister Mulumbet, an RN, became the nursing supervisor of our hospital when that post was nationalized.

Months would go by without our leaving Mettu, but I did not feel isolated because people came to see us, and I was so content in the task at hand.

Among the usual courses, our students also studied diagnosing and treatment, laboratory techniques, and obstetrics during their final year. I was often on OB call at night, at which time our students gained supervised experience which would prepare them for the time when they would be assigned to work in isolated areas.

At the end of 1969, Thompson Gac, a Nuer student, was called to work at the Omo River with the Swarts. Later Luel Aklilu was called to work at Godare with the Hoekstras.

Going into unfamiliar and distant parts of the country was a big adjustment for them. It was an assignment that took them into a tribe different from their own with a totally strange language. These remote clinics had radio-telephone contact with our hospital, and also with MAF, so that cases could be referred to us and the doctors could give them advice.

Seeing these young graduates go out on their assignments was a fulfilling experience for me.[5]

One of the doctors at the hospital in Mettu had predicted about Arlene: "She'll be the salvation of our program." By God's grace, she indeed was effective in training young Africans for nursing careers.

It wasn't long after our return to Ethiopia in 1969 that we welcomed Thompson Gac, his wife, Nyaluol, and their two small sons to Omo River Post. With the arrival of this well-trained nurse with an Advanced Dresser Certificate, the medical work among the Gelebs changed hands. Bob was thankful to relinquish this responsibility to a person of Thompson's caliber, especially in extreme cases.

One day a Geleb appeared at the clinic with an urgent message: a friend had been seriously wounded by a hippo. He was being transported by

5 Ibid.

dugout across the northern end of Lake Turkana to the Omo River delta. Would the *hakim* (Arabic for doctor) come for him by motorboat?

The messenger guided Thompson to the prearranged meeting place. No dugout. They waited and waited. Twilight is brief in the tropics, and that night would be moonless. It was essential to get back to the mission before sundown, so Thompson headed back, leaving the messenger at a nearby village to await the arrival of the canoe.

As the motorboat traveled upriver, people along the banks waved and shouted, but there was no time for visiting. At one place, however, they were more insistent. Pulling in to shore, Thompson found a young lad named Torbosa whose foot had been totally mangled by a crocodile.

Back at the mission, Thompson dressed his wounds. But he knew that this was not enough; if he were to live, he would have to be flown to Mettu.

The next day, the messenger came to say that the dugout had arrived at last. So Thompson made another trip down into the delta, returning immediately to the mission. There was no time to be lost. Arrangements were made with MAF on an emergency basis to fly the two badly wounded

Thompson Gac, trained by Arlene Schuiteman at Mettu,
was the hakim *at Omo River Post for six years*

patients to Mettu. Torbosa's leg was amputated at the knee, but the delay in getting help cost the hippo victim his life; he died at Mettu.

Some months later, thanks to a generous gift from friends in Iowa, Thompson and Torbosa flew to Addis Ababa where he was measured for a prosthesis. It wasn't long before an agile Torbosa was able to stump around on his fiberglass leg, even taking part in soccer games. He attended our small school and was one of the more promising students.

It had not taken Thompson Gac long to earn the trust and respect of his patients—indeed, of the whole tribe—but Geleb customs sometimes made medical care difficult. For example, both food and water are withheld from a sick person, meaning sometimes parents refused to let Thompson give a feverish, thirsty child water with which to swallow pills.

This is a particularly vicious custom with dysentery, when body fluids need to be replenished. Thompson believed more patients succumbed to dehydration than to disease. He made some progress over the years through individual teaching and occasional public health lessons. However, customs are difficult to change before the heart is made new in Christ.[6]

Ministry among the Gelebs sought a response to God's love and the gospel of Christ that would open hearts and minds to the Truth.

The Gelebs believed in an angry God who continually had to be placated. According to their beliefs, he at one time walked on earth. One day he stopped at a Geleb house and asked for food. When he was refused, he became so irate that he left the earth and went up into the heavens. He is up there to this day, lying prone, looking down on the earth—and the Gelebs are his chosen people because they live right beneath his navel.

The ills they experience are a result of God's anger, and many goats are sacrificed to try to win back the favor of this capricious deity.

The Gelebs also were keenly aware of evil—although not "sin" as we understand it. They took measures to rid themselves and their villages of whatever it was—a curse, an evil eye, the angry God that had caused the suffering or misfortune.

One night, Bob witnessed a new moon ceremony. Donkey dung had been collected and arranged in a circle around the village. A fire was burning within the circle. At one point in the rite, brands were plucked from the fire

6 Morrell Swart, "Outstanding Dressers Serve at Maji and Omo," *Ethio-Echo*, Vol. 11, No. 3, August 1975: 7, 8. Joint Archives of Holland, Hope College.

and thrown into the darkness outside the circle. The flaming brands were supposed to dispel the evil that had been visited upon their village.

This ceremony is reminiscent of the scapegoat in Leviticus that "shall be presented alive before the Lord to be used for making atonement by sending it into the desert...."[7]

Circumcision also was practiced by the Gelebs. The ceremony was enacted as a rite of passage among young men. However, if a man had not been circumcised and he had a daughter approaching marriageable age, her marriage could take place only after the father was circumcised.

In each of these customs—animal sacrifice, the tossing of burning sticks from the village, and circumcision—there was enough common ground with the Bible to launch instruction in the Truth. Jesus Christ, the sacrifice made once and for all, took upon himself our sins and carried them away forever.

Up and down the lower reaches of the Omo River, Bob traveled by outboard, visiting villages in the several Geleb clan areas week after week, year after year. Initially, before facility with the language had been acquired, Scripture recordings, prepared with the help of informants, were used on hand-wound players from Gospel Recordings, Inc. These were a great innovation, giving impetus to early evangelistic thrusts.

However, the development of battery-powered and then solar-powered tape players by Dr. Ronald Beery, founder of Portable Recording Ministries (PRM) in Holland, Michigan, vastly improved this means of sharing the good news. PRM's first players were brought to the Omo River Post in 1968 by the five volunteers from Michigan. They were to be used as a sort of pilot project to determine their worth and practicality as evangelistic tools.

The value of these little machines was immediately evident. Used by missionaries and the Gelebs themselves, who listened over and over again in the villages, Scripture made an indelible imprint on hearts and minds.

One evening when Bob was in the village sitting by one of the dung fires, Inogitiri said to him, "I've been thinking. Geleb ways, their talk, their

7 Leviticus 16:10, *New International Version.*

customs are all wind. The talk of God that I hear on the tapes, the words of
God's Book that you tell me—that's truth."[8]

But not everyone was so moved by the gospel message.

Behind all the filth and fear and social corruption among the
Geleb people lies spiritual desolation. Waste places. Dry bones.
Death. Like the bleak fossil beds back on the ridge. Although they
are quite unaware of it, their crying need is a spiritual one. Many
shun the gospel because they have no conscious need of any other
way.

[A man] came to us full of fear and dread. He wanted an
injection. He had been cursed; someone had dug up some bones
from an old grave and had used them to curse him. Now he was very
sick and would die.

"If you trusted God, you would not be afraid of a curse," we said.

"But I am a Geleb!"

"God loves the Gelebs!"

"Maybe. But I don't want that talk. Give me an injection."

A frantic mother brought her baby the same day. Someone had
cast the evil eye on the child so that he came down with a severe
case of dysentery.

"Give medicine to take away the curse."

And with her dirt encrusted hands, she removed the filthy
goatskin from around the equally filthy baby.[9]

The good news had not yet infiltrated her superstition-encrusted heart.
Nor had Achew's brothers-in-law yet been moved to walk in the way of
kindness and trustworthiness, even where their nearest of kin were concerned.

Achew's wife, Nyelim, gave birth to her first child during planting
season, which is usually a season of hunger as well as of arduous toil
in the fields. Improvident use of last year's harvest leaves the
people with meager supplies, and it's a struggle to save enough for
seed.

---

[8] Morrell Swart, "Nothing Else Matters So Much." Reprinted from the *Church
Herald*, June 12, 1970: 17.
[9] Ibid. 16, 17.

This is a particularly hard period for nursing mothers. Often Nyelim didn't have enough to eat and her child grew slowly.

Achew worked to earn money to buy corn flour which we had ordered from Jimma. But one day he gave his two brothers-in-law the flour to take to his wife. It was never delivered; Nyelim's brothers ate the flour themselves, stealing food from their sister and her infant son....

Only when they know Christ will the Gelebs realize their terrible lack. When their eyes are opened and they see themselves, as we all must, against the purity and holiness of Jesus; when their ears are opened to hear him say, "I am the way (you must walk), and the truth (you must believe), and the life (you must claim as your own)," then their redemption is near.

Therefore, if we give a bar of soap without telling them of the cleansing power of Jesus' blood; if we give medicine without introducing the sick to the Great Physician; if we dig a well without inviting the thirsty to drink of the Living Water; if we teach about new foods without breaking before them the Bread of Life; if we give out a garden tool without trying to discover if the soil of the gardener's heart is ready to receive the seed of the Word, we will not have fulfilled the mission of the church, nor obeyed the command of Christ to "go into all the world and preach the gospel to the whole creation."[10]

When our school opened for the first time in October 1970, we knew these principles had to be carried over into the field of education. There were only six students at first. ("We don't want our children to become educated; who will watch the goats?") But even so, right from the outset, this school did more than duplicate government efforts to introduce the three Rs; it included a long-term program for training students in Christian citizenship. We had Ethiopian teachers of God's choosing: Assefa Zewdi and Timotewos Jerkab. Faithfully and admirably supervised monthly by Dottie Rankin from Mizan Tafari, these teachers carried out their roles with Christian grace and patience.

School attendance ebbed and flowed with the seasons, but the program demonstrated quite satisfactorily that children without benefit of pre-

10 Ibid. 17.

A Geleb family is baptized at the Omo

school orientation—no books or pictures, no paper or pencils—indeed could master the basics and even acquire a thirst for knowledge. It certainly broadened some children's horizons and stimulated their thinking. However, I must add that sewing and carpentry classes were generally more popular than academics.

Simultaneously, Bob was holding special classes to deepen inquirers' understanding of the Christian faith. The response was gratifying. We prayed that many soon would be prepared for baptism.

And it was so. The Holy Spirit truly was at work among us. The crowning day of our initial six years on the Omo River came on April 25, 1971, when our first baptismal service was held at the water's edge.

We had some discussion about the mode of baptism. With so grand a river flowing by our door, the usual Calvinist custom of sprinkling hardly seemed appropriate or even adequate. Immersion was risky at best and could be dangerous, considering the Omo's crocodile population. (In fact, among wildlife conservationists, the Omo River delta was known to be one of the last strongholds of the world's largest crocs.) Finally, pouring was pronounced the most acceptable and practical mode—pouring Omo River water from a Geleb gourd over the heads of new believers.

Twelve people, representing three tribes, were baptized that day: Korie, Arikar, Lokwar, Achew and his wife, Nyelim, and their small son, all of whom were Gelebs; Akol and his wife, Nakademo, and Ata, who were Turkanas; and Thompson's wife, Nyaluol, and their two sons, Cuol and Jaal, who were Nuers.

It was a time of rejoicing and praising the Lord. The church in Geleb country had come into being—and what God had begun, he would bring to completion.

Three months later, on July 25, there was one more note of joy and encouragement—all because of what God was doing here. Gabite, his wife, Tufa, and little son, Akol, were baptized as a family. And Korie's wife, Meerkoin, also had the "water of God" poured on her head. Korie had said that he wanted his wife to be baptized, too, so that they would no longer be divided.

After the service, we all went up to the school (which also served as the Christian meeting place) for the sacrament of Holy Communion. A small loaf of thick *durra* porridge represented Christ's body, and tomato juice, his blood. It was the first time that Gelebs had sat at the table of the Lord. They learned what it meant to "remember Christ's death."

In June of that year, two other events took place that made us realize anew that "time like an ever-rolling stream bears all (one's children) away."

Our daughter, Chloe, was married to Mark Young on June 4 at the mission chapel in Addis Ababa. Mark's parents, who were medical missionaries in Yemen, were there, as well as siblings of both the bride and groom. Bob officiated. He was assisted by Don McClure who had baptized Chloe twenty years before at Akobo in . The newlyweds returned from their honeymoon in time for Jack Swart's and Kay Young's graduation from Good Shepherd School on June 9.

It was a busy, happy time for both families, except for the "bearing away" of one's children. However, ties were strong and love abounded regardless of time and distance.

Following the wedding and graduation, we went to the United States for a few months. Jack was enrolled at Northwestern College in Orange City, Iowa, where he was a student for a year before his life took another direction.

We also greeted two new grandchildren, Brandon Reid Borschel and Christie-Ann Marie Powell, who were born in 1970. The third generation of our immediate family now numbered three, and we praised God for each new life.

Our fourth grandchild, Jon Karl Hill, was born as we flew over the Alps on our way back to Ethiopia that November. How my heart had longed to be able to remain stateside a while longer! I chafed at stern plane schedules and reentry visas. Jon would be two years old before he met his maternal grandparents.

Christmas 1971 was especially memorable. There were Geleb, Nuer, and Turkana Christians with whom to celebrate, as well as a fellow American. Dr. Beth Marcus, who was at that time the Secretary for Adult Voluntary Services with the RCA's General Program Council, had come to Africa for a firsthand overview of RCA work and to assess the need for future volunteers.

So it was with a keen sense of joyful fellowship that we all attended a Christmas service of praise and worship, and then sat down together for a feast in the mission yard. Leafy branches had been brought in and laid neatly and thickly on the grassy ground in the shade of *mye'de* trees. We all sat on mats around this "table." Families brought what they could: boiled whole grain, *durra* porridge, corn, beans, peanuts boiled in their shells, and stewed chicken. The *piece de resistance* was a roasted sheep, the gift of a Jewish guest we'd entertained just a few days before.

All these things were placed on platters or banana leaves on the table, and we feasted sumptuously. The joy and praise of the occasion made everything taste the more sweet. Never again would the celebration of Christ's birth be a lonely festival for the missionaries at Omo River Post.

In 1972, Julie Strong gave up the editor position of the mission newspaper, *Ethio-Echo*. In ten years under her leadership, it had become a notable publication in mission and church circles. Now, after twenty-one years in Ethiopia, Julie and her family were relocating to the United States. Who would carry on as editor?

"Morrie, will you do it?"

We were in Addis Ababa. The Executive Committee had been pondering the future of *Ethio-Echo*. And one morning, Mal Vandevort approached me with that startling inquiry.

My first reaction was: Me? Impossible! We live five hundred miles from Addis Ababa. Mail deliveries are erratic. How would we ever be able to solicit articles and pictures, receive the manuscripts, edit them, send them off to the printer, do the proofreading, etc., and maintain any kind of a subscription schedule?

And then Mal added, "Will you do it if Glenn Noble helps with the Addis end of things?"

With that, my answer had to be, "I'll try it."

The job had its appeal. And the wide acclaim, which *Ethio-Echo* enjoyed through the years that Julie Strong was editor, made the challenge exciting.

Polly Kurtz also offered her assistance. So we would do our best as a team to maintain the same high standard and purpose: to help keep the church informed about what God was doing through his people in Ethiopia.[11]

For the next five years, this responsibility proved to be my greatest joy and satisfaction. But it was not entirely "my thing." For it could not have been done without MAF and those faithful ones in Addis Ababa who indeed did see each issue through to completion, including the mailing. To them I remain deeply grateful.

[11] *Ethio-Echo*, Vol. 9, No.1, July 1972: 8. Joint Archives of Holland, Hope College.

XIII
Omo Windmills
and Teppi Tapes

The central theme of Geleb conversation was cattle. Their most persistent ambition was to acquire more livestock; sheep and goats were used for meat and sacrifices, and cattle were acquired by raiding and killing neighboring tribesmen. The overabundance of small stock was the main reason their land was so overgrazed. With cattle-raising tribes on all sides, tsetse fly to the north, and Lake Turkana to the south, the Gelebs were hemmed in with no room to expand.

Ecologists had predicted that, because of the increasing difficulty in providing pasture for their herds, the Gelebs one day would become an agricultural rather than a pastoral people. They already were farmers to an extent, depending upon the annual rise and fall of the river to water and enrich their gardens.

Every year the bottom lands and riverbanks became green with growing grain. Bird-chasers posted themselves on high platforms every few hundred feet to keep away the great flocks of *queleas* and weavers that could strip the ripening heads in no time. Most years, the harvest was plentiful. The threshed and winnowed grain was stored in spherical, grass-covered bins set up on platforms in the village, out of reach of herds. That was the time of year when the people danced in the moonlight. Well-fed, they were exuberant.

Then, inevitably, would come the quiet nights when the grainstores were empty, and people became dependent primarily upon their cattle for

194

sustenance: for milk, blood, and an occasional feast of meat. Cattail roots and waterlily pods, found in abundance down in the delta of the Omo River, were also a source of nourishment during the lean time—a period they accepted as part of the rhythm of their lives.

While there is virtue in acceptance, one wonders if it commendable when children are ordered: "Stop crying! Gelebs are always hungry this time of year. After a while, there will be food again."

But even the Gelebs began to see this state of affairs could be avoided—especially after observing the results of irrigation by a Dempster windmill in the mission garden.

Geleb country had several assets: the Omo River with its ample, year-round supply of water, unlimited arable land, and winds that blow from off the lake most of the year. This combination provided the God-given potential to help solve the Gelebs' annual hunger problem.

Therefore, in response to their recognized and expressed needs, the Food From Wind project came into being. Thanks to the generosity of several RCA individuals and congregations, three more Dempster mills were imported and installed in Geleb fields. Enthusiasm for this type of irrigation was high. Hand pumps had been tried as a means of irrigation in the school garden and on a few Geleb plots. They worked well but took a lot of physical energy and had only limited capability.

At that time, a *Reader's Digest* article about windmills on the Greek island of Crete showed the Lassithi Plateau crowded with cloth-sailed mills. Intrigued, we made plans to visit Crete on our way back to Ethiopia after a brief furlough in 1973.

We rented a bright yellow VW in Heraclion. Our route took us along the sea and then south into the mountains. We drove through olive groves and fruit orchards; along narrow, precipitous mountainside roads; and finally, through a pass in the highest range. From there we could look down on the plateau.

What a sight! As fascinating as the *Reader's Digest* coverage had been, the real thing was awesome. The high plain was abloom with hundreds of white cloth-sailed mills. It was like beholding vast acres of giant lilies.

Soon we were down in the midst of them. Each small plot had its own windmill pumping water from its own well. Closer examination revealed simple construction with materials we were sure were available in Addis Ababa. After taking numerous photos of shafts and gears and other crucial parts of the assembly, we completed our journey to Ethiopia and Omo River Post.

Soon after our arrival, we were dismayed to learn that the Gelebs were on the warpath. Warriors were gathering by the hundreds in Nyememeri, the village on the other side of the airstrip. They came from every clan of the tribe, out for blood and lots of cattle.

Apparently, while we were on furlough, the Bumei tribe fifty miles to the north came and drove off many of the Geleb cattle. This was done in retaliation for a terrible massacre the Gelebs had carried out among the Bumei some months previously. Now revenge was being planned again—a never-ending cycle of getting even.

To strengthen the warriors physically, several steers were slaughtered for daily feasts; and to sustain their resolve, tribal elders harangued the young men about the glories of such events.

The plan of attack was laid out, but for days they delayed because there had been no rain. Every day they prayed to their gods for rain so that there would be water along the way to Bumei country. Thirst was the most feared enemy on such an expedition. However, the skies were never clearer.

Finally they could wait no longer. The last steer was killed on Sunday afternoon, and after all the men had marched ceremonially through its dung, they headed north. They had sent spies a few days earlier who reported that there was a large Bumei encampment between the EthioSudan border posts. So the Geleb warriors headed for that encampment, confident that the police wouldn't bother them. Early Tuesday morning was the time set for the attack.

The sun rose blood red that morning, and there was a smoky, fog-like pall over Nyememeri. Bob made the remark, "If we were superstitious, these signs would mean something to us." As it was, we had a feeling of impending disaster.

On schedule Tuesday morning, the Gelebs opened fire. The Ethiopian police responded with machine guns. Two police were killed, seven Bumei were slightly wounded—and the Gelebs, immediately demoralized, ran, scattered, and headed for home. They had lost several of their number from serious wounds, and they lost even more from thirst. They returned with not even one goat.

The Gelebs were a subdued people. They had lost face as a tribe reputed to be fierce and invincible. Our prayer for them became all the more focused on God's promise: "I will give you a new heart.... I will give you new and right desires—and put a new spirit within you. I will take out your stony hearts of sin and give you new hearts of love."[1]

When those disturbing weeks were over, it was a relief to us all to turn our attention to more peaceful and useful pursuits.

Unknown to us, the Pollocks had visited Crete shortly before we did, and it wasn't long until Ted was down on the Omo with drawn-up plans for a Cretan windmill. He and Bob collaborated in launching this new phase of the Food From Wind project that would put in Geleb hands a mill much less expensive than the imported variety, and presumably simple to operate and maintain.

The first one was placed near the school garden where volunteer Glen Crabtree (who came from Sheffield, Iowa, with his wife Lois) supervised and trained Geleb men in the planting and irrigating of individual plots. It was a huge success. Enthusiasm increased. Requests came for many more mills.

Bob's dream—shared now by the Gelebs as well—was to plant cloth-sailed mills up and down the Omo in arable areas that would lend themselves to irrigation.

But who would manufacture the mills? Ted Pollock had gotten the project "off the ground" and, while he would continue making the components at his station, other responsibilities now called him elsewhere. Bob had too many calls upon his time to give adequate attention to the task. But the mounting interest must be responded to with consistent production. Who could give full-time to this work?

The answer couldn't have pleased us more.

Our son Dick had graduated from Good Shepherd School in June 1973. He was now in Nashville, Tennessee, taking a course in welding, and his wholehearted desire was to return to Omo and help his dad.

Dick arrived in June 1974, well qualified in both aptitude and training, and for fourteen months, he gave himself enthusiastically to welding up

---

[1] Ezekiel 36:26. Scripture quotation taken from *The Living Bible*.

towers and wheel frames for the mills. Besides the straightforward construction, to quote from a letter to one of his sisters: "I've been doing a lot of experimenting with different types of pumps and attachments and guides for the mills, too. I still have a lot of experimenting to do and a lot of windmills to build. I feel I did the right think in coming out here to help Dad in his project." Dad and Mom thought so, too!

The local interest in windmill irrigation endured; it was proving to be no fly-by-night idea that would soon fizzle out. Really, the keenness of the Gelebs for the project amazed us. The genuineness of their response was seen in their willingness to assume a percentage of the cost commensurate to their means, and in their industriousness preparing the land and caring for their gardens, particularly in light of the fact that gardening traditionally was women's work.

Each mill was a package deal. When a Geleb asked for one, he received, in return for his nominal payment, not only the mill but also a set of garden

Food From Wind Project:
A cloth-sailed Cretan windmill

tools and a cassette player from Portable Recording Ministries in Holland, Michigan. Remembering that "man does not live by bread alone," we were determined that Food From Wind should also supply food from the Spirit. The windmills became gathering places that afforded great evangelistic opportunities. So, with the players and cassettes of Bible teaching at each site, the Word was planted and bore fruit in Geleb hearts.

The project prospered with the able assistance of many volunteers (among them, the aforementioned Crabtrees and also Harold and Irma Roos from First Reformed Church of Denver, Colorado, who spent three months with us), and the financial and prayer support of numerous churches and individual friends in the homeland. A grant also was sought from a relief agency in England, called OXFAM, that sent engineer Peter Fraenkel to evaluate, advise, and report. At the time Peter came in 1975, "some nineteen mills of various types were operational and under the control of local villagers, and a further five were in operational condition on mission land for cultivation, experimentation, or demonstration. Eleven further sail windmills had been completed and awaited installation for villagers requiring them."[2]

From the start, and with an eye to the future, Bob knew that it was essential to train a Geleb in windmill maintenance. Careful observation revealed that Achew, of all the workers, had an aptitude for such responsibility.

Achew, already a Christian, faithful, and "ungelebly" industrious, soon learned how to use a variety of basic tools. When he had mastered the art, Bob gave him a tool set of his own. Achew could be counted on to be on hand when windmills needed repair.

According to an article written by Gavin Bennet for Kenya's *Sunday Nation*:

> [The Gelebs] are extraordinary because they live on the brink of great bounty and yet they have chosen, quite simply, to starve.
>
> Their homeland...looks no more than a waste of sun-blasted rocks and sand....But that hellish desert is made of rich alluvial soils, and right through the middle of it flows the giant Omo River....
>
> The implications of fertile soil, unending sunshine, and abundant water are clear enough to modern agricultural man. Perhaps the

---

[2] Peter Fraenkel, *Food From Windmills*, (Intermediate Technology Publications, Ltd., London, November 1975) 1.

simple, semi-nomadic [Gelebs] hadn't realized the potential, or didn't know how to harness it.

Not so. They had been given the know-how and the means to turn their desert into a garden. It came in the form of an American missionary called Bob Swart who, unlike many peddlers of piety, realized that, among the starving, food for the stomach would have to precede food for the soul.

When he arrived...he found a people for whom hunger and famine were as much a way of life as their beehive-shaped huts....

Swart stumbled across the theoretical answer and then with amazing energy, turned it into a practical one....

The delightfully international combination of American missionaries, British financial and technical assistance, and a windmill design from Crete subsequently produced a fairy-tale "ending."

Along the bank of a broad, brown river in the heart of Africa appeared a line of twirling windmill sails; and in the middle of the desert appeared pawpaws [papayas], bananas, mangoes, and vegetables in great, gorgeous, green profusion.

The mills wrought an agricultural and, to some extent, a cultural revolution. [Geleb] men who hitherto had scorned such a menial task as farming, were swiftly persuaded to cultivate maize and other crops....

They were taught to farm and look after the source of their bounty—the mechanical mills. Many found both new concepts hard to grasp, but some picked up the idea quickly and were selected to teach others.[3]

As the tape ministry flourished on the Omo, so it did at the Godare among the Mesengo. The Hoekstras had used records initially, just as we had. But

[3] Gavin Bennet, "The Most Extraordinary Tribe [sic]," *Sunday Nation* (Kenya), March 30, 1980: 18, 19. Joint Archives of Holland, Hope College.

with the advent of the small, easily carried cassette players, the ministry was vastly enhanced.

At first, we simply loaned cassettes and players to anyone who might say, "I live across the river" or "I live behind that mountain. May I take a machine to my family so that they also may hear the good news?" A few days later, the machine would be returned with stone-dead batteries, but you knew that in another village, the gospel had been preached.

Later as some became Christians, the players were increasingly placed in the hands of the more deeply committed. This made the technique doubly effective. Now not only the machine spoke, but when its message had been heard, the new believer could say, "This is indeed God's message for us. I believe it and you should believe it also." The lowly cassette enables the new believer to witness intelligently, and at the same time, as he hears the message over and over again, he becomes grounded in the truths of the Christian faith.

I think of the day Elong, a strapping Mesengo, nearly middle-aged, came in with his player and dead batteries. As he began telling his experience, he drew from his bag a string knotted some one hundred ten times. He slowly fingered the knots until he reached a larger knot somewhere near the middle. Looking up, deeply satisfied, he smiled and said, "These are all Mesengo, but from this knot on are Dannier people." Through the use of the cassette and the bilingual Mesengos on the border of the tribe along the Bacco River, Elong had been preaching to a tribe that had previously not been reached with the gospel....

Having seen the effectiveness of this method among the Mesengos, we felt God calling and giving vision as to how this method could be used to reach our remaining areas.

[So] when the Evangelistic Committee of the American Mission met some months ago to consider the Unfinished Task in southwest Ethiopia, the group responded affirmatively to this challenging statement: "Using cassettes and planes, our entire area can be effectively reached in the next eight to ten years."[4]

[4] Harvey Hoekstra, "Teppi Tapes Tell It on the Mountains," *Ethio-Echo*, Vol. 10, No. 2, February 1974: 1, 2, 3. Joint Archives of Holland, Hope College.

As a result of these deliberations, the Hoekstras moved from Godare to Teppi in 1972 and, with the help of volunteers, set up a base for a far-reaching, three-pronged tape ministry. On the front gate, the whole program was succinctly described in two words in tall letters: TEPPI TAPES.

> Our new base is...a rapidly growing market town in a heavy coffee-producing area where as many as ten tribes come together. We are situated directly beside the government airstrip used regularly by Ethiopian Airlines DC3 aircraft. This location enables us to produce tapes in the various languages and, with the use of MAF planes, to itinerate efficiently to a growing number of small airfields.
>
> Besides evangelization, the tape ministry also seeks to make a real contribution to the national educational effort. In cooperation with the Ministry of Education, a language teaching program has been developed on cassettes. The aim is to enable each of the tribal groups to learn to understand and speak the national language, Amharic. Once having laid the foundation by the use of oral Amharic lessons, we expect to move forward into literacy.[5]

(An openness to literacy was embraced by a government official, as Harvey described in a letter:

"When this plan was presented to the official in the Ministry of Education, the man stood up behind his desk and said with some emotion, 'Mr. Hoekstra, this is a plan that all Ethiopia needs. Could you give us a ten-year plan? We will give you blanket permission for the district.'

"Perhaps for the first time, permission was given to open a mission station on the basis of something other than having to operate a school and clinic. Teppi town had both, and God opened the door for us through the cassette program....God be praised!")

> The third phase of our ministry is in the field of medicine. When the first small airstrip was finished and we made our initial landing, we found hundreds of people on hand to welcome us. They received us warmly and listened eagerly to the gospel from previously prepared cassettes in their own language. At the same time, we discovered that many among them were needing medical care. Some too ill to travel by mule or on foot were flown to the Mettu

5 Ibid.

hospital. As other communities have learned of this service, they have begun to prepare airfields to make it possible for the plane to serve them also....

Ethiopian team members, the medical dresser, Isahak, and the evangelist, Getachew, go out every Monday to return on Friday. Men such as these are, in a sense, doing the real work, and we missionaries increasingly look upon ourselves as enablers in a training program.

An exciting and significant feature of the tape ministry is its cooperative endeavors with the historic Ethiopian Orthodox Church. From the beginning, we have recognized that in many of the areas where we are working, and particularly in the towns, the Orthodox Church has a presence.... We believe that in a cooperative program, we may share in providing Bible study materials on cassettes to encourage and stimulate the local priests and religious leaders in the ministry. Also, with cassettes in the languages of the people in the surrounding areas, these leaders are given a tool that enables them to share more effectively in the work of evangelization.

In recent conversations with Orthodox Church officials, one of the leaders said, "This is God's time for us to work together, so that

Harvey Hoekstra with a leader of the Orthodox Church

what we have not been able to do by ourselves, we can accomplish together until all our people have the opportunity to become truly Christian...."

These are exciting days to be alive and witnessing to Jesus, to be open to new relationships, new patterns of activity, with great expectations as we sense that this is God's time. He is powerfully revealing himself to be alive and full of love and mighty to save men![6]

The Hoekstras' move to Teppi did not mean the abandonment of the witness to the Mesengos at Godare.

Al Smith grew up on a farm in Maple Lake, Minnesota, "just over the hill from Harvey Hoekstra's home...." He graduated from the University of Minnesota with a degree in agricultural engineering. So when the Hoekstras were home on furlough in 1970, on the lookout for someone to assist at Godare in the field of agriculture, Al was the likely candidate.

Finally in 1972, after experiencing many months of "hopes aroused and hopes dashed," Al and Beth Smith arrived at Godare for a two-year term. Al supervised the work in the school gardens, assisted any of the Mesengos who asked for help, and carried on the inevitable general maintenance. Beth taught English to third-year students and had a sewing class for girls. Among other new experiences, she learned to "make bread and cakes from scratch."

Mary Visscher, who with her husband, Dr. Harry Visscher, and two children visited RCA personnel in Ethiopia over a two-week period in 1973 for the purpose of making a documentary film, described their arrival at Godare:

Al and Beth are a young, almost newlywed couple, braving it out as volunteers....We got an idea of what a plane means to the missionaries when we saw Beth run up and hug our pilot [mission general secretary Harold Kurtz]. Her questions came fast: Do you have our mail? Did you bring meat? (We're so sick of tuna fish!) Could you please bring us a case of Coke sometime?...[7]

---

6 Ibid.

7 Mary Visscher, "Our Ethiopian Adventure." Reprinted from the *Church Herald*, April 27, 1973: 5.

But Beth spoke of their real desires when she said, "We both wanted to help people in some way and serve the Lord. We feel this is a great learning and growing experience."

Harry and Pat Miersma arrived in Ethiopia February 25, 1973. Harry Miersma had spent the summer of 1966 at Godare. This had exposed him to missions firsthand, and though he later went into business, the Lord spoke to him again and again about returning to the mission field. Finally he sold out, went to Kansas State University for a degree in psychology, and in 1971 enrolled at Multnomah School of the Bible in Portland, Oregon, for the one-year graduate course in intensive Bible study.

Pat Shanahan, as the daughter of an Army officer and then as an Army nurse herself, knew what it was like to live in exotic places and to experience life in developing countries.

She was commissioned as a second lieutenant Fort Sam Houston, and then volunteered for Vietnam. For fourteen months, she served in the 27th Surgical Hospital in Chu Lai just south of Da Nang.

> We cared for Vietnamese as well as GIs. God used that experience to convince me that he wanted me to go to the mission field.... [I saw] the spiritual darkness and hopelessness of many who had never heard of Christ....
>
> When I returned home in June 1971, I enrolled at Multnomah for the one-year graduate course....[8]

From this point on, the lives of Harry and Pat began to have one focus: Ethiopia. Married in 1972, they were commissioned January 25, 1973, at New Life Community Church in Artesia, California.

They arrived in Ethiopia a month later. Their first assignment was to work beside the Hoekstras at the new post in Teppi. But when Al and Beth Smith returned to the USA in 1974, the Miersmas became responsible for the work at Godare.

The work was overwhelming, especially after the fellowship of the Teppi Tapes team. Every bush missionary can empathize: isolation, loneliness, strange sounds bombarding one's ears, conversation limited to smiles and gestures.

[8] "Ethio-Echo Proudly Presents:" *Ethio-Echo*, Vol. 10, No. 1, September 1973: 7, 8. Joint Archives of Holland, Hope College.

Harry and Pat tried for several months to learn the Mesengo language; they gave it their best efforts. However, never having had any training, their attempts, according to Pat:

> ...were lacking in organization and efficiency, and were for the most part frustrating. Now we praise God for his wisdom in sending us to the Summer Institute of Linguistics at the University of Oklahoma for nine weeks this past summer. Having lived among the Mesengos, longing to tell them about Jesus and not being able to, we were much more highly motivated throughout SIL's strenuous program.
>
> During the last week of our training, we watched a demonstration of exactly how to go about eliciting data from a[national] informant, and then how to organize and analyze the information. As we watched the demonstration which put together all that we had learned and made it practical for us, it was as though the Lord were lifting a tremendous burden from our shoulders. With relief, we could see ahead and at least know how to begin to learn Mesengo effectively.
>
> At this writing, we've had two and a half weeks of daily study with our Mesengo informant. In that time, we have collected more data and obtained a better grasp on the language than we had during our whole first year.
>
> Now our deepest desire is to learn to communicate with the Mesengos at such a level that we can begin Bible study with them and disciple those who are already Christians. Since our return, we've sensed an even deeper hunger for the Word of God, and an eagerness on the part of the Christians to know Jesus Christ in a fuller way.
>
> So we praise the Lord for SIL and the new "equipment" it has given us for the work among the Mesengos—and for his continuing faithful performance in our lives and theirs.[9]

Language study for the Miersmas was blessedly interrupted for a time by the birth of Amy Lynn on January 5, 1975.

[9] Pat Miersma, "Miersmas Give Thanks for SIL," *Ethio-Echo*, Vol. 11, No. 1, February 1975: 8. Joint Archives of Holland, Hope College.

During the early 1970s, as the church in mission moved ahead in the Ethiopian rain forests, lowland deserts, towns, and high plateaus, two forces were at work that awoke missionaries and their sending agencies to an even greater urgency in getting on with the divine task entrusted to them—that of spreading the good news of God's love in Christ Jesus.

XIV
Moratorium and Revolution

The year: 1971.

The place: a hotel conference room in Milwaukee, Wisconsin.

The event: the Reformed Church in America Mission Festival. Hundreds of delegates were in attendance, including the Swarts.

The keynote speaker: the Rev. John Gatu, general secretary of the Presbyterian Church in East Africa.

Gatu used the platform of our denomination's celebration of missions to launch a stunning bombshell. If he meant to shock, he was eminently successful.

> "In this address, I am going to argue that the time has come for the withdrawal of foreign missionaries from many parts of the Third World, that the churches of the Third World must be allowed to find their own identity, and that the continuation of the present missionary movement is a hindrance to this selfhood of the church."

Confessing that he was speaking for a minority of overseas church leaders, he criticized American missionaries for their cultural imperialism and domination of African church life. He proposed a withdrawal of missionaries to permit African churches and Third World churches in general to achieve a sense of their own identity.[1]

---

[1] Arie Brouwer, *Reformed Church Roots*, (Reformed Church Press, 1977) 156.

At the close of Gatu's address, the conference room was buzzing. Reaction was mixed. But generally, delegates were seeking honest responses that would help give direction for the future. Most sought a rebuttal for the validation of continuing witness for Christ throughout the world. Would someone speak and be heard?

Bob and I drifted to the periphery of a gathering of church leaders who were pondering the substance of the speaker's recommendations. Upon our arrival at the scene, Arie Brouwer asked, "Bob and Morrie, how do you see this? What is your response to the concept of a moratorium on missionary activity?"

After some thought, Bob "observed that even if Gatu's remarks were true for much of the Third World, 'there is also a Fourth World'"[2] out there that will need missionary witness and leadership for some time to come.

The concept of a Fourth World, and the fact of Christ's open-ended mandate to "go and make disciples of all nations...and I will be with you always to the very end of the age,"[3] gave comfort for the present, and a solid, Scriptural perspective for the future of missions.

However, the issue continued to simmer on the continent of Africa and came to the fore again in a press release from Lusaka, Zambia, on May 21, 1974, that stated:

> The Third Assembly of the All Africa Conference of Churches ended today with an endorsement of a moratorium on aid to churches in Africa "as the most viable means of the African churches being given power to perform its mission in the African context."
>
> The Rev. Gatu, who first startled stateside churches with the moratorium proposal four years before, said at the conference:
>
> "Our present problems can only be solved if all missionaries can be withdrawn in order to allow a period of not less than five years for each side to rethink and formulate what is going to be the future relationship."
>
> This statement has caused much concern among churches in the States to whom the Great Commission is as compelling a directive today as it ever has been....

---

2 Ibid.
3 Matthew 28:19, 20, New International Version.

Church leaders have responded in editorials, articles, and addresses in varying degrees of sympathetic understanding, caution, and conviction. Throughout the following sampling, however, runs a thread of warning to the church to beware lest the moratorium proposal be misconstrued, lest Christ's commission be declared null and void—even for five years— when MOST of the world's people TODAY have yet to hear the good news and respond to it.[4]

Dr. Alan Tippett, who was a missionary for many years and a teacher of anthropology at the Church Growth Institute of Fuller Theological Seminary, made these comments in an editorial in *Missiology*:

There are…mission fields where institutions and personnel are still far too paternalistic and foreign, and where local church identity is thereby hindered.…But to cut off support suddenly to a community trained for years to be dependent is to court disaster. Many young churches themselves have protested against this.…

Used wisely…a moratorium might well be in accord with the divine will; used as a generalization, it could limit the Holy One of Israel.…

There is a time for missionary thrust, and a time for withdrawal, but every situation must be judged on its own merits. The Christian mission must go on. Situational problems must be researched, but the moratorium must not become a cliché for the notion that the day of mission is dead.[5]

Mr. Paul A. Hopkins, [at that time] an executive of the United Presbyterian Church USA, in an article in *Concern* [quoted] this statement of the general secretary of the AACC, Canon Burgess Carr: "The simple truth about the moratorium is that we African Christians have no desire to be the channel through which the continued domination of Africa is assured."

Mr. Hopkins goes on to say that "moratorium is not in any way a rejection of the Christian faith. We Westerners have a view that

[4] Morrell Swart, "Churchmen Respond to Moratorium Proposal," *Ethio-Echo*, Vol. 11, No. 1, February 1975: 3. Joint Archives of Holland, Hope College.
[5] Ibid. (Used by permission from *Missiology*, July 1973). Joint Archives of Holland, Hope College.

unless we evangelize, the church cannot grow. That idea is simply out of date. The church in Africa is growing faster than in any other continent. At the Methodist Church Conference of Bishops in Salisbury, Rhodesia, early this year (1974), the African bishops said that henceforth Africans would take care of evangelization in Africa....

"The fact is that Africa in particular needs people in three broad categories:

"Health care: doctors and nurses

"Teachers of technical trades

"Food production: agriculture and animal husbandry.

"The list does not include evangelists because the African churches believe they can adequately fulfill the work of evangelization. But they do ask that technically qualified people we offer them be people with a deep commitment to Jesus Christ, ready to show his love through work and deed in all their work."6

The above statements and the following excerpts from a report in the *Reformed Ecumenical Synod News Exchange* show a confusing discrepancy and confirm Dr. Tippett's tenet that generalizations can be "either valuable guidelines or pernicious principles according to the way we use them."

Writing in the August *Outlook*, Iyortyom Achineku, former principal of the Reformed Theological College of Nigeria and [at that time] studying at Westminster Theological Seminary, Philadelphia, countered the cry of "Missionary, go home." Although Africa is rapidly becoming more Christian than the West (40.6 percent by a 1972 count), Mr. Achineku emphasizes that the Great Commission is by no means exhausted in Africa.

According to Mr. Achineku, theological education is a most urgent and neglected need of Africa. The churches in Africa are overcrowded and do not have enough ministers to go around. Some congregations are made up of as many as fifteen worshiping centers. [Because of this], Christians see a pastor only seldom. And, he says, in most cases, services are led by people who have never darkened the door of an elementary school. Especially, educated

6 Ibid.

Africans suffer in this situation, for there are few educated ministers to meet them on their level.

Fund-wise, he proposed that "evangelical churches launch an extensive scholarship program to produce competent teachers for colleges and seminaries in Africa. Personnel-wise, he asked that they increase and upgrade programs for theological education within Africa. In this regard, he discussed education by extension for lay leaders...."

After reading this report, many may well ask: If there are not nearly enough African pastors to nurture adequately vast numbers in even the Christian communities, how can the African churches hope to carry on all the work in evangelism?[7]

Ato (Mr.) Wagari Gemtessa, station manager of Ethiopian Airlines in Jimma, Ethiopia, and a strong leader in the evangelical church, was a delegate to the AACC at Lusaka. In an interview by letter, Ato Wagari shared his opinion of the moratorium proposal:

Question: Ato Wagari, would the withdrawal of missionaries and funds strengthen the national evangelical church of your country?

Ato W.:...It could be beneficial to those who have had the opportunity to train their leaders and have anticipated such a decision for a long time. It would be simultaneously detrimental to those who have had no opportunity of getting exposed to the avenue of training local leaders to fill the place of missionaries when they withdraw for one reason or another.

Question: Would the carrying out of this proposal help the church to take hold of her responsibilities in evangelizing unreached Ethiopian people?

Ato W.: In fact, the moratorium proposal was previously initiated by those developed churches in other African countries who, I am sure, must have sufficient reason for such dynamic actions. But as far as our country is concerned [right now], this may discourage most of the evangelical churches who fully or partially depend on missionaries, be it financial support or personnel....

---

[7] Ibid. (From the *Reformed Ecumenical Synod News Exchange*, September 10, 1974).

Question: Would the church welcome such an opportunity to test her own strength both in providing personnel to carry on the mission of the church...and in supporting the whole program of the church?

Ato W.: I am sure it would be very sour to swallow for the churches who depend fully on the missionaries in running the whole program.... However, to me, the proposal must be welcomed either partially or fully. What I mean here is a cut-off of either personnel or funds, depending on the strength or weakness of the individual church.

Question: Would the proposal be welcomed in some areas but not in others? Would it strengthen some areas but weaken others?

Ato W.: Oh, yes. The applicability of the proposal varies from church to church, and likewise from area to area. As I have clearly said, some churches are ripe and others are not. Those that are ready should accept [the challenge], and the rest should sincerely consider it for the future since it is impossible to stand on one's own feet without such a bold action.[8]

In an editorial in the *Church Herald*, editor Dr. Louis H. Benes sheds additional light on the issue and exhorts the church to continued obedience to Christ's command:

"...the African call for a moratorium ought not to be misunderstood....Some of the African leaders feel that some missionaries have, at times, held leadership posts long after they should have handed them over to the nationals, and that the national churches would grow much faster if they had to make it on their own, if they would themselves become missionaries to their own people.

"But quite a different message came out of the International Congress on World Evangelism meeting in Lausanne, Switzerland, [last summer]....The African participants there, even though they listened to a dialogue in which Mr. John Gatu of Kenya was also present, strongly rejected the idea of a moratorium on Western funds and missionaries to Africa. Mr. Gatu retreated somewhat

[3] Ibid. 3, 7.

from his earlier strong position. There he said he was not in favor of an immediate cessation of missionary activity and funds, and that it should not be permanent if it does occur three or four years from now.

"But other African leaders from a number of countries rejected the idea of even a temporary moratorium. One of them, apparently representing many others, said, 'We must help John Gatu find a way to develop the indigenous church in cooperation with missionaries so that all of us can work together as the body of Christ.' And at the close of the congress, thousands of the participants pledged themselves 'to pray, to plan, and to work together for the evangelization of the whole world.'

"But whatever Mr. John Gatu, or any other church leaders in American countries or countries overseas, may say, there is another Voice coming down through the centuries from Olivet saying, 'Go!' And our primary allegiance as Christians and as churches is to him, Lord of the Universe, and Head of his Church. The church's task, in Kenya or Indonesia, or the United States, remains unfinished as long as there are those who have not heard and have not responded to the gospel....

"The inclination, or the temptation, to surrender our missionary responsibility either around us or abroad, is due to a very disastrous misunderstanding of what the church really is: the body of Christ, chosen and appointed by him to 'bear fruit' and 'to preach the gospel to every creature.'...

"The very real question confronts us today, as our missionary force overseas is slowly being depleted: What kind of a heritage are we going to bequeath to those who follow after us? How faithfully are we responding to the Great Commission? These are questions that wait for an answer...from every last member of our churches in this generation."[9]

In the same editorial, Dr. Benes gives further substance to his remarks by quoting two Christian statesmen: Dr. Stephen Neill, who interprets the evolution of relationships in the missionary endeavor in developing African

[9] Ibid. September 6, 1974.

countries; and Bishop Lesslie Newbigin of India, who points the church again to world mission:

"The old generation," explained Dr. Neill, "worked happily with the missionaries, without any sense of rivalry, and laid the foundations of the great Kenya churches of today. The middle generation, of which John Gatu is a member, have bitter memories of the colonial epoch, and found the missionaries standing in the way of the nationals' desire for leadership. The younger generation, now at the universities, are no longer interested in either the colonial or the anti-colonial mythology, and the only questions they ask, about either an African or a foreigner, are: Is he competent? Does he know how to teach? How to lead?"

And Bishop Newbigin had this to say: "It remains the inescapable truth that we have a world mission, not because we choose to have, because we want to have, or because we are fit to have; but simply because we have been entrusted with it by Another. We are compelled to think about our mission to the world, simply because the church is that body which, not of its own choice—but of the Lord's choice—has been appointed for that mission."[10]

The moratorium proposal gave Christendom a powerful jolt. Who can say we did not need it? God uses men to carry out his strategies, and at precisely the right moment in history.

May that jolt keep us all alive to the fact that the African church—as well as other Third World churches—IS in various stages of emergence. Some have come of age and are ready to become sending churches themselves. May we also be just as aware of the others for whom withdrawal would be tantamount to betrayal. Let God's voice be clearly heard in each situation so that none may stay too long nor leave too soon.

And if, as a result of the pronouncement, African churches and Western churches alike are spurred on in their worldwide evangelistic task, what finer service could the proponents of the proposal have rendered God's kingdom?![11]

10 Ibid.
11 Ibid.

While voices were raised in earnest debate over the validity of the continuing mission of the church, another revolution was coming to a head in Ethiopia.

For some time, the educated elite in Addis Ababa had been restive. Many of them had attended universities in Russia, and they returned to their homeland with heady new ideas.

Dissatisfaction with Emperor Haile Selassie's regime was exacerbated in 1973 by a terrible drought and subsequent famine which the emperor was accused of ignoring. In 1974 mutinies broke out in the military over low pay. A secessionist guerrilla war had started in Eritrea. And riots in Addis Ababa became the last straw; the emperor's absolute power crumbled.

In a letter written from Omo River Post to our children on September 4, 1974, I shared this news: "I guess there won't be any more stamps printed with the emperor's picture on them. On last night's news, I heard that there was a major demonstration in Addis Ababa Monday against the emperor, and the commentator predicted that he would be deposed within the next couple of weeks."

That prediction came true.

The *Chicago Tribune* of August 28, 1975, reported:

> During his reign, [Emperor Haile Selassie] survived the Italian invasion forces of dictator Benito Mussolini, a revolt by his palace guard, the decolonization of Africa, but not a coup by youthful military officers that overthrew the government in September 1974.
>
> The tiny, bearded figure in the back seat of the blue police Volkswagen took a last lingering look at the walled National Palace.
>
> There was no band, no military salute, no cheers, no fanfare. Only a chorus of 400 students who ran after the car shouting abuse.
>
> The "Lion of Judah" and "King of Kings" had fallen. With him fell one of the world's last absolute monarchies and a history dating back 3,000 years.

The August 28, 1975, issue of the New York *Times* spoke of him as a "storied figure. He was the 225th Emperor of Ethiopia in a line that he traced back to Menelik I, who was credited with being the child of King Solomon and the Queen of Sheba, identified in Ethiopia as Queen Makeda."

These quotes are taken from articles appearing in newspapers just after Haile Selassie's death a year after his overthrow. He was eulogized at length in the world press. But the *Ethiopian Herald* gave his demise cursory attention. The headline announcing the event was all but obscured among items of revolutionary interest. Communism was well on its way to revamping the structure of government and dictating its ideas and strategies to the masses.

But it was hardly a smooth transition. There was much resistance to land reform and urban renewal programs; it was not easy for people to accept the nationalization of all industries, businesses, schools, and air services (MAF excepted). The new government had its hands full, and Ethiopia was in turmoil.

Our newsletter of January 1976, written in the USA, shed light on the position of the church and missions during this time:

> The Ethiopian Orthodox Church, steeped in ritual and tradition, has now been stripped of all her wealth and power. Some say she is now awakening to the realization of her true responsibility to preach the gospel.
>
> Several of the Orthodox Church's holy days are no longer national holidays. Other groups are being recognized: this year, for the first time, Muhammad's birthday was celebrated as a national holiday.
>
> The evangelical churches—the indigenous churches that have grown out of the various mission societies working in Ethiopia—have joined together in an unprecedented way to strengthen their work and witness throughout the country. This phenomenon illustrates an old Ethiopian proverb: "When the dogs are alone, they fight among themselves. But when the hyena comes, they join together."
>
> Mission activities have not been directly curtailed thus far. The Sudan Interior Mission...did suffer a setback in her evangelistic outreach program as a result of the land reform pronouncement that people claiming land rights cannot be otherwise employed. So MAF was busy for a while this year flying Ethiopian evangelists and

their families back to their home areas so they could lay claim to their land.

But as far as we know...no directives have been aimed at the missions themselves. We have heard, however, that the Derg (the ruling committee of one hundred fifteen members) considers missions valuable only for their medical services and community development projects. We can be thankful for this much, and we must be ready to seize the opportunity to spread the "good tidings of great joy" while there is yet time.

Geleb country...has not really been touched yet by all these changes....They are aware, however, that the emperor is gone—the emperor who visited them a few years ago and handed out clothing and Ethiopian dollar bills, and who was gracious and considerate of Geleb chiefs when they traveled all the way to Addis Ababa to air their grievances.

They know that all is not well in other parts of Ethiopia. But it really doesn't worry them; Geleb country and the struggle for existence—that's all they know.

Ethiopia, once so proud of being the only African nation free from foreign domination, and having once boasted the distinction of being the oldest Christian nation in the world, had sold its soul to an atheistic regime.

XV
Fallout from the Revolution

In September 1975, we went to the United States in high anticipation: Jack Swart and Deb Schoolmeester were to be married on the twentieth in Edgerton, Minnesota, with Deb's pastor, the Rev. William Kroon, and the groom's father presiding. We welcomed our first daughter-in-law wholeheartedly into our family.

Larry and Linda McAuley were in charge at Omo River Post in our absence, working along with volunteers Bob and Linda Bowman from Calvary Reformed Church, Ripon, California. The McAuleys were Presbyterians who had taught at the mission school in Dembi Dollo, Ethiopia, for two years. After this helpful stint on the Omo, they would be returning home to Illinois to launch out on their own in farming. An excellent arrangement had been offered to them, too good to pass up. This, however, was not the end of the McAuleys' mission career.

Our furlough concluded at the end of December. Bob went back to Ethiopia alone. Two more grandchildren were expected during the next two months and I didn't want to miss out for the sixth and seventh time in being on hand to exercise my grandmotherly prerogatives. (Our fifth grandchild, Shawn Renee Young, had sprouted on our family tree in May 1974)

On January 1, 1976, we welcomed Laura Yvonne Young into our family. And on February 29, we were delighted when Jeffrey Marc Hill joined big brother Jon. While a large part of my heart had gone to Ethiopia with their

219

grandfather, the joy of being there to celebrate the ongoingness of the generations was beyond description. I reveled in it and praised God for it.

Shortly before my return to Ethiopia, I received a letter dated March 19, 1976, from the Rev. Glenn Bruggers of the RCA's Grandville, Michigan, office. He wrote:

"I have learned that Arlene Schuiteman has been transferred from Mettu to the Central Nursing School in Addis. I talked by phone with Pat Miersma [now in the United States]. They left Ethiopia several days earlier than originally planned and so did not know much about Arlene's movement...."

Change had begun at Mettu, but God had been preparing his people to face the inevitable.

As far back as 1970, the Holy Spirit was working in powerful ways at Gore, the mission station only twelve miles from Mettu.

In July of that year, church leaders at Mettu planned a spiritual life conference and God's movement became evident also in that community. People were coming to the hospital chapel with an urgent desire to pray. Lives were being changed drastically and the church grew rapidly.

Arlene recorded that "in the church we witnessed the awesome power of God as people were healed or delivered from demon possession. Christians were tithing and the church accounts increased from one dollar to five hundred dollars...."

"Moratorium" was not on the lips of these Ethiopian Christians, but the mood of the times was upon them, and the Holy Spirit was working.

> In 1971 when the missionaries had been at work in Mettu for only seven years, the church leaders met on their own accord to discuss the future of the Mettu church. Then they called us to say that quite a bit of the work of the church was still being carried on by the missionaries. They often called on us to help them with planning, providing transportation or funds for various things. The doctors were often called on to preach. Church funds were kept in a missionary's home, and therefore the paying of pastors' salaries and keeping the accounts fell upon the missionary.
>
> They of their own accord, praise God, decided that they must handle these affairs and not be so dependent upon the foreigner. They reminded us that we come and go....They sensed the responsibility and were facing the challenge. We as missionaries

had brought the Word, our testimony, and our witness, but we were helpless to bring new Life. It was God, through the power of the Holy Spirit, who had pointed them to Jesus Christ, the Way, the Truth, and the Life....

In October 1972, I was back in Mettu after a year's furlough....A class of second year nursing students was hard at work....We also had an Ethiopia doctor in the role of provincial officer of health...as well as seven Ethiopian registered nurse-midwives and the trainees, some of whom stayed on to be employed here. The goal of Ethiopianization was moving right along.

The revival in this area continued to move into the villages around Mettu. One Sunday as I approached the church, I saw dozens of sticks and fetishes lined up on either side of the entrance. These had all been brought from a little village called Seygo....Demie, a young evangelist, had been witnessing in that village. God used him in many healing miracles. A man born deaf was hearing; a man lame for three years was walking; others were delivered from demon possession. When people saw these miracles, they brought their fetishes and accepted Jesus Christ. Our pastor went to visit the village and found one hundred twenty believers, many of whom were converted Muslims....

One of my former students, Thompson Gac, was working at the Omo River with the Swarts. During my Easter holidays, I made the two hundred fifty mile trip by MAF Cessna to see him at work. I spent each morning with him at the clinic. A flag was raised to indicate that "the doctor" was in. I watched Thompson as he listened to the patients' complaints, and as he examined them one by one. It was obvious that he had gained the confidence of the people...as he communicated freely in the language so strange to my ears.

Dysentery, malaria, and conjunctivitis are the most prevalent infections. Improved sanitation and hygiene, with emphasis on preventive medicine, are keys to solving many of the health problems here. Understanding the people and their customs, then gaining their confidence, is the first step....

From Godare, where another of the graduate students was at work, we received a patient for surgery at Mettu. She was a witch doctor who was blinded by cataracts. She lived deep in a forest area, and although she was only fifty miles from Mettu, she had no way of knowing what the world outside her forest environment was like. But she wanted to see; she agreed to go by MAF plane to Mettu for the operation.

I shall never forget her arrival and the fear she exhibited as she was admitted to the hospital. We had removed the hospital bed and placed a mat on the floor to help her feel a bit more at home, but still, everything was so strange to her.

That evening, I found her sitting on the veranda, calling on the name of her god. It seemed she felt forsaken and wanted him to know where she was. Finding someone who spoke her language helped the situation, and soon she had her surgery. She went back to her home with her sight restored....Later we learned from Harvey Hoekstra that her spiritual eyes also had been opened![1]

In February 1974, the American Mission gathered at Bishoftu for the annual association meeting. As this conference ended and we returned to Addis Ababa, riots broke out in the city. We were ordered by the American Embassy to remain on the mission compound and to be prepared for evacuation. One U.S. Army plane was standing by in Addis Ababa, and other planes were on call. After several days, the city returned to normal.

Students all over the country were restless, impatient for reforms to take place.

In May 1974, there were strikes throughout the land. People were wanting higher salaries. The post office went on strike and mail service became unreliable. Nineteen top government officials, including the prime minister, were arrested.

In September of that year Haile Selassie was deposed. A year later, he died.

In spite of these difficulties, the nurses' training school at Mettu had an excellent year under Arlene's teaching.

All our students passed the national exam, and one of ours had the highest grade in the country. What joy to announce this good news

---

[1] Arlene Schuiteman, "Ethiopia Notes," n.d. Joint Archives of Holland, Hope College.

to them on the night that we had planned the graduation party! Twenty-two people were at my house for the feast of Ethiopian food. Each student received an alarm clock and a collection of photos of themselves.... The students went home for the Christmas holidays.

As 1976 began, it was a special time of remembering God's faithfulness and loving-kindness to me. My heart was full of praise.

The church leaders had been planning a five-day Festival of Praise to celebrate the Ethiopian Christmas which comes on January 7. The main preparation was in fasting and prayer.

The festival began on Christmas Eve in our hilltop church on the outskirts of town. A few candles and a small kerosene lantern were the only lights. We had come to worship Jesus, the Light of the World. How the rafters rang! And what joy!

Two large tents had been put up near the church entrance to hold the overflow crowd on Christmas Day. Three Ethiopian guest evangelists came, and there were meetings every morning, afternoon, and evening with lots of good solid teaching as well as times of worship.

The festival was far more [dynamic] than we could have imagined. The forces of evil were, in fact, bound, and God opened the windows of heaven and poured down his blessings.

The final meeting was a communion service. The Mettu and Gore choirs were combined into a forty-voice chorus, with our little portable organ, two accordions, two guitars, a drum, and a tambourine for accompaniment. With hands joined, we sang with the choir to worship Jesus, our Savior, Lord, and King. We all felt the truth of the words as we sang "We Are One in the Spirit."

The nurses' school classes resumed after the vacation and we successfully completed the first term.

News kept coming from our little village churches where persecution had begun. One after the other was in trouble, and two of the churches were destroyed.

Our prayer meetings now took on a very serious kind of instruction as our elders began to prepare us for the difficulties ahead. Prayer meetings in designated homes met in different parts of the town.

The last day of February 1976, I was in the hospital supervising a student who was on obstetrics. He had just delivered a baby. It was 7 p.m. The provincial medical officer came to say that I had been summoned to appear in Addis Ababa at the Ministry of Health at once....The next day, I made arrangements to fly to Addis Ababa.

There they informed me that I was being transferred to be on the staff of the Central School of Nursing in Addis Ababa. I was assured that I had not failed in carrying out my responsibilities in Mettu, but I could not be told the reason for my urgent transfer....They reluctantly allowed me to return to Mettu to do my packing, but urged me to take no more than one week.

One evening the church had a special love feast that I will never forget. The elders served roasted lamb and bread to around seventy-five people. Individuals chose to read Scripture promises; we sang, we prayed, we shed some tears, but rejoiced in the love of God which binds us all together.

Ethiopian friends suggested that I leave as unannounced as possible for my safety....I left at 5:45 p.m. in our VW Jeep with Presbyterian missionary Kert Hultgren following a truck partly loaded with beeswax and topped off with my personal and mission possessions.

I arrived in Addis Ababa on Friday afternoon just inside the allotted time, and reported to the Ministry of Health at once. I was told to report to work at the large, modern, city hospital on Monday morning....I lived in the mission guest house for three months until the Hultgrens vacated their house. Then I moved in....

There was so much unrest in the city. My house was near the university, and some of my Mettu friends who were students there frequently came to my house to escape the stress-filled atmosphere of the campus. The usual quiet African nights were now interrupted by nearby gunshots, and it was not uncommon to see dead bodies on the streets.

Then I noticed one man who was present wherever I went. He seemed to be following me. Could this be a KGB spy? (I heard later that the pharmacist at Mettu had been a KGB spy tracking me as well)....

In September 1976, I was involved as a delegate in meetings at which major changes in the health services of the country were being debated....The slogan was: "The Needs of the People, Not the Pride of the Professional." Sometimes I was the only foreigner there and I felt uncomfortable—and it gave me an eerie feeling to see the same young man at almost every meeting I attended.

God continued to give me a deep peace and I was not afraid. One morning as I was driving to work, I was about to cross a bridge over a small stream. I sensed that something was wrong, so I made a sudden U-turn. A bus that was crossing that bridge only minutes later was blown up. I knew keenly that my guardian angels were at my side.

On October 15, 1976, my contract for working in the Ministry of Health would expire and we sought to renew it. I continued my teaching responsibilities in Addis Ababa, and was appointed to travel to Mettu to administer the national examinations to the class which I had left so abruptly in March.

Before I left the city, I was assured that the contract renewal was ready for signatures and I fully expected to have it upon my return from Mettu. Instead, I was informed that the contract had been refused.

The refusal was a sign to me that it was time to leave Ethiopia....My exit visa came on January 24, 1977. I left Addis Ababa on February 1. As I was airborne and had a last glimpse of a city and country that I loved, I wondered if God had some other place in Africa where my life and witness could be used.

My heart ached for my Christian friends, several of whom were in prison, being persecuted for their faith. I was free to leave; they weren't. Suddenly I felt extremely weary, and I knew I needed to be home in Sioux Center, Iowa, to recover from the stress of the last several months.[2]

Indeed God did have another place for Arlene Schuiteman to serve in Africa.

---

[2] Ibid.

During all these months when we were following Arlene Schuiteman through joy and trial, there were comings and goings of other RCA personnel in Ethiopia.

Harry and Pat Miersma were being plagued with health problems and eventually felt led by the Lord to return to the United States and pursue another calling. They left Godare in mid-1976. God gave them another daughter, Pam, and a son, Michael, and a new direction in ministry that blessed others. After special training, Harry and Pat served for many years with Wycliffe Bible Translators as counselors and consultants, encouraging and strengthening missionaries in Papua New Guinea and in several countries in Africa through workshops and personal appointments. The response to their workshops, counsel, and consultations made this among the richest of their personal and professional experiences.

When the Miersmas left Ethiopia, the mission asked Harvey and Lavina Hoekstra to move from Teppi and return to Godare. They demurred, but when they were reminded that they were the only people in the world who could speak the Mesengo tongue, they knew what they must do. They returned to Godare for six months.

When they finally left Godare in December 1976, the last words they heard at the plane were spoken to Lavina by a young Mesengo woman, the one who had come with the first string having thirteen knots, indicating that thirteen women had said, "Aragem, tie a knot on your string for me. I want to become a person of your Jesus."

Aragem had been crying behind a big tree. She came over to the plane. The door was still open. She said to Lavina, "Nyijobi (Lavina's African name), you come back. But if I don't see you again, I'll see you one day in Jesus' house."[3]

The Hoekstras will carry the joy and hope of Aragem's words with them until they meet again "in Jesus' house."

Harvey and Lavina had hoped to extend the cassette ministry to other African countries while continuing to be based in Ethiopia. But God had an

---

[3] Harvey Hoekstra, "A Few Dates and Events from Ethiopia," January 19, 1994. Joint Archives of Holland, Hope College.

alternate plan for them, and they instead directed PRMI's World Cassette Outreach program. This position took them on frequent trips to Africa and Asia in a variety of roles: as consultants, instructors, encouragers, and as "Mr. Fix-it." While still carrying these responsibilities, Harvey was the recipient of two honors. In 1987 he received his well-earned doctorate in missiology from Fuller Theological Seminary. His dissertation won him the Donald Anderson McGavran Award for excellence. (The treatise was subsequently published in book form under the title, *The World Council of Churches and the Demise of Evangelism.*) In 1979 he was elected president of General Synod of the Reformed Church in America.

Ten years later, still highly enthusiastic over the value and effectiveness of the cassette ministry, Harvey founded Audio Scriptures International (ASI), a program targeting people groups all over the world with special focus on displaced persons who have sought refuge outside their homelands.

PRMI and ASI merged in 1996 to become Audio Scripture Ministries, greatly increasing the scope of the cassette outreach.

So God, unfolding his grand design, expanded the vision born in Africa to become a dynamic global ministry.

To the Father be praise for the way in which he leads his workers from field to field—to plant, to water, to reap, in order that his full harvest may be realized in due season.

XVI
Still They Come—and Go

Although the times were unsettled and uncertain, Ethiopia still was accepting new missionaries. Three more RCA couples entered the country in 1975.

Al and Sue Schreuder came to Ethiopia with all the enthusiasm of youth under divine orders.

Al actually had spent a summer in 1968 with the Hoekstras at Godare to help with the hydram water system. Beyond that, it turned out to be a many-faceted short-term experience that exposed him to missionary life in the bush and revealed what serving in a cross-cultural situation was all about.

Most important, it was the summer that the Lord touched his heart and challenged him: "I remember lying awake at night, listening to the jungle sounds, thinking and praying about whether the Lord might want me to become involved. A fire for missions was kindled in me and a desire to serve him full time."[1]

God's protection in two accidents that summer—one having to do with a snapped cable and the other with a deadly snake—further confirmed Al's suspicion that the Lord had exciting plans for him if he would follow his beckoning hand.

---

[1] Al Schreuder, from a report, May 8, 1995. Joint Archives of Holland, Hope College.

In the spring of 1975, nearing the end of his second year at Western Theological Seminary, he and his wife, Sue, left for Selly Oak Colleges outside of Birmingham, England, for four months of missionary training under many fine teachers—Bishop Lesslie Newbigin among them. They had opportunity to make friends with people from many nations. They learned something about how to adjust culturally, and to see that the American way was not necessarily the only or the best way of doing things.

Al and Sue arrived in Ethiopia in mid-August 1975. Housing was at a premium, but happily there was room for them out at Good Shepherd School (GSS). While there, they became good friends of Bill and Jan Van Auken, an RCA couple from Holland, Michigan, who were teaching at GSS that year. (The Van Aukens had been volunteers at Omo River the previous year.)

(Jim and Betty Hoekstra also taught at GSS. From 1970 to 1973, Jim taught seventh- to ninth-grade math, social studies, and physical education. He coached basketball, soccer, and track and field as well. Betty was a school librarian. In 1975 they returned for another two years. This time, Jim headed up the athletics department. Betty was secretary to the principal.)

Verne and Lorraine Sikkema also happened to be in residence on the GSS compound at that time in a transitional situation. Al Schreuder remembers that they learned all of Verne's jokes and had to laugh "even the tenth time that we heard them." While not on the biblical list of spiritual gifts, Verne received the gift of humor, and no one ever left his company without enjoying a good laugh.

Laughter helped the Schreuders through the year of Amharic language study. Both were excellent students, at the head of their class. This paid off for Sue: when she missed her final exam because of the birth of their daughter Becky, her teachers decided she could skip the exam. But the number two student found that he was "allowed" to take his exam the following day!

That was also the year that Al played catcher for the inter-mission softball team:

> I remember the first team practice when they wanted to see if I could hit the ball. I was very nervous, as I didn't know more than one or two others on the team, and I was determined to exhibit my youthful strength.

I lined one of Verne's first pitches down the third base line, hitting an old man in the chest, knocking him down. Everyone was very concerned, since he was one of our coaches.

I approached him with great reluctance. Finally the old man rose to his feet, rubbing his chest. He turned and asked me if I had hit the ball.

"Yes," I weakly replied.

"Good," he said. "I'm glad we're on the same team. But next time, warn me so I have time to get out of the way!"

And Don McClure gave me an infectious grin that I was to come to love. It was the beginning of our friendship.[2]

A week after Becky was born, Al received a radio call from Harvey Hoekstra asking him to come to Teppi. The understanding had been that Al was to do the second year of his internship from Western Seminary under Harvey's tutelage, to learn all the ins and outs of the Teppi Tape Ministry, and the ups and downs of being a missionary.

It was at this point, however, that the Hoekstras had been reassigned to Godare and plans had to be changed. So Al packed up a few things, kissed his wife and baby, and caught an MAF plane to Teppi. The orientation was brief:

> Harvey gave me some keys, showed me around the place, demonstrated how some machinery worked, spent two hours talking over lunch, and then boarded the plane for the return flight to Jimma. I was on my own. Sue joined me three weeks later, accompanied by the Van Aukens who had helped her pack and came to help us get settled.
>
> Being on our own was both a blessing and a trial: a trial because I made some foolish mistakes; and a blessing because I learned quickly from my mistakes and was able to develop my own theology of mission work from personal experience.[3]

Here's one example, on the light side, of a lesson learned:

---

2 Ibid.
3 Ibid.

I couldn't get the kerosene fridge to work properly. Bill Van Auken suggested that we call Omo since Bob Swart was an expert on kerosene fridges. Bob agreed to talk with me at 9 a.m. after the regular broadcast. (Little did I know that anyone requesting a special radio call would have lots of eavesdroppers listening in. I think the whole mission heard!)

Bob reviewed the basic steps of refrigerator maintenance, and I assured him that I had tried them all several times. He then said to try turning the fridge over and then setting it back on its feet again. I asked if I should empty the fridge first or not. Bob replied, "That's up to your wife!" We all laughed.

Bill suggested that Bob might really be serious and perhaps we should try it. We emptied the fridge, turned it over, replaced it on its feet—and it worked perfectly! The mixing of the cooling fluids did the trick.

We spent the next year directing the Teppi Tape Ministry and recording the New Testament on to cassettes in five local languages: Mesengo, Keffa, Sheko, Amharic, and Oromo. We visited the several translators who were also evangelists in their home areas, flying with MAF to check on their ministries when they were not recording in Teppi. These same areas had regular bi-weekly visits from our medical team.

Not long after our arrival in Teppi, MAF flights were suspended for several months because of the government's refusal to renew their flying permits. Once the permissions were again granted, I had to visit all the airstrips by walking the length of them to check their condition before MAF could make any landings. It was while doing one of these checks that I got into trouble.

Two workers and I were flown to a strip that had already been checked and approved. During the next three days, we walked to three other strips, repairing holes and washouts. On the fourth day, MAF was to fly in to take us back to Teppi. What we did not know was that word had only recently reached this particular area informing the people that MAF did NOT have permission to fly. And anyone flying into the strip was to be arrested!

When I had seen the local governor just two weeks before to make sure we could repair the strips, he assured me that I did not need written permission; verbal permission was sufficient. He was, even then, in the process of sending letters to all the centers under his jurisdiction informing them that MAF could fly again. But the word had not yet reached this area!

The villagers, therefore, sent a message to the nearest police post, and the next morning we were arrested shortly before MAF's arrival. When the plane touched down, those on board were immediately arrested also, until they could prove that they had a valid permit to fly—which they were able to do. Then they loaded most of our equipment and left.

But we were still under arrest. We were marched that afternoon for about five hours to the nearest police post. The sergeant wanted us to sleep in the jail where the floor had just been resurfaced with mud and cow-dung. A sympathetic school teacher, however, invited us to spend the night at his house, assuming responsibility for our safety and care, and promising not to let us escape.

In his home, I at last began to understand the biblical custom of footwashing. A young servant boy came, removed our shoes and socks, and then gently washed our feet. It soothed and refreshed us. The entire time, I thought about Jesus as he washed the disciples' feet and how good it must have felt, though they surely experienced the same discomfiture I had at having someone else wash my feet.

During a delicious supper of Ethiopian food, and for a couple of hours afterwards, I debated the positive and negative aspects of democracy and communism with our young communist host. What an experience!

Early the next morning, a police corporal arrived to march us to the governor's village, over ten hours away. (We learned that the corporal was a believer from the Maji area. He was reluctantly serving in this remote outpost.) We could see that his rifle was heavy. Since our loads were light, we took turns carrying it—until we neared our destination.

We were about a quarter mile ahead of him when he shouted for us to wait for him. He was afraid we would embarrass him by carrying his rifle into the village while he straggled behind. So he took his weapon and we were marched into town "under guard."

The following morning I was taken before the governor who apologized to me for not having given me written permission two weeks before. He was really sorry about the whole episode.

That afternoon a passing MAF plane was contacted by radio. The pilot was able to fly us to Teppi as he was returning empty to his base in Jimma.

As the spring of 1977 progressed, it became increasingly obvious that our time in Teppi was limited. The local government officials were repeatedly asking for papers, explanations of our ministry, and copies of documents. It was also becoming more and more difficult to leave Teppi to visit the believers in outlying centers. Following many weeks of prayer, we decided to leave Teppi before the government forced our departure.

The last few days of our sojourn there, we lived in an emptied house. Evenings were spent in prayer with groups of believers who came to share their love with us. They asked to be remembered in our prayers. On the day we left, we turned over the house keys to the government representative who promised to "guard carefully" the mission property in our absence.

During our short term in Teppi, we learned many lessons, and we gained lifelong memories. We learned about worshiping in a Pentecostal-type church. We learned about sharing with nationals: sharing our possessions and also receiving from their limited stores what was given with open, generous hearts.

We learned about faithfulness in prayer, and healing through the Holy Spirit: miraculous healings of incurable diseases—and also the lack of healing of one of the most faithful prayer warriors, who was given grace to accept that the Lord was not going to heal her.

We learned about God's faithfulness in caring for his children through difficult times, and the oneness that can exist in the body of Christ.[4]

One of the last things that Al did at Teppi was to express in writing his faith and hope for the future of the church and the outreach centers:

4 Ibid.

As we leave Teppi to complete seminary, one verse seems to summarize all the thoughts and plans, sorrows and joys, mistakes and triumphs that we have experienced. It is found in 2 Timothy 2:2: "And what you have heard from me before many witnesses entrust to faithful men who will be able to teach others also."[5]

This verse explains one of my goals of the tape ministry: to train faithful men and women who will be able to teach and share with others also. We feel that this goal has been accomplished through God's power. There is a body of believers here in Teppi who will carry God's message long after the missionaries are gone.

Indeed, there are many in the Teppi Church of over two hundred who are able to lead others to Christ. When we first came, the elders of the church were a small and somewhat reticent group. But now they are leading services and teaching in the nearby Guri Church.

Beharu and others are teaching literacy so that people can read God's Word themselves. And there are many women who share the truths of the Bible with their friends and relatives after having heard these truths in the women's meetings on Wednesdays.

Kani Naro has several Sheko Bible study groups that meet regularly. He also leads a worship service in his home on Sundays. And Giramu Gabre is the lay pastor of a growing church of Keffa people at Shimarga. He continues to teach and preach effectively.

The work has spread well beyond the immediate vicinity of Teppi. In Meti, there is now some interest in starting services there. Others in Shosha are asking that someone come and teach them. And the Mocha people are still asking that a missionary or evangelist come and teach them about Jesus Christ.

[So, since the believers] have received training, tapes, and other materials to help them teach, now is the time for them to carry on God's work here.

We claim the promise of Philippians 1:6: "And I am sure that he who began a good work in you will bring it to completion at the day of Jesus Christ."[6] To God be the praise and glory.[7]

5 II Timothy 2:2, Revised Standard Version.
6 Philippians 1:6, New International Version.
7 Al Schreuder, "Indigenous Evangelism Will Continue," *Ethio-Echo*, Vol. 12, No. 4, March 1978: 7. Joint Archives of Holland, Hope College.

Al and Sue and baby Becky visited us at Omo River Post in April 1977, when Bob had the privilege of baptizing Becky, not in the river, but according to RCA custom. Becky also took her first steps to celebrate the occasion.

Al did complete his seminary training. After pastoring a church for a time, he and Sue were called to the RCA work in Chiapas, Mexico. The Lord blessed them with three daughters and a son.

The Doorenboses came to Ethiopia via missionary service in the Arab world.

Harvey Doorenbos grew up on a small farm in Morrison, Illinois. Life on the farm instilled practical, mechanical, and agricultural knowledge, as well as the blessings of godly parents who taught discipline, self-reliance, and the Christian way of life.

Margaret Hospers spent her childhood in a parsonage in central New York state. She and Harvey met at Hope College, and together they were led to consider career Christian service: Harvey, in medicine; Margaret, in teaching.

After Harvey finished surgical training at Butterworth Hospital in Grand Rapids, Michigan, they were assigned to the Arabian Gulf as missionaries of the RCA. They arrived there, with sons Dirk and Keith, in 1965. After language study, they made their home in Muscat, Oman.

Harvey wrote that they "thoroughly enjoyed the challenge of that work. However, oil revenues began to stimulate a very rapid and needed development in Oman, and, after 1974, my services were no longer essential to that country's medical program. We therefore accepted transfer in July 1975, to Dembi Dollo, Ethiopia"[8]—even though they were told that it might be for only two or three months because Americans were not appreciated by the new regime. However, they were able to stay for two years and made significant contributions in their areas of expertise: Harvey, as the only doctor/surgeon on the hospital staff for over a year; Margaret, as a teacher

[8] Harvey Doorenbos, "RCA, Church of Scotland, Serve With U.P.s at Dembi Dollo," *Ethio-Echo*, Vol, 12, No. 4, March 1978: 14. Joint Archives of Holland, Hope College.

at Bethel Evangelical Secondary School where she taught mathematics to grades seven through ten. Dirk and Keith were students at Good Shepherd School in Addis Ababa.

Margaret expressed their reactions soon after they arrived: "The whole family has fallen in love with Ethiopia and are grateful to have been transplanted here. The wonderful mission family in Dembi Dollo has made us feel at home. We pray that each of us may bring praise to the Lord through our lives and service."9

Jean R. Orr Memorial Hospital at Dembi Dollo was a busy place and for many years had filled a tremendous need in that largely rural community. Excerpts from Harvey's 1976 report reveal the scope of medical service in that part of the world:

> The most prevalent medical problems relate to intestinal parasites, filaria, skin infections, pregnancy, and nutrition. Public health, therefore, is of much greater importance to the community than hospital services. However, the hospital is very important for the more seriously ill and serves as a center for laboratory and x-ray studies, physician consultation, and training.
>
> The outpatient department attended to 24,000 patients....In addition, prenatal clinic was held one afternoon each week for an average of 60 women per clinic.
>
> 1,348 patients were admitted to the hospital....Of the 50 beds, 9 are in the isolation unit for tuberculosis....369 women delivered in the hospital, but 34 had stillborn babies. With 11 sets of twins and one set of triplets, there were 288 live births.
>
> The laboratory maintained its active pace through the year, doing more than 20,000 tests....The x-ray department provided us with 369 sets of x-rays....Practical training is being given to more of our staff to have more technicians able to handle the x-ray machine.
>
> The department of surgery has one major operating room and one minor room. The minor room is used for outpatient surgery, certain diagnostic procedures, and most orthopedic procedures. Infant circumcisions and tooth extractions were the most frequently done procedures....

9 Ibid.

The consultations and eye surgery done during the one-week visit of an ophthalmologist were greatly appreciated by the community....A dentist plans to come in the spring for about six weeks to teach dressers the basic care of teeth and proper methods of extraction....

Finally, our greatest thanks is to God Almighty who has blessed and directed this work. The healing that has been experienced is from the mercy and goodness of the Great Physician. Physical healing is only a part of the goal of this hospital and only a part of what the Great Physician wants to give. Each of us needs spiritual health as much as physical health, and we endeavor to share the good news that Jesus Christ has come to give every person this spiritual wholeness. We pray for an even closer relationship between hospital and church to more effectively express this wholeness of body and spirit that is the Spirit of Jesus.[10]

The same year that the Doorenboses were relocated from Oman to Ethiopia, Paul and Marcia Leemkuil were accepted as missionaries of the Reformed Church. They, too, were assigned to work at Dembi Dollo, and arrived in September 1975.

Paul had majored in mathematics at Northwestern College in Orange City, Iowa, but because he had grown up on a farm and had expressed an interest in gardening on his application form, he was assigned to teach agriculture at the Bethel Evangelical Secondary School (BESS). It proved to be an interesting, challenging, and exciting assignment as he worked with BESS students on a variety of farming projects, which included building a dam for an irrigation system and plowing with oxen.

Marcia, who had received her R.N. diploma from the Sioux Valley School of Nursing in 1971, was the nurse at the hospital, working with Harvey Doorenbos. In 1975–1976 Harvey was the only doctor and Marcia the only R.N. working with a good staff of Ethiopian dressers. Besides helping with medical treatments and in surgery, she also kept inventories, unpacked supplies, and saw that medications got to the dispensing units. Those were busy and satisfying days for her.

10 Ibid. 15, 16.

Marcia fondly remembered a little boy named Rufael who had club feet. His parents had abandoned him; the hospital was the only home he knew. Marcia also cared for *Keis* (pastor) Gidada during his last days. *Keis* Gidada Solon had been one of seven children in the Solon family, all of whom were struck down with smallpox in 1906. Of the seven siblings, Gidada alone survived, but he had become completely blind. He lived as a beggar, but begging was not God's purpose for Gidada's life.

The American Mission opened work in Dembi Dollo in 1920. Through contacts with the mission, and by the power of the Holy Spirit, Gidada's spiritual eyes were opened, and he beheld his Savior. He became a witnessing Christian, traveling on his mule along the trails of Oromo country, taking the message of salvation to even the remotest village.

During the Italian occupation [1936–1941] when missionaries had to leave Ethiopia, Gidada's ministry became even more earnest and urgent. *Keis* Mamo joined him and the two were used mightily by the Spirit. New communities of believers sprang up around the countryside. The handful of Christians which the missionaries had left behind became a body numbering in the thousands.

Like Paul, Gidada suffered severely for his faith. Like the first century Christians, the new believers persevered through persecution, strengthened by Gidada's example.

Through all his years, *Keis* Gidada was a faithful pastor, active in evangelism and counseling. He often visited patients in the mission hospital, making rounds from bed to bed with a word of comfort and encouragement.

Keis Gidada will be sorely missed by all upon whom his words fell as a benediction.... But we also rejoice for him, knowing that after seventy years of blindness, he is at last on the "other side of darkness," face to face with Jesus Christ whom he loved and served so well.

To God be the praise for the long life and Christian ministry of *Keis* Gidada Solon![11]

---

[11] "God Calls Pastor Home,"*Ethio-Echo*, Vol. 12, No. 3, February 1977: 1. Joint Archives of Holland, Hope College. (His story is told in an autobiography entitled *The Other Side of Darkness*. The narrative, dictated by *Keis* Gidada, was recorded by Presbyterian missionaries Ruth McCreery and Martha Vandevort, and edited by Dr. Marion Fairman.)

Keis Gidada's son, Dr. Solomon Gidada, was at that time the director of the Bethel Evangelical Secondary School. Solomon also was a good friend to the missionaries at Dembi Dollo, and he often entered into their activities.

During the Christmas break of 1975, a small expedition was organized, a sort of orientation trip for stalwart new personnel. It was to be done on foot down the long escarpment to the town of Gambela (where, twenty-five years before, Bob Swart and Harvey Hoekstra had had pork and beans and corn-on-the-cob for breakfast with Captain Dibble). They would see another part of Ethiopia where American Mission folks were at work. Paul and Marcia Leemkuil, BESS teacher JoAnn Griffith, Dr. Solomon, and a few students who came from that lowland area made up the company.

Marcia remembered the beautiful country they walked through that first afternoon; the black darkness that surrounded them as night fell; the fear as they crossed a wildly rushing river on a fallen tree—in the dark; and the roughness of the trail as they stumbled over exposed tree roots. "Keep following" was the watchword as they pressed on through the night—until at 2 a.m. they "stopped under a mango tree and collapsed for a few hours of needed rest."

At dawn, they continued on their way down the escarpment, walking through soft sand and being nibbled mercilessly by sandflies—finally arriving at Gambela about 3 p.m. They were all tired and thirsty, but had the satisfaction of having accomplished the feat.

In Gambela, they observed mission partners at work: Presbyterians Dan and Jane Reynolds and Connie Hall in their medical outreach; Marian Farquhar and Robb McLaughlin in the areas of literacy and evangelism. They also "participated in a joyful worship service with Nuer and Anuak people."

From Gambela, the Leemkuils flew to Gore and taxied on to Mettu for a brief visit with Arlene Schuiteman. They were encouraged by fellowship with her as she shared about her work and held a Bible study in her home.

The next lap of this Christmas-break orientation trip took Paul and Marcia to Addis Ababa on a crowded bus over rough roads through the scenic countryside, all to the accompaniment of loud, blasting music.

> This was our first visit to the city since our arrival. There was so much to discover as we met other missionaries and learned about

their work—as well as to find out for ourselves where to look for household necessities and supplies for the agricultural projects.

We returned to Dembi Dollo with one hundred hybrid chicks which we hoped to raise and distribute in the community. We mothered them all the way, holding them on our laps lest they get too cold in the flight. But for all the tender care we gave them, in flight and at Dembi Dollo, only about a third survived; the hybrids just weren't as hardy as the local variety. But the survivors grew and were strong and impressive.[12]

The hens were just beginning to lay when something came up that made it necessary to distribute them immediately: the Leemkuils' temporary visas expired before they had been granted permanent ones. So they had to leave the country in order to be granted new temporary visas.

They were advised to take a short holiday in Kenya, which they did. They took advantage of this "enforced vacation" to visit some of Kenya's well-known game parks, thinking that they might never again have such an opportunity.

Word finally reached them that their visas had been granted. They returned to Dembi Dollo, taking with them garden seeds from Kenya, and fruit trees, grapevines, and strawberries they had found at a nursery in Addis Ababa. They hoped that the produce from these plants would improve the diet in the BESS dining hall and possibly bring in some needed income for the school. The gardens were flourishing.

The church still was spiritually strong and alive in spite of coercion on the part of the local officials to force young people to attend political meetings that were scheduled at the same hour as church services.

The school year was over when Paul and Marcia received word that once again their permanent visas were being denied. They would have to leave Ethiopia, and this time they should be prepared to stay out of the country for a while.

In Addis Ababa we were invited by the Dan Reynolds family to join them on a two-vehicle safari through southern Ethiopia and down into Kenya....The third evening, we arrived at the border town of

<hr/>

[12] Marcia Leemkuil, from a report to the author, April 12, 1994. Joint Archives of Holland, Hope College.

Moyale. In the heat of the night, on a bed of sand out under the stars, we were reminded just how far out in the middle of nowhere we really were. Yet God's presence was there and his protective hand was holding ours.

How does one describe the northern territory of Kenya with its wind, heat, sand, and unending miles of barrenness?

When we arrived at a remote town called Garba Tula, we learned that the missionaries serving in this mission/government school had been praying specifically for a math teacher and a nurse to join their staff. We were given an invitation to serve as that teacher and nurse for as long as we were available.

Once again, God had provided. He had opened a door where we had seen none!

We set up housekeeping in half of the school's clinic building. I arranged the other half as an infirmary and clinic for the students.

Paul was introduced to his classes and the Kenya curriculum math texts. And I was also asked to teach some religion classes.

Our time at Garba Tula proved to be a rewarding experience as we both felt that God used us to impact the lives of the young people there.[13]

One "extra curricular" event stood out for them:

The rains came as a refreshing relief from the heat and dust, but our river grew and grew, not only in size but also in power. When a bus came through at night and attempted to cross on the concrete (Irish) bridge, it was swept over onto its side, tossing the passengers about and throwing some of them out of the vehicle.

At midnight Paul and I found ourselves part of the rescue effort. While the men threw out lifelines to pull people from the swirling waters, I received permission to open up the infirmary and take people in for the night. Our small room was soon packed with cold, wet bodies. We did what we could to make them comfortable, sharing blankets, and giving them *chai* (hot tea with lots of milk and sugar) to drink. Not knowing how to talk with them, this was all we could do to show them God's love.[14]

13 Ibid.
14 Ibid.

The Leemkuils' permanent visas for Ethiopia finally came through. They arrived back in Dembi Dollo just in time for Christmas, 1976.

> We slipped right back into our previous positions. The undercurrents of political unrest were becoming more noticeable. We were still quite free to do our mission work, but some precautions were being taken. For example, when we made a cycle trip down the escarpment to Gambela during Christmas vacation, Connie Hall asked me if I would like to join her on an immunization safari in March. She had been advised not to make medical trips alone.
>
> In March Verne Sikkema flew me down to Gambela in one of MAF's Cessnas. After final shopping and packing, Connie, her Anuak helper named Paul, and I were off the following morning to travel across the hot, desolate plains in her little Honda truck. In each village, word was sent out that there would be a clinic that day with immunizations for the children. Paul helped Connie teach health lessons. Bible stories followed.[15]

They pitched their tent close to the village. From that vantage point, they were able to observe the tribal dancing games at the end of the day that included feats of high jumping—and to hear the accompanying sing-song chants. This was the tribe's evening entertainment.

During the evening, too, the herders returned with their cattle. Dung-fires were lit. Children rolled in the ashes of old fires and adults smeared the powdery ash on their bodies as an insect repellent to keep the voracious mosquitoes away.

When it was dark enough, Connie and Marcia would go down to the river to wash away the dust of the day. One of them stood guard, on the lookout for lurking crocodiles.

The schedule continued village by village until they were nearly at the Sudan border. There they found old friends Robb McLaughlin and Marian Farquhar busy at work in literacy and evangelism.

The safari soon was over. It had been exciting for Marcia to have had a part in this outreach and to see people eager to learn to read and equally eager to hear the gospel.

Not long after her return to Dembi Dollo, her husband Paul was invited to visit Adura where Chuck and Mary Alice Jordan served among the Nuers

15 Ibid.

in the areas of evangelism, medicine, and agriculture. Here Paul was able to see another station in operation and to experience a bit of another culture. It was a joy and an eye-opener to see the people and the way of life in the lowlands. What they had been exposed to in the highlands was totally different.

During the spring of 1977, Marcia was expecting their first child and had hoped to deliver in Dembi Dollo before their anticipated furlough. MAF, however, soon would be leaving Ethiopia, and the Ethiopian Airlines schedule was sporadic. Therefore, it seemed sensible for them to leave as soon as possible.

So they packed up, closed their house, and went to the Doorenboses' home for the night, anticipating their departure the next day on a DC3. Then came a startling order:

Paul would not be allowed leave Dembi Dollo. He was being held under town arrest which permitted him to go only to and from the school. Our mission was also in the process of turning over the hospital and the mission compound to the government, in response to their demand. Suddenly it seemed that all we had feared—and rejected as impossible—was actually happening.

Although it was not easy to leave Paul, it seemed the only sensible way to go. A pregnant woman, or possibly having a newborn baby to care for, would surely complicate any emergency evacuations. Besides, the Doorenboses were now planning to go to Addis Ababa in two weeks for Dirk's graduation and then continue on to the United States.

That night, with tears of frustration, and wondering what the future held, Paul and I repacked our bags. Questions plagued our minds: How long would he have to stay? What had he done wrong? What would be required of him?

The next morning we learned that the Ethiopian Airlines flight had been cancelled. In fact, the next three or four flights failed to come in. Would the Doorenboses miss Dirk's graduation? Would I still be permitted to fly? We kept our ears tuned for the deep drone of an approaching DC3, ready with bags packed at all times.

Finally, two weeks later, the plane was coming "today." We drove to the police station for our routine clearance to leave. But our clearance this time was anything but routine.

After checking through all our baggage for anything they thought we should not be taking out of Dembi Dollo, the "Red Guard" settled on our slides and proceeded to look through each one in their dark, dingy office to see if we had photos of events that they considered harmful to their cause.

Now we began to wonder if we would make it to the airstrip in time for the plane. Soon the DC3's deep drone was within hearing distance, and still we did not have our release papers.

Finally, in desperation, I entered the office and pleaded my case: I needed to fly now and go home to my family in the United States. I'm not sure if it was sympathy for me, or if they were just ready to let us go, but the release papers were obtained.[16]

(Margaret Doorenbos' interpretation of the capitulation to Marcia's pleas was that the officers were afraid that Marcia might give birth right there in the police station. Margaret also added that she and two Ethiopian teachers were permitted to go to Addis Ababa with the understanding that Dr. Solomon Gidada would be imprisoned if these school staff members did not return. They did return.)

It was a fast trip to the airport. We made the plane, and Harvey, Margaret, and I were on our way to Addis Ababa where we attended Dirk's graduation. It was the last senior class to graduate from Good Shepherd School.

Then I flew on to the United States, arriving in mid-June. There at home, I was surrounded by my loving, supportive family.[17]

Marcia described the long weeks for those left behind at Dembi Dollo:

These were the days of making settlements to government demands, turning over properties, withstanding a bombardment of anti-American sentiment and complaints—and hours of quiet boredom for Paul as he finished existing work, the school year ended, and the time of waiting was extended.

On July 15, 1977, Tamar was born. A telegram was sent to Paul, but he did not learn of his daughter's birth until the eighteenth, our

16 Ibid.
17 Ibid.

fifth wedding anniversary. It would still be six weeks until Paul would finally be released.

But even his departure was not without suspense. After takeoff from Dembi Dollo, Paul, in conversation with Ato [Mr.] Gutama of the American Mission office in Addis Ababa, was cautioned by look and discreet gesture to hold his tongue. Later a thunderstorm threatened to make them turn back. But God's hand of protection was at work, and they reached Addis Ababa safely.

In short order, final arrangements were made for Paul to leave Ethiopia. He was soon on his way home to us.

A chapter in mission history was ending.[18]

18 Ibid.

XVII
More Farewells

"On March 27, 1977, the Rev. W. Don McClure entered the realms of glory. He now abides for eternity with his heavenly Father whom he loved and served so wholeheartedly for so many years."[1]

The radio transmitter (RT) crackled the morning of March 27, 1977, as we waited for the scheduled mission "net" to begin. When Harold Kurtz's voice came on from Addis Ababa, the news he gave was beyond belief: Don McClure had been shot and killed by Somali guerrillas at Gode in the Ogaden region of southeast Ethiopia!

In the late 1960s, while Don was general secretary of the American Mission in Ethiopia, Emperor Haile Selassie asked him that personnel of the mission "supervise the medical and educational work in the city of Gode, which was just now being built."[2]

Over Don's protests concerning personnel cutbacks and budget cuts, and his suggestion that perhaps another mission would be more able to undertake this task, the emperor merely "smiled gently and said, 'I am not asking the other missions, I am asking the American Mission to conduct the work along the lines of your Anuak project on the Sudan border.'"[3]

---

1 *Ethio-Echo*, Vol. 12, No. 4, March 1978: 1. Joint Archives of Holland, Hope College.
2 Charles Partee, *Adventure in Africa*, (Grand Rapids, Michigan: Zondervan Publishing House, 1990) 395.
3 Ibid.

To make a long and fascinating story short, Don and Lyda, upon retirement in 1971, became volunteers in mission and spent the rest of their years, even after the overthrow and death of the emperor, carrying out his wishes at Gode.

Now, only days before this couple was planning to retire to the United States, a bullet took Don's life.

In the final issue of *Ethio-Echo* that was published in the United States in 1978, Lyda and Don Jr. (also a missionary in Ethiopia) shared some of their thoughts:

> Although we, and many around the world, feel the tremendous loss of a husband, father, and tireless, energetic, and obedient servant of our Lord, we feel that God's tender and powerful hand reached down to lead him to his reward that night of March 27. The Somali guerrillas, who thought that they had the power of life and death in their hands, were only pawns of our loving Father's will.
>
> We feel it appropriate that Don should die and be buried among those whom he loved and served at Gode. The simple but moving ceremony at his grave struck deep into the hearts of the hundreds who were present.
>
> Many asked, "Why leave his body here among his murderers?" The reply is simply that these are the ones to whom he was sent and whom he loved. His death was part of his life, and as such, we are confident that "my Word will not return unto me void." HALLELUJAH!...
>
> Don would have said this is not the end, but the beginning. A time to face the odds with courage, to expand our vision, to renew and redouble our efforts; a time for strength and decisiveness, a time for obedience; a time to hold up the burden of a torn world and see not murderers, but God's children in need.[4]

And in that spirit, we have woven into the tapestry of this story the last bright thread of Don McClure's life as it touched ours. Humanly speaking, no other person could have had such a remarkable influence in bringing together our two churches in ministry in Africa—and in being instrumental

[4] Lyda McClure and Don Jr., "Many Pay Tribute to Don McClure," *Ethio-Echo*, Vol. 12, No. 4, March 1978: 1, 2. Joint Archives of Holland, Hope College.

in opening doors for further service as curtains were drawn behind us. This narrative hardly could have been chronicled without Don as a key figure.

Throughout the mission, Don's death was uppermost in everyone's mind. It was hard to take it in: that such vitality, such lively enthusiasm could have been snuffed out so precipitously. Don had gone to Glory—but we were still here. And there was still so much to do.

Thompson Gac and his family had moved from Omo River Post in early 1976. Thompson now ran the clinic at Adura River Post where the Jordans (formerly of Nasir and Akobo in) were stationed. We missed Thompson sorely; he had been a colleague in the truest sense of the term. In September of that year, I wrote to our children: "We continue to miss that family very much. Thompson was such a friend and advisor to Dad. He knew how the Gelebs think and was able to help Dad in so many ways. And Nyaluol was a good friend to me, too."

But they had longed to return to their people. Though we were sad to see them go, we were thankful for the six years they had been with us, and they left with our blessing.

So Bob once again had the responsibility of the clinic on his shoulders for the next several months. But before his shoulders sagged under the burden, the Lord provided a highly qualified, experienced person to take over this demanding work: none other than our good friend from Sudan days, Lillian Huisken.

After leaving in 1964, Lillian served variously in Eritrea; at the mission hospital in Muscat, Oman; as matron at the hospital in Mettu, Ethiopia; at Pokwo, Ethiopia, among the Anuaks; and then back to Oman where she was the nursing superintendent of a maternity hospital.

"But in June of 1976, she again heard the call of God to return to her first love, Africa. She now was sent to work with Robert and Morrie Swart at the Omo River station in Ethiopia."[5]

It took several months for Lillian's visa to be processed. But at last it was granted. It took an additional two months, however, for her to make the

---

[5] Eugene Heideman, "When the Missionary Leaves: The Mission Goes On" (a mimeographed paper of three pages). Joint Archives of Holland, Hope College.

journey from Addis Ababa to Omo River because small planes had been grounded, and hope ebbed and flowed as to their status. But finally, at the end of October, she was able to come by another means, and we welcomed her to Geleb country with thanksgiving.

Since Lillian had studied Amharic during her previous stint in Ethiopia, she was able to communicate with Lokwar, her Geleb assistant and interpreter. Together they made a fine team, both at the clinic and in village visitation. We were so grateful to God that he had provided a professional again to carry on this ministry at Omo.

Another RCA couple was to have joined us to supervise the Food From Wind project. John and Caryl Busman were appointed in 1976 and had gone to Selly Oak Colleges in England, in hopes that their visa would be forthcoming. We kept hearing that the permission papers lacked only one signature.

But that signature was never penned—and the Busmans went to Kenya instead. We were so disappointed. However, God had his plans for us all firmly in mind and under control. All would be well.

In an April 1977 newsletter, I updated our friends and supporting churches on several facts of the Omo River program:

> The wind at Omo continues to blow, and the windmills pump water out of the river, mostly to irrigate fruit trees this time of year. The Gelebs have just harvested their annual crop of sorghum grown in their traditional bottomland gardens along the river. But when their stored grain diminishes, farmers will again begin to think of planting corn and beans in their windmill gardens, all of which are on higher riverbanks. Each year a few new people ask for mills. Thanks to the generous response of the churches last year, they are available.
>
> Mission dependence upon Missionary Aviation Fellowship was brought into sharp focus last fall when the Ethiopian government grounded their planes for three months. Ironically, Ethiopians, more than missionaries, suffered from the lack of MAF services. Many sick people could not be flown from mission clinics to

hospitals, for even emergency flights were not permitted. Ethiopian evangelists serving in remote areas were without supplies for several weeks. The theme of mission RT broadcasts during that period was "How to get from here to there"—back to the good old days of traveling by mule and shank's mare in some areas.

Everyone rejoiced when the ban was lifted in mid-December and Cessna wings were flying again.

Our Ethiopian teacher, Timothy Jerkab, is with us again for the fourth year. Lowland country is the end of the earth to most highlanders, and each year when Timothy tells us he'll be back, we know that his decision has been God-directed. This year, he brought with him his bride of three months. Hiwan (which in Amharic means Eve) has had a fifth-grade education—a good qualification for a teacher's wife. She also knows some English and is learning more as she attends my English class each morning along with three Geleb students.

Enrollment at the school has doubled this year, which is encouraging. But when there were only six on the roll last year, you can see that it isn't a flourishing institution yet. Slowly, slowly!

Interest is high in the shop classes Bob has twice a week with the older students. First they made bow saws. Then they used their saws to make a workbench under a tree near the school. A wood vise was the next project. Others of an equally practical nature are lined up for the future.

The school garden is lush with papaya trees, mangoes, guavas, and bananas. Corn, peanuts, and sweet potatoes are coming. So the boys have a hearty snack every morning. We're sure these good taste treats they're becoming accustomed to now will influence at least a few future farmers of Ethiopia.

A few weeks ago, Akol arrived here after a two-day walk from Ileret in Kenya. Akol is half Geleb and half Turkana (a tribe just over the southern border west of Lake Turkana). He worked here for many years. He became a Christian. Three years ago, he returned to Kenya to look for work in his own country.

Lately he has been working at a new Africa Inland Mission outpost at Ileret. Many Gelebs live in that area. At our church service that Sunday, Akol taught our little congregation three Christian songs which he had translated from Turkana into Geleb. The new songs went over big!

But his main purpose in coming was to ask for a tape player and several cassettes of Christian messages in Geleb. So, a couple of days later, with a bag of personal belongings over one shoulder and a tape player over the other, he set off again for Ileret to share these treasures with the Gelebs on the Kenya side of the border.

In these uncertain days, it is a comfort to be reminded (as we were, albeit unconsciously, by Akol) that missionaries are expendable—that God does not leave himself without a witness. Peter and John were "uneducated, common men," but people "recognized that they had been with Jesus."[6] And that, after all, is the highest qualification for effective service.

The month of May brought more uncertainty. Though MAF had been flying since December, calls upon their services had dropped considerably. Many stations with itinerant outreach programs had had to be closed down due to local harassment. It seemed increasingly likely, too, that all MAF planes might be confiscated by the Ethiopian government.

Tom Frank from MAF's London office was asked to come and assess the situation. "On arrival, Tom found the consensus of the missions and of our own staff was that MAF should leave....Staying could no longer effectively help missions or churches; the restrictions were too many."[7]

So application was made to the government for permission to fly MAF's five planes out of the country.

On May 9, Harold Kurtz flew down to Omo River Post for a brief time to hear about our immediate future. Without MAF in the picture, the situation at Omo could become untenable. What was our thinking, and that of all the staff, on this matter?

---

[6] Acts 4:13, Revised Standard Version
[7] Stuart King, *Hope Has Wings*, (London: Marshall Pickering, Imprint of Harper Collins Publishers, 1993) 247.

The school year was nearly over, so teacher Timothy felt it would be well for him to fly home to Ghimeera country while he could. Besides, his wife had preceded him in order to be in her parental home for the birth of their first child.

On April 30, I had been busy getting breakfast and suddenly realized I was a few minutes late in turning on the RT. I rushed to do so and heard Dr. Mary's voice from Ghimeera (Mizan Tafari) saying, "Morrie, what do you mean by being late when I am just bursting with news!" The news was that Hiwan had given birth to a son early that morning.

Timothy was almost speechless with joy when we told him. He had dreamed that he had a son, so his dream had come true. Two or three days later, a message came from Hiwan asking Timothy, according to Ghimeera custom, to name the baby. Timothy said, "His name is Ephraim after Joseph's second son." Ephraim means: "God has made me fruitful in the land of my affliction." Timothy's "affliction" was that he was there at Omo without his wife and child. But MAF's tenuous presence in Ethiopia would unite the family sooner than Timothy thought.

It was about time for Lillian Huisken's furlough (counting the years she had been in Oman). So she also decided that it was time for her to go. And Ted and Dolly Pollock, who had planned to spend some weeks with us finishing up various projects before their retirement, came to the same conclusion, especially because of Dolly's health. She'd had surgery for a brain tumor seven years before. She was doing well, but was on constant medication. It would not do for them to be stranded at Omo indefinitely.

As for Bob and me, Harold agreed at that time that it would be acceptable for us to stay on. Our larder was well stocked. There was still so much that needed to be done—which would always be the case, of course. And all was peaceful and non-threatening on the Omo. So with Harold's blessing, we elected to remain for the foreseeable future.

On May 19, their last flight to Omo River Post, MAF whisked our friends up and away. In a May 22 letter to our family, we wrote:

> All American Mission staff have pulled out of Adura, Gilo, Godare, Teppi, Surma, Chebera, and Maji. We heard Mary Alice Jordan counsel Thompson on the radio from Addis to be careful with the medicines he has [at Adura] because there may not be anymore. It is a sad situation, and sadder still, Ethiopia is becoming another country of faceless masses.

The Swedish Philadelphia Mission, located about fifty miles north of Omo at Kibbish, also had made the decision to remain. But the director thought personnel should leave for several months and make only periodic visits to encourage Ethiopian staff. So, without these good friends in the area, we were left somewhat "higher and drier." But we had no qualms.

The day came for MAF to leave Ethiopia. Permission finally had come through...

...in answer to many prayers....It seemed a miracle....But the planes weren't out of the country yet.

Three aircraft from Jimma flew up and joined two in Addis Ababa. It was the very last day of May when the planes gathered in front of the control tower to take off. Seppo Kurkola [one of the pilots] went to hand in the flight plans. The controller studied the stamped and signed permissions from the Civil Aviation Department.

"*Ishi, ishi*" (OK, OK), he said. "Everything seems to be in order." He paused and looked up. "But you want to take five aircraft out. You can't leave just like that! I must confirm these permissions before I let you go."

Suspense. He dialed on the old black telephone. He managed to get through to the Civil Aviation Department. A conversation in Amharic followed. He put the phone down and smiled, "You may go!"

The planes taxied out to the take-off point and stood in line, one behind the other. The first plane called for clearance from the tower. It didn't come at first. Then at last it did. The second plane called for its clearance. But now the tower replied, "Just go, go, go." The controller seemed in a hurry. He didn't want to wait for any more formalities.

The five planes were soon flying in loose formation south-westward out of Addis Ababa, an unusual sight and sound in the early morning skies. Ethiopians below looked up and wondered what was happening.

As the capital was left behind, our pilots listened to their radios, hoping there would be no call ordering them to return. Fortunately, none came. Towards the southern border of Ethiopia, however, other calls did come. Most people who had seen the planes flying over would not have known what it meant, but Bob and Morrie Swart, the missionaries at isolated Omo, knew all too well. MAF had been their lifeline.

"Mike Alpha Fix, Mike Alpha Fox," came Morrie's voice. She was using the MAF call sign as she made contact with the planes on the mission frequency. "This is Omo River station. We are sad to see you all leaving, but we are grateful you're able to get your planes out safely. We're praying for you. Good-bye."

Other stations came on the air. They'd been listening out, too. Their voices joined in the sad farewell.

Seppo told me a long time later: "I don't think I've ever been so moved as by those messages that day."

The next day one of Kenya's leading newspapers, the *East African Standard*, had a front page banner headline: "Five Mystery Planes Arrive from Ethiopia." It was a while before the Nairobi authorities understood what had happened.[8]

That day, May 31, 1977, was indeed a sad one for all who had been served so faithfully, selflessly, and with unfailing cheerfulness for so many years by this remarkable organization. We ourselves had depended on MAF pilots and planes, in both Sudan and in Ethiopia, for twenty-seven years. They had been a vital link to the outside world—for mail, supplies, guests, medical needs, and personal transport. Each plane was a familiar "bird"; each pilot, a loved friend.

Happily, this was not the end of our relationship.

[8] Ibid. 248, 249.

XVIII
Last Days at Omo

MAF was gone.

But we still had our radio transmitter that gave us daily contact with the mission in Addis Ababa. It helped us keep abreast of what was going on in the capital, both in the political arena and at mission headquarters. How grateful we were that this means of communication still was possible.

Now we looked forward to some extra time at Omo. We wondered if God was giving us this opportunity in order to get back to our prime reason for being there. In a letter to our mothers, dated May 23, 1977, I wrote:

> The windmill project, worthy as it is, has of necessity taken too much of Bob's time because we have not been able to get more personnel in here to take it over. There is not too much to do now on the new mills that Ted Pollock prepared for assembling. Then we are going to concentrate on getting some new tapes ready with Scripture and messages. I started working on this already this morning. There won't be any way that the people can get new batteries for the tape players after we leave, but if they are used well, and enough people hear them, it will have been worth the effort.
>
> While Waryaluk (former schoolboy, now a teacher in a village school down in the Omo delta) is here this month, Bob is going to use him and a couple of others in going over some Scripture verses

that were translated a long time ago. They no doubt need to be revised. They'll also be working on making the above-mentioned tapes....Waryaluk and Lokwar (who helped Lillian Huisken in the clinic) know some Amharic. So, with the Amharic Bible and the English Bible and everyone's knowledge of the Geleb language, they ought to get along fairly well, at least with the basics.

The small group of believers—some fifty in number—that we would be leaving behind eventually, would be in special need of this material for continued teaching and encouragement in their Christian walk. Following in the Way amid traditional influences would not be easy. But we were confident that elders Achew and Koriye, the most mature members of the Geleb church, would be guided by the Holy Spirit in being examples to the little flock.

On May 29, I wrote to our children:

> When we hear over the RT of all the problems that other folks are having at their stations, we marvel at the tranquillity we are enjoying here. We've had no "static" from anyone yet. We can only conclude that God is giving us some extra time, and we are trying to make the most of the opportunity. This week Dad hopes to finish the seven new windmills he and Ted were working on. He just has to assemble and install the intake of five of them now. I've started writing scripts and then Dad will get the material translated and put on tapes.
>
> The foreign presence in Ethiopia continues to dwindle, according to today's world news on BBC. All British, Egyptian, and American military attaches, and half of those in the U.S. diplomatic service, have been given seven days to leave the country. This is not surprising in light of the Ethiopian quest for Cuban and Russian assistance.

But for all the peacefulness of our situation and our hopes for further ministry, our time at Omo River Post was cut short—not by a directive from the government but by our mission's general secretary, Harold Kurtz.

Before the Kurtz family left Addis Ababa on June 5 for a three-month furlough, Harold suggested that, because of stepped up military activity in the country, it wouldn't be wise for us to remain. As the mission head, he felt responsible for our well being. We respected his judgment and were ready to bow to his counsel.

> We're sad at the prospect of leaving because it could well be that we won't see Omo and the Gelebs again, and we've been here almost as long as we were in Sudan. I didn't think we'd ever feel about Ethiopia as we did about Sudan, but somehow our roots have gone down pretty deep. We still have seven years before retirement. If we don't return here, we wonder what God has in store for those years. We leave it to him; he'll show us in good time.
>
> Our bags are packed. Our folks in Addis Ababa are working on getting a chartered plane to take us out sometime this week.

We were told that a plane would be coming for us on June 9. However:

> On June 8, the district administrator from Jinka arrived on the opposite bank of the Omo. He shouted over to Bob that he wanted his Land Rover ferried across the river so that he could go on to Maji for a meeting. The mission ferry, prefabricated by friends at Trinity Reformed Church in Holland, Michigan, and powered by an outboard motor, was the only means of transporting cars across the river, and Bob was the only safe operator.
>
> Bob informed the official that, while he'd be more than willing to ferry him across, he'd have to find some other way to return because we were scheduled to leave the next day.

At that point, Bob was told, in no uncertain terms, "You'll have to change your plans!"

There was nothing else we could do. Bob ferried the Land Rover, the district administrator, and his entourage across, and they headed off to points north.

We sent word to Addis Ababa to cancel the next day's chartered flight and asked that they try to make another booking for two weeks hence. This delay gave us a bit more time to work on cassette tapes and new teaching messages. We were thankful. Actually it was rather idyllic, if not ideal, to be there by ourselves. I described those days in another letter:

June 19: Friday was the last day of school. Waryaluk had carried on in Timothy Jerkab's absence, and while we can't vouch for the quality of his work, there certainly was a good and happy spirit the whole month that Waryaluk was the *astamari* (teacher), and the students caused him no problems.

I went over to the school about noon and gave out a few little treasures that had once belonged to Jack and Dick—some tiny cars and a few tonettes (small black plastic flutes). The children seemed pleased.

This past week, Bob made and installed hand-pumps on all seven of the new mills that have been put up recently. Now when the wind doesn't blow, the farmers can irrigate anyway—with a bit more effort.

One afternoon, Bob went up to the mill sites and discovered that a strong whirlwind had rushed across the fields, whipped one of the windmill wheels right off the tower, and flung it into the river! It had also picked up a little boy and thrown him into the river. Fortunately, a Geleb man was there at the time. He rescued the boy and retrieved the wheel.

When Bob got there, the rescuer told him what he had done and asked, "Now what will you give me?" Oh, oh, oh! When will a Geleb do anything for anybody without thinking he should be paid for it? We know the answer: only when they know what Christ has done for them—and freely!

We hear that the administrator is back from his meeting. We hope he'll come here to the mission tomorrow to be ferried back across the river. When that is accomplished, we think we'll be free to go whenever a plane can come for us.

The administrator did come within the next few days. But before he would drive his Land Rover on to the ferry, he and some local officials demanded to have a tour of the mission. They wanted to know if the generator and our two dilapidated vehicles (the twelve-year-old International Scout and an ancient Jeep truck that had seen years of service at Maji before it was driven down in caravan in 1965) were in working order. They wanted to see every room in every building. For some reason, this did not include our house.

Satisfied that they had been shown all there was to see, those from Jinka made ready for the crossing. As soon as that was accomplished, the others asked Bob to take them back to the police post. We knew that this had been prearranged because they wanted to be sure that Bob before he left paid the tax on the mission land and teacher Timothy's education tax. Bob was well aware of this and had discussed the matter with our local administrator previously.

At any rate, Bob took the men upriver in the boat. The man from Jinka was there ahead of them. He invited Bob and the local official to a meal of *wat* and *injera* (Ethiopian hot pepper stew with spongy, flat bread).

Bob paid the taxes. Then the district administrator informed him that he must leave all keys for the mission buildings. It would be acceptable to leave them with the Gelebs we'd be asking to guard the place.

There was little hope now of our being able to return. Having to give up keys meant only one thing: Omo River Post would become the police post. Our hearts were heavy at the thought.

On June 25, a chartered Air Mula plane came to fly us to Addis Ababa. After loading up at the mission, we had to touch down at the police post five miles north in order to be given clearance for leaving. The police inspected all our luggage, every inch of the plane—even the hollows of the wheel wells—to be sure we weren't taking anything away that would be useful to them, such as typewriters, radios, or guns, the latter of which we'd thrown into the river months ago. When the search was over, we were off.

Because of fighting below us, the pilot flew at an altitude higher than usual. This necessitated using oxygen masks, which was an adventure in itself. Looking down on lush green farms nestled among the hills below us, it was difficult to believe that Ethiopia's beautiful countryside was the scene of battles and bloodshed. We were sore at heart for this lovely land.

A big parade celebrating the people's militia was being held that day in Addis Ababa. No vehicles were permitted on the streets except by special permission. Air Mula was able to get its Land Rover to come to the airport, and we were whisked to the nearby Mennonite guest house. Our mission had made reservations for us for one night. It was interesting to be there with others who were also on their way out. That common bond made us friends, literally, overnight.

At the American Mission the next day, we devoured mail. Among the letters was one from our daughter Merry with a note from her husband, Don

Hill. He reminded us to have faith to "leave one's work to be finished by those who've been planted with the Holy Spirit." That was such an encouraging word, reminiscent of the friend in Khartoum, Sudan, who had said fifteen years before, "They have expelled you, but they can't expel God."

The encouragement was needed especially in that revolutionary atmosphere where newspapers blared such headlines as: "Imperialists Conspire to Landlock Ethiopia"; "Call of the Revolutionary Motherland"; "Red Campaign to Crush White Terror"; "Imperialist Pressure Will Not Deter Ethiopia's Revolutionary Struggle."

In the midst of all this furor, it was heartening, too, to remember Psalm 2:

> Why do the nations conspire, and the peoples plot in vain?
>
> The kings of the earth set themselves, and the rulers take counsel together, against the Lord and his anointed, saying,
>
> "Let us burst their bonds asunder, and cast their cords from us."
>
> He who sits in the heavens laughs; the Lord has them in derision.
>
> Then he will speak to them in his wrath, and terrify them in his fury, saying,
>
> "I have set my king on Zion, my holy hill."[1]

Sometime after the emperor was deposed, I said to Bob, "Please, if we must leave Ethiopia, let's not go to another country; let's just go back to the States."

A man of few words and of a cautious nature, his response was merely, "Oh?" He was not about to commit himself—or us—to a promise. God's will and purpose certainly would have to be considered.

As it was, when the time of our leave-taking actually came, neither of us was prepared to bid farewell to Africa. Our thoughts rambled in unison:

"What about the Africa Inland Mission's outreach work among the Gelebs at Ileret, Kenya—that place up near the Ethiopian border—where Akol had come from when he wanted cassette tapes? Maybe they could use our help

[1] Psalm 2:1–6, Revised Standard Version.

there. Why not make our years of Geleb experience available in another part of the tribe? Let's go see!"

Was the Lord directing our thoughts? We had to find out. So our first stop on our homeward way was Nairobi, the capital city of Kenya.

One noon we had lunch at the Jacaranda Hotel with two couples of the Africa Inland Mission: Don and Doris McKenzie and Howard and Doris Andersen. Don at that time was director of personnel in AIM's Nairobi office. The Andersens were missionaries at Gatab in the Northern Frontier District.

We had a delightful visit. Bob and I learned something of the nature of the Africa Inland Mission; our new friends, in turn, heard a bit about our background, particularly of the last few years at Omo River Post. Then we posed our question. It was an exciting moment; the answer, in large measure, would determine our immediate future.

"Would the Africa Inland Mission welcome us in assisting in their outreach work among the Gelebs way up there in the Northern Frontier District at Ileret?"

Don's reply startled us.

"You know, Howard and Doris, in addition to their busy program at Gatab, have been making the long trek up to Ileret every couple of weeks. We as a mission have been praying for seven years for the Lord to send someone to live there!"

What further confirmation did we need?

We left Nairobi with a song of praise—and in company with Keith Doorenbos. His parents were on their way home for a brief furlough. Because Good Shepherd School now was to become the Rest and Recreation Center for Ethiopian troops, Keith was on his way back to Kodaikanal School in India which he had attended when his parents were serving in Oman. We flew together as far as Bombay, where our ways parted. We were somewhat bewildered by the milling crowds. But nothing bothered us too much. We were on our way to the United States, eager to see family and friends once again—and to get on with the new venture before us.

The last years of the American Mission experience in Ethiopia are summarized in a report that Harold Kurtz, on leave in the United States, wrote for the final issue of *Ethio-Echo*.

Phone calls kept following me around as I was doing mission interpretation in the Northwest. [We] arrived at the Pittsburgh airport [in late July] en route to the New Wilmington Missionary Conference, only to find an urgent request to call our Africa office....Definite word had come from Ruth McCreery in Addis Ababa that the Revolutionary Council of Dembi Dollo had demanded that the mission turn over the hospital to the government within fifteen days. The mission doctor [John Knowles] had been accused of malpractice, his life threatened, and he was virtually under house arrest....

I left for Ethiopia on the first of August...to do all that was necessary to secure the release of the doctor and other personnel in Dembi Dollo [which included RCA's Paul Leemkuil]. The [Presbyterian] Program Agency said to me, "Do whatever is necessary, for we know we can count on our church to give all necessary support in working out the release of our personnel. We hope for a turnover to the Ethiopian churches which will provide for continuation of the work begun and a healthy, ongoing relationship."

I returned to Addis Ababa to find "Yankee, Go Home!" signs on the street corners and shops....All missionaries were being accused of being CIA agents and of exploiting the people. This was all part of a policy we had heard about earlier: to not expel missionaries but to destroy reputations through propaganda, and then through harassment make it impossible for them to continue service....

After about a month and a half of negotiations over wage and hospital settlements...Dr. Knowles...was finally relieved by an Ethiopian doctor and flew out to Addis Ababa on September 19, being the last of the missionaries to assemble there. [Paul Leemkuil had been released a couple of weeks earlier.]

In the meantime, I continued to work on the practical and legal aspects of making a complete turnover of personnel, equipment, projects, and institutions to appropriate Ethiopian agencies....

I can still only marvel at the way the Lord enabled me to complete that process in a manner I never would have believed possible....I had felt earlier that, no matter what, I would probably be leaving the country with people and communities on my conscience; but, by his grace, I felt that an adequate provision was made in every case.

By the middle of November, I was involved in the final "wrap up" and made reservations to fly out to my family on the seventeenth. Imagine my surprise after I had checked my luggage, gone through customs, etc., when at passport control they told me I was on the "black list" and they couldn't let me leave the country!

While I waited the fifteen minutes [it took] for them to locate the letter which revealed the cause for which I was being held, "my sins paraded before me"! It was a great relief when I found out that the letter was from the Ministry of Health, and that they wanted to make sure I had settled financially with them over the Dembi Dollo Hospital. I had done that and a letter of clearance was already in the works.

By the next day I was cleared, and it was with a great deal of relief, mixed with deep sorrow and heartache, that I felt the wheels of the jet lift from the Addis Ababa runway.

As I left, seven of our missionaries remained behind under the care of the Mekene Yesus Church.... [Among them were] Dr. and Mrs. Harvey Doorenbos, who had accepted the request of the Mekene Yesus Church to work in a former German hospital in Aira in western Ethiopia, since the Dembi Dollo Hospital was now in government hands....

Many will want to know what happened to individual stations. The rundown is as follows:

1. Stations which went into the hands of the government through local harassment and pressure, if not confiscation, were Godare, Teppi, Omo River, and Surma.

2. Stations which were turned over to a synod of the Mekene Yesus Church were Dembi Dollo, Pokwo, Gilo River, and Ghimeera.

3. The Chebera station had been overrun by "bandits," so we don't know its condition. However, it was officially turned over to the Ethiopian Orthodox Church Mission.

4. The Adura River work among the Nuer was basically turned over to the Ministry of Health....[2]

[2] Harold Kurtz, "Mission Head Informs, Encourages, Exhorts Us All," *Ethio-Echo*, Vol. 12, No. 4, March 1978: 1, 4, 5. Joint Archives of Holland, Hope College.

Harold closed his report by exhorting us to pray for Ethiopian Christians as they...

> ...struggle to find their way through the maze of a continuing violent revolution. The challenge is great in speaking the "Word of the Lord" during a time like this. The Ethiopian Church is a mature church with a great potential, and we must not fail her in her hour of need. Christians there have an extremely crucial role to play as ambassadors of love and reconciliation.
>
> And they continue to carry a great vision for the days ahead which can be summed up by a verse from Jeremiah, quoted to me by one of their leaders: "For I know the plans I have for you," says the Lord, "plans for welfare and not for evil, to give you a future and a hope."[3, 4]

In this manner the American Mission as an entity was dissolved. But the Ethiopian Church, during the ensuing years of revolution, moved on from strength to strength by the power and grace of almighty God. To him be all the glory!

Our brief furlough was nearly over. Negotiations between the RCA's General Program Council and the Africa Inland Mission had been completed. We were ready to leave for Kenya the first week of October when another phone call came from Nairobi asking us to delay until AIM had our visas in hand. We had been living in one of the mission houses in Holland, Michigan. Now it was needed for other occupants. Friends arranged for us to stay in a staff apartment at Camp Geneva on Lake Michigan while we waited. There we spent long and peaceful days—and met Steve Kragt, a young man who was in charge of maintenance at the camp.

A born handyman with a fine Christian demeanor, Steve exhibited the qualities of which great volunteers are made. A challenge was put to him, and it became obvious to us that this Camp Geneva detour on the way to Kenya had been in God's Book of Plans!

3 Jeremiah 29:11, Revised Standard Version.
4 Kurtz, "Mission Head Informs," 5.

Three weeks later, word came that the necessary papers had been issued, and all things seemed ready. We were eager to be on our way.

On October 26 we sent out our last "Omogram" with the glad news to all on our mailing list that God had opened before us another "wide door for effective work."[5]

> The Geleb tribe straddles the border on the east side of Lake Turkana—the very same tribe with the very same language as those among whom we lived in Ethiopia. Our twelve years of experience with the Ethiopian Gelebs have prepared us, as nothing else could have, for further service in Kenya, and the Africa Inland Mission has welcomed us warmly. In fact, we were told that they'd been praying for seven years for someone to come to work among the Kenyan Gelebs.
>
> We will still be missionaries of the Reformed Church in America; there will be no change in the relationship between us and our supporting churches, or Partners in Mission. Our membership in the AIM will be only as associates.
>
> With visas now in hand, and a telephone call of confirmation from Nairobi, we are ready to leave for Kenya. We shall fly from Chicago Sunday evening, October 30, and will reach Nairobi the following Tuesday morning.
>
> So, in the words of Paul, our thoughts go Geleb-ward: "Here for the [second] time I am ready to come to you. And I will not be a burden, for I seek not what is yours, but you; ... I will most gladly spend and be spent for your souls."[6]
>
> Please pray that, in a special sense, we may be reckless spendthrifts!

With all hurdles cleared, we soon entered Kenya through that wide open door, thankful to have some years yet, as well as health, to spend and be spent in Africa for the sake of the gospel.

---

5 1 Corinthians 16:9, Revised Standard Version.
6 2 Corinthians 12:14–15, Revised Standard Version.

The Dispersion Years

In light of successive expulsions and relocations of RCA personnel and colleagues, the mission field seemed like a chess board. We were being moved from square to square, but hindsight showed it was not by an amateur who sometimes made errors in judgment or needlessly sacrificed chess pieces to the opponent. Rather, we were in the hands of the Master Player who knew just which moves to make. The constant shifting of position was part of the Master's strategy for spreading the Word, for planting the seeds of the gospel, and for strengthening his church. He would see to it that those left behind, tended by the Holy Spirit, would increase in faith and numbers.

The RCA missionaries of Sudan and Ethiopia now were dispersed to work in several African nations, carrying out the Lord's purposes according to his master plan.

XIX
Living on a Dune

It was November 9, 1977. We were in Kenya, flying north for a brief preview of Ileret.

What a beautiful flight! When we took off over Nairobi in the small Africa Inland Mission (AIM)-Air Cessna, we looked down upon hundreds of blooming jacaranda trees. The thick clusters of their lavender-blue flowers gave the city a gentle glow. Farther on, we flew over neatly ordered tea plantations and forests of African pines and Rift Valley lakes.

While the countryside north of Nairobi is mountainous, it soon falls away to the vast plains of the Northern Frontier District (NFD), a wasteland of desert and thorny scrub with cones of ancient volcanoes here and there, and rivers of frozen lava. It's a fascinating landscape.

Out of the flatness, just east of the lower end of Lake Turkana, rises Mount Kulal, a huge, sprawling, now-peaceful volcano that dominates the scene. Because we'd had a late start that day, we would be going only as far as Gatab on Mount Kulal. It was a rule, strictly adhered to, that MAF and AIM-Air planes must be on the ground an hour before Africa's sunset and sudden nightfall.

Gatab, located near the top of Kulal, is a Samburu settlement as well as the site of an AIM mission station. On staff were Howard and Doris Andersen, Paul and Betty Lou Teasdale, and two nurses, Betty Steinbacher and Lou Cameron.

267

The mission airstrip is one of those thrillers with one end dropping off into a deep gorge. Our pilot, Mike Grinnell, was no novice; he brought the plane in with confidence in his skill, and with faith that Another was in command.

How the wind blew there! That night it howled and moaned hour after hour, and when morning came, clouds were rolling and billowing through the compound and over the airstrip. No one would have guessed that there was a breathtaking view of Lake Turkana to the west.

We waited until noon that day before boarding the plane. Howard Andersen was flying to Ileret with us. Mike revved up the engine, and we sat and sat, waiting for a break in the cloudy waves that continued to pour over the mountaintop. Finally, between one billow and the next, we took off, out over the gorge that was completely hidden from view and north to Ileret near the Ethiopian border.

We landed on the government airstrip on top of a long dune. At the west end was the Kenya police post; at the other end, about a mile away, was the mission site that boasted two corrugated tin buildings: one for the caretakers and the other, dubbed the Safari House, for the use of missionaries on their monthly visits from Gatab.

Much to our surprise and delight, we found our old friends, Akol and Nakademo, at Ileret. (They had been with us at Omo River Post.) While the men visited with some of the people, Nakademo invited me to her house and served some wonderful beans she had just cooked. They were tasty and I was hungry!

That afternoon, Howard took us on a tour of the projects that had been started at Ileret long before we had ever heard of the place. It was about 1970 when the Africa Inland Mission began making periodic medical and evangelistic flights into the area from Gatab. Then, in response to reported hunger conditions, Paul and Betty Lou Teasdale began a fishing scheme that would provide food and cash for the people of Ileret. Down near the lake, Paul built a cement block fish shed, a small shop, and a house for the African in charge. Howard wanted us to see this project first.

We rode in an old Jeep down to the warehouse beside the lake where fishermen brought their catch (mostly tilapia) which they had sun-dried. The fish then were pressed and bundled in sacks for shipment across the lake to Kalokol in Turkana country, then sent to markets in Kenya and Uganda. The project was a viable, odoriferous one!

Then we drove to the pump house at the edge of a riverbed, which was chronically dry except when it rained in the hills to the east. The sandy riverbed soaked up rainwater like a sponge and held it in great underground pools. This water was pumped to tanks that supplied the whole community on top of the dune.

Water from Lake Turkana—fed by many rivers, principally the Omo at its northern extremity—has no outlet, making it brackish and unfit for sustained consumption. Water in the southern reaches is so full of algae that, from Mount Kulal, the lake appears to be a beautiful shade of green. Hence its nickname: the Jade Sea.

The brief orientation to Ileret made us eager to begin. We assured the people—the Daasanach—that we would return in about a month.

Our pilot flew us back to Gatab along the east shore of the lake, low enough so that we could see scores of crocodiles sunning themselves in the late afternoon rays, and myriad water birds of all varieties: ducks, geese, cranes, and herons. We landed on the mountain strip just before the fog rolled in, covering everything in a thick, damp blanket. We praised God for holding back that cloud, resting along the summit, until the plane had safely descended.

During our weekend in the Northern Frontier, we sensed two messages from the Lord. Inevitably, our thoughts kept returning to Omo River, wondering if we might have gone back there in spite of indications to the contrary. But we believe that God spoke to us clearly about this subject.

The first message came as we stood on the dune looking northwest toward Omo. Nakademo was with us, pointing out a place on the horizon that she said was the delta village of Edboron, where there were a few Christians. I looked and looked, straining to see the place. A few minutes later I looked again, and a heavy rain was falling way out on the lake between us and Omo. It was as if God had drawn a curtain across that area to remind us—or assure us—that our home from now on was Ileret.

The second message came to Bob in a dream that night at Gatab: Bob was in a room with several other people and kept asking one person after another if he could go back to Omo. Each person gave an indefinite answer, and finally, in frustration, Bob said, "I just want to know: yes or no!" Then from another room an invisible source answered, as if over a loudspeaker, "No!"

Our interpretation of these events gave us a joy and a peace of heart that we hadn't known before. After months of wondering if it were only man's voice we had obeyed in leaving Omo, or if it were really God's voice speaking through the man—in this case, Harold Kurtz—now we knew! We believe that God heard and answered our prayers for assurance and wisdom in this matter. "If any of you lack wisdom, let him ask of God...and it shall be given him."[1]

Back in Nairobi, that peace prevailed during the long days of preparation for the big move to Ileret.

Since "wheels" were a major consideration, Bob had ordered a new Toyota Land Cruiser. We were relieved when it passed inspection and became our reliable means of transport.

This Land Cruiser was a rough, tough, unstreamlined, four-wheel drive pickup that served us well for the better part of ten years, faithfully taking us over incredible terrain—miles and miles of washboard highways, deep-rutted, muddy byways, bare rock outcrops—and through swift-flowing rivers, treacherous salt flats, and trackless wastes. It was a great vehicle!

Because we were starting from scratch, we scoured the city for beds and mattresses, chairs, tables, and dressers, and many cartons of groceries. Having lived in the bush for nearly thirty years, the planning wasn't too daunting; it just took time to find our way around an unfamiliar city, all the while driving on the left, or, according to our British friends, the "correct" side of the streets.

Eventually everything was accomplished.

As for orientation, the powers-that-be advised us to stay for the annual AIM Conference held at Kijabe, AIM's largest mission station and home of Rift Valley Academy, where missionary children receive their education. It was a golden opportunity to meet hundreds of new colleagues, to learn how this mission organization conducts its business, and to be inspired and refreshed throughout the program. It was the first of many conferences that we attended, each one a highlight of the year, with superb speakers and leaders and some four hundred in attendance.

We also met John and Caryl Busman, the couple who had been slated for Omo River but were prevented by the lack of one signature.

While still waiting for the elusive Ethiopian visas as they studied at Selly Oak Colleges in Birmingham, England, the Busmans finally were advised to proceed to Kenya to find something temporary to do until the visas came through.

---

[1] James 1:5 Revised Standard Version

So it was that in March 1977, John and Caryl became the first representative missionaries of the RCA in Kenya. They inquired with many different organizations about using their particular skills in agriculture. The Rural Development Office of the National Christian Council of Kenya (NCCK) put them in touch with Herbert and Ruth Andersen of the Africa Inland Mission, stationed at Kalacha at the edge of the Chalbi Desert in the Northern Frontier District. Herbert (brother of Howard) and Ruth were going home for a year's furlough. Someone was needed to supervise a new project in the nearby Huri Hills.

The Busmans traveled to Kalacha to see the Andersens and to learn more about their responsibilities. The project had to do with tree-planting, improving pasture land with better grasses, and experimenting with catchment basins for providing water for cattle in the area.

It was a task that John and Caryl felt they could handle. They returned to Nairobi for an intensive course in "survival Swahili" and subsequently became part of the NCCK's development effort in the NFD.

The Andersens helped the Busmans settle into their home in Kalacha and soon departed for the United States. Kalacha at that time consisted mainly of a few dwellings and humble shops, huddled in the desert near an oasis of palm trees and a spring of fresh water.

The inhabitants of this dry land were the Gabbra. They passed through Kalacha with their herds of camels, sheep, and goats, taking them to water at the spring.

The Busmans enjoyed getting to know the Gabbras. John worked with a small crew to build roads, improve water supplies, and plant trees. They started a tree nursery, collecting seeds from trees in the area. The local people thought they were "slightly balmy" to offer to pay them for bringing in seeds that could be had for nothing!

In cooperation with a United Nations project, they also collected plants from around Kalacha and the Huri Hills and helped to formulate a land-use management plan for the Gabbra.

Because they had the only means of vehicular transport, John and Caryl often were asked to take people on what they called "*huko* safaris." *Huko* is Swahili for "over there somewhere." Such general directions usually took the driver over endless tracts, through formidable terrain. The safari could be an all-day affair as the truck wandered the countryside, usually to bring patients from small, scattered settlements to the dispensary in Kalacha for medical treatment. The Busmans always took a guide with them since there were no defined paths to the nomads' camps, nor any road signs.

Human beings were not the only ones who needed help. One time John used the project's four-wheel-drive Bedford truck to pull a camel out of quicksand. Caryl said, "The camel had sunk in up to his neck and a rope had to be tied around that to extract him—fortunately, alive."[2]

It was during this interim assignment, packed with unaccustomed adventures, that the Busmans made their way down-country for the conference at Kijabe where we met them. It was one of those "it's about time" experiences after so many months of correspondence, praying, waiting, and hoping.

But now we could see why, in God's foresight and wisdom, he had dashed those hopes and said no to the Busmans entering Ethiopia and yes to Kenya. They belonged in Kenya for now, surely in answer to the Andersens' prayers for well-qualified personnel to carry on in their yearlong absence.

John, born in Pipestone, Minnesota, was raised on a farm in nearby Chandler. He earned degrees in engineering physics from South Dakota State University and agricultural engineering from the University of Arizona.

Caryl was born and raised in Williams, Arizona. She earned a degree in botany from the University of Arizona. Both John and Caryl became keenly interested in studying African plant life as a source of food, fuel, and medicine. They saw a challenge in using technical resources and skills in ways that improve the quality of life for the rural poor of the undeveloped nations. But they were also aware that they had much to learn from the Africans. As Caryl pointed out, "My contact with African Christians and with various development projects has made me increasingly aware that we Americans do not have all the answers to spiritual or technical issues. There is a lot that we can learn from others so that together we can grow."[3]

With that mindset, both John and Caryl were able to blend teaching and learning into rich experiences in development.

Because Kalacha is located on the way to Ileret, the Swarts and Busmans made plans to travel north together following the mission conference. After one more foray to the marketplace for last-minute purchases, we were ready to start out.

---

[2] John and Caryl Busman, from a report to the author, August 1992. Joint Archives of Holland, Hope College.
[3] Ibid.

Our previous trip to Ileret, flying high above the Northern Frontier District, had been quick, smooth, and impersonal. Now we experienced the real thing. We saw at close range the starkness of the NFD in all its moonscape barrenness. We felt the bumps, the withering wind, and the "burning of the noontide heat." We smelled and tasted the dust of the road. In it all, we sensed the joy and excitement of being on the right track, on our way to the place where we fully expected to spend the next seven years— that is, until Bob was of retirement age.

John and Caryl were good guides. We reached Kalacha after two days of travel, having spent the first night at the mission at Loglogo. Because our new friends had offered to accompany us all the way to Ileret, we all rested for a few days and then started off into territory unfamiliar to all of us.

We had an interesting trip, to put it mildly. It was bewildering trying to traverse the game park along Lake Turkana because of a confusing network of tracks that led variously to lodges, to paleontologist Richard Leakey's new research camp at Koobi Fora, and to scores of dig sites. We made a few wrong, time-consuming turns, but at last we made it to Ileret.

Upon arrival we went directly to the police post to report our presence and intent. The inspector was cordial as he welcomed us to Ileret. He knew that we were hot and tired, so he invited us in to his veranda and served us juicy, tinned pineapple and good hot tea. How much we appreciated his thoughtful kindness.

The following day, December 23, Daasanach friends presented us with a goat. We understood its significance: it was to be butchered and roasted, not only as a gesture of welcome, but also to be enjoyed as a feast for all who would gather for the occasion.

There is nothing to compare with the flavor of goat meat prepared according to Daasanach custom. Large pieces of the dressed meat were skewered on sticks driven a few inches into the ground and tipped toward the open fire. The chunks crackled and hissed, turned brown and crispy, sealing the juices inside. And the air was redolent with a marvelous aroma.

We furnished the tea (called *chai*, which is boiled with milk and lots of sugar), and together with several Daasanach workers and friends, we ate heartily of the delectable fare. It was a pleasant, friendly time—a pre-Christmas gala, and an auspicious beginning to our sojourn at Ileret.

However, we had not yet come to stay; we had to make one more trip to Nairobi for further supplies, and to meet a plane that would be arriving

January 4 to bring our first volunteers to assist us in getting established at Ileret: none other than Jack and Deb Swart! How excited we were, and how eager to see them again!

Their plane arrived and we could hardly contain ourselves for joy!

This was Jack's first return to Africa since he had graduated from Good Shepherd School in Ethiopia in 1971. It soon was evident that he was in his element. He wanted to share with Deb the Africa he loved so that she could, as far as possible, enter into his past and understand his sub-Saharan enthusiasms. So we were all concerned that this would be not only a homecoming for Jack, but also a heartwarming experience for his wife.

What had led to this commitment as volunteers?

During the three years before their marriage in 1975, Jack had worked first in southwest Minnesota as a hired hand at one of Edgerton's large dairy farms. He later joined a building crew, starting out as a "gofer," but by 1977 he had become the crew's foreman. God was preparing him for practical missionary service.

Following high school, Deb had had training as a dental assistant and now had a good job in nearby Pipestone.

Bob and I visited Jack and Deb in the fall of 1977, challenging them to consider going to Ileret for a few months to help us get started. When they found out that they could go out under the RCA's adult volunteer program, and that their respective employers would grant them four-month leaves of absence, they knew that this was what the Lord wanted for them.

Jack and Deb arrived that January night bedraggled and tired after the long Pan Am flight. But the next morning, when Deb looked out of the guest house windows, she was revived by the African flora: "hedges made of daisies, jade plants the size of bushes, and poinsettia TREES."[4]

Deb went to town one morning with Jack and Bob. While they purchased building materials for a house at Ileret, she sat in the truck and watched the people going by, all dressed in colorful clothing. "I said colorful," Deb remarked, "not matching. Obviously clothes were worn for covering the body, not for making a fashion statement!"[5]

---

4 Deb Swart, from a report to the author, June 1996. Joint Archives of Holland, Hope
    College.
5 Ibid.

She took in all the sounds of the thronging city: the talking and singing—all in languages she could not understand. And when she heard English spoken by an African, "it didn't sound the same, but I liked it."[6]

Eventually all the buying was finished and food for the next four months was packed. There were cartons of canned foods, sacks of flour and sugar, butter in tins, fresh vegetables wrapped singly in newspaper, eggs in stacks of open trays. New ideas, new ways, new foods for Deb to see and taste and marvel at. We discovered that we need not have been concerned about Deb's response to Africa. She took every new experience in stride and was a good sport throughout those early days when she was bombarded on every side by mini-shocks to her senses.

The trip to Ileret took the usual three days. We camped one night out in Africa's starlit darkness, listening at intervals to the distant roar of lion, the occasional whoop of a hyena, and strange birdcalls. We slept, too, more than we realized.

On the third day we arrived at Ileret, that exotic night now only a memory. We lost no time in getting Jack and Deb set up in their paradome, which was a portable, ten-sided room, about twelve feet in diameter. Being quite round, it took the Ileret winds fairly well—much better than our already well-used tent that had been loaned to us kindly by friends at Loglogo. Its poor canvas had to be mended and patched regularly; its fibers just couldn't stand up to the wind's constant buffeting.

But we wouldn't be tenting for three years at Ileret as we had at Omo River. Jack and Deb had come to help build our house. With plenty of sand and stone available locally, and steel, cement, and roofing brought in by truck and even by small plane, work was begun immediately.

By the time February rolled around, the foundations were in, cement blocks were all formed and cured, and everything was ready for our master mason friend, Carl Brouwer, and his wife, Lorraine. The floor now could be poured and the walls laid up.

Besides assisting Carl in the cement work, Jack put his carpentry expertise into practice: he made all the cabinets for the kitchen and the washrooms. In her memoirs, Deb wrote that "Jack loved working with his hands, with his dad, with people he understood and had come to love. Ileret wasn't Omo, but you could almost see it from there."[7]

6 Ibid.
7 Ibid.

The women not only helped me prepare meals; they also kept busy with sandpaper and paintbrushes. Bob was available for any job that needed doing, but his special responsibility was welding up all the window frames, and later making screens for each window and the long front veranda.

So with all this lavish assistance, our carefully but simply designed house took shape before our eyes. It looked like a palace after the months of tent-living.

At the close of the day, after supper and showers, we would sit out under the stars in quiet fellowship with one another. BBC World Service, heard on our little shortwave radio each evening, helped keep us in touch with what was going on in other parts of the world. And then it was time for bed. When they were alone, Jack and Deb would talk and talk about the day, about what they were doing and learning. "Those days at Ileret," Deb declared, "strengthened our relationship and helped us focus on what was most important in life. It was the best of times for us."[8]

The Swarts and Brouwers had to leave all too soon. It had been a richly rewarding three-month experience for all of us—living and working together on the crest of that windy dune, enduring the sting of sand blowing with the strong, hot, easterly gales, and luxuriating in the cooler air that came off the lake every afternoon. Bob and I had no words to express our thankfulness. We looked forward to spending the rest of our missionary years based in this lovingly constructed house.

We also wondered if the Lord would use the dune as a "launching pad" for Jack and Deb into future service in Africa. Deb had passed her orientation with flying colors; Jack already had the necessary bent. We would be watching with keen interest for further developments.

There was much at Ileret to remind us of Omo River. We had the lake instead of the river, but often we could see a definite line in the water where the silt-laden Omo had surged afresh into the blue-gray Lake Turkana. Across the lake to the west was the same mountain with its small central peak we had gazed upon so familiarly from Omo. On a very clear day, we could even make out the Kibbish Hills that had been part of our northern horizon.

Of course there were the Daasanach themselves. Their settlements were scattered sparsely here and there among the scrawny thorn trees down off the dune. But by far the largest local concentration was located on the sloping duneside just below the Ileret police post. It was an amazing sight!

[8] Ibid.

Usually tribespeople settle as far as possible from government centers; they don't want to live under the scrutiny of official eyes. It was obvious that the Ileret situation must have been the result of an exceptional circumstance. They were there for protection.

Tribes other than one's own are traditional enemies; tribal languages in our experience have but one word for stranger and enemy. And no matter in which country we were living, there was the same overriding drive: to rustle cattle from neighboring tribes. If men on either side were killed in the process, well, it was worth the price of a good haul, or even the hope of one.

Apparently the Gabbra to the south had been on the warpath some time previous to our arrival. So for safety's sake, several hundred Daasanach had huddled up close to the police post—and stayed.

The post was also the home of a government-run clinic. The government dresser tended to the simple needs of the local populace.

By special arrangement, a nurse from Gatab or Loglogo, or sometimes even a doctor from the Medical Center at Kijabe, came by AIM-Air in a supervisory capacity to assist the government personnel in any way necessary. We looked forward to these twice-a-month visits, not only for the good fellowship, but also because the plane brought mail and fresh supplies to restock our larder. We had a radio-telephone that kept us informed about flight schedules and whom to expect. This was a blessing!

The medical service soon expanded to include the Daasanach settlement of Ilolo right on the Ethiopian border. It was hoped that word about these regular clinics would spread to the nearest Ethiopian villages so that they, too, could benefit from this help.

Beyond the Daasanach encampment near the police post, where the great dune began to slope away toward the lake, stood a gnarled old tree. How it had survived axes and herds to remain the one significant shade-provider on that section of the dune was a marvel of arboreal endurance. It was in the shade of this leafy canopy that we chose to meet on Sunday mornings for worship. Never mind that calves and goats chose to meet with us; no one paid any attention to their quiet browsing.

A young Daasanach named Yerkoi had been helping us with further language study, translation of key passages of Scripture, making cassette tapes, and composing Christian songs. He seemed to have a calling for evangelism as well. So together with Paul Lotadei (a Turkana Christian who was in charge at the fish shed) and Akol, Bob had valuable assistance in planning and implementing these weekly gatherings, to say nothing of outreach into the countryside.

Contact with the larger segment of the tribe in Ethiopia continued, as had been our hope. In our March 1978 newsletter, I included this item: "Our thoughts often go over the Ethio-Kenya border to Omo. Four young friends from there have come to see us, and a few days ago, one of them took back with him the first of the new cassette players that the Brouwers brought from Portable Recording Ministries. It's a comfort and a joy to know that the lines of communication are still open."

In July Waryaluk, Waleta, Amaluk, and Akula appeared at our door. Such a pleasant surprise! We were especially happy to see Waryaluk, who had carried on as the teacher at Omo after Timothy Jerkab left. He gave us a report on the changes that had occurred. He said that the entire mission compound had become the headquarters for both police and civil government. Both he and Achew had been put in jail for a few days because of the responsibilities in caring for the mission after we had gone.

Waryaluk also told us that a group was still meeting for worship each week. Another interesting item had to do with boxes of Gideon Bibles that had arrived at Omo shortly before we left. We had given out several of the Bibles and had left a pile of them on our dining room table, knowing that the police would find them.

Waryaluk said that the police had been selling them! Our comment was: "Gideon Bibles are free, but if people are willing to buy them, and if the police in that now atheistic state are willing that the Bibles be distributed by whatever means, they are worth every penny. Who can reckon the value of the Word of Life?"

These young friends were with us for the Sunday meeting under the tree, at which time Yerkoi preached on John 3:16. Bob taped the whole service and sent it back to Omo as an encouragement to the Christian community there.

On another occasion, we had the pleasure of welcoming our friend Achew to our home. As we sat having dinner together, he gave us further news of what had happened just after we left Omo River Post.

Achew told us that we had no sooner flown off in the Air Mula plane than the police made a beeline for the mission. As previously mentioned, they had had a tour of every building with the exception of our house. Now they demanded an inspection of the missionary residence, every corner of it.

Because they were suspicious that we might have planted traps or explosives in strategic spots throughout the house, they ordered Achew to go ahead of them to open every cupboard door and drawer in every room.

How Achew laughed as he told us this amazing account of mistrust. The communist mindset had jelled already.

Achew also told us that the police had entered his house and confiscated all the tools and other paraphernalia Bob had left with him to keep the windmills in repair. They accused him of having stolen the goods. This is probably the moment when they jailed him and Waryaluk.

It was a sorry tale.

August 1978 brought a great change in Kenya's history: President Jomo Kenyatta died. His death occurred during the week that the Busmans came up to Ileret for one last visit before proceeding to another assignment in Kenya, and when the Word of Life team came to hold an evangelistic campaign. This group was made up of Kenyans, mostly of the Kikuyu and Samburu tribes—young people in their teens and early twenties. They held meetings at Ileret, Ilolo, and at a large cattle camp some miles south of Ileret.

When news came over the radio that President Kenyatta, a Kikuyu, had died, concern that bordered on fear was etched on every young face. *Mzee* (the Old One) had presided over the affairs of Kenya for fifteen years. None of the team could remember their country being under any other rule, and they were afraid. They had heard of the chaos in other African nations when the leadership was disposed of or deposed, and they were keenly concerned for their own land.

They asked us, "What happens in your country when the president dies?"

We tried to reassure them that all would be well, though our words were based more upon hopefulness than confidence at that point.

As more news followed, it was disclosed that the vice-president, Daniel arap Moi (a Tugen, which is a subdivision of the Kalengin tribal group), had been sworn in as acting president before the word of Kenyatta's death was broadcast to the country and the world. So we knew that an otherwise inevitable intertribal power struggle had been averted.

It wasn't many weeks after this event that we began to hear about unusually heavy rains in Ethiopia's highlands. Every river was in flood. We had been noticing that the line where the Omo's silty water met the grayblue of Lake Turkana was moving steadily southward and that the level of the lake was rising significantly.

Then the old "grapevine" began to hum with the news that Omo's banks were being washed away by the high, rushing water, and that most of the windmills had been destroyed as one by one the torrent toppled them into its mighty stream. We were heartsick over these unwelcome tidings.

Gavin Bennet and his group later made their Round Lake Turkana Expedition:

When the Turkana Expedition reached Numa Meri (Nyememeri), we saw piles of tangled, twisted steel tubing and a few buckled and broken windmill sails lying in the fruitless dust.

The missionaries had long since departed...under circumstances that encouraged them to abandon all they had built: a couple of stone houses, a geodesic dome, a workshop full of tools and spares and welding equipment and generators. An old American Jeep. [It was probably our fifteen-year-old International Scout.]

All these are still there. The buildings now house the District Officer and the local police chief. The DO drives the Jeep. The tools and spares are scattered around the workshop which is never used.

One windmill remains. It is in the police station yard, and around it stand maize, pawpaws [papayas], bananas, and mangoes, fruit literally dripping off the branches....

The bulk of the [Daasanach] people have taken the collapse of their dream philosophically. No longer are they learning to irrigate and set up farms. Now they are learning Marxism and setting up committees.

The overall situation is distressing and depressing. Yet it is not without hope. That one windmill is still turning, still spewing water from a short length of hose pipe into a hand-dug channel, still sustaining a rich crop of fruit, still standing high and conspicuous....

And its silent message is getting through. A drill master, sent there to train the ragtag regiments of the People's Militia, as taciturn a man as you are ever likely to meet, was moved to nod at the windmill and the river and say: "These are the wars we must fight now."[9]

For all intents and purposes, the Food From Wind project lay in ruins, and there was no one on the scene, or on the horizon, with the vision, expertise, or any other means to lift it out of the "fruitless dust." Not yet!

In late December 1978, we received a cable informing us of Bob's mother's death. She had not been herself for several years, so we could not grieve. Now we praised God for his mercies that made her mind was sharp again and her step as lively as ever.

The new year brought us more volunteers: Steve Kragt, Ross Slagh, and Larry and Linda McAuley. Steve had been in charge of maintenance at Camp Geneva in Holland, Michigan, when we were "stranded" on Lake Michigan's shores during the fall of 1977. Ross was the son of good friends in Zeeland, Michigan. The McAuleys were being pulled back irresistibly to Africa after a three-year stint on a farm in Illinois. Larry told us that when he rode the tractor over acres and acres of farmland, his heart was really in Africa. He would talk to himself in Daasanach sentences, recalling all he could from his experience on the Omo in 1975. He and Linda were compelled to return, if only for a brief visit.

Bob and I had gone to Nairobi to meet this group when they arrived from the United States. We thought that the trip back to Ileret overland would be a great experience for the novices and one that the McAuleys surely would appreciate.

On the way north, we stopped to see the Busmans who had been transferred to Rhapsu when the Andersens returned to Kalacha. They were to oversee an irrigation scheme on the edge of Meru National Park. The scheme was sponsored by the Methodist Church under the National Christian Council of Kenya. It had been started to provide a means of livelihood for Boran and Somali nomads who had lost their herds in the *shifta*, or bandit, wars in the 1960s. The Busmans told us that the farmers in the area raised wonderful bananas and papayas as well as corn and red chili peppers. (When they transported the chilis to Nairobi, no one wanted to ride with them because the dust from the chilis was so strong that it made people choke and sneeze.)

[9] Gavin Bennet, "The Most Extraordinary Tribe," *Sunday Nation* (Kenya), March 30, 1980: 19. Joint Archives of Holland, Hope College.

John and Caryl worked with a group of farmers to form a management committee so that the project could run strictly under local supervision. Unnecessary items were sold and operations were streamlined so that a viable scheme could be left in place.

One of the major difficulties faced by the farmers was the periodic decimation of their crops by wandering herds of elephants and Cape buffaloes from the neighboring game park. The park rangers were not always amenable to paying compensation for such damage, especially since they suspected that these same farmers might be poachers! But from time to time, the rangers issued blank shells to be fired when the marauders would approach. However, the animals soon became accustomed to the sound that did them no harm, and eventually they paid no attention.

John and Caryl enjoyed seeing the animals from the park literally at their doorstep. They also liked to go to the lodge in the game park on occasion for a cold drink and a look at the tourists. In fact, our last glimpse of the Busmans was at the lodge. They were sitting at a small table, sipping cold Coca-Cola and watching tourists.

From personal experience, we can tell you that it's an interesting pastime. The run-of-the-mill tourist is a breed apart, well worth the price of admission. When we were in Nairobi, sometimes we would have lunch or just a cup of tea "under the thorn tree" at the New Stanley Hotel, and we would watch the tourists start out for the game parks.

They emerged from the hotel feeling conspicuous, if not uncomfortable, in their newly-purchased, extremely expensive, khaki outfits which were a must in some circles for proper safari-going. The line of zebra-striped combi- busses waiting at the curb soon were filled with eager sightseers, and off they'd go on an adventure they'd never forget.

Some discomfited residents of Kenya gladly availed themselves of T-shirts with "I AM NOT A TOURIST" emblazoned boldly across the front.

When their three-month assignment at Rhapsu came to an end, the Busmans went home to the United States, wondering what further surprises God had for them in the future.

From Rhapsu it took us two days to reach Ileret with our volunteers. With this team of young people, we had a rich supply of expertise, energy, and willingness at our disposal. We always marveled, each time a group came to us, how God had chosen just the right people to tackle the jobs that needed to be done. This team was no exception. Many projects were completed, such as shelving in the workshop, a ceiling in our house, and the erection of a clinic building at Ilolo.

The response to the mission medical outreach at Ilolo had been heartening, from both medical and evangelistic standpoints. So it seemed right to put up a small structure as a practical symbol of our commitment to this community up there near the Ethiopian border. It was a great help too for the medical safari staff to have a shelter in which to see patients during their bimonthly visits.

Once again our gratitude for the timely and excellent assistance of our volunteers was boundless. We were sad when they had to leave us, but our hearts overflowed with praise for all they had accomplished.

There was another compensation: the plane that came for the McAuleys brought Paul and Marcia Leemkuil and baby Tamar from Sudan. (How this blessing came about is described in a later chapter.)

Our son Dick, after two years at Northwestern College in Orange City, Iowa, now was studying in Tulsa, Oklahoma, at the Spartan School of Aeronautics. Donna Giles, a good friend whom he had known in Ethiopia, was working toward an associate degree in nursing at East Tennessee University.

On one of his trips to Tennessee, Dick and Donna began seeing one another in a new light. Before long they were engaged and planned to be married in June 1979—that very year! They wondered if we could be there!

We started immediately to make plans for a forty-five day excursion that would take us to the wedding in Tennessee and from coast to coast to see all our family, including two new grandchildren: Sarah Amber Hill had been born in October 1978 in Oregon, and Justin Robert Swart in Minnesota in May 1979.

Donna's parents, the Rev. Ray and Effie Giles, had been missionaries in Ethiopia, so both families shared a common bond in background and interest. We were all pleased with this turn of events.

Both fathers presided at the lovely ceremony on June 9. Jack, a brand new father as of May 30, and his sister Gayle sang together beautifully. And all in attendance rejoiced at this happy occasion.

Our forty-five day junket soon was over. We had accomplished our mission, delighting in each family visit. We even attended a few sessions of General Synod, which met at Hope College that year.

Once back at Ileret, we continued to make tapes for local and over-the-border evangelistic outreach. A new informant had appeared on the scene, and he was able to give expert help both in translation and reading for recording. So this phase of the work prospered.

One day Lokwar, an Ethiopian Daasanach, came to see us. When approached about taking a few tapes back with him, he demurred: "I'm afraid. If I go back with these tapes in my hand and the authorities catch me with them, they'll take them away and throw me in jail. I'm really afraid. I cannot take them."

Our hearts were heavy, but we understood his dilemma. Imagine our surprise and pleasure when the same lad came back a few weeks later and said, "I am ready now to take some cassettes with me. I am not afraid."

Lokwar left in a day or two with a bag outfitted with a new tape player, a solar battery, and several tapes. We saw him off with great joy.

In November joy filled us again at the family level when we received a cable from Chloe and Mark Young with the news that James Robert had been born. Renee and Laura now had a brother, and our grandchild count had risen to ten.

Another message reached us that November. Much to our delight, our good friends, the Rev. Glenn and Phyllis Bruggers, were planning to visit us. Glenn had been appointed to the Africa desk on an interim basis following John Buteyn's retirement. In order to understand more clearly what was required of him, he needed to experience Africa firsthand.

We went to Nairobi to welcome them and then proceeded to introduce them to the rigors of travel in the Northern Frontier District. They took it in stride with grace, good humor, and avid interest.

However, if you should ask Glenn and Phyllis about the highlight of their NFD safari, they might tell you about a refreshing bath in an idyllic natural spa surrounded on three sides by sheer rock cliffs from the top of which baboons looked down, chattering in high glee!

We didn't know it at the time, but Glenn and Phyllis were our last visitors at Ileret.

We were at the point in our local ministry where we began to dream of putting up a shelter in which to meet on Sunday mornings as well as a house for a pastor. The shade of the tree was fine, but the wind! Surely a simple meeting place could be built easily and quickly—a structure that would be open at the sides between five-foot walls and the roof, allowing for plenty of ventilation, but offering protection from the persistent, often gale-force winds.

We received permission from the County Council. The District Church Council and the Town Council approved the project. Building materials were ordered. More volunteers from First Reformed Church in DeMotte, Indiana, were poised to come as soon as they received positive word.

In early December we went down-country for the annual mission conference. Immediately upon arrival in Nairobi, we sent a cable to the volunteers to let them know all permissions were in hand and the light was green for them to come the end of January. There seemed to be no obstacles.

We thoroughly enjoyed the weeklong conference held at Kijabe. Now that it was over, we looked forward to our return trip to Ileret. We wouldn't have much time to prepare for the work group: staking out the buildings, making cement blocks, transporting materials to the site, etc. We hoped the materials already had reached Ileret in our absence.

On December 11, we were having lunch at Mayfield, AIM's guest house in Nairobi, when a mission official came in with a message for us: a directive had been received by telephone from the provincial commissioner (P.C.) at Embu that the Swarts were to "vacate" Ileret immediately. We were incredulous!

We had planned to leave for Ileret the next day, but changed those plans so that Bob could drive up to Embu with Jonathan Hildebrandt of AIM's personnel office on December 13 for an appointment with the P.C. It turned out to be a short interview. All the P.C. would say was that it wasn't in the best interest of the Kenya government for us to remain there. Nor were we permitted to work anywhere in Kenya where there were Ethiopians. We had permission to go up to Ileret one last time to retrieve our belongings. "You should be able to do that in two days!"

We thought despondently to ourselves, "Here we go again! But at least we aren't being ordered out of Kenya!"

Before we left Nairobi for Ileret, we had several offers from both AIM Kenya and AIM International of positions in other locations that we might wish to consider. This was so heart-warming and reassuring. All our mission family in Nairobi, and along the way through the Northern Frontier District, were most encouraging and supportive. The news had reached every corner of the NFD.

When we arrived at Ileret and the home that so many loving hands had built for us, we discovered that all of the building material had come by truck in our absence. This included one hundred eighty-five bags of cement. In light of this, Bob asked by radio that Jonathan Hildebrandt and the AIC bishop, Ezekiel Birech, try to reopen the matter with the P.C. and request an extension of three months so that the cement blocks could be made and the buildings put up.

The men did have another interview at Embu. The result was hardly encouraging: the P.C. was willing to reconsider, but there would be no action for thirty days.

It was not easy to compose a second cable to the volunteers, who were doubtless already preparing to come. There was no way, even if there should be a reprieve, that we could be ready for them by the end of January. Our hearts were heavy. The circumstances were quite different from our previous uprooting experiences, yet it all seemed so strangely familiar. It was a difficult thing to leave Ileret.

We returned to Nairobi, sharing a cheerful Christmas with the Andersens at Kalacha on the way. How we would miss these dear NFD friends!

Those were painful days of uncertainty. The gracious hosts of Mayfield, Jim and Gloria Orner, gave us a room where we could stay indefinitely. We had made a decision not to seek another assignment yet, but to do all that was possible to obtain a reversal of the Kenya government's order. Our greatest desire was to return to Ileret.

We waited. There was no action on the part of the P.C. at the end of thirty days. In fact Bob learned from Jonathan and the bishop that in their second interview with him, he was very reluctant even to discuss the matter or to give any reasons. Only when pressed did he give what he called a hypothetical case. It was in the form of a question: "If an ambassador from another country told your government that there were CIA agents at the border, wouldn't it be right for your government to send them away?"

In other words, we were being accused by the Ethiopian government of being spies. (My own wry comment, privately expressed, was that they had confused AIC [Africa Inland Church] with CIA!) So we began to suspect strongly that there was dim hope of our going back to Ileret as long as the communists were in power in Ethiopia.

Yet hope dies hard. When the P.C. was asked if it would do any good to appeal higher, he said it would not because "the order came from the highest level." But Jonathan wanted to probe those higher levels anyway.

So began a test of patience when appointment after appointment was made and broken. But if patience was what it would take to get us back to Ileret, we were willing to have it tested to the utmost.

We were guests at Mayfield for six months while all this was going on. Only at the end of that time did we know what God required of us, and where he was leading.

XX
Steps Toward Decision

The interval that Bob and I spent in Nairobi following the orders to leave Ileret was a roller-coaster experience of hopes raised and hopes dashed. It would have been intolerable if we had not been certain that God was somehow working out his purposes, even in this period of waiting; and if we had not had opportunity to do more than just wait.

In January 1980 we were available to be of help to the Hoekstras. They had been scheduled to visit missions in Malawi and Zambia as representatives of Portable Recording Ministries in order to repair several faulty tape players.

But when Harvey was suddenly in need of emergency surgery, they were unable to carry through with this commitment. The Swarts to the rescue! We were free and eager to assist in this mission.

With the necessary spare parts in hand, we flew south. We soared above the clouds, but shortly after crossing the border into Tanzania, we could see the majestic and glistening white top of Mount Kilimanjaro, the highest mountain in Africa. It rises over 19,000 feet and is always covered with snow.

Our first destination was Blantyre, Malawi, where we were guests at the Southern Baptist Mission, a charming compound with all kinds of tropical trees, a profusion of flowers, and hospitable, friendly missionaries. Work on the players began immediately and continued through the next few days.

On Sunday our hosts took us out into the country to one of the rural churches—a narrow building made of bricks covered with mud mortar and roofed with poles and grass. The people were so friendly, and what singers! They sang antiphonally and in harmony. It blessed our souls.

The white-haired pastor, who was about eighty years old, was still strong and a forceful, dramatic preacher. We couldn't understand what was said, of course, but it was enough to be there and to marvel and praise God for the sufficiency of Christ for all people.

The pastor invited us all to his home for a meal after the service. We sat visiting with the pastor while his spry little wife prepared curried chicken and *nsima*, which are cakes of very thick cornmeal. We ate the *nsima* by breaking off bite-size pieces and dipping them in the chicken broth. It was delicious.

Before we left to return to Blantyre, two women took our hands and, gently swinging our arms, sang a little farewell song, "Go with Jesus." It had been a very joyful day!

Our mission accomplished in Blantyre, we then flew to Lusaka, Zambia. Upon arrival, we were whisked off in a VW Bug and taken ninety miles southwest to Chikankata, the location of the largest Salvation Army mission post in the world. The compound housed a two-hundred-ninety-bed hospital, a secondary boarding school for five hundred students, and a studio where Christian programs for the Zambian Broadcasting System and Trans World Radio (Swaziland) are prepared and taped.

Bob was soon at work assisting in the repair of tape players. At the Sunday morning corps (church) service, our host interviewed us with the intent of instilling more interest in cassettes and the myriad possibilities of using them. The next day, Bob attended a brainstorming session about organizing a seminar on tape ministries in Lusaka for interested people from neighboring countries.

It was stimulating to be exposed to other mission programs and to sense anew the worldwide scope of the Great Commission. It was also sobering to be in Zambia during the history-making period of guerrilla warfare carried on by Joshua Nkomo's Patriotic Front.

Just a few weeks before our visit, one of the Chikankata ambulances was destroyed when it hit a land mine. There it sat on the compound, a complete wreck. Though the driver and passenger had been blown out of the vehicle, neither was seriously hurt. A patient, who was in the back seat, had been transferred to a more comfortable car. If he had remained in the ambulance, he surely would have been killed. Many similar stories of God's care for his own came out of this conflict.

When we returned to Nairobi, there seemed to be a slight chance of our going back to Ileret. At least Bishop Birech had not given up hope. He had written a letter of appeal to the assistant minister in the Office of the President, giving nine good reasons for the petition. Reason Eight is perhaps worthy of quoting for posterity:

"The reports of the police, district commissioner, and district officer on the local level have all been good concerning the conduct of Rev. and Mrs. Swart. They know of no reason why these kind, old people should be asked to leave." The bishop's gentle words warmed our hearts.

Another new development was the resignation of the province commissioner who had issued the original order. How we snatched at any tidbit of news that would bolster our optimism! But the days and weeks passed, fruitless but not hopeless.

In February of that year, I wrote in a letter to our children:

> It's an ever more wonderful experience to keep surrendering the helm of our lives to God's direction. I often think, Jack, of that picture by Holman Hunt that we gave you years ago—the one of the young man at the ship's wheel. Behind him was Christ with one hand on the young man's shoulder and the other hand pointing the way. It's the picture of a truth that holds for all people of all ages, for all who put their lives at the Lord's disposal and trust him for direction. It's a great adventure in faith and in life, and as far as we're concerned, it's the only way to go.

Our relatively free days made it possible for us to take in a few special events. On February 16, a group of us started out from Mayfield and drove down to Voi on the road to Mombasa. Voi was in the path of a total eclipse of the sun. Seven years before, in June 1973, we had traveled from Omo River Post south to Lodwar in Kenya to witness the same phenomenon. That total eclipse lasted for seven minutes. Having once beheld such a glorious sight, we were eager for an encore.

This time it was four minutes long, but nonetheless awesome: the gradual darkening, the appearing of stars at 11:25 a.m., the birds roosting quietly in the trees, and the marvelous halo and diamond ring spectacle as the moon completely covered the sun. Night at noon!

As the light returned, the birds began singing as they do at dawn. Beneath the trees where sunlight filtered through, each tiny patch of light was crescent-shaped, and flowing shadows covered the ground.

My response to all this could be described as worship, not of the drama, but of the Creator manifested in its wonder.

Invisible to mortal eye,
The moon moved 'cross the sapphire sky
To keep her rendezvous with one—
Her source of light, her sovereign sun.

How silently she made her way
Unerringly along a ray
Held out as scepter by a king,
A mystic, royal welcoming.

The heavenly bodies kept their tryst;
As earth's light dimmed, behold! they kissed.
Spellbound, we watched a wondrous thing:
Lo, 'round them shone a diamond ring!

Returning light revealed the earth
To marvelous signs was giving birth:
Fleet shadows flowed like dappled streams;
Gold crescents filtered through the leaves.

The years have passed, yet lingers still
That sense of worship, the awesome thrill.
At whose behest are such joys given?
Our Father, God, the King of Heaven!

In Christ we see the scepter raised;
Respond, O heart, and be amazed
That such a One should beckon us—
That in his courts he'd reckon us.

But, as the Lord liveth, it shall be!
We'll tryst with Him eternally—
The Source from whom all light springs:
Our God, our Savior, King of Kings!

—MFS

The waiting and hoping continued. On March 16, the assistant minister called the Africa Inland Church office. Bob and Jonathan Hildebrandt and Bishop Birech were to meet the minister at the parliament building at 11:45 on March 18. The minister would explain the situation to them. Then they would have lunch together.

The meeting did not take place. It seems that a half hour before the engagement, President Moi had asked this man to go to Zambia on the 2 p.m. flight. The minister said he would make another date when he returned. He never did.

About this same time, a missionary friend told us he had been talking with someone in the Office of the President and the subject of Ileret came up. The official's estimate was: "They will never get back there; they are political subversives."

In early April we heard that the bishop and two church elders went to see President Moi on various church matters. When their business was finished, the bishop dismissed the elders so that he could talk privately with the president about several things, including the Ileret situation. President Moi declared that he had not heard anything about this. He said, "The Department of Immigration should be handling this." He put a call through to Immigration but there was no answer.

We were loathe to let discouragement set in, but as time went on and we seemed no nearer to receiving a definite answer, other alternatives began to look more inviting. There were several that appealed to us. We began exploring the possibilities.

The RCA's General Program Council (GPC) was seeking, after an absence of many years, to join hands again with the church in the southern Sudan. The moderator of that church, the Rev. John Jok, sent word to us, saying, "We, the church, will accept you back so that you can complete the task you did not finish before. We will be glad to have you come back if you are willing to suffer with us." Glenn Bruggers and John Buteyn of the GPC urged us to plan a survey trip to Sudan as soon as possible.

Two other prospects were presented to us in casual conversations over the dinner table at Mayfield. Desmond and Virginia Hales, AIM missionaries who were based in the town of Eldoret in western Kenya, told us about an area in the northwestern part of the country, close to the Uganda border, where the AIC was hoping to start work among an unreached, remote segment of the Pokot tribe. It was in a settlement called Alale.

The other field for consideration lay in the opposite direction: in southeastern Kenya among the Muslim Orma people.

All three of these proposals appealed to us, not only as places where we might relocate, but also as a means to challenge the RCA, in response to the call of African churches, to expand its involvement in the mission program in that part of the world. Perhaps in the two latter cases, the RCA and the AIC could work together on a partnership basis. It all sounded attractive and exciting. Hearing of these needs was as if the still, small voice of God were speaking in answer to our earnest prayer for his leading.

We began to make plans for three survey trips.

The first was to Alale. Desmond Hales went with us.

We found the Pokot chief of that district sitting by the roadside among some of his older constituents. He was eager to join us in a walking exploration of the area, the primary purpose of which was to locate a site for an airstrip for the use of future medical safaris. After dismissing two sites as less than ideal, the third showed real promise, with unlimited length, good soil and good drainage, and few trees.

We inquired, too, about the water supply. The chief said that there was a well a few miles away where the Pokot pumped water for their daily needs. But up on Lorsuk Mountain was a spring. It was a tortuous hike up that mountain, but well worth the effort. There it was—crystal clear water flowing continuously from an opening in a rocky rise on the mountainside. At that moment a dream was born.

Before we left Alale, Desmond talked to a number of people gathered under a tree where we had first found the chief. He spoke in Swahili about Jesus Christ, with the chief interpreting in the Pokot language. "Yu hai!" Desmond exclaimed. "Yu hai!" He lives! He lives! If we hadn't believed it before, that proclamation surely would have persuaded us!

It had been a tiring but exhilarating, day. Our mutual positive response to the visit to Alale left us wide open to the leading of the Lord to that place. But we still hadn't heard anything definite about Ileret.

We arrived back in Nairobi on April 26.

Two days later we had our answer. Desmond had come from his home in Eldoret. He told us that Claudon and Gladys Stauffacher, a retired missionary couple, had stopped at their house a few days before. The Stauffachers had had dinner with President Moi. (President Moi was baptized and nurtured in the Africa Inland Church and knows personally several of the older missionaries.) They approached him about the Ileret problem. His answer was the word we'd been waiting for, though not what we had hoped. He said, "They will not get back there until there is a change in the government in Ethiopia. The Ethiopians were complaining that they were trying to Christianize their Marxist state. We have advised the AIC to cover the work with Kenyans."

That was as direct a communication as we could hope to have, and since it came from the highest office in the country, we accepted it as God's final word to us as far as Ileret was concerned.

This message was confirmed when we met veteran AIM missionary Earl Andersen at the Nairobi Baptist Church one Sunday in May. He told us that he had seen the president's secretary who gave him the same report that we had heard from Desmond.

Disappointing, yes, but mingled with a kind of relief. Our striving ceased, and the surveys and searchings could continue with single-minded purpose.

I wrote a letter to my mother on May 10, 1980.

> We're finding it so hard to know where God wants us; there are so many voices giving what they feel are clear directives. The church wants experienced people at Alale in the west. We met a Kamba pastor this week who wants us—not anyone else—to open new work among the Orma. Ron Beery and Harvey Hoekstra are persuaded that we are the ideal ones for the tape ministry in Sudan. John Buteyn of the RCA's General Program Council would rather see Bob in a teaching-training program in Sudan. And John Jok, the Nuer moderator of the Presbyterian Church, has cordially invited us to join them there. We feel as if we are being torn limb from limb in this quest. We've never experienced anything like it before.

To top it off we received a "thus saith the Lord" letter from John and Gwen (Adair) Haspels, Presbyterian Mission kids from Ethiopia and Sudan, respectively, now serving at Pibor, Sudan, under ACROSS. They were sure that we were destined to return to our first love among the Murle people. Obviously, the temptation was great.

With all the calls from the Sudan quarter, we knew that we would have to visit that country—if we could get a visa. But it was advisable for us first to make a trip into Orma territory to get a feel for that area and a sense of what the Lord wanted of us and the RCA mission outreach in Kenya.

So on May 11 we flew with Michael Donovan of the AIC office to Malindi on the coast where we were met by AIM missionary Van Davis. By three o'clock we were prepared to start off: north as far as Hola and then westward. Van and Musa, an evangelist, traveled with us. The coastal area had a decidedly Arab flavor, and anyone, if asked, surely would declare himself to be a Muslim.

We drove as far west as Waldena, a small, dilapidated police post seemingly in the middle of nowhere. The most impressive building was the quite new, four-room school. The most ramshackle structure was one that had been an AIC church.

Some years before, the AIC had sent two pastors to Waldena to evangelize the area. Unfortunately the potentially effective strategy did not work. The pastors were not compatible. One left, and the other dabbled in unworthy and illegal matters, and the ministry among the Ormas floundered and fizzled out. It is a sorry chapter in AIC history.

But that evening we met in that poor church building. At the special request of two Christian police wives, Musa led a service in Swahili, preaching from John 10, in which Jesus said, "I am the door" and "I am the Good Shepherd." Several were in attendance. The occasion must have been a spiritual feast for them all.

We returned to the coast the next day, stopping en route to visit in a permanent Orma village at Oda. Because most of the semi-nomadic Ormas had moved away from the Waldena area to find better pasture for their herds, we had not been able to see an Orma village there.

These Orma homes at Oda were like tall beehives, all of ten feet high. The firm stick frame, patterned in overlapping arches, was covered thickly with grass neatly tied to the frame. The doorway was extremely narrow. In the opening, there was a curtain of thick, soft bark fiber that brushed the flies off of anyone entering the house.

One quarter of the round interior was partitioned off as a bedroom, the bed being a raised platform with a cowskin mattress. To one side was a set of shelves. Two slender bundles of long withy sticks, each bundle bound together with palm fiber, were placed upright on the floor two feet apart and fifteen inches from the wall. The tops of those bundles were tied to the curve of the wall about eight feet up. Between the wall and the bundles, short sticks were tied to make shelves. Here the woman of the house kept her pots and gourds and her firewood. We were amazed at such ingenuity.

After a delightful meal in one of the Orma homes, we continued on our way, satisfied that our visit to this part of Kenya had been most worthwhile and would be helpful as we sought God's plan for the next step.

Our Sudan visas were granted. We marveled! This had to be the Lord's doing because we knew that our names were on that country's black list, as was true of all who had been expelled in the early 1960s.

We flew to Khartoum on June 4. The sole purpose for going to the northern capital was to have an interview with the Rev. Ezekiel Kutjok, a Shulla from the South who was the general secretary of the Sudan Council of Churches. It was important to contact this church leader. We wanted to hear about his ideas and concerns for the expansion of the work in the southern region. Were we just dreaming to think that the South would ever be wide open again to expatriates working together with nationals in the strengthening of the church? Kutjok spoke encouragingly and gave several suggestions about where the RCA could make a vital contribution.

It was a mutually helpful interview. We knew as we flew from Khartoum a few days later that his blessing would be upon whatever could be done to encourage and build up the church in the South.

In Malakal we stayed on the MAF compound. Our hearts ached as they had in Khartoum over the deterioration of the town. The roads and buildings were crumbling; even the people on the street had a faded and despairing look about them.

But when we went to the house of the Lord, we found a difference! On Sunday morning we gathered with Anuak and Murle Christians in the sanctuary that held so many memories for us. Now it was bat-infested and full of decay, but the joy of these African Christians was contagious. The very fact that Anuaks and Murles, traditional enemies, were worshiping together filled us with praise. God in Christ had broken down the tribal barriers. We relished being there in their midst and thanked God for his faithfulness.

Especially wonderful to us was meeting Otung's daughters.

One day a woman named Sarah came to the home of our hosts to discuss the matter of a flight. When I heard her name and looked at her carefully, I asked, "Are you the daughter of Otung and Abongo?" She replied that she was.

I then told her that I was *Nyingu*, my Anuak name meaning Child of a Lion. She remembered, and we had a happy reunion. Two of her six sisters were in Malakal at the time and all three came to see us one morning. Leah

Nyakili, Sarah Aja, and Rachel Anuk were tall women, attractive, married, and all active Christians.

Thirty years before, they were children at Akobo. Their father, Otung, allowed them to go to school. Wilma Kats was their teacher. She had much to do with the shaping of their lives.

In those days their mother served food to her husband on her knees, according to Anuak custom. Now these stately women, her daughters, were not afraid to stand in the presence of men, even taking part in the church service, because of the freedom they had found in Christ.

From Malakal we were to fly southwest to Juba, the capital of southern Sudan. However, because of the urgent call we had received from Pibor, we asked MAF if it could make a diversion and fly southeast to the land of the Murle, and it agreed. On the appointed day, we boarded the Cessna with a certain amount of subdued excitement. Would we really see Pibor again after eighteen years?

We flew over the boundless savanna, dissected into several vast plains by the Nile, Sobat, Baro, and Pibor Rivers. It was all so familiar: the home territories of the Shulla, the Dinka, the Nuer, the Anuak, and the Murle.

As we circled over Akobo, our very first home in Africa, it was obvious that we could not land because of a very wet airstrip. But from the air, we could see the impressive hospital that was being built in the name of the Sudan Council of Churches. It would be an eighty-bed complex.

We could also make out what used to be the Chapel of Hope, given with such joy and sacrifice by Hope College students in the fall of 1949 during the annual Missions Emphasis Week. It was now lying in ruins, a result of hostilities that had devastated so much of the South.

Clouds had been building up around us, clouds that already had dumped rain on Akobo. But visibility was good—until we were about halfway between Akobo and Pibor. The clouds suddenly dropped from the heavens all the way to the ground in front of us. It was as if God had let a curtain fall right before our eyes. This curtain extended as far as we could see in every direction. There was no way that we could fly through, or around, that dense fog.

Again Bob and I sensed that God had sent us a message: "Returning to Pibor is not my will for you. Others are there now by my direction. You are to go elsewhere."

Of one mind and heart, we said, "Let's proceed to Juba." So the pilot veered toward the southwest and headed for the city in Sudan's southernmost province, Equatoria.

We heard later from John Haspels that all had been clear at Pibor that afternoon. They had even heard the plane approaching and wondered why it never arrived. So it was that the lure of John's "thus saith the Lord" letter was canceled by a silent Cloudy Pillar whose message had thundered loud and clear.

In Juba we stayed at the ACROSS staff house. Bob had interviews during the week with several men of position regarding tape ministries and other areas of service in which the RCA might consider joining hands with the Sudanese Church. What a privilege to meet with these strong leaders whom God had called out to guide the church in the South through persecution, political upheaval, and a tenuous reconstruction.

One Sunday morning a young Sudanese pastor stood before his people and said, "We used to think it was only the white man's work to spread the gospel. Now we must commit ourselves to God and take up the responsibility of sharing Christ with our people."

We returned to Nairobi on June 24, still in a quandary over our future, knowing only that Pibor was no longer an option.

On July 8, our secretary for Africa, Glenn Bruggers, called to tell us of Wilma Kats' death. We mourned for this longtime friend and rejoiced for her. Now she was well!

Glenn also wanted us to know that the RCA would back us fully whether we felt the Lord was leading us to or to Kenya. We heard those words with gratitude.

Bob drew up a list of pros and cons that helped to clarify our thinking. As a result, and in answer to the prayers of many months, we told Jonathan Hildebrandt on July 14 that we sensed strongly that we were being led to stay in Kenya. Ultimately both of us had responded to the needs in the two unreached areas in Kenya: Alale and Waldena. It had been a long journey of the soul. Now we had peace.

A stirring scene took place at the end of 1979, when the Kenya branch of the Africa Inland Mission was bowing out of its administrative position in favor of the Africa Inland Church.

> As part of the ceremony, two men stood on the platform: a Kenyan pastor and a mission executive. They stood for an emotion-packed moment, embracing, as the pastor on behalf of the Africa Inland Church, pleaded that expatriate personnel stay and help....

> In the present climate of coups and apartheid, marching Islam, and maneuvering Marxism, Africa is a prime battleground for the Christian faith. African churches have sprung up in every country. Some are struggling to maintain their own identities in the face of tribal tradition and other hostile pressures. It's going to take the concerted efforts of Christ's church in the world, serving in the power of the Holy Spirit, to help stem the anti-Christian tides that are sweeping over this continent, to help strengthen the churches as they "stand in the gap," and to assist in the proclamation of God's redemptive work in Jesus Christ.[1]

Under this mandate, and that of the Great Commission, which is valid "until the end of the age," we moved forward in the direction God was leading. This meant that the work of the RCA would be expanding in Kenya; the RCA and the AIC would be working in partnership, with personnel from both churches serving together at the new outposts.

All this was negotiated first between the RCA and AIC Bishop Ezekiel Birech and later at the regional levels. The RCA proposals were accepted wholeheartedly, and Bob and I gave thanks that the church at home had the vision to commit itself to further outreach.

In this tremendous step of faith, the AIC/RCA Joint Projects was born.

---

[1] Morrell Swart, "African Churches Pulsate with Life." Reprinted from the *Church Herald*, September 5, 1980: 19.

XXI
Triumphs and Trials
at Alale

After a month of Swahili study in August 1980, we made brief excursions west to Alale and east to Waldena for regional church meetings. Then we were ready to take the next step. The long period of waiting and wondering made us realize anew how precious it was to have work to do. Every cell within us was clamoring, "Let's get going!"

Our strategy, since we could not be in both places at once, was to open Alale first: see to all the government and church transactions, choose a site, clear the airstrip, provide for a water supply, and put up at least temporary housing. Taking care of these preliminaries would free new personnel to apply themselves to studying the language and getting to know the people and their customs and cultures without having to deal with time-consuming details of launching a new mission post. Our hope was that within two years all would be ready, with personnel on site, so that we could move across Kenya to Orma country and go through the same process there.

Rob Przybylski and Gary Melcher, from First Reformed Church in DeMotte, Indiana, were our first volunteers at Alale. They called themselves second-generation volunteers because they both had parents-in-law who had volunteered in Ethiopia. So they had had some orientation before they left home.

These two strong young men were a real asset in helping us "get our act together" that month of October 1980. They accepted the rough camp life and the hard work with grace and cheerfulness—a God-given volunteer attitude for which we always were so thankful. It ministered to us.

Doc Propst was with us the first few days. Seventy years old, his parents had been AIM missionaries in Kenya; so had a grandmother. For years he served as a medical doctor, itinerating throughout the country. He and his wife, Lila, had seven children, most of whom became missionaries.

During his later years, Doc gave up his medical work and put his expertise into water development projects. His skill was much in demand. To Africans, who considered his water wizardry to be nothing short of magical, he was fond of saying: "I can't create water, but I can take what's there and do something with it."

Doc was impressed with the spring up on Lorsuk Mountain. He estimated that six thousand gallons of water a day flowed out of that mountainside. With that kind of production, he thought it would be a feasible project, even though it would require three to five miles of pipe to take the water down to the proposed mission site and on to the community. He realized it would also be a tremendously challenging undertaking for that part of the world.

Doc returned to Nairobi on a truck that had delivered a load of freight, including sections of a prefab tin house (*rondavel*) that the men put together in a few hours. The house was oval in shape, twenty-one feet long and fourteen feet wide. This would be our living quarters for the next two years. How spacious it seemed after sleeping in a pup tent for several nights.

"Clearing" was the name of the game those first weeks at Alale. A two-mile track from the main road into the airstrip and mission site was cleared of brush. Work on the airstrip took several months, due to the many candelabra euphorbia trees—giant, thick-trunked, spiny cacti with a milky sap that stung both skin and eyes—and the Pokot themselves.

About thirty laborers were hired for the job. They worked with a will, but one of their fellow Pokot was causing a problem. Every day a man sat under a certain tree at one end of the strip. He had a bee log in that tree and was not going to permit workers to chop it down. The matter finally was settled through the chief, and the man moved his bee log to another tree away from the strip, his source of honey still intact.

But that was not the only obstacle. Right in the middle of the strip were two other controversial trees. Some years before, goats had been sacrificed in religious rites under those trees, and superstition held that if they were cut down, the people who had made the sacrifices would die. So the chief said he would find out whether the people were still around, and if they were, another sacrifice would have to be made to remove the curse.

Finally, after lengthy investigations and no further complaints, the trees came down. The strip was completed by the end of February 1981.

While the clearing was still in process, we had an occasional foretaste of things to come. One day the Sikkemas flew over on their way back to Sudan. They buzzed us twice, flying low over the airstrip. The second time around, they dropped our mail.

We had been expecting them, but the actual event exceeded all expectations. The familiar MAF Cessna, the first plane to make a pass over our unfinished airstrip, flown by dear friends—well, our appreciation almost overwhelmed us. We thanked God for joys like this that mingled with the day-by-day plodding and sent us yet again on our way rejoicing!

While all this was going on at Alale, our thoughts wandered often to Edgerton, Minnesota. The "further developments" that we were watching for in Jack and Deb Swart's life were materializing at an astonishingly rapid rate.

Baby Justin was teething and fussing one Sunday evening in September. So Deb stayed home with him while Jack went to church. When he returned after the service, he found Deb in Justin's room rocking him to sleep. In a stage whisper he said, "When you're finished, I want to talk to you."

The request wasn't so unusual, Deb remembers, but the urgency of his voice was like nothing she had ever heard before. She knew it must be a compelling matter. Soon she was able to lay Justin in his bed and join Jack in the living room.

"What do you have to tell me, Jack?" she asked.

"We need to look into serving overseas as missionaries," he replied.

"We NEED to?"

"Yes, we need to."

"Why?"

"Because tonight God told me to use my skills in another place in this world."

"Okay, honey. What do we do?"

"We must contact Wycliffe Bible Translators. Tonight at church, a young woman talked to us about her experiences as a support person for Wycliffe in Mexico. I have this strong feeling that God wants us to do the same sort of thing."[1]

[1] Deb Swart, from a report to the author, June 1996. Joint Archives of Holland, Hope College.

Three months later, Jack and Deb and little Justin were on their way to Sudan, fully supported by the RCA. However they would not be working at this time with Wycliffe or its overseas counterpart, Summer Institute of Linguistics (SIL). Support staff for SIL had already been provided, and applications to SIL elsewhere had not been fruitful.

But the RCA, hearing about these closed doors, had called Jack and Deb to ask if they would consider going to Sudan under ACROSS (Africa Committee for the Rehabilitation of the Southern Sudan), which needed builders. They took one look at each other and, without further hesitation, answered, "Sure!"

Once this commitment was made, applications and official documents were processed quickly. On January 21, 1981, this Swart family arrived in Nairobi where ACROSS had its headquarters.

Happily we were able to be there to welcome them. It was a joyful reunion. Deb truly seemed as glad to be back in Africa as Jack was; the months at Ileret three years before had infected her with a love for this continent.

They had expected to be on their way to Sudan within a few days, but there was an unexpected delay. It was something we had not anticipated when we named Jack after his father.

ACROSS had applied for visas for the three of them. Deb's and Justin's visas were readily granted; Jack's was denied. The name of John Robert Swart had been put on Sudan's black list at the time of the 1962 expulsions. (We marveled again that we had been permitted to enter Sudan just a few months before.)

Bob and I had to return to Alale before the matter was settled. We felt for this enthusiastic young couple who were so sure they had heard God's "Go ye!" and in obedience had gone. Their faith was being tested, and so was ours.

One Saturday morning in February, we received a message from Jack on the mission radio: he wanted to talk with us that evening. We were elated later that day to hear Jack's happy, exultant voice saying, "I've got some good news!"

There had been no word from Khartoum, but the Sudan Embassy in Nairobi gave him a visa anyway. A few days later, the family flew to Juba on an ACROSS plane, flying by way of Alale. The plane circled twice, flew across the airstrip, waggled its wings, and headed north. Reminding the

Lord of what a precious cargo was on board, we watched the plane until it was out of sight. Our children were on their way to beginning their own missionary career—their faith intact, and ours stronger than ever.

About this time, a Land Rover (rugged British, four-wheel-drive vehicle) arrived at Alale with a team from Norconsult, a Norwegian group that assists in development projects. They had heard about the water source up on Lorsuk Mountain and wanted to assess the situation for themselves.

They were impressed with what they saw and fully agreed that the project of piping water down the mountain should get underway as soon as possible. They even thought that NORAD, a Norwegian government aid agency, might have some funds available to assist.

But we actually applied to Food for the Hungry/Canada on the matter of underwriting the project. Our hope and goal was that, with a drop of twelve hundred feet from the spring, the water, flowing solely by gravity, would bring a new quality of life, not only to the mission staff houses and proposed dispensary, but also to many in the Alale community.

Consider this scene: Bob and I went to the borehole a few miles from the mission late one afternoon. Women were there pumping furiously, sweating profusely, panting with the effort—for a cupful of poor quality water every three or four pumps. Pails, plastic jugs, and gourds all had to be filled. And we came with our five-gallon jerrican. Two donkeys ambled into the enclosure to sip what they could from the foot-shaped hollows in the muck where a little spilled water stood.

We took our turns pumping the big wooden lever. It took a while, but at last, long after sundown, all the containers were full, and the women were glad for a ride back to their villages with their precious water.

Was it any wonder that our thoughts turned more and more to the spring on Lorsuk? To make available to our neighbors a source of good water, easily obtained, would be a service of incalculable value—for better health, and for a degree of the abundant life God means for his people to enjoy. But it would be a few months before this dream would be realized.

By this time, and as part of the AIC/RCA Joint Projects agreement, Ronald and Alice Chomom with their little daughter Chemutai had joined the Alale team. Ronald and Alice were Pokot. Both were Bible school graduates and were therefore a gift to the evangelistic thrust in the Alale area. We praised God for them. When we went to the United States in May for a brief furlough, we were thankful to be able to leave the Alale mission and its incipient program in their care.

Going home this time held special significance for several reasons. First of all, we were happy to meet two more new grandchildren: Robert Newton Powell, born the previous October, and Leah Rae Swart, born in January. These little ones were two more jewels among our treasured family.

Then on May 10, Bob and I—mystified, humbled, and thrilled—attended the one hundred sixteenth Hope College commencement to receive honorary doctor of humane letters degrees from Hope's president, Dr. Gordon Van Wylen.

The annual Mission Emphasis Week, when support for mission projects held high priority among the college students, was a thing of the past. But to us, this presentation was evidence of Hope College's enduring interest in and recognition of the dynamic mission enterprise of the Reformed Church in America, both at home and abroad. It was a very glad day!

About now, good news was coming from Larry and Linda McAuley. God was speaking to them about a career commitment.

Larry's initial interest in missions began during his high school years and was further swayed by attending the Presbyterian New Wilmington Missionary Conference each summer for three years. Out of these conferences came an opportunity to spend a summer on the Colorado River Indian Tribes Reservation in Parker Dam, Arizona, with the Summer Services Program. As a result, the cause of missions became an established preoccupation which led him, after receiving a degree in agronomy from Kansas State University, to Dembi Dollo, Ethiopia, for two years, along with Linda, who had graduated from Sterling College in Kansas with a degree in elementary education.

Larry told us that he felt "strangely detached" while at Ileret in 1979. They had become disenchanted with life in the United States and were hoping that spending a month at Ileret would give them some direction, perhaps hearing God speak to them in no uncertain terms; but it didn't happen.

Once back in the United States, though, God continued to nudge them, bringing missions to their minds until they couldn't have ignored his will if they had tried. They began to think about committing themselves in earnest to mission service.

The United Presbyterian mission agency had no openings for them at that time. So the McAuleys were about to sign up with the Africa Inland Mission to go to Zaire to work at Rethy Academy (a missionary children's school) and in translation, when they received a letter from Bob Swart with an invitation to join the ranks at Alale, to bring the good news of Christ to the Pokot through the ministry of agriculture and community development.

Larry remembers how thrilled they were to receive that letter. Things moved quickly for them: an interview with the RCA's Al Poppen; meeting the rest of the staff at the New York City office; deputation, packing, a sale, and "suddenly we were on our way! AFRICA! This is where God wants us! What a joy to know that we were smack-dab in the center of his will!"[2]

The McAuleys traveled to Kenya with us in September and soon were deep in the study of Swahili.

Happily, we found Jack and Deb in Nairobi when we arrived. ACROSS had been given a contract with the Dutch government to build clinics in the Pibor area, and Jack, who had been in charge of building projects in Juba, was asked to supervise this new undertaking. They were in Nairobi for a brief holiday before proceeding to Pibor, and to purchase supplies for several months in the bush.

Before we went back to Alale, we made one more foray into Orma country. There were nine of us in all, including other missionary colleagues and two Kenyan AIC pastors. We were welcomed heartily by the police and teachers and the local Orma leaders. At the evening meeting, the pastors held a service by lantern light in the old church building. At the close, the young police officer stood and said, "We are very much glad that you have come. Our big problem is that we have no church leaders. The Orma people are difficult, but God can do the impossible. We are glad you have come so that light may come to the people here."

We found the chief several miles east of Waldena. He had a scribe write a letter for him, giving his approval to our coming sometime in the future. In Hola, the district headquarters on the Tana River still further east, Bob and the nurse, Rose Schwarz (who soon would be making monthly excursions to the Orma) were able to see all the officials necessary to get authorization to work at Waldena. We were elated! We thanked God for expediting the matter of written permissions. We looked forward with keen anticipation to opening work in the area in a few months, in the name of the RCA and in partnership with the AIC.

So, with the essential letters now in hand, we returned to Nairobi and, shortly thereafter, to Alale.

---

[2] Larry McAuley, from a letter to the author, October 19, 1995. Joint Archives of Holland, Hope College.

It was becoming more obvious to us that the spring on Lorsuk was a major factor in the establishment of the Alale mission post. Without a good supply of water for a school and a clinic, to say nothing of mission personnel, we might as well forget about this outreach effort. Some events that took place in October were crucial in this regard.

The McAuleys came on October 17 for their midterm break from language school. Doc Propst arrived two days later. The spring was revisited.

Because of drought conditions below and the often foggy atmosphere up the mountain, Pokot farmers had taken to clearing land above the spring for planting corn. This was in violation of government decree that the forest on the mountaintop should be preserved. President Daniel arap Moi had broadcast over the radio urging administrators and chiefs to get people off the tops of mountains and give them alternative sites for planting.

But the clearing continued. This adversely affected the water supply up there. When Doc measured the spring's output this time, one of its outlets was producing only a quarter of what it had the year before!

This was so discouraging. We were facing another critical question, too: would Food for the Hungry/Canada come through with funds for this project? We had had no word from them since visiting their headquarters the previous summer.

On October 21 we all convened for a heart-to-heart discussion. We considered fully and frankly the pros and cons of either scrapping the whole scheme, or continuing with plans for piping the water, with the possibility that the spring would dry up after a few years. Did we want to go ahead, hoping that the authorities would take action in moving the few people from the crucial catchment area and then start in on a major reforestation effort? Or should we pull out for a few years, initiating the work among the Orma now and revisit Alale later to see how things were progressing or regressing on Lorsuk?

Our hearts felt like lead. There were so many negatives and unknowns. What was God's will in all of this? We prayed earnestly for his wise direction.

At last Doc Propst boomed out in his big, kindly voice: "We've got to make a decision. What are we going to do?"

There was a long silence as we all waited for an answer.

Finally, Bob boldly declared, "I'm ready to risk it!"

It was a turning point—the step of faith that perhaps God was waiting for. Everyone seemed to take heart after that and we proceeded to make positive plans.

The very next morning, we received via mission radio a cable from Canada: "All systems go." The financial grant would be in the bank by the end of November.

Also, at a community meeting that same morning, the chief, sub-chiefs, and tribal elders showed, for the most part, a genuine desire to cooperate. Doc drafted a letter of agreement. Several copies were made. The chief signed them. They were distributed to the district commissioner, the district officer, the clerk of the city council, and the local authorities.

Larry McAuley offered his services to the forestry department for a massive tree-planting project in the watershed area on Lorsuk, to be implemented after the first of the year when their Swahili course would be finished.

So, to echo the cable from Canada, all systems were indeed go! The burden of indecision had been lifted and we looked to the future ministry at Alale with increased assurance of God's gracious hand upon us all.

Pastor Ronald Chomom's being with us meant that evangelism could be an immediate, vital part of the mission program. In preparation for various kinds of meetings, an area was cleared in the shade of a large, leafy thorn tree. Sturdy forked sticks were pounded into the ground and flat-sided logs laid across them for benches. They served very well. The Pokot gathered there readily, particularly on Sunday mornings. Ronald also visited in the villages in the vicinity. The seed of the gospel was being sown.

With 1982 soon upon us, and the imminent arrival of the McAuleys and several RCA volunteers to propel the water project from dream to reality, it was incumbent upon us to have everything ready: prefab houses on site; beds, food, forty tons of two-and-a-half-inch pipe; and a track cleared as far as possible up Lorsuk Mountain for the trucker hauling the pipe. All preparations were completed on time, and it wasn't long before we were singing "Hail, hail, the gang's all here!"

Another group from First Reformed Church of DeMotte, Indiana, came to help. Verne and Lorraine Sikkema's son Milton was among them as well as the pastor, the Rev. Jack Boerigter. Besides the DeMotte team, two couples had come from Bayshore Gardens Reformed Church in Bradenton, Florida: Harold and Hank Stauble and Marvin and Shirley Brandt; and Tom Larink from Grand Rapids, who had come out for a longer term of service in Sudan but would have some orientation with us first. Doc Propst was there, too, for the very specialized task of "capping" the spring and working on an unbreakable water tank for the community.

So with our large crew, plus several Pokot workers, the venture moved along smoothly and steadily. The spring was cleaned out prior to being capped. The laying of the long pipeline proceeded, starting at the mission and advancing gradually up the mountain.

While all this was going on, the kitchen corps served forty-five to sixty meals a day and baked bread daily to keep the hard-working teams nourished and strong. This whole project was a huge undertaking for this remote outpost.

During this time, the RCA's new secretary for Africa, the Rev. Warren Henseler, paid us a visit. The timing was such that Bob was able to introduce him not only to Alale, but also to Waldena. We were sure that such an overview, though brief, would be helpful to him in his recently acquired position.

On March 1, the last of the pipeline was laid amid great rejoicing. The work had been tough! Carrying heavy pipe up brushy mountain inclines had taxed everyone's endurance. Aching muscles, blisters, and fatigue had plagued the men. But God had renewed their strength and determination every morning. As the final length of pipe was put in place, the men stood on the mountainside and sang the Doxology, giving thanks to God. What a moment!

This project had been a physical feat; it was also a spiritual victory. Prayer played a large part in the whole process. We learned shortly after it was completed that the mountain-dwelling Pokot had offered sacrifices to insure that the project would fail and we'd all leave. So we could look back and see our October doldrums in their proper perspective: the "principalities and powers" were in conflict with God's purposes. We were sure that prayer was instrumental in God's getting through to us during that memorable meeting, and then for enabling the whole team, together with the Pokot workers, to accomplish this tremendous task. Then we understood more clearly than ever the truth and dependability of God's promise: "As I have planned, so shall it be, and as I have purposed, so shall it stand."[3]

Shortly after the spring was capped, the mission and community tanks were erected and the pipeline to the Alale community center was laid. Many hundreds of people now had the blessing of abundant, pure water.

With significant rainfall in April, Larry McAuley and Tom Larink, assisted by a few Pokot men and forestry employees, were able to get nearly a

3 Isaiah 14:24, Revised Standard Version.

thousand young trees planted on Lorsuk's denuded slopes. The healing of the spring's catchment area was begun.

Sunday morning attendance at the outdoor services continued to increase, making it necessary to fashion more log "pews." More and more, Pastor Ronald went out in the villages after sundown when the people were more apt to be at home. Sometimes he and Larry went off on their motorbikes to more northerly reaches of the tribe to spread the good news of the Savior's love.

With the airstrip cleared, the water system in working order, all government and church-to-church agreements in hand, a Kenyan pastor and his family on staff, and the McAuleys amazingly well oriented to life at Alale, Bob and I began to make plans for moving on to Orma country in August. We had hoped that a nurse would be in residence at Alale by this time. But this not being the case, the McAuleys agreed to carry on the medical work at the first-aid level for a time. Eventually they were able to hire a young man named Daniel who had been trained as a "patient attendant." It was three years before a qualified nurse joined Larry and Linda to round out the ministry there.

Before we left the land of the Pokot, our daughter Chloe, her husband Mark Young, and their three children from Dhahran, Saudi Arabia, wanted to see for themselves all that was going on at Alale. They came on June 16, Bob's sixty-third birthday. What a grand celebration!

Two days later, the morning dawned beautifully clear. All of us—nine adults and five children—were planning to climb Lorsuk that morning to see the newly completed installation halfway up her side. We had heard gunshots during the night, but didn't think much about it. If Karamojong raiders had come across the Uganda border just to the west of us, they were after Pokot cattle. We had no cattle.

While I prepared a big skillet of scrambled eggs for breakfast and Chloe watched toast brown under the grill flame, the children ran in and out of the house. Mark had walked out to the gate.

Pastor Ronald, carrying his bow and arrows, approached Mark and said quietly, "I think we should take a walk in the forest." Not comprehending his meaning, Mark took him to Bob. Ronald repeated his warning.

Bob immediately took action. He told Mark and Chloe to get their valuable documents together to carry with them, and to remove the remainder of their belongings from their tent to our house which could be locked. Bob gathered our important papers. I turned off the stove, put the toast in a bag, and filled a thermos with water. McAuleys were doing the same sort of things.

We left the compound none too soon. The armed Karamojong raiders, four to five hundred strong, descended upon the mission minutes later. Apparently they had passed the mission during the night, had found no cattle, and were now returning to Uganda. This raid, we understood, was in revenge for one the Pokot had made only two weeks before on the Karamojong, killing thirteen people and burning a village. The feud between the two tribes had a long history.

As we made our way into the bush, the sound of gunfire exploded over us. We all ducked and ran—through gullies, over rocks, dodging thorn bushes, hoping that we were distancing ourselves from the warriors, praying that they weren't spread out through the woods.

Things quieted down quickly, but we continued running until we were perhaps a quarter of a mile from the mission. We crouched together under a low scrub tree and counted heads. One was missing. Where was Tom?

As we waited, not speaking, catching our breath, the children munched on toast and needed drinks. Then we began hearing new sounds: the banging, crashing sound of rock on metal. The marauders were breaking into the houses, shooting off locks, and smashing windows.

There was nothing that could be done; we could only sit helplessly and wait, thanking God that our pastor had given us warning, that our lives had been spared, and praying that Tom was hiding somewhere unhurt.

Perhaps forty-five minutes passed. Then we became aware that a gun battle had begun at Amakuriat, the next police post. Because there were no more sounds from the direction of the mission, Bob and Larry decided to return cautiously to see if it would be safe for us all to go back.

After what seemed an eternity, Bob reappeared. We could return, he said; the danger was past. "But just sit a minute, and let me warn you about what you're going to see. When Larry and I first arrived back at the mission, we were angered to see that with the Karamojong gone, some Pokot were in the yard looting. We yelled at them. They dropped everything and ran. As we moved closer, we could see that the Karamojong had ransacked the entire mission. Everything is in a shambles. Expect to find everything stolen or broken. Mark and Chloe, I saw your suitcase all cut up and completely empty. Everything in the houses has been turned upside down. The tent is gone, except for the poles and the flooring.

"Before we go, let's praise the Lord for his mercy in sparing our lives." Bob prayed, and we all joined in heartfelt thanks to our God that each of us there was safe.

We hadn't walked far when who should appear but Tom! Joy and relief showed on every face. He had merely run in a different direction. Incredibly, in his hand he was carrying his camera and a paperback copy of *Huckleberry Finn*! "I thought we'd go in the woods, there'd be time to read a while, and then we'd return," he explained. "I left my wallet, but grabbed the book!"

Humorous incidents like this kept us all going as we surveyed the wreckage around us. The place looked as if a tornado had struck: all windows were smashed, and the looting of cloth items, foodstuffs, camping gear, cooking utensils, cameras, and typewriters was thorough. Yet these were just things, and again we could only praise God for the safety net that he had spread for us. We learned later that several police, Pokot, and Karamojong had been killed in the ensuing battle at the police post.

Our thoughts turned to Ronald and Alice and their two little girls. Had they escaped unharmed? They didn't show up for some time. But at last we saw Alice with the children walking toward their house. They had run into the woods on the other side of the airstrip, hiding deep among the trees. Ronald had hidden for a while and then had followed the raiders from a safe distance to check on their movements.

Bob and Larry were relieved that their Toyota trucks were still functional. The side mirrors were gone, and each had a smashed cab window. But the tires were untouched; the engines had not been tampered with.

Nor had the three-thousand-gallon water tank been touched. Bullets had ripped through the houses, as evidenced in chairs, walls, and closets; bullets so easily could have ruined that fine tank.

Around noon, some men from Amakuriat drove up to ask Bob if he could help some of their wounded, among them a policeman, a few women, and some children. Bob and Mark, who is a physician, went to see if anything could be done. The wounded were in great need of hospitalization. So Bob and Tom took them to Kapenguria, three hours away. They arrived back that evening. The patients had survived the long, rough trip and were now in the hospital. Word came later that the policeman had died.

Of the hundreds of raiders, twenty-one had been slain when Pokot warriors ambushed them on their way back to Uganda.

All thoughts of climbing Lorsuk had evaporated. We spent the next few days trying to restore order to the compound, replacing broken window panes, taking stock of what remained. We made a quick trip to Nairobi with the Young family, who had to fly back home to Saudi Arabia, and at the same time we replenished some of our supplies to carry us through until we would leave for Orma country in August.

On July 2, Doc Propst flew in with a representative from Food for the Hungry/Canada. He wanted to see the installation at the spring as well as the community water tank and pump that Doc had designed for rugged durability and that was filled by gravity flow from the mission water tank. The representative was well pleased. "You are to be congratulated!" he exclaimed. So we were certain that he took a good report back to the home office in Canada.

Tom flew out with the plane that day; he needed more clothing. The McAuleys left the next day for an already scheduled and well earned vacation, and to celebrate their tenth wedding anniversary. Our pastor and family went home to Kapenguria for a few days.

Bob and I had no qualms at all about remaining there alone. Hadn't we spent more than thirty years in similar bush situations? Wasn't the Lord there with us? Alale seemed to be a peaceful place now that the Karamojong had retreated across the border.

Following the raid of June 18, when seven of the local police were killed, President Moi gave orders for all police personnel to be withdrawn from the Alale location. He said that these men didn't know how to fight raiders, so he would see to it that the Pokot themselves were armed.

Bob and I were having supper Sunday evening, July 11, by the light of two kerosene lanterns. I had just gotten up to cut some cake for dessert when our little tin house exploded with gunshot. We dove to the floor. Bob had the presence of mind to extinguish the lights. He braced a chair against the door with its back caught under the doorknob. Shooting into the house continued, and the attackers began to bombard our flimsy dwelling with rocks. The newly repaired windows were again being shattered.

I whispered to Bob, "What shall we do?"

He said, "Pray!"

So we prayed aloud to God for protection and deliverance.

At one point, as we huddled on the floor together, I felt something sticky on Bob's trousers, and my first thought was "blood!" But it turned out to be strawberry jam. One of the bullets had smashed through a tin on our pantry shelves. There was jam spattered all over the house.

Our assailants finally demanded money and sugar. The previous raiders had nearly depleted our sugar supply, but by standing almost literally on my head in the sugar barrel, I was able to scrape up a few pounds. Bob handed some money quickly through the partially opened door. And then all was quiet. Our attackers had left.

Not feeling safe in the house, we grabbed two small shoulder bags containing precious documents, and a sleeping bag which had been returned after the first raid, and took once more to the woods.

As we were leaving the house, we could hear the Pokot sounding the call for help from village to village. It was an eerie sound, and not having heard it before, we weren't sure whether it was coming from friends or enemies. We decided it was the better part of wisdom to stay away from the house that night. We had no idea, either, if we had been assaulted by Karamojong or Pokot bandits.

Lying on the ground under a tree, with our sleeping bag over us, our trembling hearts again were filled with praise for God's mercies. We had suffered not a scratch.

Soon we were aware of a glow around us. Was the moon already rising over Lorsuk? It seemed too early. I rose up to look. No moon—not even its heralding brightness. We accepted the manifestation for what it surely was: a sign of God's presence round about us, and we were comforted.

(Sometime later, we received a card from Arlene Schuiteman, sent after she had heard our news. On the card was printed this reassuring thought by Mother Basilea: "In the night of fear and despair, a light rises resplendently. It is Jesus.")

At dawn we returned to the house. A Pokot worker was already there. He was relieved to see us; he hadn't known if we were alive or dead. We counted bullet holes in the house walls and then sent a message by mission radio to Nairobi to let them know our circumstances. We also asked them to call Desmond and Virginia Hales in Eldoret to inform them that we would be coming later in the day. We had a little breakfast and then started packing. We needed to get away. It was a decision we had made during the night.

Bob hadn't been well and the night out in the cool dampness, together with the shock and stress of the evening before, set him back considerably. As we started getting things together for our departure, a few Pokot friends gathered around, and when they saw that Bob had no strength to carry things out to the truck and trailer, they proceeded to help. In spite of himself, Bob had to smile at the higgledy-piggledy way they packed the vehicles. But we were both so grateful! By noon we were ready to leave. It hurt to say good-bye to the friends there, and to lovely Alale. We certainly hadn't expected to leave so precipitously. We had planned to be there when the others returned. But under the circumstances, we wondered if they actually should return at this time. We would see them downcountry.

In one of the towns along the way, we found Pastor Ronald and Peter Maru, another AIC pastor, beside the road waiting for a taxi to take them to Kapenguria. They were astonished to see us, and even moreso to hear what had happened at Alale. It was a real blow to them. We became their taxi to Kapenguria.

How Bob managed to drive all the way to Eldoret that afternoon I do not know, except that God gave him strength beyond his own. Desmond and Virginia had been expecting us and welcomed us lovingly. Bob went right to bed in the haven of an upper room and stayed there for a week.

In Eldoret we had time to reflect on recent events at Alale. Psalm 91 had become very real and meaningful to us, for God showed himself powerful on our behalf. Surely we had been sheltered under his wings; he had given his angels charge over us; he answered when we called on him. The message of the hymn "Under His Wings" became patently real to us.

Some people question the matter of persevering in trying to serve an apparently ungrateful people. From our own experience, to hear a word of thanks in any language, or even to see a person's face light up because of what one has received, has been far from the normal reaction. In fact, we learned not to expect gratitude for anything. What about Christ and the ten lepers? One thankful heart! That is a high percentage for tribal folks.

However, we believe that in obedience to the Great Commission, we must go where God leads, to love and serve in a Christlike way, realizing full well that that way is rarely welcomed, appreciated, or even tolerated in some cases—the witness, more often than not, rejected. The witness by life, word, and deed is the task committed to us; the "new creations" are the work of the Holy Spirit.

Service cannot be limited to those in whom the seed of faith has shown evidence of bearing fruit. Even as God sends rain on both the righteous and the unrighteous, services such as medicines and water systems cannot be withheld until the whole community is Christian.

In a letter from the Vogelaars in Egypt, Harold stated: "…we seek to bear a Christian witness. That very task requires us all to love and serve the world for whom Christ died—before the world accepts, not on condition that it accept. We are not alone in this, but we are often lonely."

And often it is the development programs, these evidences of caring, that first prepare the ground to receive the seeds of faith.

On July 17, Desmond Hales and two members of the regional church council went to Kapenguria, where they were joined by Pastors Ronald Chomom and Peter Maru, to meet with the district commissioner and the chairman of the county council to discuss the Alale situation. Government authorities assured the Africa Inland Church that they would do everything possible to make the area secure.

We took leave of our good friends in Eldoret on July 19 and drove to Nairobi, where Paul and Erma Lehman were waiting to welcome us at the Mennonite guest house. The Lehmans had been Jack's and Dick's dorm parents at Good Shepherd School. They were now the hosts at the gracious, rambling guest house that had been built decades before to house the British Officers Club. We basked in the peace and friendliness of the place.

It so happened that the McAuleys were there also, refreshed after their vacation, and so distressed to hear of the second incident at Alale. How would this affect their "call" to that needy area nestled up against Lorsuk and Kachagaleu?

On Saturday, July 31, Bob and Larry started out for Alale to retrieve the rest of the things we would need at Waldena. They planned to stop at Eldoret that night. Linda moved in with me for the duration of our husbands' absence.

Early Sunday morning, August 1, we were awakened by a barrage of gunfire in the distance. I remarked to Linda: "I wonder if the cause of this will be newsworthy enough to appear in the papers."

When we went to breakfast, we were astounded to hear that a coup to overthrow the government of President Moi was in progress. Newsworthy enough, indeed! There was palpable apprehension in the air. The Voice of Kenya (VOK) radio station was taken over by the dissident air force early in the day, and a brash announcement was made that the government of President Daniel arap Moi had been overthrown.

Three hours later, VOK was back under its former control. Kenyans were told to keep calm because *Nyayo* still lived! (*Nyayo*, meaning "footsteps" in

Swahili, was the watchword of President Moi's regime.) Gunfire was heard throughout the day.

Not being able to travel about in the city that Sunday morning, we had a beautiful worship service out on the lawn of the guest house. We were so aware of God's peace around us in the midst of the city's turmoil. As we prayed and sang, two bombers zoomed deafeningly over Nairobi several times, and late in the afternoon, we heard heavy artillery fire at the air force base to the east.

The coup attempt was a failure. Four of the ringleaders fled to Tanzania. Seventy-one air force men had been killed. The looting in the city was disastrous for many shopkeepers, most of whom were Asians. The whole downtown of Nairobi was in a shambles.

Linda and I wondered about Bob and Larry. When they returned on August 8, we learned that they had been delayed in Eldoret for a day because of the coup attempt, but otherwise had no problems in traveling. They had been more concerned about us, having thought that they had left us in a safe place. And they had! Again, we all had been protected "under his wings."

Tom was now studying Swahili in preparation for further service in Kenya. The McAuleys and the Swarts made a brief trip to Waldena with two loaded vehicles and trailers to seek out at least a temporary mission site where we could set up, in a few hours, a metal storehouse in which we could leave our gear, in anticipation of our return later in September.

On September 1, Bob and the McAuleys left Nairobi for another trip to Alale. It was imperative that the mood of the Pokot be assessed. During the Swart-McAuley visit the month before, the people admitted that the bandits of the second attack had been a few renegade Pokot. So the men laid down certain conditions that must be met if the Pokot wanted missionaries to return to Alale: the culprits must be apprehended and disciplined; the families involved must return the money that had been taken (it had been cash for workers' wages); and the Pokot, who are well aware when raids are imminent, would be responsible for warning the missionaries who were there to serve them.

How had the Pokot responded to these conditions?

When Bob returned to Nairobi, he had encouraging news. The community of Alale had rallied around the mission in a tremendous way, and not only in word. It had not been able to apprehend the attackers because they had fled across the border into Uganda. But their parents had been ordered to sell enough of their cattle to make up the full amount of cash in repayment for what had been taken. The chief had handed Bob a paper bag containing seven thousand shillings in one hundred shilling notes. Full payment!

The tank up on the mountain had been vandalized, probably by the irate, illegal farmers up there. The Pokot themselves had repaired it as best they could. They had also had a big *baraza* (meeting) at which the people promised that such a thing would never happen again. They would help protect the mission.

Word also came while they were there that the warrior age-sets of the Pokot and the Karamojong had agreed to be at peace.

With all of this encouragement and goodwill in evidence, the McAuleys had perfect peace about staying on at Alale. Following such adverse events, this was a first step in a steady walk of faith.

God confirmed this decision in a remarkable and beautiful way: he let Larry and Linda know that, after ten years of marriage, they would at last have a child. Their joy and thanksgiving knew no bounds. Luke was born in April 1983.

XXII
Into South Sudan
Again—and Out

Details surrounding the Leemkuils, Sikkemas, Busmans, and (Jack and Deb) Swarts were described in earlier chapters, but there were further developments in each case.

Paul Leemkuil arrived in Iowa from Ethiopia in 1977. It was a joyful reunion with Marcia after many anxious months, and Paul at last met his daughter Tamar who was then six weeks old.

A few months later, the Leemkuils were asked by the RCA Board of World Missions to consider an assignment to Doleib Hill in South Sudan.

With the establishment of the Africa Committee for the Rehabilitation of the Southern Sudan (ACROSS) in the 1970s, the door into that needy country had opened a crack, and even the churches were able to request personnel from overseas for certain purposes. The Shulla Presbyterian Church of Doleib Hill already had asked for someone to assist in teaching at the Bible training school. Presbyterians Bill and Lois Anderson had returned to Sudan in response to that call. Now the church had requested a teacher for the vocational aspect of the school's program, the purpose of which was to teach the young pastors a trade that they could use to help support themselves until their churches could provide more fully for them. This would be Paul's responsibility.

The Leemkuils' travel documents were ready in mid-January 1978. With their six-month-old daughter, they embarked on what they termed their most "difficult and challenging adventure in mission."

319

They flew to Khartoum, arriving at 4:00 a.m., and were met by a blast of heat. Once through customs, they took a taxi to the Acropole Hotel where they collapsed, exhausted by the heat. The Iowa winter they had left behind hardly prepared them for such torrid temperatures.

With no friends in that capital city, the Leemkuils were quite on their own and felt lost in the midst of all the strangeness. They walked the streets, locating some shops where they could purchase necessities, all the while looking forward to the journey south when they would join the Andersons at Doleib Hill.

The day of their flight to Malakal finally came. Upon arrival, they again felt lost; no one was there to meet them, for whatever reason. At last a car from the Lutheran World Federation came to pick up its own personnel who had come on the same flight, and kindly took the Leemkuils to the church compound of the Presbyterian Mission. Late in the afternoon, Bill Anderson came to transport them out to Doleib Hill.

Marcia's first impressions were that...

> ...the Hill had hardly a hill, as the whole area appeared to be a flat, never-ending plain. But the *doleib* designation was certainly apropos, for the only trees in sight were *doleib* palms in the little village we were to call home. We would be living in a duplex. It was a shelter over our heads, but it needed lots of repair. The walls had cracked. The wooden frames of doors and windows had been eaten away by termites. The house also needed a ceiling as a shield from the sun's heat on the tin roof.
>
> We were situated on the bank of the great Sobat River. During the dry season, the water receded several hundred feet from our front door. In the rainy season, the whole area became a swamp; the Hill was surrounded by water.[1]

With the rains nearly upon them, Paul and Marcia concentrated those first weeks on getting the house in order, and laying in food supplies from Malakal for the six months when the road would be impassable—supplies such as one hundred kilos of flour, fifty kilos of sugar, a four-gallon *debe* of goat cheese, and kerosene for the lanterns.

---

[1] Marcia Leemkuil, from a report to the author, April 12, 1994. Joint Archives of Holland, Hope College.

Happily their household goods arrived before the wet season began, so they were able to set up housekeeping. They had also received seeds for a vegetable garden.

Marcia described Doleib Hill as "a place with a story to tell" because many had served there for decades to make Christ known. Now it was a place of hardship and devastation as a result of ten years of civil war.

Shortly after our arrival, we were shocked when the Andersons shared the news that they would be leaving for the States with no intent of returning to Doleib Hill. On the day of their departure, Paul took them to Malakal in a fiberglass boat that had been repaired for the occasion. On the way back, the boat began to leak and the motor gave out. But God was watching over Paul and he was able to make his way home. Now we were truly on our own.

Shawish Nywalo was in charge of the Bible classes. Paul, due to the lack of all tools except the few he had brought with him, turned to agriculture for his vocational teaching. A nursery was set up and fruit trees were started. Gardens and fields were planted. Irrigation ditches were dug for the coming dry season.

During the early stages of our gardening, we were short of food. So when our cucumber vine produced prolifically, we made "cucumber stew" on which to survive until our other plants began to bear fruit.

Over one hundred papaya trees were planted. The citrus trees from another era were pruned and fertilized. The corn and bean patches were growing. Eventually all produced abundantly, and we brought in fruit and vegetables by the wheelbarrow load.

But all was not well. At mid-term, all the students decided they would no longer take part in the vocational training. There seemed to be no way to convince them otherwise. So our role became nothing more than that of caretaker of the gardens.

In September, after six months of isolation at the Hill, I made my first trip out to Malakal with Paul. We rode the Honda 80 cycles that had come in our freight. Tamar was packed in a backpack slung over Paul's shoulders. The road was far from dry. We went through long stretches of water which sometimes covered the engines.

It was a difficult trip, but I believe Paul realized how hard the long time of isolation had been for me and how much I needed to get out. In Malakal we visited Verne and Lorraine Sikkema. That was so refreshing to us.

That December we were able to have the Sikkemas and some new-found friends from the Lutheran World Federation in our home for Christmas. They brought, as a very special treat, all the ingredients, and ICE, to make ice cream. What a wonderful time of fellowship that Christmas Day was!

In January 1979, I developed a severe ear infection. Since there was no local medical help, we decided to go to Nairobi. During the period of treatment, we were able to travel to the Northern Frontier to lend a hand to friends in various places, among them Bob and Morrie Swart.[2]

We welcomed the Leemkuil family to Ileret with open arms. They arrived on February 15, on the plane that took Larry and Linda McAuley out after their happy and productive month with us.

Paul proved his usefulness in short order, taking up where Larry had left off. First of all, he made a fine youth chair for year-and-a-half old Tamar—a chair that we were thankful to have for many future occasions. Paul also turned a "hole in the wall" in the hallway into a linen closet with shelves and sliding door. And in the shower room, he built a medicine cabinet.

Each one who came to Ileret left his/her mark of skill and industry, and our home atop the dune became less and less a mere dwelling of cement and steel, and more and more a monument to God's love as shown through his people, our friends and family, who gave of themselves so unstintingly. The memory of all the dear hands that had worked so hard made our precipitous leave-taking at the end of that year all the more heartwrenching.

Although we didn't know it at the time, God had a great plan for Ileret. All love's labor was not lost!

Upon returning to Doleib Hill, the Leemkuils had many more anxious days when Tamar developed high fevers. It wasn't long before their supply of antibiotics had been depleted, and still the fevers ravaged Tamar's little body. Marcia bathed her in cool water in an attempt to control the high temperatures—all for nought.

2 Ibid.

Finally, in desperation, they made their way downriver opposite the place where the Jonglei Project was in operation. (They were digging a canal to divert some of the Nile waters for irrigation purposes.) Crossing the river in a dugout, they went to the Jonglei compound and asked for medication to treat Tamar.

They were so helpful. They examined Tamar, gave them the necessary medicines, and then took them back to Doleib Hill on their big barge. Love, compassion, and benevolence are not attributes solely of missionaries!

That April the Leemkuils were honored by visits from the Rev. Paul Hopkins from the Presbyterian mission board and the Rev. John Buteyn, at that time the Africa secretary of the RCA's Board of World Missions. Paul and Marcia shared with these men their difficulties and frustrations with the situation at the Hill. There seemed to be no solution.

A request for another assignment in Sudan was not forthcoming, so the Leemkuils made a decision at the end of May to return to the United States where they lived for three years until a new opportunity overseas opened up for them.

Verne and Lorraine Sikkema were in the United States on furlough at the time MAF flew so dramatically out of Ethiopia into Kenya in 1977. So their immediate plans had been changed drastically.

For six months, they assisted at USMAF's headquarters in California. Their special task was to check out new candidates for MAF missionary service. But in January 1978, they were transferred to Malakal, Sudan, where MAF was resuming work—which was the reason the Sikkemas were there while the Leemkuils were posted at Doleib Hill.

Five years before, Verne had flown to Sudan on a fact-finding trip, visiting old familiar places, and delighting in seeing old familiar faces. He reported that Malakal was still recognizable, but that Doleib Hill looked like a ghost town. Most of the buildings had been destroyed. The school and two of the larger houses had been burned. But the church was still standing, and services were being held.

When he flew to Pibor, the first person he met was Nyati.

He is still radiant, although they told me his mind was affected while he was in prison. I couldn't detect it. The hospital and

Roodes' house seem to be in good shape, but the Swarts' house was in ruins. The Arcon house (where Hostetters and Hoekstras lived) needed much repair, with its screens torn and its ceilings down.

I should add that over three hundred new believers were baptized the week before our visit. So the seed sown long ago is bearing fruit. The Holy Spirit has continued to work.[3]

At Akobo, Verne started to walk to the mission. But as he approached the market area, some of the merchants recognized him.

I was suddenly surrounded with folks hugging me and shaking hands. It was tremendous to be greeted so warmly by Arabs, Anuaks, and Nuers alike. I never did get to the mission.

In 1962 when I left Akobo, I wondered if I would ever be coming back in an MAF plane. Now when I did return, it was not only in such a plane, but I was the pilot! Thank the Lord for his leading in our lives.[4]

Now the Sikkemas were posted in Malakal on an assignment both thrilling and disheartening: thrilling to be a part of the reopening of Sudan after years of civil war, when hope was running high that peace really had returned to the land; and disheartening to be living in the midst of decay and destruction where once there had been beauty and order.

But they were there under orders. MAF had been given permission to provide air service for the Sudan Interior Mission as it once again opened work in what had been the Blue Nile Province. That all this had come to pass was a source of real wonder, and all those who had been called back during this period worked with a will to serve in all ways possible, to make the most of the opportunities before them.

Another trial for the Sikkemas was being so far from their youngest daughters, Arloa and Charlotte, who were attending high school in Jos, Nigeria. Letters were infrequent. They had much concern for them. But both girls graduated from that school and then went on to college in the United States.

---

[3] Verne Sikkema, "Report on Sudan Visit," 1973. Joint Archives of Holland, Hope College.
[4] Ibid.

After four years in Malakal, the Sikkemas again were transferred, this time to Kenya. Another MAF couple replaced them in February 1982, but they stayed only eighteen months. By that time the Sudan Interior Mission personnel had left. A few Presbyterians had come and gone. The MAF plane sat idle for much of the time. And the state of affairs in that country again was beginning to deteriorate. The next phase of Sudan's civil war was about to begin.

The surprise that John and Caryl Busman had been waiting for turned out to be an opening in Sudan for them in 1980. The Sudan Council of Churches (SCC) needed someone to finish out the term of a Lutheran couple who left for medical reasons.

The Busmans entered Sudan by way of Khartoum and then headed for Juba in the far south. There they assumed responsibility for the Rural Development Office of the SCC. They considered it a privilege to work with Sudanese colleagues in Juba and to be in Sudan at a time when people were free to travel throughout the country.

Their work continued to focus on things agricultural: importing hoes and other garden implements, as well as improved vegetable seeds to distribute to farmers through a network of rural churches. Caryl said that almost everything in Sudan had to be imported; the only locally available things were fresh fruits and vegetables, meat and eggs, and ground sorghum flour.

John and Caryl were encouraged to see the variety and quality of vegetables for sale in the local market improve dramatically with the introduction of good seeds.

They also spent time and effort training lay leaders in rural churches in some development skills.

In 1982 the Busmans returned to the United States in order to pursue further education. John's doctoral thesis focused on the problems of irrigation in Third World countries. Caryl completed work for a master's degree in the social sciences with an emphasis on the role of women in development.

With this aspect of their own training behind them, John and Caryl were ready to accept their next directive. In January 1988 they began working in Somalia in the Horn of Africa.

Mogadishu seemed to them an enchanting city—much more Mediterranean in character than African, thanks no doubt to the Italian influence when Somalia, then known as Italian Somaliland, was ruled by that European country. Houses were built in the villa style, and copious use was made of Italian tiles. Children they met on the street addressed them in Italian, and nearly all cafes and restaurants included pasta on their menus— although the Somalis had introduced their own ideas as to how pasta could be eaten. It was not uncommon to see them eating it along with bananas!

Although the Busmans were in Somalia for only a short time, they came to respect the so-called proud, fierce Somali people. Except for narrow bands of agricultural land along the rivers where farming was possible, they found that Somalis depended mainly on their herds for survival, and that dependency demanded a nomadic lifestyle. This made working out any sort of a development strategy a challenge.

One project John and Caryl monitored was a refugee forestry effort in an area called Luq. Sponsored by Church World Service, the program was initiated among ethnic Somali refugees who had fled the turmoil in the Ogaden region of southeastern Ethiopia and settled in camps in Somalia.

The Busmans worked among them in helping to find agricultural options and in supporting ongoing forestry projects. The Somali in charge of the overall project discovered that refugee women did better planting and raising tree seedlings than did the men. But, regardless of who did the planting, trying to encourage anything to grow in one of the hottest and driest places on earth, and without protection from the marauding herds of sheep and goats, was a nearly impossible task.

Trial plots of trees showed which species stood the best chance of survival. So John and Caryl focused their efforts on collecting data from those plots. And they encouraged local farmers with land along the river to raise trees as one of their crops.

Another project had to do with a type of stove that burned wood more efficiently. Given the design, Somali craftsmen carved these stoves from soapstone or molded them from clay. The Busmans noted, however, that though the stoves were for sale in the marketplace, hardly any of the families who manufactured them used the stoves themselves—because the women didn't like the way they cooked!

The sojourn in Somalia was interrupted briefly when John was asked by the Tanzania Church Council to come for a month to advise a group of rice farmers how to make the most of the meager water that was available. Ironically, during that month heavy rains fell, flooding rice fields and causing farmers to plant their rice in water more than three feet deep!

Caryl visited several Mother's Union groups of the Dodoma Diocese of the Church of the Province of Tanzania to help them formulate possibilities for women's projects. She remembers one particular visit she made on foot: "It was an experience to make the journey at night, unaided by flashlight— five women playing follow the leader through the blackness of an African night." They were all thankful to reach safely the village where they were to stay.

This was the Busmans' first experience in Tanzania. They were glad for the opportunity to see firsthand how the *Ujamaa* (socialism) experiment was working. This was their assessment:

> It was evident that the initial enthusiasm had worn thin and people were devoting more time and effort in tending their own private plots of land than they were the communal plots of the *Ujamaa* villages. Even so, it seemed to us that there was a greater sense of national identity in Tanzania than we had encountered elsewhere in Africa—a hopeful sign for the future.[5]

Shortly after the Busmans returned to Somalia, they realized that they weren't accomplishing their objectives. They had wanted to locate an area outside of Mogadishu where they could organize a development project for the resident Somalis themselves rather than supervise refugee projects.

So, because their philosophy of development clashed with that of the project leader, they felt they could not in good conscience continue. With regret that they hadn't been able to do more in Somalia, they said a sad farewell to Africa and soon were on their way to the United States and, eventually, to other fulfilling missions in Pakistan and Cambodia.

John and Caryl gave themselves wholeheartedly for the cause of the more abundant life in Africa.

[5] John and Caryl Busman, from a report to the author, August 1992. Joint Archives of Holland, Hope College.

It took AIM-Air pilot Dale Hamilton seven hours to fly the Swart family from Nairobi, Kenya, to Juba, Sudan, that day in February 1981 when they flew over the mission at Alale. It was a long, hot flight for them all. They were so glad to get out at last and stretch. But the heat! Deb said it was like a blast furnace. While waiting to go through customs, Justin drank up their water supply in no time.

Deb had embarked on this journey with some trepidation. Glad as she was to be back in Africa, she had heard that Juba was neither a pleasant nor an easy place to live. But her faith came to the rescue. She reasoned:

> We knew our call had come directly from God, and it was too obvious that we were going with him ahead of us. And Jack was so happy and excited and at peace that I caught that from him and trusted him—and God! After all, people do live there, and we'll survive there, too. Right, Jack?
>
> "Right," he replied. And that became my attitude, and Juba became my home. But that first night in Juba I thought I was going to melt. People told us it was the hottest February they could remember. Thanks![6]

They soon moved into an Arab-style home: white stucco with high ceilings and small windows, and a wall surrounding the yard. It was a duplex that they shared with an ACROSS family from England. Ceiling fans added to their comfort.

Soon after their arrival in Juba, Jack and Deb asked of the SIL director how ACROSS had learned about Jack and Deb. He told them that since the position they had applied for with SIL had been filled, he went across town and gave their application to the director of ACROSS. He liked what he read about them and telegraphed to the RCA his request that they come and work with their organization. Jack's first project was an example of cooperation between Christian groups and the frustration of dealing with an uncooperative, basically hostile, government.

The Bible Society wanted to move from Khartoum to Juba and would need a new office building and storage room in its new location. Now that ACROSS had a builder on its team, it was in a position to offer his services.

---

[6] Deb Swart, from a report to the author, June 1996. Joint Archives of Holland, Hope College.

Jack gladly accepted the assignment. But he soon discovered that the Sudan government did not share his enthusiasm for the project. The authorities opposed the undertaking; they used all kinds of stall tactics. And the application process dragged on and on.

One day Jack was reading in his Bible the account of the importunate widow who eroded the judge's resistance to her claims for justice until he capitulated and gave her all she wanted.

Jack determined to apply that teaching to his situation. He went every day to the government offices, asking how things were going, making sure that his application papers were indeed "in the works," and generally, as he said, "making a nuisance of myself." Between visits to officialdom, and believing that the necessary permission would be forthcoming, he gathered together all the building materials: sand, stones, cement, blockmaker; and large, shallow water tanks in which to mix cement by hand. All would be on site and ready to go when approval finally was given.

At last, after four months, Jack returned home, bursting into the house with the permits in his hand. Praise God for his faithfulness!

The Bible Society was able to move to Juba in December of that year, and Jack and Deb felt blessed to have had a part in making it possible.

While Jack was so busy for ACROSS and the Bible Society, Deb had some difficulty finding her niche. Walls around everyone's home were barriers to new friendships. Language was another obstacle. But Jan Burpee of ACROSS was a great help to her, as well as Megs McLaughlin. (Megs and her husband Robb were there to work on the translation of the Old Testament into Nuer.) They helped with the market, and Megs encouraged her to relax and accept her present sole role as homemaker until another avenue of service opened for her.

This happened one day when Jan asked her if she would like to assist her in caring for a baby that had been brought to the Juba hospital. He was an orphan and needed more attention than the nurses were able to give him. Justin could go with her, so she agreed. Deb recalls that it truly was a Third World hospital...

> ...the likes of which I'd never seen before. But I guess my mothering instinct took over, because once I had that baby in my arms, I forgot the unpleasant smells and scenes around me. So from

then on, while we were in Juba, Justin and I went every weekday
to bathe, play with, and just hold this baby boy.[7]

In July 1981 ACROSS colleagues Ron and Judy Bodenhammer, who were
working at Pibor, invited the Swarts to visit them. Until that time, Jack had
been thrilled enough just to be in Sudan; they hadn't given Pibor more than
a passing thought. But when they received this invitation to come on the next
plane, they did not hesitate.

Flying over the vast sudd and huge expanses of waving elephant grass and
the endless savanna was awe-inspiring. And then the pilot suddenly exclaimed,
"There it is!"

"There what is?" asked Deb.

"Pibor Mountain!"

"Where?"

"There!"

"That rock?"

"Yes, that's Pibor Mountain," Jack answered.

Pibor Mountain was just a great outcrop of rock standing sentinel in the
surrounding plain. It had been the source of all the stone used for building
our houses thirty years before, and on top was a place for picnics. Just an
outcrop, but it was filled with childhood memories for a young man coming
home.

> Now Jack is really home! It was an emotional moment for him and
> for me. We hugged Justin and told him that this place was part of
> his roots, too. We walked through the town. Jack pointed out the
> remains of government buildings and even spots where Murle
> friends' huts once stood.[8]

An outboard motorboat was waiting for them at the river's edge, and soon
they were around the bend and pulling up in front of the old mission site.
Jack's one recorded comment was: "The trees don't look as tall to me
anymore!"

Two ACROSS couples were serving at Pibor at that time: the
Bodenhammers, as agriculturists; and Dr. Sam and Ginny Cannata, as
medical personnel. The Cannatas were living in the Roodes' old house; the

7 Ibid.
8 Ibid.

Bodenhammers in the Hostetter/Hoekstra house. The former Swart house, the most heavily damaged during the disturbances, had been partially rebuilt and was occupied by Jon and Barbara Arensen who were working under SIL and engaged in translation of the New Testament into the Murle language, continuing the work started by Paul Hostetter and Harvey Hoekstra.

Many of the Murles remembered Jack and commented that he had grown up to be a fine young man with a wife and son. They all asked about the other members of the family. Jack constantly was reminded of happy times and situations as he was growing up in that out-of-the-way place.

Deb remarked that it was a wonderful time, and she was so full of praise to God for allowing her the privilege of visiting Pibor and actually seeing where Jack had spent many of his early years.

Not long after returning from their three-day trip to Pibor, the ACROSS director approached them with an amazing proposal: that they consider moving to Pibor to start up a new project. They were so surprised; they hardly knew how to respond. Jack was in the midst of building for the Bible Society; Deb was happy in her ministry at the hospital; and they were making friends in Juba. Nor did they want to be swayed Pibor-ward for sentimental reasons; it had to be from the Lord. So their initial response was negative.

The following week, the director came again. He explained more fully what was behind his request. Jack and Deb listened with new understanding. The Dutch government had given the Sudan government a grant to build four medical clinics in the Pibor district. Sudan knew that the Dutch would require accountability for the project, so it had asked ACROSS to be responsible for the whole job.

Sudan also realized that it could not expect any of its own skilled workers in the North to live and work in the South. The director said that the ACROSS board had agreed unanimously that Jack would be the man for the assignment because of his background and experience, and because he had proved himself capable of handling, with persistent diplomacy, sticky situations with government officials.

So Jack and Deb prayed with more openness of heart and mind. At last the answer came clearly: they should move to Pibor.

The move was accomplished on October 28, 1981, their moving van being an AIM-Air Cessna. Even their 250 Honda motorcycle and kerosene refrigerator made that flight!

The Cannatas had moved over into one half of their house to make room for the Swarts. This "duplex" was different from the one they had occupied in Juba, but it proved to be a happy arrangement. The house, though, was in serious disrepair, and the many cracks and crevices were wide-open entries for unwanted creatures. Even in their heyday, these houses were not critter-proof, but years of disuse and weather and local wars had exacerbated the situation.

Justin was taught right away to empty out his shoes every morning before he put them on, and to look between his sheets before getting into bed each evening. He had no problems.

One of the first to greet Jack and Deb at Pibor was our old friend and colleague, the evangelist Lado. He remembered Jack as a child and was overjoyed to see him as a man with a family. Jack had told Deb about Lado. She was so glad to meet him. She said:

> Many thought Lado was a bit deranged, but I don't think so. His heart was right with God. He carried a solar-powered tape player every day, cranking the handle and playing the songs we had recorded at the weekly church service. Lado had a brightness in his eyes that was always there.[9]

Because most of the building supplies for the four clinics had to come all the way from Nairobi, and some from Juba, Jack had to plan carefully in order that it could be delivered by truck during the dry season. Three huge trucks arrived in January 1982, and more came in February. The work could proceed.

Eventually there would be clinics at Pibor, Likwangole, Pochalla, and Gumuruk. Besides providing these buildings, the Dutch government also sponsored the training of eight students who one day would staff these clinics.

While it was not required of her, Deb set out to learn the Murle language. With the help of the Arensens, she made good progress, and before long, as she said in her own words:

> I believe the Lord loosened my tongue and opened my mind so that I could teach basic Bible truths, greet people correctly on the path,

9 Ibid.

help Dr. Sam in the clinic, and visit with my women friends.
Precious days and joys![10]

That Christmas, Jack and Deb received many love gifts from RCA
churches and friends. They prayed about what to do with those gifts. The
answer came: they would write down all the indigenous Christian Murle
songs, check them well, type them, and have them printed at the Africa
Inland Mission's print shop at Kijabe, Kenya.

They collected one hundred sixteen songs and choruses. Many of them
had been composed by the songmaker, Ngachor.

It was a glad day when the plane brought not only their mail and fresh food
order, but also the box full of paper-covered books of Murle songs. What a
treasure!

John Kajach, born to Ngachor in 1961, now was a grown man. He had
been brought up by his mother in the Truth, but it wasn't until he came to
Dr. Cannata one day that he actually took the step of faith. John had broken
his arm in a fall from a mango tree. Dr. Cannata had set it, put a cast on it,
and then shared his faith so effectively that in a few weeks, John accepted
Christ as his Savior.

Dr. Cannata continued to disciple him until his faith was strongly
established and he truly lived in the power of the Holy Spirit. The following
year, John became a student at AIM's Moffat Bible College at Kijabe,
Kenya. (His tuition was paid for by Dr. and Mrs. Al Roode. Though the
Roodes had left Pibor in 1961, they continued to be missionaries to the
Murles and made it possible for several young Murle evangelists to be
trained at Moffat Bible College.)

Life at Pibor was both restful and busy for Deb. While Jack was supervising
the building of the clinics, she had her own special ministries that gave her
much satisfaction. On Saturdays, she gathered children under a big, shady
matungtoch (tamarind) tree and taught them the Way, the Truth, and the
Life. And on Tuesdays, she met with women in a nearby village for Bible
study and prayer.

It was a social time, too. It was wonderful to get to know these
women. I remember when I told them that I was pregnant with our
second child. They were overjoyed and told me they'd been

10 Ibid.

praying for another child for me. I especially felt their love and care during this time.

One day a friend and I were discussing childbirth, learning from each other. I told her I'd like to deliver this baby at Pibor. She gave a little gasp and responded, "Oh, Deborah, you can't do that!" She went on to say that they all know I love them and that I'm a strong woman. "But you are not a Murle. You should do the things that white people do when they have babies and not try to be a Murle."

I was touched and we hugged. I'll never forget that.

That same woman accepted Christ as her Savior. What a joy to see her rebirth in Christ and to see her rise above her circumstances! After she received Christ, she told me that she now knew what it was like to have her "stomach satisfied." [To the Murle, the stomach is the seat of the emotions.] She said, "I'll always live in this hut; I'll always be a poor Murle. But now I know the peace of God in my stomach."

She learned how to read, and when I left for Nairobi to have our baby, I gave her all my teaching primers so that she could teach many other women.[11]

Deb and Justin left Pibor on March 5, 1983. Jack joined them in Kenya on April 14. The clinics were finished to the point where Jack's Murle foreman could carry on and see the job to completion.

I was delighted to be there with them during this time. We all stayed at the Mennonite guest house. Deb and I walked every afternoon before supper. On one of these walks, we talked about names.

"There's only one name that both Jack and I really like," Deb said. "It's Craig. Do you think Adrienne would mind if we'd use that name if our baby is a boy?" (My sister Adrienne had lost her twenty-seven-year-old son Craig seven years before.)

"Deb, I know she'd be thrilled. There is no doubt in my mind about it," I replied.

On April 23, Jack took Deb to Nairobi Hospital. That afternoon, he returned to Justin and me, uncharacteristically inarticulate with the joy welling up in him. He picked me up, swung me around, and finally said, "We have another son. His name is Craig Webber. Deb and Craig are doing well."

[11] Ibid.

What glad news! Justin was happy to have a little brother. And Adrienne was elated that they had named this new child Craig.

The little family of four went to the United States in May for furlough, fully intending to return for another term at Pibor. The new clinics would have to be furnished, and both Jack and Deb were dreaming of an expanded ministry among the Murle, including training in carpentry, masonry, and adult literacy, as well as producing a wide variety of printed material for use in these programs.

But these dreams were never realized. Two days before the Swarts left Kenya for the United States, the Sudan People's Liberation Army (SPLA) shot its way into Pibor, came across the river, and set up its headquarters in what had been the Swart/Cannata house. Fortunately, all personnel had left as a result of having been forewarned. But it was a very difficult time for those who had evacuated and for the Murle who had nowhere to go—and for Jack and Deb who had left so much of their hearts in Murle country.

One incident that occurred during this time made international news. ACROSS people John and Gwen Haspels—the same John who wrote us the "thus saith the Lord" letter—were up in the Boma Hills southeast of Pibor. They became hostages of the SPLA. Gwen and their children were permitted to leave after a few days, but John and a few companions were held for two weeks under life-threatening conditions. They found their hope and confidence in God through daily worship and reading of the Word.

The news of their eventual release was broadcast worldwide. When the Haspels family returned to the United States, John appeared on "Good Morning, America." During the interview, John stated that they had every intention of going back to Africa. Incredulous, the interviewer asked why he would want to do that? His reply was, simply, "Because there is no safer place than where God wants you to be."

The whole of Murle territory soon was under rebel control. No missionaries would be going back to Pibor for a long time. Jack and Deb felt as if they had lost their moorings, adrift on a sea of uncertainty. But not for long.

In August they were visiting in Holland, Michigan. They met with Dr. Ronald Beery, founder and president of what was now called Portable Recording Ministries International (PRMI). He informed them that PRMI was about to begin a ministry in Kenya. Even as they were meeting together in Holland, Dr. Harvey Hoekstra was in Kenya interviewing African candidates for the directorship of the new outreach.

If Jack and Deb were interested in becoming part of that ministry, Ron suggested that they consider going to Nairobi first to build a soundproof studio, and then to be a recordist. This offer appealed to them. Would the RCA second them to PRMI?

The church answered in the affirmative. The Jack Swart family's next move would be to Nairobi, Kenya.

XXIII
A Tutor in Zambia

Arlene Schuiteman had left Addis Ababa in 1976 weary of the ferment in Ethiopia that had affected her life so drastically, and sick at heart over the persecution and imprisonment of many of her Ethiopian associates. She was thankful to be on her way home to family and friends who would rally around her and help restore tranquillity to her disquieted spirit. As the plane lifted her above the fragrant eucalyptus trees of the capital city, Arlene wondered: "Will I ever return to Ethiopia? Will God send me to another country? Or am I saying farewell to Africa?"

After eighteen months at home, Arlene realized that it was improbable that she would ever return to Ethiopia, the nation whose pride for centuries had been that of being the oldest Christian nation in the world—the nation now under ever-increasing bondage to Godless communism.

Indeed, Ethiopia was a closed chapter for her; but not her missionary career in Africa. Early in 1978 God began showing her that there was another place in Africa where he wanted her to serve him.

God worked behind the scenes through a missionary doctor in Zambia who had visited Mettu in Ethiopia and observed my work there. This doctor knew of a need for a nurse instructor in their mission hospital at Macha in the Southern Province of Zambia.

The director of the Brethren in Christ Mission contacted me and also the Rev. Glenn Bruggers, our RCA mission representative.

There were phone calls, letters, and interviews. In my heart, I knew that God was leading me back to teach nurses in Africa. I was ready to respond. The RCA was ready to facilitate my answering that call.

The Church Mission Association of Zambia (CMAZ) handles the recruiting and processing of applications and work permits for all the mission hospitals in the country. My application was sent to CMAZ, but by the time it arrived there, another nurse had filled the post.

This was disappointing and confusing news for me, but I was told that the CMAZ was also needing to supply an instructor of nurses (tutor) for another place in Zambia: St. Francis Hospital, administered by British Anglican missionaries in Katete in the Eastern Province.[1]

Arlene responded favorably to this opening. But that call to Macha had been so strong and had seemed so right. Was God leading her to Macha in a roundabout way, via Katete? She rested in the promise: "In all your ways acknowledge him and he shall direct your paths."[2]

On August 19, 1978, Arlene was in the departure lounge of the airport in Frankfurt, Germany, waiting for her flight to Lusaka via Nairobi. Suddenly she heard the announcement for a plane about to depart for Addis Ababa.

I longed to go on board that plane, but the door to Ethiopia had closed and a door to Zambia had opened.

I boarded a plane for Nairobi where I waited several hours for a flight to Lusaka, the capital of Zambia. Prior to 1964, Zambia was known as Northern Rhodesia. Fourteen years had passed since it had become an independent republic within the British Commonwealth. There was a one-party system; Kenneth Kaunda was the president. I was told that the country was comparatively stable politically. After having been uprooted from Nasir in the Sudan during their civil war, and again from Ethiopia during their revolution, political stability sounded like music to my ears.

Little did I know that in a short time, the Zambian army would be mobilized!

[1]Arlene Schuiteman, "Zambia Notes," n.d. Joint Archives of Holland, Hope College.
[2] Proverbs 3:6, King James Version.

In Lusaka the blooming tropical trees, the early morning bird songs, and the familiar smell of grass fires all welcomed me. Katete was still three hundred miles from Lusaka. It was located along the Great East Road that led from Lusaka to the border of Malawi. This was a smooth, hard-surfaced road that took us from the four-thousand-foot plateau where Lusaka was situated, winding downward until we crossed the Luangwa River. It then climbed back to an elevation of three thousand feet. Productive farmland was all around us.

On a Sunday afternoon, we arrived at Katete where I had come to live, to serve, and to be a light and a witness for Jesus Christ. Here I was introduced and oriented to life in Zambia and the people of the Nyanje tribe. Dr. James Cairns, the medical superintendent, and his wife Faith, were especially helpful.

The very morning that I arrived, a new class of students was ready to begin their course at the Nurses' Training School (NTS). These students came from many different tribes and from all parts of the country. All of them had passed an entrance exam and had a good knowledge of English. In the carefully structured two-year program, the students had a total of twelve weeks of theory in the classroom. The rest of the time was spent working in the hospital wards under supervision.

The three-hundred-fifteen bed hospital consisted of several one-story buildings. Each ward was in a separate unit, and all the beds were filled to capacity. Beds in the wards were so close that one person could just squeeze between them. The pediatric ward was especially full with usually two patients in a crib. Clinical instructors and ward supervisors were responsible for teaching the practical procedures. My work was to teach the theory and administer the program. It was a big responsibility, but I loved the students and I love to teach.

The work load in the NTS was heavy and demanding. Every six months, after sorting through hundreds of applications and interviewing the most likely candidates, a new class of students arrived. At the same time, the senior nurses had to pass qualifying exams in both theory and practical nursing. After graduation they were employed at our hospital for a year of bonding and further supervision. It was an excellent program, but there was no respite for the tutors. The setting was ideal for physical and emotional burnout. Relatives and friends were faithful in writing letters of encouragement, and six women from my home church were very supportive prayer partners during this time.

I had been at Katete only a few weeks when the American Embassy notified us that it was unsafe to travel the Great East Road to Lusaka. We were to stay put. I had been told that Zambia was a politically stable country. However, the neighboring country of Southern Rhodesia was in the process of gaining her independence, and guerrilla fighters from that country had come into Zambia.

This was an unsettling development for me because I was still unfamiliar with the surroundings and the people of the area. But God spoke to me. I remember just where I was sitting in my room early one morning when God assured me that he had called me to serve him in Zambia and I could trust him.

In the months ahead, the trouble intensified. By November the army had been mobilized, bridges were destroyed, and lives were being lost. Back in Iowa my mother, elderly and frail, did not like what she saw on TV. One of my sisters exclaimed, "I wish Arlene would just come home!"

In spite of the uncertainties, Glenn Bruggers and his wife Phyllis came to visit and offer encouragement. In time, Southern Rhodesia won her independence and became Zimbabwe.

High school students in Zambia were required to interrupt their education and receive military training. Some of our student nurses had already completed their stint in the national service. They were definitely more disciplined and focused in the classroom than the others. A National Service Camp was located about ten miles from us. One of the servicemen, Charles Mumba, had been used to win many soldiers to the Lord. When we invited him to speak at our Nurses' Christian Fellowship, the Holy Spirit moved some of the young women to make a decision to follow Jesus. New believers met in my house each Sunday evening for Bible teaching and fellowship. This was an exciting and rewarding time for me.

The Reformed Church of Zambia was strong in the Eastern Province. At the time my grandparents were migrating to America, others from the Netherlands had migrated to South Africa. The Reformed Church in South Africa sent missionaries to Northern Rhodesia (now Zambia) and established a church. During Zambia's struggle for independence in the 1960s, the churches were already under Zambian leadership, and the missionaries had returned to South Africa.

Leatta Weidenbach, a Presbyterian who had also worked in Ethiopia as a nurse, was my housemate. She assisted as a tutor in the NTS and also served as assistant nursing supervisor in the hospital. A new two-bedroom house, designated for the nurse tutors, was completed four months after my arrival. Leatta and I spent many evenings listening to taped sermons while we stitched drapes for all the windows in our new home. We prayed for our students, for our friends in Ethiopia, and made plans for each day's work.

We had a fine house, but we were without transport and were therefore rather confined to the hospital compound—until the Indian pathologist, who was leaving Zambia, wanted to sell his little blue 1971 Datsun. There was one condition: that his dog be included in the transaction. Well, because break-ins and robberies were becoming more common, a watchdog could be an asset. That, together with our eagerness for more independence and the freedom a car would provide, helped us make the decision. We bought the car.

Now we could drive the fifty miles to Chipata to buy fruits and vegetables in an open market. Although the road to Lusaka was not yet secure, it was reasonably safe to make the two-hour drive east to the Malawi border. We could even travel to Lilongwe, Malawi's capital. It was a beautiful, peaceful place, and best of all, we could make a phone call home!

By May of 1979, some people were making daytime trips to Lusaka again. There were several detours around areas where bombings had damaged bridges. Road checks had been set up in order to search passengers and their belongings before they could proceed. Vehicles were also sprayed for tsetse flies because sleeping sickness was endemic in the region.

It was at this time that the General Nursing Council (GNC) called all nurse tutors to a meeting in Mindolo in an area of northern Zambia known as the Copper Belt. (Copper was Zambia's chief export and main source of revenue.) Dr. Cairns thought it was important for me to participate in the meeting, and I was assured it would be safe to travel by road.

Dr. and Mrs. Cairns took me to Lusaka where I boarded a bus for the six-hour trip to Mindolo. There were no mishaps along the way. At the meetings fifty tutors were given helpful directives; we shared with, and learned from, one another.

Other conferences were being held there at the same time. We all ate in the same dining hall. During the first meal, I spotted some Ethiopian students and went to talk with them. They were taking a year's course in Christian Youth Leadership. One of them was Matthew Gichele who left Ethiopia the day before a freeze on exit visas was put into effect. He had escaped the most severe persecution in his country.

Matthew's Zambian visa would soon expire, and it was still not safe for him to return to Ethiopia. We talked and prayed about what he should do. By August 1980, thanks to the help of members of my church in Sioux Center, Matthew was on his way to Fremont, Nebraska, to begin his college education. In the years to come, he graduated with honors and went on for a master's degree from the University of Oklahoma. By 1991 he was back in Ethiopia as the East African director of the Businessmen's Committee where he is effectively instrumental in leading businessmen to the Lord.

Shortly after my trip to the Tutor's Conference in Mindolo in 1979, I was appointed to serve on the General Nursing Council of Zambia. This required frequent excursions to Lusaka for meetings and also to Kabwe in the Copper Belt for preparing and marking the qualifying exams.

On one of the trips to Lusaka, I chose to attend a church service where I met an American lady. It was one of those "steps ordered by the Lord." This person worked in the CMAZ office. She informed me that they were wondering if it was time for me to transfer from Katete to Macha.

I was shocked by what I was hearing! I had thought that God was leading me to Macha in the first place; then another tutor had filled that post. But I learned that she had stayed for only one year of the three-year commitment, so the position was again open.

This conversation made an immediate impact on me. It was one of those unforgettable moments when I sensed that "God was in this." Was he really directing me to leave Katete?

Before I returned to Katete, I went to talk with Ira Stern, the director of the Brethren in Christ Mission in Lusaka. He confirmed the need for a tutor at their hospital in Southern Province, and he warmly urged me to consider going to Macha.

Many thoughts went through my mind. This was a time for fasting and prayer. I appreciated the six-hour drive alone back to Katete.

Leatta, whose term of service was soon ending, concurred that the move to Macha was right. The Cairns advised me to delay making a decision until after a brief furlough I would be taking in September 1980. The time at home would give me opportunity to look at this matter more objectively, as well as to investigate the cause of my severe headaches and to spend time with my aging mother whose health was deteriorating.

During furlough I was treated for malaria, amoebiasis, and filariasis. I also had sinus surgery.

The decision to transfer from Katete to Macha was made with the help of Glenn Bruggers after considering all the ramifications of such a move. And we were assured that this was God's direction for me.

The furlough was too short to visit all my supporting churches, so I prepared a slide presentation with taped commentary. My sister Grada and Sena Rensink, a former teacher of mine, continued to share the story of Zambia long after I was back in Africa.

It had not been an easy leave-taking. My mother's health had declined so much that, although she realized I was leaving, she could no longer respond. This was the last time we would see each other.

When I returned to Katete, our gardener was slashing to keep the jungle from creeping into our yard. Gwyneth Tyson, an experienced British nurse tutor, had arrived and was ready for orientation. The next six weeks, the task of delegating my responsibilities occupied most of my time. It was decided that both Leatta and I would leave as soon as the senior class had graduated in February 1981.

That January I knew that I had guardian angels watching over me. After attending a meeting in Lusaka, I was traveling back to Katete. I stopped at a gas station where two burly men were the attendants. No one else was in sight. While one man filled the gas tank, the other checked the oil. The Datsun's hood blocked my view of the engine, but there was a small crack through which I could see that the man's hands were not where they should be for checking the oil. So I stepped out of the car, leaving the door ajar and my purse perched on the front seat. The man moved to check the oil. As I put the hood down, the other man sidled up to the open door and my purse. I offered a quick prayer; he seemed frozen to the spot. I quickly slipped into the car, paid my bill, and said, "Cheerio." With a sigh of relief, I thanked the Lord for his watchful care over me.

It was a gorgeous morning. After three hours, I had crossed the suspension bridge over the Luangwa River and had begun to climb the curvy road through a forsaken forested area when the car began to sputter and pop—and then stopped. Again I prayed for help. First, a huge truck pulling two trailers lumbered by without stopping. Next, a yellow pickup cab with the words "Road Inspector" on the door came along. Two Zambian men got out and asked, "Are you all right?" I told them what had happened. They saw, upon opening the hood, that a wire had been disconnected at the very place where the gas attendant had been tampering. They reconnected it firmly, and the problem was solved. Once again I was so thankful to God who brought them along at the right time in that isolated place.

Soon after this experience, I made the move to Macha in Southern Province, traveling west to Lusaka and then south on a hard surfaced road toward Choma. This was the original trail, the Line of Rail, along which David Livingstone, the missionary/ explorer, had traveled. He gave thirty-three years of his life to exploration so that the gospel might come to all tribes. He also exposed the horrors of the slave trade. Livingstone died in 1873 while kneeling in prayer at his bedside where his workers found him. His heart was buried in Zambia (then Northern Rhodesia). One can see his statue near the famous Victoria Falls located only a two-hour drive south of Choma.

At Choma I left the road and turned west on a rough track for another forty miles. Macha was really in the bush! Why would anyone start a mission so far from the Line of Rail? It was a center where many Tongo people lived and this was where the Tonga chief had decided the first missionaries should settle.

The first missionaries were two women from the Brethren in Christ Church who arrived by oxcart from Southern Rhodesia seventy-five years ago. They had come to start a boys' school. The first year their only student was the son of the Tonga chief. But gradually the numbers increased. Over the years the small hut used as a school was replaced by proper primary and secondary schools. And the small clinic developed into a two-hundred-ten-bed hospital and a nurses' training school with students at four levels in the curriculum.

A church with a Zambian pastor had been established. English was the national language in this post-colonial country, and services were interpreted from Tonga into English for the people of other ethnic groups. Each Sunday evangelistic teams went to the outlying villages to conduct services.

One Sunday I went with one of the teams to Walkete. Only one woman appeared. She said that everyone else had gone to a funeral in the next village. We proceeded over the rough, dusty trail for several miles, reaching Hamoshinka Village where many people were sitting in groups on the ground. Some men, including the father, were busy making a small casket for the two-year-old daughter who had died of malnutrition. Inside the house we joined the women who sat surrounding the corpse.

Wailing increased as more people arrived. Again we took our place outside under a shade tree, waiting for the casket to be finished. More neighbors, friends, and relatives came, walking and wailing.

Finally the men carried the casket into the house. The body was placed inside and the box was nailed shut.

The father had three wives. Wife number two, the mother of the dead child, was pregnant. Wives number one and number three brought big pails of water which they carried on their heads as we followed the casket to the burial site. The freshly dug grave was so deep that as we approached, we could hardly see the head of the gravedigger. Shovels and pickaxes lay on the mound.

The tiny casket was carefully lowered into the grave. The father placed in the grave an old white tin cup which was pierced with a spear. A late arrival, a teenage girl, came running, screaming, refusing to be comforted. Some sang a few songs, the pastor led in prayer, Scripture was read. There was a short message. Then the father spoke words of thanks. Dirt was shoveled into the grave. One elderly man kept a sharp eye on things to see that all details were carried out correctly.

The buckets of water were brought near. Men washed their hands over the mound. An old woman sprinkled the remaining water over the grave, and several women patted the mounded earth with their hands. The paternal grandmother separated herself singing her own lament: "Why am I left instead of this little child?"

The pain and sorrow were real, but because some were believers, there was also hope.

In September, during a weeklong conference, new church members were baptized. Prior to the communion service, a footwashing ceremony was held. This was a new experience for me. A sermon based on John 13 was preached, after which the men and women went to separate rooms. Quietly, and in an orderly manner, women directed us to sit in groups of twelve. The person next to me girded herself with a large Turkish towel tied to the waist. She proceeded to wash my feet in a basin. Afterwards she rose from the kneeling position, shook my hand, and kissed me. Then I proceeded to wash the feet of the woman next to me. So it continued around the circle. In less than an hour, all had reassembled in the sanctuary, and the communion service began.

My work assignment at Macha was similar to what I had done at Katete. This included upgrading the Zambian Enrolled Nurse

Training School. The three immediate goals were to improve the staffing, the dormitory conditions, and the students' behavior and attitudes. To these I added my own prayer that the students who did not yet know Jesus Christ would be confronted to make the choice to follow him.

The mission also set a goal to Zambianize the missionary posts as soon as possible—to replace each foreigner with a Christian Zambian well qualified for the job.

After I had been at Macha for three years, some of our goals had been realized. The medical superintendent, Dr. John Spurrier, had worked hard to get the grants necessary to make improvements. The dormitories had been repaired and redecorated, and new beds and mattresses purchased. Students were taking pride in keeping their residences neat and clean.

A new building with a large classroom, tutors' and secretary's offices, and a student lounge had been built and dedicated. Teaching materials and students' syllabi had been revised. Aptitude testing had been introduced, and from twelve to sixteen new students were accepted twice a year. The new assessment procedures were begun with ward supervisors' involvement. Student Representative, Discipline, and Education Committees met regularly. There were a minimum of discipline problems.

The teaching staff worked in a cooperative and congenial manner with the medical and nursing staff of the hospital. This made it possible for the improvements to be made. The increase and continuity of teaching staff had been the Lord's gift, and although we often faced difficulties, God helped us to pull together. Four Christian Zambian registered nurses were on the hospital staff, and a Zambian nurse, Glynis Masanduka, was on our NTS staff. Mr. M. Kalambo was the new Zambian hospital administrator. Zambianization had begun.

When my home church in Sioux Center, Iowa, asked what they could do to help people at Macha, I told them that we needed a drilled well. Funds were sent to drill a well two hundred seventy feet deep. This gift covered the cost, too, of pipes and pumps. (And enough money remained to purchase a ton of powdered milk for malnourished children!) On several occasions in the coming years, it was this well that provided water to the community when other sources ran dry.

My suggestion of a well for Macha came out of my own experience with drought the previous year. In November 1982 we had some early rains. The farmers planted their maize (corn) which grew to six inches—and then the drought hit. The maize withered, and all our gardens dried up. We were forced to ration water. There were over two hundred patients in the hospital, fifty-four student nurses, two hundred forty secondary students, plus staff for these institutions—all of whom needed water!

A reservoir had supplied us with water, but when that went dry, a tank of water was delivered each day, water which had been siphoned from a swamp near Choma. The secondary students were sent home for their holiday. The beautiful poinsettia hedge which bordered my yard died, and the lawn was nothing but bare, dusty ground.

The severe drought continued through 1983. Although it started to rain all around us, none fell on the Macha area. Now, six to eight tanks were brought from Choma daily. Our faith was tested as we continued to pray for rain.

Then an amazing thing happened. We were told that water was gushing into the reservoir! We ran to see for ourselves. Apparently water from a distant catchment area, where rain had been falling, had emptied into the streams feeding our reservoir. To us it was a miracle.

Later we had six inches of gentle rain and all of nature soaked it in. Eagerly, and yet hesitantly, we put water in the bathtub; it seemed as if we were wasting water for a bath! We vowed never again to take this precious gift of God for granted, but to use it conservatively.

One Sunday we had a thanksgiving service especially to thank God for the rain. Church members carried stones to be used to erect a small monument near the reservoir as a reminder of what God had done on that particular day. In the future when someone would ask, "What is the meaning of this heap of stones?" (reminiscent of the Old Testament event recorded in Joshua 4), it would be a testimony of the wonderful way God supplied us with water and filled the reservoir in just a matter of hours. The heap of stones is there to this day.

The frequent trips to Lusaka for General Nursing Council meetings were tiring, but I realized their value. They helped me stay current with changes that were introduced by the Ministry of Health (MOH). One such meeting was a two-week seminar, called for the purpose of revising the curriculum of the Nurses' Training Schools.

An effort was being made to deliver health care to the poor people in the rural areas. The motto was: "Health for all by the year 2000!" We were directed to focus on training our students for working in the Rural Health Centers. We had actually been doing this already, since Macha is in a bush setting, and our students received their practicum in public health by participating in Mobile Clinics which covered a radius of forty miles.

It was the aim of the NTS staff, of course, to prepare the students well for their future responsibilities and ministries. Besides classroom teaching and practical experience in the wards and clinics, annual retreats for spiritual growth and renewal were planned. Special guest speakers were invited to present Christ and to encourage Christian students in their daily walk.

But no matter how hard we try, not all eventualities can be covered in the training process. I received a letter from a recent graduate who was just starting out in her profession:

"I am now posted in Northern Province. The Provincial Medical Officer (PMO) took me to four health centers and said I could choose which one I would like to work in. The one in the highlands is run by Catholic missionaries. It is nice, but the means of transportation is horrible. It frightened me very much. It took four hours to cross Lake Banweulu by boat. When we were in the middle of the lake and could not see the shore, a hippo rose six meters from the boat. All twelve of us in the boat were quiet, looking at the hippo's ears and wide mouth. Our hope of surviving was gone, not only because of the hippo, but also because of the water. The PMO then knelt in the boat and led us in prayer. The hippo turned, disappeared, and rose again twenty meters away. We saw it a third time, but then it was very far away. We took a different direction on our return trip. I chose not to work there.

"But I chose Tungati Rural Health Center. There is a Men's Ward, Women's Ward, Labor Ward, Outpatient Block, and Treatment Room. The only attractive thing here is that food is cheap. The chief brought a hen and some cornmeal. Villagers gave me some peanuts and tomatoes. The lady I work with gave me a charcoal stove."

Letters such as this showed us what our task as tutors involved. We prayed that we would prepare them well. But how does one fit into the curriculum a course on "The Fine Art of Crossing a Lake Infested with Hippos"?

In November of 1986, I had some special guests: Dr. William Brownson, then president of General Synod, and his wife Helen; and the Rev. Warren Henseler, our secretary for Africa. People who had regularly listened to Words of Hope were happy to meet the person whose voice they had known so long.

As we were touring the hospital wards, Dr. Brownson was drawn to one of the patients, Dick Mbewe, who was recovering from corrective surgery on his foot. A few years earlier, this teacher had attempted suicide because of depressing family problems. He had climbed an electric light pole and tried to electrocute himself. During the extended hospital stay, his right arm had been amputated, but his foot had been spared. He will always carry the scars of that experience, which he refers to as his "thorn in the flesh." It is through that incident that Dick Mbewe came to know the Lord. Now he eagerly shares his faith.

As a result of that contact with Dr. Brownson, the offering at the next General Synod was designated for building a house for him. Dick eventually graduated from Bible Training School and worked as a chaplain and evangelist in the Macha hospital. Later he moved into the new house with his two little boys, Douglas and Derrick. They were my neighbors.

When guests came to visit, I tried to arrange a drive to the Victoria Falls at the Zambia/Zimbabwe border. I was glad to be able to take the Brownsons and Warren Henseler to that wonderful place. It's both a physical and a spiritual refreshment. As we approached the falls, we could see the spray twenty miles away. The Victoria Falls are twice the depth of the Niagara Falls, and the mile-wide river rolls into the chasm with a deafening roar. One of the most imposing phenomena in the world, it is known locally as the *Mosi-oa-Tunya* which means "the smoke that thunders." A plaque marks the area. It reads: "Mightier than the thunder of many waters, Mightier than the waves of the sea, The Lord on High is Mighty. (Psalm 93:4) God is always greater than all our troubles."

I had to remind myself of that truth many times during the inevitable ups and downs of teaching and administration. Shortage of staff was a chronic trial. It was a real boon when Dr. Philip Thuma, who had grown up at Macha and later graduated from Johns Hopkins Medical School as a pediatrician, became a regular instructor, sharing the teaching load. And God provided volunteers on short assignments to fill the empty posts. One volunteer, Rhonda Postema, from Wyoming, Michigan, gave three consecutive summers, using her many skills, working hard and willingly in any way she could. And Nancy Lammers' visit resulted in her providing a photocopying machine which greatly lightened the office load.

Another area of concern was the soaring costs of food staples. The price of a sack of maize increased by 125 percent, and the price of a sack of *kapenta* (very tiny dried fish) increased from 90 to 240 *kwacha* overnight. People and institutions were having difficulty paying for these increases. Sacks of dried beans, dried *kapenta*, ground maize, and boiled cabbage were staples on our menus. If the food was not tasty, the students would complain. So I made it a habit to stop by the kitchen and sample the food each day. Onions and tomatoes, when available, improved the flavor.

The year 1986 was one of much heartache due to conflicts among the staff. Most graduate nurses throughout Zambia preferred to work in the city hospitals, so staffing in all the country hospitals was becoming more and more of a problem. Yet the GNC had made two recommendations which exacerbated the situation: first, students would no longer be allowed to work the night shift or carry a large share of the load for staffing the wards. And second, by way of implementing the first, we had to provide a more reasonable working schedule for the students' practical experience in the hospital, and correlate this more closely with the theory.

The changes were resisted by some and urged on too quickly by others. Levels of stress rose sharply. It was also recommended that there should be only one intake of students each year. This meant that classes would be double in size, but that the work load of the tutors should decrease. It took time for all these issues to be resolved.

Then another cause for deep concern reared its ugly head. With the decrease in tuberculosis in 1983, our TB ward had become almost empty. Plans were underway for converting this ward for some other use. But then, at first inexplicably, the number of tuberculosis patients increased again. One of our new students was also diagnosed to have TB. We were not yet aware that the signs we were observing would become more and more frequent—and would later be recognized as AIDS.

In the years ahead, this disease would take a heavy toll. In 1986 we had eight cases of AIDS in our hospital; by August 1987 we already had fifty-five cases with nine deaths. It was a time of heightened distress and grief—a time when it was comforting to realize that God is indeed always greater than all our troubles!

Retirement was now approaching. During my last year at Macha, David Chikoti, a Zambian RN, joined the NTS staff as a clinical tutor. Sometime later, Glynis Msiska (nee Masanduka) returned as a qualified tutor. (Her husband became the first Zambian physician on the hospital staff.) And Heidi Froemke, who had been on the NTS staff for a few years, was oriented to take over my position.

One other place had to be filled; the housemother was also retiring. Who would take her place? After many months of waiting, a twenty-seven-year-old Tonga woman, who had grown up in the Macha area, came as a direct answer to prayer. Patricia Matoomana soon proved to be a real blessing to students and staff alike.

So the stage was set for the ongoing performance of the medical work at Macha. The whole cast was in place, brought in from the wings by the Divine Director, and now ready to play their respective roles in the high drama of their mission.

Before I left Macha, I experienced once again the intervention of that Divine Director in my life.

On April 27, 1988 I had a close call as I was traveling to a meeting in Lusaka. The forty-two miles of dirt road from Macha to Choma were usually somewhat of an adventure, especially at the end of the rains. Tall, uncut grass bordered the road which had recently been graded; it was smoother than I had ever see it.

I was making good time at forty-five miles an hour. Halfway to Choma, at a bend in the road, a big blue truck suddenly came around the curve at breakneck speed on MY side of the road! There was no way, humanly speaking, to avoid a head-on collision.

I shouted, "God, help!" And he did. Somehow I braked and turned off the road. Providentially there were no trees, stones, holes, or ditches right there. I bumped up and swung around while the truck screeched past me. I heard a pop. I couldn't believe I was still alive.

I got out of the car. The truck had disappeared around the bend. My car was not damaged except for the sideview mirror which had been hit and shattered. (That was probably the pop I'd heard.)

I couldn't stop praising God as I continued on my journey to Choma. My eyes fell upon the Scripture verse taped on the dashboard: "He shall give his angels charge over thee, to keep thee in all thy ways."[3] And "His eye is on the sparrow and I know he cares for me" flashed into my mind.

On my return trip after the meeting, I stopped at the site of the Close Call and looked at the tracks which were still visible. I felt as if I were standing on holy ground, for surely God had come to my rescue there.

The final year in Africa was made more difficult because many of us were coming down with repeated attacks of malaria. The pattern of the rainy season that year, and the fact that the disease was not responding well to the usual treatment, left us ill much of the time. A new drug, mephlequin, plus fansidar was prescribed. This combination made me very sick with the side effects of ataxia and dizziness. But it did prevent further attacks for several months.

[3] Psalm 91:11, King James Version.

Now it was 1989 and I was sixty-five years old. It was time to retire. I could go with a peaceful heart, knowing that the work I was leaving behind would be carried on by a staff as surely called to their positions as I had been—good and faithful servants of the Lord Most High.[4]

So the curtain comes down on Arlene Schuiteman's autobiography in African settings. She was a loved and respected teacher, nurse, and friend who truly walked in the way of Jesus Christ. Hers was a life of exemplary missionary service.

[4] Arlene Schuiteman, "Zambia Notes," n.d. Archives.

XXIV
They Stayed in Ethiopia

Dr. Harvey and Margaret Doorenbos returned to western Ethiopia in May 1977 following their older son Dirk's graduation from Good Shepherd School in Addis Ababa. They returned to Dembi Dollo almost immediately lest the director of the Bethel Evangelical Secondary School, Dr. Solomon Gidada, be imprisoned because of the absence of one of his teachers.

But in June Harvey and Margaret were able to go to the United States for a brief furlough. They did not know what the future held for them.

During this interim, the Ethiopian Evangelical Church *Mekane Yesus* requested that they relocate in Aira to serve in the hospital and school there. This was a former German mission station. The Doorenboses unhesitatingly accepted this challenge, though they were well aware of the growing political tensions throughout the country as the communist regime tightened its control over all aspects of life.

The hospital at Aira was a mud-walled facility with beds to accommodate about seventy patients. Before the Doorenboses' arrival, it had become not much more than a major clinic. But when Harvey, a surgeon, became a member of the staff, the work load changed significantly, not only in numbers of patients, but also in the proportion of surgical cases. Harvey also practiced general medicine, handled administrative duties, and taught staff and students in the Health Assistant Training program.

*Walking to clinics means taking medicines (on the donkey's back)
and cooking gas (in the cylinder)*

The senior staff at the hospital had a distinctive international flavor with missionaries hailing from the Scandinavian countries, Germany, and the United States. Later, Ethiopian nurses joined the staff, while some health assistants were upgraded to become nurses after a training course. In 1988 the first Ethiopian doctor became part of the Aira medical team.

As the quality of care in government hospitals deteriorated, the yearly outpatient and inpatient census at Aira Hospital grew. Twice during their early years there, the government demanded that Harvey cover the surgical needs in an area where its own surgeons were absent.

While her husband maintained a heavy daily schedule at the hospital, Margaret was equally involved at the Lalo Aira Secondary School of seven hundred students. When "Education!" became a political slogan, she found herself also having to teach night school classes. Her students included pastors, health workers, primary teachers who had not completed twelfth grade, and a number of political cadres.

Even the poor peasant farmers were required to learn to read and write. Because the communist authorities had not prepared material for literacy classes, the church happily distributed excellent and simple Bible readers for adults.

As the years passed and the numbers of patients and students increased, the need for new facilities became critical. Prior to 1977, plans for more substantial and more spacious hospital buildings had been drawn up. But because of the country's internal turmoil, they had to be put aside for a time. Harvey eventually pursued the matter, and many trips to America via Europe included visiting financial offices of mission agencies.

At last in 1986, a Lutheran World Federation team finalized its drawings and encouraged donors to fund the project. In the spring of 1988, sites for a new school and a rebuilt hospital were turned over to a contractor, and building began. Government restrictions, import problems, local harassment, and many other obstacles turned the one-year project into a six-year ordeal.

Boons and blessings came at just the right time. At Aira the six-year trial of patience hardly had begun when assistance for the medical program arrived. Dr. Carl and Margaret Toren joined the Aira medical team in July 1988. They had come at the invitation of the Ethiopian Evangelical Church *Mekane Yesus*. What in their background had brought them to this moment?

Carl became interested in mission work when he, along with others from Hope College, traveled to Apache, Oklahoma, one summer to work with the Rev. Andy Kamphuis at Apache Reformed Church. "His commitment and example showed me that mission work was for 'ordinary' Christians like me,"[1] Carl said.

After graduation from Hope, he spent a year as a youth director at the Church of the Good Shepherd in Lynnwood, Washington, as part of the RCA's Adventure in Mission program. But by this time, he was already considering a career in medicine, feeling an urgency to be equipped to offer a service desperately needed in so many parts of the world.

A book by Ann Harrison had further impact on his life's direction. She had written a biography of her husband, Dr. Paul Harrison, distinguished Reformed Church missionary. *A Tool in His Hand* is the story of a man wholly dedicated to his God, his profession, and to his service to the people of Arabia. After reading this delightful chronicle, Carl was all the more convinced that medicine was the way to go, and that, under God's guidance, he would use such training in missionary service somewhere.

While at medical school at Northwestern University, he attended the Inter-Varsity Urbana Conference in Urbana, Illinois. "In addition to being

[1] Carl Toren, from a report to the author, August 19, 1996. Joint Archives of Holland, Hope College.

totally inspired, I connected with some RCA folk, including Dr. Beth Marcus, who told me about the work of Dr. Stan Vander Aarde in India. I arranged to finish my course work early and in 1984 visited Dr. Vander Aarde in Madanapalle and the Christian Medical College in Vellore [founded by RCA's beloved Dr. Ida Scudder in 1918] for ten weeks."[2] Carl's personal interest in missions was becoming a fixed goal.

Pediatrics became his specialty. He had heard and seen that children under five years of age in developing countries were among the most vulnerable to the assaults of preventable diseases; mortality rates in this group were distressingly high.

Carl met Margaret Crandell while he was on a medical rotation in Winnetka, Illinois. It wasn't long before they discovered that their interests were similar and their goals, identical. Margaret had chosen nursing as a career because she hoped to serve somewhere in the world as a missionary. They were married in 1985 during Carl's residency.

Two years later they applied to the RCA for mission service and had no particular area of the world in mind. A few months later, they received a call from the Rev. Warren Henseler: Dr. Doorenbos had requested that the Torens join them in Ethiopia. "Where's that?" was Margaret's bewildered response. She soon found out.

> Preparation took a little extra time since Margaret was pregnant with our first child. I started studies for a master's degree in public health, and we attended some orientation courses in Detroit, Michigan. Those courses were interrupted by Daniel's premature birth during a snowstorm and his subsequent hospitalization in Detroit.[3]

But over the next few months, while Carl and Margaret were busy packing, raising their support, and caring for him, Daniel became a thriving infant, the joy of his parents, and soon to provide an entree for them into many an African heart.

The little family left for Ethiopia in July not yet having received their visas. This caused some anxiety. But after a brief stopover in Rome, a fax from Warren Henseler gave them the word to proceed; all papers were in order.

2 Ibid.
3 Ibid.

In Addis Ababa the Torens spent three months in school to acquire some knowledge of the Oromo language. It wasn't until November that they arrived at their destination in Aira where Carl soon began his work as a physician/pediatrician.

> That first day was…I can't think of a one-word description. Overwhelming/exhausting/confusing/appalling? All fit. We get these half-histories and make half-diagnoses and give half-treatments. It was unbelievable. The health assistant is seeing other patients while we are seeing the referred patients, so they translate every other question and every other answer. Finally you get sick of it all and do a physical exam [yourself]. There are no sinks for washing hands and no tables for patients to lie on, so [you just examine them however you can]!
>
> On the basis of this half-physical exam, you arrive at a suspected diagnosis, which of course cannot be confirmed because the test isn't done here. So you proceed to treatment, which in a sense limits your possible diagnosis. No one diagnoses cancer here, because it cannot be treated anyway. All masses are TB because we can treat it. All fevers are malaria and if it doesn't respond to anti-malarials, then they are treated for typhoid. Antibiotic choices are almost always penicillin, even for diseases that don't respond usually in America, such as pneumonia and meningitis in children.[4]

Harvey Doorenbos had gone through similar trauma when he first came to Aira, so he could empathize with his young colleague and encourage him through the less-than-ideal conditions.

> Dr. Harvey and Margaret Doorenbos were our colleagues and friends during our entire time in Aira and really helped to brighten our lives. Just being the only other ones who spoke American English made them very nice to be with. We also had good friends among the other missionaries: a German physician taught me how to take x-rays on the fifty-year-old equipment, and to do C-sections.
>
> Our best Ethiopian friend was a physician who also worked at the hospital. We drank a lot of tea at his house. Margaret was honored by being named as godmother to their first-born daughter.[5]

4 Ibid.
5 Ibid.

Besides working in the hospital, Carl had two other major responsibilities: teaching pediatrics and public health at the Health Assistant School, and public health supervisor. The latter job gave him great satisfaction, but it was also a source of frustration because it took him away from the hospital and the care of very ill patients. However, when the result of surveys showed a good percentage of vaccinations given, or of a good number of latrines dug, Carl was gratified.

On the home front, Margaret was in charge of the household and made numerous adjustments, including having kitchen help, snakes in the bathroom, and biting ants. But one facet of Ethiopian life was always a pleasure for the Torens: they enjoyed hot, spicy Ethiopian food from the first experimental bite. The flat, spongy, slightly sour bread dipped generously into a variety of highly tasty stews became a family favorite, even Daniel's.

They also learned to enjoy the gentle softness of candlelight, often necessary because the generator was on only from six to ten o'clock each evening. Wait two to three weeks for mail was another adjustment to life in the bush.

Daughter Erica was born in the United States during their first furlough. Carl finished work on his master's degree in public health at that same time. Then they went back to Ethiopia—only to learn that the long civil war was becoming more of a threat. The rebels had changed their tactics. Their strategy was no longer that of moving directly south into Addis Ababa, but rather of approaching the capital from the west.

In March 1991 the Torens were in Addis Ababa for a meeting. They were making preparations to return to Aira when the American Embassy called them in.

> The embassy staff informed us that the Tigrean rebels had taken over a major city in the west and the embassy had information that the next advance would take the rebel army through Aira. They recommended that we not return, since there was a strong possibility that the rebels would bring the front line through Aira and then settle down for a long siege of the capital. If such were to be the case, we would be cut off from Addis Ababa. The embassy told us stories about previous expatriates who were behind enemy lines and had to walk to Sudan in order to get out.
>
> The prospect of a two-hundred-mile walk with two small children made us think and pray hard about what to do. In the end, though

we were concerned about all that those at the embassy had said, we decided to return to Aira anyway.

By mid-April several towns in our area were under rebel control. Then came the day in which the front line crossed Aira also. We found ourselves with a new government. This meant, among other things, having to get new ID cards. At that point all the mission and church people were telling us to leave. We decided to follow their advice.

With several other families making up a convoy of four trucks, we went south around the active front line and headed for Addis Ababa. There is one part of that convoy trip that makes us laugh to this day. The adopted daughter of one of the missionaries was three years old and right in the middle of being potty-trained. So amid all the tension and worry about rebel soldiers and land mines, the whole convoy stopped when little Tigist said she "had to go." We all watched as out came the potty and she would sit for a while, many times with no results. Her mother would look back at us, shrug her shoulders, and off we'd go again.

We made it to Addis Ababa without incident. People were still predicting a prolonged siege, so we made the decision to head for Chicago.[6]

The long siege did not take place. Rather the government army became thoroughly demoralized. It fled the country, and Addis Ababa was wide open for a new takeover, which occurred in May. The Torens were then in the United States but stayed informed. They heard that the Oromos were up in arms because the new government was dominated by the rebel Tigreans. This led to further unrest throughout Oromoland.

Carl and Margaret were loathe to bring their family back into such a situation. They waited for some news of stability, but after a year, with still no sign of normalcy, they knew they had to get on with their lives. Carl found work at a private, non-profit clinic in Chicago, and the Torens were blessed with two more children, Craig and Caroline.

Now that we are on the domestic side of missions, we miss foreign missions a great deal and wonder if God will call us overseas again

6 Ibid.

someday. I serve on the Illiana Classis Mission Committee and our family loves to play host to visiting RCA missionaries.[7]

In 1992, when the Doorenboses went home for three months, Dr. and Mrs. Robert Vander Ploeg filled in for them at Aira. As Margaret described their arrival, the Vander Ploegs felt as if they were on another planet. Everything was so different for them: the Ethiopian calendar made up of twelve months of thirty days each plus a thirteenth month of six days with seven days for leap year; the time figured from dawn to dawn, 7 a.m. being one o'clock in Ethiopia; the language, the people's names, the surgical instruments, the names of drugs, the soft-spoken voices of coworkers. Harvey and Margaret saw Aira all over again through their fresh-from-America eyes.

As for the building schedule, Harvey hoped to be able to move into the new hospital when they returned in September. But Dr. Vander Ploeg, after watching the construction process, wondered if the move would take place even a year from September! With no cement mixer, no wheelbarrows, no pulley to the top of the buildings, it meant a very slow, though steady, work pace.

The secondary school, no longer sharing the original site with the hospital, now had its own location. It was built in two years. Teachers and students moved in immediately upon its completion.

By the end of 1993, the new hospital facility was functioning. With great joy, singing, and prayer, the hospital staff moved from the old buildings to the new outpatient building in May. In August the inpatients were transferred to new wards. That same month the kitchen, laundry, maternity ward, and the surgery unit were moved to their new facilities.

For the sake of perspective, these events at the mission at Aira are placed by Margaret in their proper historical setting—the ongoing communist revolution. The fact that the church persevered through this period is testimony to the faithfulness of God and the power of the Spirit.

---

[7] Ibid.

For all our fears and concerns during any given crisis, we foreigners never suffered as greatly as our Ethiopian Christian friends, many of whom spent months or years in prison and often suffered physical or mental torture. We moved carefully, spoke guardedly, trusted very few friends or coworkers, seldom traveled or entertained guests from abroad, and lived with restrictions and, at times, extra divine protection: once in Addis Ababa I found myself surrounded by machine guns as soldiers were attempting to arrest a girl who had entered the taxi I was in. The girl gave herself up, sparing the other passengers a possible spray of bullets.

Throughout the revolution, the top government officials insisted that there was freedom of religion in the country. In reality, the local leaders did whatever they liked.

Small sects and denominations had no chance of surviving; their members tried to keep house meetings going, often to their detriment. Anyone with a charismatic interest was labeled "Pente" (for Pentecostal). Even school children with charismatic leanings were targeted and were often detained long enough to force them to repeat the grade they had had to leave. Young people who met in small groups were often jailed.

The Mennonite Church was completely shut down, all property confiscated, and most elders and pastors imprisoned. The *Mekane Yesus* Church remained open in Addis Ababa, but in Oromo areas, it was closed periodically. During those times, young people's choirs, prayers at school and hospital, youth attendance at church for any purpose, Bible classes in the church school—all were forbidden.

And even when the church was permitted to open its doors, sports events, which demanded compulsory attendance by all youth, were scheduled at the very same hour. A funeral or a wedding was an occasion for preaching and singing. Despite a ban on public hymn-singing, many hymns became "wedding songs" as the groom escorted his bride to his home. A number of marriages were blessed by a pastor in a home because the church was forbidden for such use.

It wasn't long before the synod offices, with their printing equipment, transport facilities, and foreign funds became suspect.

More church officers and pastors were imprisoned. The offices closed completely following a raid against all Oromo resistance leaders. Imprisonment often lasted two or three years. Other prisoners became the pastors' "congregations." When they had opportunity, many pastors spoke boldly to the officials about the Lord's work and the inability of any power to work against the Holy Spirit.

Two German pastors were put in prison for disobeying an order not to preach in a certain village. We missionaries held an evening prayer meeting to plead for their release. During the meeting, two nuns seeking overnight accommodation in our home came and knocked at our door. They reported that the two Germans were sitting at the roadside waiting for someone to take them to the mission. The nun's car was too small for two more passengers, but they brought the joyful message.

How similar that evening was to Peter's release from prison as recorded in Acts 12! We scheduled prayer meetings for several other evenings after that for the sake of Ethiopian pastors who had not yet been freed.[8]

There were two rebel "fronts" at this time: the Tigre Liberation Front (TLF) which had been fighting for years for Eritrean independence from Ethiopia, and the Oromo Liberation Front (OLF). The Oromo, in whose territory our missionaries served, are by far the largest ethnic group in Ethiopia. Their animosity toward the regime of the Amhara, Emperor Haile Selassie, had simmered just below the boiling point for decades. Now they began to organize themselves as counterrevolutionaries. Their tribal passion now was boiling in earnest.

Often in conflict with one another, the TLF and the OLF ultimately worked together for the overthrow of communism in Ethiopia.

In late 1990 the TLF from the north began a wider swing of liberation throughout the country and, with other rebel groups, completed a government takeover in early 1991 simply by chasing away the present worn-out, disillusioned, military group.

[8] Doorenbos, "Notes from the Doorenboses regarding Ethiopian experiences: 1977 to 1996," n.d. Joint Archives of Holland, Hope College.

In the spring of that year, missionaries from outstations and other towns in our area began to move toward Aira under embassy orders to evacuate. [It was at this time that the Torens left.] Our Aira foreign community dropped from over twenty to only five by the time all had departed.

As the new Tigre-based government became established in Addis Ababa, the OLF, which had fought alongside the TLF in the liberation of this western area, proclaimed itself as a government of its own. Education became secondary to the struggle for *Oromiya*, a homeland for the Oromos. This group felt for over a year that they were in control, leaving us foreigners confused as to which government and government officials we should deal with.

Because the OLF did not participate in establishing the new government in Addis Ababa, but rather withdrew from the elections and the temporary coalition government in 1992, they were labeled "outlaws" who needed careful supervision. So the OLF movement was suppressed. Even at this writing, this subjection is felt, because all the people in this area are Oromos.[9]

As all this bewildering turmoil was splitting Ethiopia apart, the Doorenboses' son Dirk died in a motorcycle accident in the United States in May 1991. It was several days before the word got through to Harvey and Margaret on their mission radio, and by that time, Addis Ababa was surrounded by the takeover troops and travel was prohibited. That left their son Keith and his wife to handle the funeral arrangements and settle Dirk's earthly affairs.

Dirk was a graduate of Hope College. He had come to Aira for Christmas in 1981, and in 1983 he spent a year in volunteer water development work in Tanzania. In August 1988, he went to Nevada for graduate study, earning a master's degree in May 1991. Dirk had been investigating work, utilizing his expertise, in Saudi Arabia as well as in East Africa at the time of his death.

The Doorenboses' great comfort was the assurance that "when Dirk was born December 10, 1969, we had placed him in God's hands, and we know that he remains there forever."

Life for the Doorenboses went on. In 1994 the secondary school opened with a good enrollment, though not enough teachers. One problem was that

9 Ibid.

the university was unable to train adequate numbers of educators for all of Ethiopia's schools. In addition, many teachers were leaving their profession for more lucrative jobs in offices and government departments. The situation was becoming critical.

Encouraging things were happening, though, at the Onesimos Nesib Bible School (ONS) in Aira. This school, named for an Oromo who translated the Bible into *Orominya* during the latter part of the nineteenth century, and run under the auspices of the *Mekane Yesus* Church, was established in 1972 for the training of evangelists and, eventually, pastors.

Giving hope to the community in 1994 was a class of forty students sent out to do practical field work as part of their training. And at Easter time, one hundred eighty-eight young people became members of the growing, vibrant church at Aira.

Also during 1994, Merle and Karen Vander Sluis of Fellowship Reformed Church in Holland, Michigan, began their assignment in Ethiopia, bound for Aira after six months of Oromo language study in Addis Ababa. Merle earned both his undergraduate and graduate degrees in science from Western Michigan University in Kalamazoo, and Karen completed nurse's training in Kalamazoo and earned a bachelor's degree in health studies at Western Michigan University.

The Vander Sluises came to Ethiopia with considerable experience both at home and overseas. The Peace Corps had lured them during the first year of their marriage in 1965. They served in India for two years in an applied nutrition project in a Lutheran-run leprosy hospital.

Their next venture took them to Tehran, Iran, where Merle taught science, Karen cared for the health needs of teachers, and both were dorm parents at a high school.

For another five years, they worked with Christian Reformed Church Home Missions teaching Navajos and doing pediatric nursing in New Mexico. A short-term stint in the Dominican Republic, followed by teaching in international schools in Jordan and Colombia, rounded out their previous overseas sojourns. Just prior to taking off for Ethiopia, Karen managed a health clinic for migrants in Holland, Michigan.

So they brought valuable experience with them to Aira, but they still had to plod through language study along with the novices. The Vander Sluises, like the Torens, also expressed confusion over the Ethiopian method of telling time.

At the end of May, the Vander Sluises moved to Aira. Having visited Aira at Christmas and Easter, now they were ready to become residents in Oromo country and get on with their new life and mission.

Though they had lived in several developing countries, each one had its own typical way of life with which a newcomer had to become acquainted. Even provinces, and districts within provinces, had their own way of doing things.

They learned early that "grains, wheat, and *teff* (a fine grain), needed to be bought on market day, cleaned, and taken to the mill to be ground, and that spices are pounded by hand."

Buying a live chicken that would have to be dressed, and a chunk of beef for stew and hand-ground hamburger, were new things for them. They learned, too, to boil drinking water for twenty minutes and then pour it through a filter. Life at Aira had begun in earnest!

Soon after their arrival, Merle started teaching ninth-grade biology to fill in for a teacher who had become ill. He was amazed at the quietness of classrooms even though there were seventy students in each of his classes.

Karen also plunged right into her medical role:

> I have driven our two public health assistants to the village nearby to give immunizations. I love getting out there and trying to speak Oromo with the mothers—but I need to learn and practice so much more! For the first few weeks we will sort and clean the public health office at the hospital and go out and meet some health workers in nearby areas.[10]

Writing in February 1996, Merle and Karen still were marveling over their long Christmas celebration, expressing appreciation for MAF's services, and telling a bit more about their life and work at Aira:

> Christmas was quite an event for us because we celebrated it in December, the Ethiopians celebrated it in January, and our latest mail is still delivering Christmas cards. We certainly appreciate mail.... We do not get very much outside news except for what we hear on Voice of America or through shortwave radio contact with other mission stations and with Mission Aviation Fellowship.

[10] Merle and Karen Vander Sluis, from a newsletter, June 6, 1995. Joint Archives of Holland, Hope College.

*Medical personnel from Aira Hospital make periodic
trips to outpost clinics*

[MAF had made a slight change in its name, from Missionary to Mission.]

The Mission Aviation Fellowship flights are important for us because they often bring mail. When the plane comes, we have to get the cattle and people off the airstrip....

Most of the crops are harvested (coffee, *teff*, corn, *nugi oil*). Now is the time for my coworker and me (Karen) to get busy because the people are not working in the fields and they have time to attend meetings. Duressa and I have finished health classes in one church and will start in another church this week. We call it a "deacons' program." It involves twenty volunteers. They are trained to go into the communities to promote good health practices and sanitation. They are also encouraged to visit the sick and the elderly. The first group was very enthusiastic in class. Now we will see if that enthusiasm can be put into action.

Merle is keeping busy with teaching biology. The students are very quiet and reluctant to ask or answer questions, but we hope that as time goes along, they will become more responsive.

Daily I go out into the countryside, weaving my way around cattle, goats, sheep, donkeys, and, of course, many children....Merle still gets out on daily motorcycle rides, finding new trails to explore. Interestingly enough, we came upon an old set of horseshoes. Horseshoes has now become a favorite game with the teachers.[11]

While the Vander Sluises were becoming part of the Aira community, the political situation in the country hardly was improving. In fact in 1995 it began to look as if history might be repeating itself. There was talk in high places about adhering to "the government line"—or else! It was becoming evident that the new regime's methods were similar to those of the communists. And the church was again the center of much suspicion because it had organizational capabilities to implement plans and propaganda. As medical director of the hospital, Dr. Doorenbos was...

...summoned and questioned concerning the employment of a doctor who apparently is considered "an enemy of the government." He was reportedly dismissed from three other work sites for this very reason. Now the government has ordered the hospital here to get rid of him.[12]

Yet, in spite of such interference, the hospital moved ahead in its mission under the Lordship of Christ. The 1995 report, compiled by Dr. Doorenbos, is statistically impressive, especially when one realizes that the staff consisted of only four doctors, seven nurses, and twenty-three health assistants (sometimes referred to as "barefoot doctors").

Outpatients numbered 74,396 for the year, 42,000 being newcomers. There were 4,328 patients admitted; 810 women came for delivery. The surgical suite performed 2,738 operations which included 1,000 eye cases and 400 OB/GYN procedures.[13]

The school also was the target of government restrictions. It took all the resources of heaven to carry on under such conditions. Christians were being hampered in meeting their objectives:

[11] Vander Sluis, from "A Missionary Letter," February 20, 1996. Joint Archives of Holland, Hope College.
[12] Doorenbos, from "A Missionary Letter," September 26, 1995. Joint Archives of Holland, Hope College.
[13] Ibid. April 13, 1996. Archives.

Patients sometimes come to the Aira Hospital by "ambulance"

The secondary school director has been told that we must follow political lines in our teaching and our curriculum, and "the government curriculum does NOT include the teaching of the Bible." School has been functioning for a week, and Bible teachers are still not appointed. The stockroom shelves hold two hundred forty beautifully bound Bibles for use in the classes—a gift from a partner church in the U.S. Will they be used?[14]

Margaret later wrote that this order was never received in writing, so they ignored it. An Ethiopian pastor was appointed to the school staff, and Bible classes were being taught.

[14] Ibid. September 26, 1995. Archives.

In latter years, still serving with joy but with increased concerns about the mood of the times and what it bodes for the future, letters from the Doorenboses became more contemplative. Completing her eighteenth year of teaching twelfth-grade English, Margaret wrote:

> There were thirty students in my first class; there are ninety-one seniors in two sections this school year. In some respects, it has become boring. The curriculum has been the same for eighteen years, and the students have become less and less capable as the years roll by. Why is that?
>
> The government put more emphasis on quantity than quality in education. Without high enough standards to meet the university entrance requirement test and without any alternative industry or craft shops to which to turn, high school students began to see education as futile. Thus it is very difficult to motivate the students to inquisitive pursuit in the sciences, to creative writing in the arts, or to wider vistas through reading material outside their assigned curricula.[15]

With retirement looming, Harvey and Margaret expressed their love for the work at Aira and the need for someone else to catch the vision, whether national or expatriate:

> We left Michigan for the mission field thirty years ago. We have lived in Bahrain, Oman, and Ethiopia....What a privilege we have had to work with the churches and their outreach into unevangelized areas! But now that privilege will end in this decade. Who will meet the many needs we see as yet unfulfilled? It does not have to be foreigners. However, expatriate missionaries bring with them not only their particular skills, but also a connection with the worldwide fellowship of believers. Through that connection, Bibles get printed for tribal groups, literature is sent for young Christians, supplies for special medical or educational needs are provided, and the local church is richer for its fellowship with an international network of Christ's people.
>
> Who will meet their needs? Have you considered sharing your talents farther afield? Have you prayed earnestly for that skilled

15 Ibid. April 13, 1996. Archives.

man, that professional woman, that young family who wants to go but needs to overcome concerns about living and working abroad? Have you invested in missions?

You (our RCA supporters) have nurtured us in our mission service through prayer and writing and kindnesses too numerous to mention. Now let us look together to the future and consider those willing to meet the challenges of the twenty-first century abroad as well as at home.

Meanwhile, we will continue to educate here in order that young Ethiopian doctors, new school teachers from Aira, newly-trained health assistant students, and young Christians may become tomorrow's leaders in Christ's work.

Your partners in Christ's work,

Harvey and Margaret[16]

In 1997, Harvey and Margaret Doorenbos were honored by Hope College as recipients of its Distinguished Alumni Award.

---

[16] Ibid. February 22, 1995. Archives.

XXV
Our "First Love" Still Beckons

"Ah, land of whirring wings which is beyond the rivers of Ethiopia;...Go, you swift messengers, to a nation tall and smooth...whose land the rivers divide."[1]

Commentaries say that this passage refers to an ancient land in the Upper Nile region south of Egypt, a land called Cush; and the whirring wings are locusts. Though it is a prophetic description of a tense period in Old Testament times, I like to reinterpret it in our own experience: Upper Nile is our familiar and loved province; whirring wings are those of myriad varieties of river birds; tall and smooth people are the inhabitants of southern Sudan.

Waves of missionaries have traveled up and down the Nile; have come and gone, and come again, yielding themselves to the summons of the Lord and to the curious allure of this land west of Ethiopia.

So we go back yet once again to the RCA's "first love" in Africa, Sudan, which continues to beckon and whose call we have heeded, even in perilous times.

In October 1982 a remarkable young woman arrived in Upper Nile Province, a woman whose faith, commitment, and determination saw her through many unusual—and sometimes less than agreeable—situations.

Barbara Kapenga was born in Vellore, India, the daughter of RCA missionaries to Oman, Jay and Midge Kapenga. She graduated from

1 Isaiah 18:1, Revised Standard Version.

Kodaikanal School in India in 1972 and Earlham College, Richmond, Indiana, in 1976. Interestingly, God used the Peace Corps to give Barbara her life's direction.

> When I applied to the Peace Corps, one question in their form was to list your first three choices for posting. I wrote "anywhere by Africa." A week later they called and said there were three posts available: Niger, Upper Volta, and Tchad...and I'm still in Africa![2]

Barbara served the Peace Corps in Tchad, or Chad, as a teacher of English to junior and senior high school students.

In 1981 she received her Master of Arts degree in religion from Yale Divinity School, as well as her high school teacher certification.

Seconded by the RCA in January 1982 to the Mennonite Central Committee (MCC) for service in Cairo, Egypt, Barbara and all the other members of the MCC team found themselves black-listed for unknown reasons. At this time she was invited to Sudan by the Department of Religious Affairs in Juba, Equatoria Province.

On her way to Sudan, Barbara had a layover in Nairobi where she stayed at the Mennonite guest house. There she found the Alale contingent, still reeling but recuperating from the recent assaults at the foot of Lorsuk Mountain. Tom Larink was now studying Swahili; the Swarts were laying plans for moving on to Orma country; and the McAuleys were waiting for the green light to return to Alale. We were all refugees in a sense, and all in transition under God's direction.

When Barbara finally reached Sudan, she was assigned to be the matron of girls as well as the religious education teacher at the Teacher Training Institute in Malakal. This was a boarding school at the high school level with an extra year tacked on to train primary school teachers. It was touted to be the finest school in Upper Nile Province, but it left much to be desired. With only ten teachers for a thousand students, a principal who spent the entire year in the North, and a deplorable lack of funds, it was an impossible state of affairs. And the "cheating on the national exams was incredible!" Barbara said.

With responsibility for training those who would be teaching Christianity both to Christians and non-Christians in the public schools, Barbara felt

---

[2] Barbara Kapenga, from a letter to the author, March 18, 1996. Joint Archives of Holland, Hope College.

keenly the frustration of her position. She knew that she could not continue dealing with other elements of boarding life that she was unprepared for: hysteria, kidnappings, deaths, supervision of discipline, witchcraft, etc. It was all beyond her experience and orientation.

After a year she moved to Doleib Hill to join Bill and Lois Anderson, who had returned as staff members of the Giffen Bible School. Among other activities, she and Bill introduced a TEE program for both Doleib Hill and Malakal areas, using materials put out by the Sudan Evangelical Church. This was a much happier period for Barbara. But even so, tensions again were building up in southern Sudan, and her sojourn at the Hill was brief.

> Andersons were away. I woke up early one morning and looked out to check that the Jonglei Canal base camp lights were shining some kilometers away. If I could see them, I would know that all was okay. But this morning I saw only fires. Then I heard shots and mortar thumps.
>
> Later that morning, refugees began pouring into Doleib Hill. We heard that the foreigners had gotten away on barges. BBC announced that evening that several had been kidnapped, and I recognized the name of a friend who had been killed. Our Land Rover had come in earlier that afternoon and had seen the truck behind it explode on a mine.
>
> I waited two or three days. Then the principal drove me to Malakal (not by the road). There I had two offers: a Lutheran World Federation flight to Nairobi, or a seat on the French attaché's charter plane to Khartoum.[3]

She flew to Khartoum with the French attaché, and then on to the United States for a respite between missionary adventures.

What happened to the schools Barbara left behind? The Teacher Training Institute in Malakal was closed because of the rebel activity. It became a barracks for a time and then apparently an Islamic school for girls.

The Bible school at Doleib Hill attempted to go on functioning, but several months after Barbara left, the site was the scene of a battle and almost everything was destroyed. The school was moved to Malakal.

It is not easy to see God's hand in such sad endings. But we know he can see beyond the apparent finale, and he will continue to work out his purposes for his people in Upper Nile.

[3] Ibid. August 5, 1996. Archives.

Barbara was soon on the go again. Always ready for the challenge of filling in where she was needed, she accepted a call to teach third-grade English, art, and first-grade sports at Al Raja School in Bahrain, an island off the coast of Saudi Arabia in the Persian Gulf. Flexible by nature, she didn't let the fact that her certification was in secondary education deter her from teaching at the primary level. Her command of Arabic made her an invaluable teacher wherever she was assigned in the Arab world.

After a year in Bahrain, she returned to Sudan, this time to the Arab North.

When Roger and Carolyn Schrock became World Mission Associates with the RCA in 1991, they came with several years of experience in Africa serving under the auspices of the Church of the Brethren. They had had no notion, when they were undergraduates at a Brethren-affiliated college in Kansas, that missions in Africa would become the major focus of their lives—and soon.

According to Roger, "We were expecting to go into volunteer service during the Vietnam war. And then to seminary, and finally into the pastorate."[4]

But in April 1967, the Schrocks were asked by their church to go to Nigeria to teach in a mission school. With only twenty-four hours in which to make a decision, they pondered and prayed until they had the answer. They graduated in May, were married in June, and in September left for Nigeria, where they spent three years at the mission school.

This term of service was followed by a five-year stint as administrator for the mission's health care system. Their two sons, Jon and Jedd, were born during this period.

Then, after pastoring a small church in Minnesota for three years, they were called to go to Africa again, this time to staff a rural health program in western Upper Nile Province in the war-ravaged southern Sudan. As representatives of the Church of the Brethren, they were responsible to the Sudan Council of Churches and the Ministry of Health of Upper Nile Province. The people whom they served were Bul Nuers.

[4] *Daily Courier News*, Elgin, Illinois, July 4, 1987. Joint Archives of Holland, Hope College.

The Schrocks first lived in Bentiu on the Bahr el Ghazal while a house in Mayom, seventy miles west on the Bahr el Arab, was being built for them. (Much of this area at one time was under the ministry of the American Mission with which the RCA was affiliated for many years.) They found a strong Presbyterian church in Bentiu as well as in Wang Kai and in Ler where the RCA's Roxanna Sarr had worked for a short time in the 1950s. But overall, churches in that part of the province were young, small, and had suffered much. Roger and Carolyn tried to be supportive of the pastors and evangelists and looked forward to helping establish a congregation of believers in Mayom.

The Schrocks' first worship experience was in Wang Kai on Easter Sunday. They remember gathering at the church at 8 a.m., before the heat of the day, with a group of about seventy: Presbyterians, Catholics, and Brethren. The Catholic priest in Bentiu later explained that during the civil disturbances in Sudan, Protestants and Catholics came together and agreed that, since they all worship the same Christ, they should join in their celebration instead of being in competition.

The first year in Upper Nile was one of orientation which included the necessary discipline of language study; learning about the people, their customs, culture, and needs; the new experience of home schooling their children; and working through the planning aspects of the health program, writing up reports, and figuring out the budget for a two-year period.

In early 1981 Roger and Carolyn and their sons moved to their new home in Mayom which was to be the center for their health care work. Because more staff was expected, they had to oversee the construction of more homes, offices, workshop, and storage buildings. Well construction and a cattle vaccination program also were initiated with the help of competent, concerned Nuer men who were learning to carry more of the project load.

Writing at Christmas time that year, the Schrocks put their story in an historical setting:

> When one resides in Sudan, it is easy to become discouraged with the prospects for peace as proclaimed by the Christmas angels. President Sadat of Egypt has just been assassinated; Libya is involved with a war in Chad; Uganda is still suffering from sporadic fighting; and Ethiopia and Eritrea are still at war. These are five out of eight of Sudan's neighbors who are involved in war or great unrest. Such tensions, of course, spill over into Sudan.

When one couples this African scenario with the renewed
pressure of President Reagan to sell weapons to many countries in
this part of the world, a person begins to wonder if the holocaust
can be far off! May God's Spirit move in people's lives that peace
on earth may not be just a chant of angelic voices from on high, but
a reality in our earthly lives.[5]

At their first Christmas service at Mayom, Roger was able, with the help
of an interpreter, to tell the story of Christ's birth simply and clearly. Many
had never heard this wonderful news before. "Roger is a good storyteller,"
Carolyn said, "and is able to relate the lowly birth of Christ to the lives of
these cattle people who do not live so very differently from those in
Bethlehem long ago."[6]

An evangelist soon joined them at Mayom and plans were made to build
a simple structure for the steadily increasing numbers of believers and
inquirers, and for protection from wind, sun, and rain.

With the arrival in 1981 of another couple whose expertise lay in water
resources and health education, well-digging soon was underway, with the
villages providing the labor and funds for cement. The expatriates were
responsible for guidance and transportation, as well as for providing the
handpumps.

By January 1982 the first Mayom well was in use, providing pure water for
many families who previously had been using contaminated water from the
river or swamps. The handpumps arrived and were installed on the wells as
they were completed. Enthusiastic villagers continued to organize themselves
and collect money so that they, too, could enjoy this benefit. The Schrocks'
hope was that the number of stomach disorders would soon diminish.

By August three wells were functioning; four more were in the process.
Other projects included the planting and cultivation of a demonstration
garden and the beginnings of a nursery for fruit tree propagation; an animal
husbandry expert on the team was hard at work vaccinating thousands of
cattle for rinderpest; and an American doctor, also new on the staff, was
training local people as paramedics to learn about health management and
the use of several medicines for in-village care.

[5] Schrock, from a newsletter, November 1981. Joint Archives of Holland, Hope
     College.
[6] Ibid. January 28, 1982. Archives.

Recognizing his leadership skills, and since the project at Mayom was now well staffed and well launched, the Church of the Brethren asked Roger in 1983 to fill its position of Africa representative. After much thought and prayer and long-distance communication with the Sudan Council of Churches (SCC) in Khartoum, Roger accepted this new task because both he and Carolyn considered it to be a call from God as well as an effective avenue for serving Sudan and all of Africa.

The Schrock family soon settled in Elgin, Illinois. Roger's responsibilities took him on frequent liaison trips to Africa. On his first visit back to Sudan, he consulted with the SCC concerning the ongoing Primary Health Care Program at Mayom, and actually was able to spend some hours at their former home where he was relieved to find all team members safe, confident, and eager to work in spite of rapidly deteriorating security in the whole southern region.

A few months before, the president, without holding a plebiscite, had split the South into three regions. Then, by presidential decree, Koranic Law was made the law of the whole land. These events raised concern for Christian leaders in southern Sudan.

The question was raised among Sudanese church leaders: "Is it safe for U.S. missionaries or church workers to be in this country?" The response was: " Will you remain faithful to God's call to be in mission?"[7]

With that challenge ringing in his ears, Roger took up his God-given burden of directing, coordinating, and facilitating the continuing mission program of his church in Africa for the next seven years.

> It is evident that the Schrocks operate out of a sense of call. That is, if the church calls them to serve, they feel it is their duty to respond, if at all possible. It is this belief that has made their lives a bit more exciting than the average family.
>
> What is the next call? That's a tough one. "In the past, the call has come before I was ready to leave the job," Roger said. "I don't know what the next call will be."[8]

Three and a half years later, in 1991, that question was answered.

7 Ibid. November 28, 1983. Archives.
8 *Daily Courier News*, Elgin, Illinois, July 4, 1987. Joint Archives of Holland, Hope College.

We have responded to a call from the New Sudan Council of Churches (NSCC) to return to the southern part of Sudan. The NSCC is trying to enable the churches that are living in the liberated area of Sudan (under the control of the Sudan People's Liberation Army, or SPLA) to carry out their mission and ministry. Roger has been asked to be their Executive Secretary, and Carolyn will likely work in either communication/interpretation or in education.[9]

By September, with both Jon and Jedd now attending Manchester College in North Manchester, Indiana, and their Elgin home having been rented, the Schrocks once again moved to southern Sudan. Their new home was in Torit in the southernmost province of Equatoria, east of the Nile and not far from the Uganda border, a savanna area with the Imatong mountains in the distance.

This new call is a large challenge for us. The needs of the churches in the liberated areas of southern Sudan are many. Since this current conflict has been in process for seven years, nearly a generation has missed out on education; for the three to five million people, there are only five or six hospitals functioning with extremely limited supplies; the infrastructure has largely been destroyed—and thousands are becoming Christians.

This means that many new churches are developing and there is almost no trained leadership to help disciple the new Christians. Last year I visited one congregation [numbering in the thousands]. They told me that I was the first person representing the church to visit them in five years. They asked, "Don't our Christian brothers and sisters outside care about us?"

We are being challenged to work with the churches to find ways to respond to these many needs. We are excited that the Church of the Brethren, the Presbyterian Church USA, and the Reformed Church in America are cooperating in supporting us and seconding us to the NSCC.[10]

9 Schrock, from a newsletter, January 1991. Archives.
10 Ibid.

The Schrocks' home in Torit was equipped with solar panels on the roof, allowing twenty-four-hour electricity for lights, computer, and a sound system. Solar power also was used to pump water from a bore hole to a high water tank, and pure water ran from the tap. These amenities made life in Torit pleasant following strenuous days at NSCC headquarters.

Roger soon discovered that the office of executive secretary was a multifaceted position. In addition to attending meetings, working with church leaders, consulting with the donor partners, and caring for financial matters, he also supervised the erection of more staff housing and acted as tour guide for visitors who wanted to see the southern Sudan firsthand.

As Communication/Interpretation Coordinator for the NSCC, Carolyn provided a vital service for the overall program. One of her most important contributions was producing a quarterly newsletter, NSCC News. As the only printed material published in the area, it was put together primarily to encourage Christians throughout the SPLA-controlled region and to connect them to the larger community of Christians. It was circulated also to those interested in the NSCC.

Communication to the outside world was necessary, too. The three supporting denominations had to be kept informed about the plight of the Christians in the South. Monthly communication had to be sent to NSCC's many other partners in Europe and the United States and Canada. This sometimes included press releases and urgent appeals for funds.

Another assignment for Carolyn began with the formation of the NSCC Peace Committee, the purpose of which was to "offer opportunities for individual congregations and communities to focus on what the Bible teaches about peacemaking and how Christians can live that out in their local situations."[11] It was a challenging and exciting prospect for the months ahead.

Many of Carolyn's days were spent serving as hostess, a role she played graciously and compassionately.

Unfortunately, and to the Schrocks' dismay, the lawless disorder in the South continued to worsen. They poured out their hearts in a 1992 letter written on vacation in Nairobi:

> The war has displaced thousands of Sudanese, and the NSCC has been drawn more and more into relief work. We have organized

[11] Ibid.

some local interchurch committees who can receive relief aid from donors and carry responsibility for local distribution. Some of the displaced have moved three times in the past year. That explains why so much relief food is needed: they are not in one place long enough to plant and harvest.

The government has made a major dry season offensive into the South, recapturing towns it had lost years ago and trying to break the morale of the rebels and local population. As a result, the fighting has come close to our town, Torit. We were expecting heavy aerial bombing, which thankfully never came. But shelling was heard in the distance and the battle front came to Lyria forty-two miles to the west.

The NSCC and other agencies decided to begin moving to safer areas. We had already planned to have a vacation in Kenya, so we kept to the original plans and are presently anticipating five restful days at the Mombasa coast.

We left our house pretty much intact. There were a few days of emotional roller-coaster, not wanting to think about our home being destroyed, knowing that it was a possibility, yet wanting to be able to feel that material possessions are minor compared to the lives of friends and coworkers we left behind. Today the news is that things are calm and relatively safe in Torit, so we calmed down and are ready for the beach tomorrow.

We have struggled with the ability to maintain our pacifism as we are daily bombarded with military talk, hatred, and insecurity. We have wrestled with how to live amid war and not be overwhelmed by it.... We are still convinced that we should not run away from violent situations, but instead find ways to live our pacifism in the middle of it all. Pray for us as we try to live the Brethren witness in these trying circumstances.[12]

Within a few months of returning to their Torit home, however, Roger and Carolyn found it necessary, along with thousands of southerners, to become refugees themselves. They moved to take up what they hoped would be temporary residence in an apartment in Nairobi, a sanctuary from an increasingly life-threatening position. They continued to carry on their

[12] Ibid. May 23, 1992. Archives.

NSCC obligations from Kenya's capital city, traveling in and out of Sudan as their work dictated, and choosing the times and places of least danger.

Living now at the source of supply, the Schrocks became more personally involved in relief work: relief coordination meetings, relief purchases and shipments—and more communications to the outside world to spread the word of Sudan's terrible dilemma.

In October Roger participated in a monthlong advocacy tour of Europe and the United States and Canada:

> He and Rev. Sirisio Oromo visited church, government, and U.N. groups and met with Sudanese in exile. It is hoped that the case of Sudan can be elevated to debate in the U.N. Security Council. We must try to find a way to stop the war in Sudan and the severe human rights abuses occurring there....
>
> The future is uncertain, but we continue to plan for a fifteen-day "peace tour" of Church of the Brethren folks coming to learn about the problems in the Horn of Africa and to examine what further peacemaking roles the church might have in this setting. We are planning for a third NSCC General Assembly early in the next year, and we are looking forward to adding some new staff to help lighten the load for the rest of us and to make a greater contribution to the tremendous needs in Sudan.[13]

In April 1993 the Schrocks reported renewed fighting east of the Nile in southern Sudan:

> It is hard to avoid feeling hopeless, but our NSCC teams continue to plug away at community development education along with identification of priority needs through the churches. It is a slower process than doing emergency relief imposed from outside agencies, but we hope it will have lasting effects and build dignity and self-reliance in the long run. It is so good to have an eleven-member staff now instead of the three or four of us that struggled along for the last two years.
>
> But PEACE is what is needed to allow the work to go forward with continuity. Relief is useless without a hope for peace.[14]

13 Ibid. Christmas 1992. Archives.
14 Ibid. April 17, 1993. Archives.

Roger and Carolyn were beginning to feel by this time, though, that the
Sudan situation was getting more world attention:

> All of our hard work in communication and advocacy is beginning
> to pay off, along with the work of other groups. It is hard to quantify
> this kind of contribution, but our feeling is that we have had some
> success in our efforts and have made some difference....
>
> The time for home leave is coming soon....We will be present at
> the Church of the Brethren Annual Conference. We will also
> contribute to the Presbyterian Church USA General Assembly in
> Orlando, Florida, and a Reformed Church in America gathering in
> Wisconsin.[15]

In the fall of 1993, they again picked up their work with the NSCC with
all its countless aspects. As a result of their having told the Sudan story "to
the world," they were receiving an almost overwhelming number of visitors,
all of whom had to be cared for and oriented for their travel to southern
Sudan. They, too, wanted to have a firsthand view of the suffering in the
South.

At that time there seemed to be a positive movement toward some
reconciliation between the factions of the SPLA:

> This involves a lot of work on the part of Sudanese church leaders,
> so we also get involved in support roles. Pray that this initiative will
> come to a positive conclusion as a step on the path for peace for
> Sudan. The people have suffered long and dramatically....Pray for
> wisdom for the church leaders as they manage this reconciliation
> process....Also pray for President Moi of Kenya as he is to host the
> political reconciliation talks between the SPLA factions with the
> hope that it might lead to mediation between the government of
> Sudan and the SPLA.[16]

Because of the Schrocks' wholehearted concern for the Sudanese people,
for the cause of peace in their land, and out of love for the Prince of Peace,
they devoted themselves to the easing of hostilities and the establishment of
peace.

[15] Ibid.
[16] Ibid. Christmas 1993. Archives.

But in August 1994, after a long "desert" experience, they wrote these heartbreaking words:

> For our long silence, we apologize. These intervening months have been a prolonged time of discouragement for us, and we have not had the emotional energy to share these difficulties broadly.
>
> Grief is perhaps the only word to describe our sorrow and pain for the continuing displacement, family separation, and lack of stability all around us. We grieve for the Sudanese, but we also grieve for our own loss of close community with those we are now more geographically separated from. We have always gained strength from the joy of the African Christians as we lived among them. We miss that community support. Gradually we are building a new community of Sudanese who are in exile with us.
>
> It has been a slow process for us to come to the realization that we may not see the end of this struggle soon. We cannot sustain the hope that our presence can bring an end to the pain around us, but rather we are learning to share the joy of knowing God's abiding love in the midst of that pain. This is all a part of the lessons we are learning about what peace is.[17]

In January 1995, the Schrocks shared these insights:

> The problems and challenges of Sudan have not diminished. The factionalism has continued, and this has meant more suffering. The government of Sudan continued the war by treating all, civilians and combatants alike, as legitimate military targets.... Both sides of this senseless war believe that the solution lies in some type of military win. The people in both the North and the South are very tired of the killing, but the leaders seem more concerned about power and control than in the welfare of the people.
>
> Certainly there are major problems in the society, and until some sense of justice can prevail, there will be no hope for lasting peace. Please pray that the peace of God can reach the hearts of many who must forgive their enemies and trust God's control for the future. Both Christians and Muslims believe in God's Word. If only we could live out God's teachings![18]

---

17 Ibid. August 20, 1994. Archives.
18 Ibid. January 1995. Archives.

During Holy Week of 1995, the Schrocks compared those last days in Jesus' life with Sudan and their own condition:

> The Triumphal Entry: We, too, have experienced some of the acclamation for our work and ministry here. Several weeks ago, the General Assembly of the NSCC elected Dr. Haruun Ruun (who had been the Deputy Executive Secretary) to be the next Executive Secretary. We rejoice in this selection and celebrate that the NSCC is now well enough established that the church leaders felt it was time to call a Sudanese to this important post. At the time of the election, some very affirming words of appreciation were given to us by the church leaders. That was an uplifting experience.
>
> Maundy Thursday: It is very depressing when we learn of Sudanese leaders who have been "bought by Khartoum" to betray their own people. We know that many more persons will be destroyed by this war which is prolonged and escalated by such betrayal. The lure of silver and power is just as real today as it was in Christ's time.
>
> Good Friday: In Sudan we have met people who have faced the difficult decision of whether to offer their lives in order that others may live. A recent example is a group of women in Mapuordit who so badly want this war to end that they have offered to sacrifice their lives if it will somehow bring the political leaders together to find a way for peace.
>
> Easter Morning: Sometimes it seems as if we are locked into Good Friday in Sudan. But then we listen to the Christians as they tell the wonderful stories of how the church is growing at a fantastic rate in spite of the persecution and suffering, and we know that Easter is being experienced throughout the year in Sudan. The good news of Easter is that Christ lives and that those who believe in him shall also live. We have seen and experienced this reality in a way that never was so real to us in our own culture. There is hope in spite of all the hells that are thrown at persons: war, famine, loneliness, greed, anger, broken relationships, disease. Christ is alive, and we see and experience this reality in new and poignant ways in Sudan. The Easter story is one that needs to be shared.
>
> The Emmaus Road: After the Easter event, the disciples were not sure about the future. As they walked along the Emmaus Road,

they were trying to figure out what all the recent events meant for them. We, too, are walking along the road to Emmaus. We do not yet know what is next for us. As we journey along, we hope that we will be able to recognize the Spirit's presence with us, and [like those disciples] be uplifted.[19]

That summer, while on home leave, the answer to "What next?" was given. As stated in the October 1995 *RCA Today* bulletin insert: "Roger Schrock has been appointed as the RCA's coordinator for mission stewardship in the Synod of the Heartland, and supervisor of the RCA mission programs in the Middle East, effective October 1."

Throughout the transition period, Roger and Carolyn felt that God was opening and closing doors. When this particular door opened before them, their response was enthusiastic:

...we are glad to have been called to a work that uses Roger's skills and experience but also presents new challenges for growth. He will need to re-focus from Africa to the Middle East and will need to learn the processes of mission stewardship. We feel blessed that these opportunities are before us.[20]

Though it had become next to impossible to serve Sudanese southerners in their devastated homeland, the thousands of southern refugees in the North were in dire need of assistance. And the door for such help was marvelously open. These people needed not only immediate physical relief from the inevitable conditions engendered by huddled masses, but also provision for the long-term spiritual well being of the many Christians who were victims of this lopsided and senseless civil war. The teaching of Christian leaders must go on; the Christian community must be built up and encouraged.

And by God's power and grace, such training was sanctioned by the northern government; in the shadow of mosques and minarets, southerners are being taught and prepared to minister among their own people.

19 Ibid. April 10, 1995. Archives.
20 Ibid. September 19, 1995. Archives.

In 1984, when it became evident that Doleib Hill was no longer a suitable place for educational purposes, Bill and Lois Anderson relocated in the North. With the cooperation and the encouragement of the Sudan Evangelical Church, and the tolerance and permission of northern officialdom, the Andersons were able to open the Gereif West Bible School near the capital city of Khartoum. RCA missionary Barbara Kapenga joined the staff there in 1985. It was the beginning of a long and effective ministry.

From this point on, the teaching careers of the Andersons, Barbara Kapenga, and the Rev. Peter and Patty Ford are solidly meshed.

It had been a circuitous route to Sudan for the Fords, paralleling that of the Doorenboses to Ethiopia.

Their interest in overseas missions had been whetted during their college years. Patty was active in Nurses' Christian Fellowship at Meyer Memorial Hospital School of Nursing in Buffalo, New York. Peter discovered his bent through Inter-Varsity Christian Fellowship at State University of New York, also in Buffalo. They actually met through Inter-Varsity's general conferences.

They were married in 1977. This was the union of two quite different church backgrounds: Peter came from the Plymouth Brethren tradition, while Patty's affiliation had been with the Roman Catholic Church.

Following marriage they lived for a few years in Rochester, New York. They found compatible Christian fellowship in First Reformed Church there, where the Rev. Louis Lotz was pastor. When he heard of the Fords' leaning toward missions, he suggested that they meet with Al Poppen in New York City, and their interest continued to grow.

Peter and Patty were accepted by the RCA mission board in 1982, following Peter's graduation from Western Theological Seminary in Holland, Michigan. Commissioned that summer, they spent the fall term in Birmingham, England, studying Islam at Selly Oak Colleges. In December they went to Amman, Jordan, for Arabic language study.

Their first assignment in the Arab world took them in 1984 to Muscat, Oman, where Peter became the assistant pastor of the Protestant Church. He not only shared in the preaching ministry, but also visited Omanis, assisted with the Arabic congregation, and saw to it that the RCA property was maintained.

Their son David was born in Muscat on May 10, 1985.

In the fall of 1987, the RCA's Secretary for Africa, the Rev. Warren Henseler, contacted the Fords about a request he had received from Bill

Anderson, who was at that time head of the Gereif West Bible School. Barbara Kapenga, then the only RCA person in Khartoum, was going on home assignment. Bill was concerned about who would replace her. Peter enlarged on Bill's request in a letter:

> [Bill really wanted] someone long-term, provided that person had a theological education and could teach in Arabic. At that time, I was the only RCA missionary on the field who met the qualifications! We had been thinking it might be time to make a switch; I always had felt called to teaching, so it did not take us long to agree.
>
> Plans were to go there the summer of 1988 after a home assignment, but our visas were delayed (partly, we surmise, due to the massive floods in Khartoum that August). We finally went back to Muscat temporarily. The visas came at last in January 1989, and we arrived in Khartoum in February.[21]

The Fords were the guests of Barbara Kapenga for the first five weeks. She was able to share valuable helps and insights in their adjusting to the new scene.

Just as moving from one tribal area to another in black Africa demands a certain amount of acclimation, a transfer within the Arab world can also be disorienting. Peter and Patty found the Sudanese lifestyle quite different from that of the Omanis: a slower pace, for one thing. The advice they would give is: "Shift into low gear and go with the (very slow) flow!"

Many foods that were available readily in Oman simply were non-existent in Khartoum. So Patty's culinary skills were brought to the fore in creating great meals for her family.

Even the language presented its challenges. Peter began teaching fairly early, taking over Barbara's course on Old Testament Wisdom and Poetry Literature.

> It was good to finally get into Bible teaching, but doing it in a new dialect of Arabic is quite stretching! I found it humbling to have to say repeatedly, "I didn't understand your question," and to see my efforts at translating class notes get substantially rewritten by my Sudanese helper.

21 Peter Ford, from a letter sent to the author, October 9, 1995. Joint Archives of Holland, Hope College.

But again, God has provided. There is a good language institute right in our neighborhood, and Patty and I plan to do some further study, especially in colloquial Arabic, over the summer.[22]

On June 30, 1989, Sudan experienced a peaceful military coup. This resulted in a clamp-down on freedoms of speech and press. The government also ordered the removal of hundreds of thousands of southern refugees from the areas in the North where they had settled. But the school in Gereif continued to operate.

While Peter taught at the Bible School and in the Theological Education by Extension program, Patty found her niche working with the Good News Club for children living near the school. She had to teach in colloquial Arabic so the children could understand her. She also taught a Sunday school class of four- to ten-year-olds, an age range that tested all of her skills for effective instruction.

In the summer of 1990 Patty organized a vacation Bible school, the first ever for the Khartoum International Church. They had a great time, she said, despite all the work and "making do" with limited resources. The weather even cooperated. They had only one minor dust storm and no major power cuts in the six days they met.

But Patty considered her most vital ministry to be with forty-five local children who gathered in a neighborhood home for an Arabic Bible Club. She had a tremendous concern for the children of Sudan. They are, as she calls them, Sudan's hope for tomorrow, for both the church and the country. Her dream was to encourage some women students from the Bible School in this sort of outreach to children.

May 1990 brought graduation at Gereif Bible School—an especially stirring event because it happened only every three years. As Peter explained, every class, with few exceptions, moved together through a three-year program. At the end of that time, having completed their studies and having qualified in the areas of teaching and preaching, graduates were prepared to be sent out as evangelists engaged in pastoral ministry. Graduation Day that year was made memorable with five speeches, ten choirs, and 1,680 bottles of Pepsi!

The Presbytery of the Evangelical Church, which owns and runs the Bible School, had at the outset selected the students for training. Now that same

---

[22] Ford, from "A Missionary Letter," May 1989. Joint Archives of Holland, Hope College.

Patty Ford leads the Good News Club

body would assign them to numerous congregations scattered throughout northern Sudan. Many expressed a desire to return to live and work in the South, but the civil war made that difficult.

Along with a new class entering the Gereif Bible School that fall, an important new development that would greatly strengthen the Sudanese church began to take shape—a dream of the Andersons and the Sudanese church leaders that at last was coming to fruition. Initially, it would be called the Khartoum Theological College. As a joint venture of the various Sudanese churches in the North, it represented a major accomplishment and would fill a need for advanced theological training.

Peter was given the special task of making the initial orders and requests for books for the college's library. "Just the right job for a book-lover like me," was Peter's response.

At the same time, the specter of the Persian Gulf crisis began to loom large on the eastern horizon. All Arab countries were caught up in what had become a threat to peace in the whole region, and Sudan was no exception.

The uncertain situation brought change rather precipitously to the life of the Ford family:

> The New Year (1991) found us involved in our usual ministries in Khartoum, while we watched with concern the countdown to renewed fighting in the Gulf. We were perplexed as to what it would mean for us. On the one hand, there was no real danger to us in Khartoum; Baghdad was a thousand miles away, and we sensed absolutely no feelings of hostility toward North Americans by the people of Sudan.
>
> On the other hand, it was known that Palestinian terrorists were in the country and that U.S. citizens would be targeted. Furthermore, the political situation in Sudan was, and is, precarious at best; events in the Gulf could spill over into unrest in Khartoum. The U.S. ambassador urged Americans to leave, at least temporarily. When the same request came from the RCA leadership in New York, we quickly flew to Nairobi on January 14.
>
> For the next three weeks, we closely followed events, talked things over with friends, and prayed. Although there were no serious incidents in Khartoum, the potential for danger would continue for at least the duration of the fighting.
>
> For various reasons we could not wait indefinitely. We had been planning to begin home assignment with extended study leave in November 1992. We finally decided to move these plans forward. So Peter returned to Khartoum for a week to pack away our belongings. We were soon on our way to the United States.[23]

Following several months of speaking in supporting churches, the Fords settled in the mission house of Addisville Reformed Church in Richboro, Pennsylvania. They lived there for the duration of their study leave. By September 1, Peter was busy at Temple University, focusing his attention on Islam and Christian-Muslim relations. Patty was taking courses in Christian Education at Princeton Theological Seminary. And David was enjoying first grade.

On February 17, 1992, just a year after the Fords had arrived in the United States, they entertained guests for tea: their Presbyterian colleagues at Gereif, Bill and Lois Anderson:

23 Ibid. March 6, 1991. Archives.

We had last seen them in Nairobi. The fighting in the Gulf and the potential dangers in Khartoum had made the future uncertain for all of us. As it turned out, the war was over sooner than anyone had expected, and the Andersons were able to return to Khartoum at the end of last March.

Our friends had much good news to share. The Bible School was continuing under the able leadership of our Sudanese colleague, Hani. Our colleague, Barbara Kapenga, had also returned [after having spent three months teaching at the Yeheywet Birhan School for Girls in Addis Ababa while waiting for her Sudan visa] and was busy coordinating the Theological Education by Extension program. But the best news was that the new Sudan (formerly, Khartoum) Theological College (STC) had started up and had begun classes with twice as many students (about thirty) as had been originally projected!

STC has begun to meet a long-standing need in Sudan for a higher level institution to train pastors leading to ordination. We have had a stake in this school from its inception. I had served on the planning committee before leaving Khartoum. A letter I wrote to Warren Henseler about the financial needs of the new venture came to him at just the right time; he was able to channel a gift of $70,000 to the college. This had been given by Reformed Church Women.

But most importantly, to us personally, we are expecting that this new theological college will be the primary focus of our ministry when we return to Sudan.

Talking with Bill and Lois made us wish we could return now! We do miss our friends and our work there; but we have no regrets about our present course of action. Studies for both Patty and me are challenging, stimulating, and definitely beneficial. While we still have a couple more years of this, we believe that we will return much better prepared to carry on a ministry among Christians living in a Muslim world. Plans are on track for our ministry to resume in Khartoum.[24]

---

[24] Ibid. March 23, 1992. Archives.

Before their graduate studies were completed, Peter was invited to return to Khartoum for three weeks to teach a concentrated course in biblical Hebrew and Greek. He was elated with what he found there:

> The new Sudan Theological College was up and running, providing pastoral training for Sudanese Christians who have completed secondary school. The staff welcomed me with open arms.
>
> I taught a course entitled "Orientation to Biblical Language." In three weeks the students learned the alphabet, transliteration, a few key words, and some grammatical terms both for Hebrew and Greek. Then I guided them in some research utilizing what they had studied. Those who did well will take full courses in Hebrew and/or Greek as electives.
>
> I went through the STC library, checking to see how many books had arrived there safely. Over the last couple of years, I have purchased or obtained donations of over 2,400 volumes, mailing them in canvas sacks. It was heartwarming to see that most of them had made it and were nicely stacked and catalogued, thanks to Barbara Kapenga. Many thanks also to Reformed Church Women who provided funds for the new books [as well as for other STC projects].
>
> And many thanks to the RCA's Central and Hope Colleges for thirty used commencement gowns and eight academic hoods which I brought with me and which will be used for future graduation ceremonies here!
>
> At the end of my visit, the students threw a small party for me..... They expressed their eagerness to see us return as a family....next year. Indeed we are now looking forward to this more than ever....I sensed strongly that God was using this opportunity to confirm for us our call to ongoing service in Sudan, especially with STC. God is doing a remarkable work through this new institution in a country still beset by civil war and ethnic/religious strife.[25]

Soon it was the end of the 1994 school year; the Fords' study leave was over. Peter still had work to do on his doctoral thesis; this he would do as time

[25] Ibid. February 1993. Archives.

permitted back in Sudan. David had finished third grade—and most exciting, he had become a big brother!

Patty had completed the necessary research papers for the master's degree program in Christian Education. Peter mailed the papers in on April 23—and two days later, Andrew Timothy was born. How overjoyed the whole family was, and how thankful to God, for this precious gift.

Patty graduated three weeks later.

In August the Fords returned to Sudan to take up their teaching ministries at what was now called Nile Theological College. There were seventy students enrolled. They were being trained in one of two streams: pastoral ministry, or teachers of the Christian religion in public schools. The latter was an amazing new addition to the curriculum. Patty explained:

> It has long been a requirement for all high school students to pass an exam in either Islam or Christianity. But until now, only Islam has been taught at school. Non-Muslim students had to study the Christian faith on their own in order to take the exam in Christianity. Now Christianity can be taught, so teachers need to be trained to teach it. In 1993 the first class of two dozen students was admitted to the college for this new two-year Christian Education program.[26]

As of December, and in addition to his teaching role, Peter was named to become Dean of Studies, a position which had been held by Bill Anderson.

> We would have preferred a bit more time before moving into such a responsibility, but our sense is that Peter's gifts and experience allow him this opportunity to offer a helpful contribution to a school which is at the forefront of Christian theological education in this country, where the needs are so great, yet where God is building his church.[27]

In 1995 the Fords suffered anxiety and sorrow as both their fathers, within just a few months, were struck down with cancer. Patty's father was treated for leukemia and became a shadow of his former active self. Peter's father became seriously ill with lymphoma which was discovered after the little family had had a lovely vacation in June with Peter's parents in Manila,

[26] Ibid. September 1993. Archives.
[27] Ford, from a letter, Advent 1994. Archives.

where they had served as missionaries for eighteen years. His passage into glory occurred in October.

On the other side of sorrow was the joy in seeing their sons grow up with healthy bodies, keen minds, and an inclination toward spiritual things; and in seeing, as their focus in ministry, the Nile Theological College turning out students well qualified for dynamic and strategic service in the suffering country of Sudan.

The first commencement was held on December 14, 1995. Twenty-three students received their degrees in a Spirit-filled, moving ceremony. For the Fords, it was...

> ...a humbling, awesome experience to participate in the first graduation from NTC. Pray for these graduates, that the visions they have, and the knowledge they have gained, will help the church here to become all that God has called it to be.
>
> We often wish we could do more to help. Yet we remember that the church's true strength and hope come not from a few missionaries who happen to work with them, but from the living Christ who came as one of them to reveal the saving grace of God, and who is present with them even in their suffering.[28]

Bill and Lois Anderson retired but continued to teach part-time at NTC. Bill also researched the history of the church in Sudan for a work called The Church in Sudan: Its Impact Past, Present, and Future.

The Reformed Church in America has every reason to praise God for its representatives in Khartoum who have given themselves for the sake of the Sudanese Church and for the sake of Jesus Christ, the head of that church. To him be all honor and praise!

[28] Ibid. Advent 1995. Archives.

XXVI
Joint Projects
Concept Unfolds

The Reformed Church in America has a long and colorful association with the Arab world. Its missionaries pioneered ministry to the people of Islam, persevering through a century despite strong resistance to the gospel.

With these faithful pioneers in mind, Bob and I faced, for the first time in our career, the challenge of opening work among Muslims. The Orma people of southeastern Kenya are not heirs to centuries of Islamic culture and tradition, as are the descendants of Ishmael; they began to embrace Islam only around the time of World War I, after Christian missions from Europe during the nineteenth century had failed to make a significant impact. Now they maintained a stout opposition to Christianity.

This was made plain in an incident related by Rose Schwarz, a nurse who had been making regular medical visits to the Ormas from the AIM mission at Mulango. A Kenyan evangelist accompanied her each time, but unaware of the Muslim mindset, the young man preached simply as he had been taught. On one occasion, the Ormas were incensed, and shouted, "God, yes! Jesus, no!" To them, Jesus was one of the three gods whom Christians worship.

While the doctrine of the Trinity is a mystery even to Christians, to Muslims it is anathema. Jesus (Isa) is merely one of the great prophets, and not as exalted as Mohammed.

Yet, in obedience to the Great Commission, a witness must be given, sensitively and lovingly, in the context of their understanding. The RCA stepped forward into this Orma field with confidence in almighty God.

Before we made our final move to Waldena in Orma country in September 1982, Jack and Deb and three-year-old Justin flew to Nairobi from Sudan for a brief break and a happy visit with us. They surprised us with a gift of two days with them at Safariland Lodge at Lake Naivasha, one of the soda lakes of the Great Rift Valley that are so attractive to flamingos.

The lodge was a beautiful place with all kinds of tropical flowers and blossoming shrubs, expanses of thick, green lawns, swimming pools, horses, and a marvelous variety of birds. Peacocks strutted around on the lawns. Mischievous vervet monkeys darted down from the stately, flat-topped acacia trees to tease the proud birds as if scolding them for their haughty ways.

We thoroughly enjoyed those two absolutely carefree, peaceful days—effective therapy after the traumatic events at Alale. We couldn't thank Jack and Deb enough for their loving thoughtfulness.

The young Swarts soon were on their way back for what would turn out to be their final few months at Pibor in Sudan. Bob and I headed east for Waldena, a trip of about ten hours, broken by an overnight stop at Mulango.

Mulango could be called Waldena's parent station. Over the years, missionaries from Mulango had made brief trips into Orma territory, attempting by various creative approaches to reach this tribe with the gospel. So sincere was their concern that at one point they brought seven Orma boys to Mulango, with their parents' consent, so that they could be educated at the local school. They housed, clothed, and fed them, and saw to it that they heard the good news of Jesus, the Redeemer.

After four years, one of these boys was baptized. Named Ali Duri, he took the Christian name of John. We were told that for a while he was bold in sharing his new faith with his people, but eventually persecution silenced him.

Twenty years before our arrival, the Africa Inland Church Mission Board (AICMB) also had attempted to reach the Ormas, sending two African pastors to Waldena. It turned out to be an unfortunate move. The pastors were not compatible, and one of them left. Pastor Mbuva stayed, and he and his wife erected a small mud-walled church building. They had a ministry of sorts for a while, though mostly among the police who came from other tribal groups.

But when Mbuva became involved in poaching and immoral matters, the AICMB dropped its support. Why he continued to live at Waldena, we will never know. He remained there for some years after our arrival, living in the ramshackle pastor's house.

We realized the prince of this world had enjoyed the upper hand in the effort to present Christ as Son of God and Savior to this tribe. On a previous survey trip, we had chosen for our home base a site on the north side of the Galole River. Orma villages, like clusters of giant mushrooms, were scattered here and there in every direction. The quite new four-room government school, police lines, merchants' shops, and the little church were well established nearby.

Our camp was pleasant in the shade of acacia trees. Bob rigged up a "shower bower" among the bushes behind our *rondavel*. Birdlife abounded, as did goats and fat-tailed sheep. We enjoyed watching the small herders urging their flocks back to the *manyattas* (villages) every evening.

Once a tiny kid had begun bleating for its mother as the flock approached the village. Kid and nanny soon were united, the mother standing still while her baby suckled. Then, to my amused astonishment, a little Orma boy ran up to the pair, grabbed hold of one of the nanny's rear legs, and proceeded to drink from the remaining "faucet"! What a picture: two "kids" sharing a mother's bountiful nourishment!

Everything about this site pleased us and we thought that we had made a wise choice—until the river informed us otherwise.

The Galole is a dry, sandy riverbed most of the year. But should it rain heavily in the distant hills, all the feeder streams flow into the dry watercourses, and the Galole can become a raging torrent, virtually uncrossable.

Such was the case that November. We were looking forward eagerly to attending the annual AIM conference at Kijabe in early December. In fact, it was mandatory that all missionaries be there. But would this watery barricade keep us from making the two-hundred-mile journey?

It would have, if it hadn't been for our old friend, Verne Sikkema.

He had flown to Waldena to check out the long airstrip on the other side of the river that Bob had cleared with the help of Orma workers. (The strip was one that the government had closed some years earlier by digging ditches across it to stop rampant poaching in the area.) Before MAF or AIM-Air could use it for passenger service, a pilot was obliged to inspect it. Verne was that pilot.

It was frustrating not to be at the strip for his several buzzings and landings. We could only listen and try to interpret the whirring, roaring sounds.

Then all was quiet.

Soon Verne appeared on the opposite bank. He shouted, "How can I get across? I want to spend the night." We could hardly believe it!

The water was still chest-deep and rushing madly. But with an Orma, like an outrigger, on each side of him gripping his hands, and his overnight bag lashed securely to an inner tube that another Orma pulled across like a floating pull-toy, Verne made the crossing intact. Never was a pilot welcomed more heartily.

While he was on our side of the river, he inspected a short strip with a dogleg that Bob had cleared in case of an emergency. It was only four hundred yards long, one-third the length of a proper strip. But Verne was sure that he could land and take off if necessary on even such a short, crooked runway.

He returned to Nairobi. We kept hoping the water would recede enough to allow us to drive across. Instead, it rose higher than ever. At the eleventh hour, remembering Verne's estimate of the emergency strip, Bob called him by mission radio and asked if he could come to our "rescue." It was his day off, but he flew in anyway and, as he put it, "snatched us out of Waldena." A pilot with less confidence and experience never would have attempted it.

It was another excellent conference. The long uncertainty of the preceding days made us appreciate more than ever the privilege of attending this annual event—for the spiritual refreshment it gave us and the good fellowship with scores of others from the Africa Inland Mission.

Along with the mixed blessing of abundant water that December, we received the happy news of the birth of Caleb Giles Swart. Leah Rae now had a little brother; Dick and Donna, a son; and Bob and Morrie, their thirteenth grandchild.

The message of the Galole came through loud and clear above the roar of its waters: we must move to the south side of the river. We set up our new camp under tall acacias well back from the river. It was comforting to know that, though the track east or west might not always be passable, at least the capricious Galole would never again hold us captive.

It should be noted that the arrival of water in the riverbed is hailed with much joy by all who live up and down its reaches, including missionaries.

When the river is dry, people dig holes in the sand until they strike water. This same water is used for countless goats, sheep, cattle, donkeys, and camels. As the water level falls, the holes are dug deeper.

A flowing river replenishes the water supply and all Ormaland rejoices. When the first surge is discovered, spreading out from bank to bank and filtering down into the sand, a few young people prance and dance ahead of it, shouting the good news; there will be enough water for several months.

Our new camp consisted of a fine tent that was our bedroom, and two *rondavels*: one for our pantry and kitchen and the other for guests and volunteers. Our dining room was outdoors in the shade of a spreading thorn tree. I did most of my cooking in that same shade, using a charcoal brazier called a *jiko*.

A *jiko*, roughly the shape of a thick-waisted hourglass, was a wonderfully versatile stove. While meat or vegetables cooked in a pot over the glowing coals, potatoes could be baked flavorfully in the lower section in the bed of ashes. The fragrance of such a meal titillated the appetite to an extraordinary degree!

Usually we had company for our open-air meals. Superb starlings are among Africa's loveliest and friendliest birds. These rufus-breasted, iridescent little beauties took it for granted on a daily basis that they were invited guests. They would perch on the arms of our chairs, and even on our knees, eyeing the food on our forks and expecting to have a share of the fare. Once an especially daring little chap lit on my raised hand which held a brownie. We rather delighted in their bold greediness, but did cover dishes of food on the table to keep them out of it.

One morning, breakfast was just about ready when I heard a little scratchy, rattly commotion. Upon investigation, I found that two starlings had been picking up and bouncing our vitamin pills on the table, and a white pill was even then rolling like a tiny wheel on the table's surface. How I laughed—and put the pills under a bowl!

In February 1983, God blessed us by sending Pastor Amos Tito to Waldena. Pastor Amos was a Pokomo from the Tana River area near the coast—a kindly, gray-haired gentleman. He told at one Sunday morning service how he had tried to ignore God's calling him to the ministry. He became a shopkeeper and was doing a good business—until thieves broke in and ran off with his whole inventory.

Rather than wringing his hands hopelessly and bewailing the loss of his goods, Amos accepted this financially devastating experience, recognizing it for what it was: a wake-up call from the Lord. He knew now that God would go to any lengths to get his attention. So, in humility of spirit, he bowed to his Sovereign's will and began preparing for the ministry.

Upon graduating from Bible school, Amos Tito had several pastorates, among them a church on the strongly Muslim island of Lamu off the Kenya coast. With this background, and having lived all his life in the Muslim-oriented coastal region, the AIC Mission Board sensed that he would be a good candidate for the Orma work. So, honoring the AIC/RCA Joint Projects agreement, it appointed this man to work at Waldena.

Pastor Amos lived in a *rondavel* near the church. In the shade of his little front porch, he set two chairs and a small table. On the table he kept a glass and a pitcher of water. It was an invitation with spiritual overtones. "Come, you who live in this dry and thirsty land. Come and drink of this life-giving water."

Pastor Amos was one of the Lord's saints, a true servant of the Most High. He made many friends among the Ormas. Surely they saw in him, if they were seeking, the very likeness of Christ. We were abundantly thankful to have him as a colleague at Waldena.

More colleagues were on the way.

On March 4, 1983, Bob and I were at the Nairobi airport eagerly awaiting KLM's arrival. Soon we were greeting our travel-weary friends, Paul and Marcia Leemkuil and their two children, Tamar and Nathan. How good it was to welcome them to Kenya! This was the "new opportunity overseas" for which they had been waiting. The General Program Council had appointed them to the Orma work.

It would be a few months, however, before they would join us at Waldena. The inevitable language study must be slogged through, and Marcia would need some nursing orientation in a Kenya hospital before she could be registered to work in the country.

But they had come, and we thanked God for providing this fine family who we anticipated would coordinate the Orma program following our retirement.

Early on in our planning for the Orma outreach, it was determined that establishing three mission bases along the Galole River would be more effective than centering activity solely at Waldena. The settlement at Titila, about sixteen miles downriver, was chosen as the second prime site. The Leemkuils eventually would locate there. But their first months in Orma country would be spent at Waldena for orientation purposes. So, high on the list of things to do was to arrange living quarters for them.

It was essential that a workshop be the next building project. Carefully planned, such a structure would make a suitable temporary home for the new family.

Help for this undertaking came that June. Northwestern College in Orange City, Iowa, had a program that prepared interested students for summer projects in mission settings. The college chaplain, the Rev. Gerald Sittser, was the guiding spirit. He led his charges well and implemented their assignments.

We were favored to have Brice Hoyt and Calvin Ver Mulm come to us out of that program. For two months these young men worked with a will at an exceedingly tedious task: fitting and fastening corrugated sheeting to an iron frame. I was sure that they would never want to bend another nail for the rest of their lives. But their unstinting labor resulted in a sturdy, practical workshop that would do very well as an interim residence.

Karen Sikkema, daughter of Verne and Lorraine, was with us for a month during this period, too. Karen had finished one of three years of teaching at Rosslyn Academy. We were pleased to have her at Waldena. She pulled her share of the work load and was good company for us all.

Their language course now behind them, the Leemkuils were ready for the next step. At the behest of the Kenya Nursing Council, Marcia began her two-month public health orientation in Nakuru on July 25. After moving Marcia to this town, which is a three-hour drive northwest of Nairobi, Paul and the children divided their time between Nakuru and Waldena. Paul wanted to get their Orma home ready for occupancy.

So all was in order for the whole family when Marcia's assignment was completed in mid-September. Paul and the children brought her home happily, along with a puppy named Snoopy, six rabbits, and six laying hens. We shared their joy.

That year we had our first Gathering. Our new secretary for Africa, the Rev. Warren Henseler, had sensed strongly and rightly the need for the scattered RCA teams to assemble on a regular basis for fellowship and encouragement. The idea was hailed with enthusiasm. Bob was tapped to make the arrangements, and on October 5, 1983, a goodly number of us gathered at the beautiful Safariland Lodge on the shore of Lake Naivasha.

Barbara Kapenga came from Sudan, and Arlene Schuiteman from Zambia. Dirk Doorenbos arrived from Tanzania, where he was working with a water development project. Harvey and Lavina Hoekstra, together with their son

Paul, were already in Kenya at the request of the Kenya Bible Society, so they were able to be with us. Larry and Linda McAuley came from Alale; Ken and Connie Shingledecker come from Daystar University in Nairobi. Marvin and Shirley Brandt joined us, too. They were about to go as volunteers to Alale to "hold the fort" while McAuleys were on home assignment. The Sikkemas from MAF headquarters in Nairobi and the Leemkuils and Swarts from Waldena made up the rest of the RCA/Africa contingent. (Harvey and Margaret Doorenbos were unable to come from Ethiopia. Jack and Deb Swart were in the United States between assignments.)

Also in attendance were: the Rev. Warren Henseler, the Rev. Al Poppen (both from RCA's New York office), and that year's president of General Synod, Dr. Leonard Kalkwarf, and his wife Beverly, from their pastorate in Pennsylvania.

What a grand fellowship! Warren had planned sessions of praise and worship, of sharing and stimulating discussion. And our schedule allowed moments for roaming the grounds to enjoy the profusion of flowers and blossoming shrubs, the quiet lake, and the sounds of African birds and vervet monkeys in the tall acacias.

The three-day idyll was over all too soon. But our VIPs were with some of us for a few more days.

The Kalkwarfs, Warren, and Al, undeterred by the prospects of a rough trip, traveled with us to Waldena. What good sports! Without the seasoning advantage of thirty-five years of living in the bush, our guests did find the journey taxing. They marveled that Bob could find his way in the dark through apparently trackless country. He seemed to be able to sniff his way along like an old hound.

At one point in Orma territory, someone had planted in the path a stick with a white cloth attached. We suspected that this was a signal of some sort. So we turned right in order to follow a less used and more roundabout way.

Sure enough, we soon were stopped near an Orma house. The family was terribly concerned for a lad who had been down in one of the deep water holes in the riverbed when the sandy wall caved in and buried him. Fortunately they had been able to rescue him. What they wanted now was reassurance that he would suffer no serious consequences and that he would indeed survive the ordeal.

Marcia Leemkuil and Beverly Kalkwarf were both nurses and examined the boy. They could find nothing significantly wrong with him, so they were able to comfort the family with a cautiously optimistic report and praise God with them that his experience had been no worse.

We reached Waldena at 9:30 that Saturday evening. Everyone was so weary that, after a quick snack of breadsticks and hot chocolate, we all retired to tents and *rondavels* and slept the night through.

The importance of our guests' visit could not be overestimated. The RCA recently had pledged support for each of the proposed three mission posts among the Orma. It was imperative, therefore, that these representatives see for themselves where, and for what purposes, this money would be used.

The third post had not yet been pinpointed. But they experienced Waldena on Sunday, swelling our congregation considerably that morning. In the afternoon they enjoyed ginger tea at the home of Sub-Chief Gobu.

Then on Monday we all gathered at Titila where the Leemkuils would live. Word had been sent ahead, so the *wazee* (elders) had assembled for a *baraza*. Ali Duri was there, too.

The village *wazee* spent some time addressing our visitors, expressing their hopes for the future of their community and their expectations of the AIC/RCA Joint Projects. They wanted a dispensary, a school, and a *duka* (shop) where they could buy things. The Muslim leader even had the temerity to ask for help in building a mosque! Ali Duri had the grace to be embarrassed over that request and told the people to stop talking foolishness.

Our hosts then served us a few slices of roasted goat meat. As we were getting ready to leave for Waldena, we heard Ali haranguing a group of Ormas. We could not understand what he was saying, but he was speaking with obvious authority.

Pastor Amos told us later that the Orma *wazee* had been chiding Ali for his friendship with Christians, accusing Bob of having put the "seal" of Christianity upon him. Ali's response must have taken more than a little courage: "If I am a Christian or a Muslim, that is my talk; it has nothing to do with anyone else."

Our American guests had goat meat twice that day. Sub-Chief Gobu had wanted to give us a goat when we first arrived in 1982. Not yet having a refrigerator, we declined with thanks and suggested he wait with his gift until some important people came to see us.

Now was the time. When Bob was so bold to ask Gobu for a goat, he exclaimed, "Yes! Thank you!" And he seemed so happy to give it.

The animal was delivered that afternoon. Our friend Mullah slaughtered it according to Muslim custom and roasted it in African fashion: large chunks impaled on sticks leaning toward the fire. I made a stew from some of the smaller pieces and served it with *ugali*, white cornmeal cooked so thick that it can be sliced.

Pastor Amos joined us, as well as Gobu and the Muslim leader, Mohammed Boru. We all enjoyed meeting together over a good meal. And I believe each one felt honored to be there.

The next day, two planes came to take our guests back to Nairobi. Verne Sikkema was one of the pilots. Dr. Kalkwarf boarded the plane with a live rooster in one arm, a gift from Pastor Amos. The Leemkuils and Swarts waved our friends off. We felt refreshed and uplifted by the events of the preceding days and ready for whatever lay ahead.

One of the subjects discussed during the weekend was the matter of our retirement. In an October 21, 1983, letter to my sister Adrienne, I wrote:

> I must say that this subject has been concerning us for some time, especially as it pertains to you and Mother (who was suffering from Parkinson's and Alzheimer's diseases). You have had the sole responsibility for Mom for so many years and my heart has really been troubled that I've not been able to share this with you more adequately. With Bob's sixty-fifth birthday approaching, I had thought with comfort that I would soon be able to relieve you and hopefully care for Mom as lovingly and faithfully and patiently as you have.
>
> Now, in this normally last year of service, Bob's vigor remains that of a much younger man, and with the new work among the Orma barely launched, it seems that to go home for good at this time would be leaving the project in the lurch.
>
> Paul and Marcia Leemkuil are next in line at the helm here, but they are still so new that it would be hardly fair, capable though they are, to leave them wholly in charge at this stage. And we have always said that we'd retire responsibly.
>
> So we told our "bosses" that if our strength holds, we'd give ourselves for another term of three years. We had the impression that Warren Henseler and Al Poppen, in welcoming this commitment, were relieved that the Orma work would continue to develop for a while yet under our leadership....

I've written this letter with a heavy heart, not because I wonder if our decision is wrong, but because of what it means to you. I wish there were some way that we could see our commitment to completion here and share your burden at the same time. I rather dread breaking the news to our children, too. They don't want their children to miss out in knowing their grandparents as they did in their growing-up years. Nor do we like not knowing our grandchildren well as they change from year to year. It's part of the price of serving overseas.

Adrienne's response was an answer to my prayer that God would prepare her to receive my letter, and a confirmation that our decision was right. She said, in essence: "You must be where the Lord wants you. I am where the Lord wants me. Please don't be concerned about us here. You have my blessing."

I answered her with these words: "I've just read your letter for the 'leventy-'leventh time. It was such a beautiful letter, so marvelously and assuringly expressed, and so full of love and understanding. Brought tears."

Really, it was like a load lifted, and peace filtered through my heart and mind.

Further confirmation as to the rightness of extending our years in Africa came in October 1984.

We had been in the United States on a six-month leave. Just before returning to Kenya in September, we spent a few precious days with Mother and Adrienne. It was not easy to say good-bye. Mother's frailty was otherworldly, her step so uncertain and slow.

It wasn't long after we had resumed life in Waldena that a message came over the mission radio that she had passed away from the brilliant New England fall colors, which she had loved so much, to the resplendent glories of heaven. It had happened on October 5, Adrienne's birthday.

Dear Mom,

How sweet the moments spent with you
Before we left for other shores;
Your thoughts had cleared, you asked for prayer—
Remembering, my heart soars.

We sat together, you and I,
Yourself encircled in my arms;
Our souls communed in love's accord—
Remembering, my heart warms.

We could not know how soon would sound
The call: Come, my child, to your rest!
For memories, I thank our God—
Remembering, my heart is blest.

Your feet now move with vital step,
Your voice has joined the praising throng;
And knowing one day we'll meet again—
In my heart's a song.

—MFS

Mother's death gave me an acceptable opportunity to witness to two
Ormas who came to say "*pole sana*" which means "very sorry" in Swahili.
Hussein came first, and then Mullah. I told them that, along with my sorrow,
I had joy in my heart because I knew that my mother was in heaven with her
Savior Jesus Christ. They listened quietly and respectfully.

While we had been home on leave, Dave and Connie Fieldhouse and
small daughter Kim from First Reformed Church in DeMotte, Indiana,
spent three months as volunteers at Waldena. What a comfort it was to us
to know that these two young families, the Leemkuils and the Fieldhouses,
were together in that remote place, encouraging one another and easing the
sometimes heavy burden of loneliness. It made our hearts lighter.

Upon our return the Leemkuils had their scheduled furlough. Marcia and
the children actually had left a few weeks early to attend a family wedding.
Just before their departure, a message came from Marcia's father with the
sad news that her mother had passed away suddenly. Both grief and joy
encompassed the family during the ensuing months, along with God's
abiding presence.

Among all the memories of 1984, drought and famine played a ravaging
role. Ethiopia was devastated by these conditions, and many of Kenya's

people suffered real hunger. The Ormas, barely able to maintain life at an adequate subsistence level in the best of times, began to languish. The plight of the children quickly became acute.

In our absence Paul and Marcia had embarked on a children's feeding program that was greatly appreciated by the Ormas, giving hope that the lives of these youngsters would be spared.

When we returned that September, Bob and I gladly continued this service as the Leemkuils had begun it: in the name of the One who loves little children. A relief agency, Food for the Hungry, was our major donor of the cornmeal and powdered milk for the daily meals at Waldena and Titila.

Two Kenyan women cooked the cornmeal in a huge *sufuria* set on three stones over an open fire while children, each with a parent, gathered around and waited eagerly, but patiently, for their full bowls of mush.

As I watched them eat, spoonful after spoonful, scraping their bowls clean, and then licking up what the spoons missed, I thanked God for enabling us to provide this life-sustaining nourishment, trusting him to use this small service to accomplish something great in the lives of these little ones.

There were some big ones now to care for, too. Dr. William Brownson was the new president of General Synod. He had chosen to visit some of the RCA work in Africa as part of his official agenda that year, and September was the month he would be arriving at Waldena.

So we spent our first days back home sweeping and dusting! After being unused for some months, our little *rondavels* needed a major cleaning. We were delighted to prepare our facilities for Dr. Brownson, his wife Helen, and a welcome return of Warren Henseler.

These three had visited Arlene Schuiteman in Zambia first. Once in Kenya, Verne Sikkema became their host pilot. With interim visits in Nairobi with the Sikkemas and Jack and Deb Swart, Verne took them first to Alale for a weekend with the McAuleys and then to Waldena.

During their short stay, we showed them all there was to see: the airstrip and clinic building at Titila that Paul Leemkuil had completed, the Waldena community, and the feeding program in operation. Pastor Amos joined us for supper the last evening. (He loved meeting our guests.)

Such visits were not only a privilege, but also a stimulating pleasure. They provided a spiritual boost in every instance. We were always grateful to the RCA for the close ties it maintained with its missionaries over the years.

We took our guests back to Nairobi in our trusty Toyota Land Cruiser. On the way, we stopped in Machakos, not far from Nairobi, to see the Africa Inland Church's Scott Theological College. (Peter Cameron Scott was the founder of the Africa Inland Mission.) We knew this institution would be of great interest to our visitors.

We arrived just in time for the chapel service. After our friends had been introduced, Dr. Brownson was asked to give a message to the student body. In a letter home, I described the occasion:

> Dear Bill Brownson! He is always ready and thrilled to preach, and he gave a gem of a sermon. We really rejoiced and praised God that this man with very special (and quiet) preaching gifts had this wonderful opportunity to encourage these young African men and women who are preparing for church work.
>
> There stood this humble but distinguished man in his travel-rumpled clothes and wearing a little old khaki jacket we'd loaned him against the wind in the back of the truck— preaching pure gold. It was so great to be able to share him.

We had counted on Warren Henseler to be with us in Nairobi the next weekend for a very special reason.

After several months of special training as a recordist at a technical school, along with some hands-on experience at Portable Recording Ministries (PRM) in Holland, Michigan, Jack and Deb and their two little boys left for Nairobi in April 1984. They would be working under PRM's affiliate, Gospel Communications Research (GCR).

Jack's first responsibility was to construct a soundproof recording studio. PRM had rented a maisonette on the compound of the United Bible Societies. Following a design drawn up by Tom Van Wynen, GCR's technical advisor, Jack built a studio within the upper floor of the maisonette. As PRM's Kenya director, Tesfahun Agidew, saw it, he built "a house inside of a house."

On Saturday, September 29, the new facility would be dedicated. It had been hoped that Warren Henseler would give the dedication sermon, but because of circumstances outside of his control, he had to leave Kenya the day before.

That Saturday afternoon, about sixty guests sat under a large carport before a cloth-draped podium. Representatives of the Bible Societies took part in the program as well as GCR personnel. And Bob Swart took Warren's place in giving the sermon. It was a mutual thrill for Jack and Bob when the son introduced his father: "Our speaker is one who is very dear to me...." Such occasions are rare in a person's life and therefore are cherished beyond the telling.

We had so much to praise God for that thanksgiving day. On November 18, Shelah Brooks Swart was born to Dick and Donna, their third child. Her birth brought the number of our grandchildren to fifteen—all priceless gifts from the Lord.

Another reason for praise had to do with rain. Orma land was parched, kindling dry after two long rainless years. A few showers fell on us in October, enough to awaken the dormant grass seeds.

Tread gently where the green grass grows:
The desert blooms not often.
Rain drops rare from Orma skies
The seeds to wake, to soften.

Faint emerald carpets shine around us—
The aftermath of showers;
But if the rain falls not again,
The grass will bear no flowers.

More rain, Lord, for this thirsty land,
For grass, for beans, and maize;
More rain, Lord, to wet the earth,
To cool the sultry days.

May water, Lord, like manna fall,
May earth produce her grain!
May Orma hands be lifted high
In praise for abundant rain!
—MFS

This prayer was answered lavishly during the next two months. The heavens opened. Way up in the mountains, as well as in Orma country, rain poured down with abandon. And the Galole River flowed for the first time in two years. The Ormas had good crops; their cattle had abundant pasture.

But there was a minor downside to this wonderful tide: it wreaked havoc on our riverbank. The unusually high river and the force of the current tore great chunks away. Day and night, we could hear thunderous splashes as tons of earth fell into the rushing water. Even huge acacia trees toppled as more and more of their root systems were exposed.

We had placed our second camp well back from the precipitous bank, but it was soon evident that our little kitchen could be in eventual danger of following the acacias downstream. Our beleaguered campsite would not survive another rampaging Galole. It was incumbent upon us to search yet again for a more ideal location.

XXVII
...and Unfolds

During our 1984 furlough, we had met a young man who was slated to join the Orma team. Roger Scheenstra was attending Reformed Bible College in Grand Rapids, Michigan, preparing for career mission service. We were impressed with Roger's earnest commitment, though somewhat concerned about his bachelorhood. But he had been in Kenya before on two summer assignments, he said, and he was undaunted at the prospect of coming out as a single missionary.

God had other plans. A lovely young woman named Susan finally said yes to Roger's proposal and yes to the Lord's call to serve in Kenya. Roger and Susan were married in May.

Because of his new status, Roger's arrival was postponed for a year, and now we anticipated his coming in early 1986—with a wife!

But 1985 held more than just great anticipation.

The Leemkuil family, now numbering five, returned from furlough in February. Tamar and Nathan were proud for us to meet their new little brother Matthew, who had been born in October 1984.

The blessing of Matthew's birth eased somewhat an otherwise very difficult few months at home. During that short period, there had been three deaths in Marcia's family; an aunt was diagnosed with cancer; and both widowed fathers found it so hard to see them return to Africa.

These circumstances tested in a powerful way the reality of Paul's and Marcia's calling. Yet, with a steadfastness born of faith and obedience, they set their faces toward Kenya. We welcomed them with thanksgiving.

That year Paul focused on completing the building program at Titila: living quarters with a workshop at the rear, and a clinic. Poured cement walls and corrugated roofing made both structures strong and practical.

Shortly before the Leemkuils returned to Ormaland, we welcomed another Kenyan to our staff. Chosen by God and supported by nurse Rose Schwarz, Joshua Chelanga came to Waldena from the Marakwet tribe in western Kenya. He was a public health worker. He and Marcia Leemkuil worked together at the clinic that had been fashioned ingeniously from a shipping container by Diguna, a German mission group in Nairobi.

Joshua was also a gifted evangelist and preacher. When Pastor Amos had to be away, he gladly and ably led the Sunday morning services. At other times, as the Spirit nudged him, he was able to witness appropriately to Orma friends. Joshua was a definite asset to the ministry among the Orma, as was his wife Leah when she joined him there after a few months.

In June we had the rare pleasure of having a grandchild with us: six-year-old Justin Swart spent three weeks at Waldena. Deb had sent along some schoolwork which we did in the morning while Marcia taught Tamar and Nathan. But the three children played together the rest of the day.

At night Justin slept in a little tent right beside ours. He was so brave and so good! But during the third week, he began talking frequently about "my brother," so we knew he was becoming eager to go home again. When the time came, we took him back to his family in Nairobi. Before he greeted his mom and dad, he made a beeline for his little brother Craig and gave him a real bear hug. He had had a fine time at Waldena, but how good it was to be home again!

In July our daughter Gayle made a nostalgic journey back to Africa, her first since she had graduated from high school in Alexandria, Egypt, twenty years earlier. Her two children were with her. She wanted Dawn and Brandon, now seventeen and fifteen, to taste a bit of the continent she loved, to experience something of life in the bush, and to break free from the provincialism to which Americans so often are prone. She hoped to broaden their horizons and enlarge their vision.

We helped that process along by scheduling brief safaris to search out possible sites for the third mission base among the Ormas. Our original plan had been to locate in the Meliloni area west of Waldena. But that whole region recently had been declared by the Kenya government to be part of a game reserve. So our hope to settle in Meliloni was dashed. Other possibilities lay to the east.

Pastor Amos was able to travel with us. We visited a settlement called Chifiri, a place that was easily accessible during the dry season. But when the rains came, the surrounding countryside, as flat as Kansas, became an impassable mire.

Asa was more difficult to access from the west because of the extremely rutted, unused tracks—body-buffeting and bone-rattling. But we arrived at the community center none the worse for the rough trip.

We were well received at both Chifiri and Asa. The possibility of the AIC/RCA Joint Projects being of service among them was appealing. Since this was just a fact-finding safari, however, we were not ready to make any decisions. It was enough to have seen the two areas and to have made contact with the community leaders and some of the populace.

We camped at Asa the second night, setting up our gear near to the police lines. But for all the weariness of the day, we had no sleep. A pre-wedding celebration was in full swing a few hundred yards away, and we endured, as well as were fascinated by, the Orma singing that began at nine o'clock in the evening and lasted uninterrupted until five in the morning. The participants must have been exhausted!

As for us, we had experienced a bit of Orma culture and wouldn't have missed it even for a good night's sleep.

Before Gayle and her children returned to the United States, Jack's family joined us for a safari to the Maasai Mara Game Reserve, a must for all visitors to Kenya. On the Tanzanian border southwest of Nairobi, the Mara can be depended upon to give sightseers live coverage of a wide variety of Africa's animals and bird species. This instance was no exception. In fact, it was the season for the annual migration of thousands of wildebeest, or gnu, from the Serengeti Plain in Tanzania up into this protected region of Kenya. It is an amazing phenomenon, one of the wonders of the world of nature.

We also visited Lion Hill Camp at Lake Nakuru, another soda lake, especially to view the flamingos. Countless thousands of them make a rosy pink margin around the lakeshore.

The most exciting moment on this safari was when Bob, without realizing it, drove over a python; he had thought it was just a large stick. But Brandon, who had been standing up looking out of the pop-top of the safari van, shouted, "Grandpa, you drove over a snake!"

Looking behind us, we could see the last three feet of it about to disappear into the brush. Jack jumped out and grabbed its tail, pulling it out into full view. It was a relatively small specimen (about nine feet long) and beautifully marked. Jack obliged the photographers among us by pulling the python out several times so all could get pictures. Then it vanished, apparently suffering no ill effects from its bruising encounter.

After all this family activity, life at Waldena seemed rather dull. But it was just a matter of mentally shifting gears and getting on with the Orma agenda.

"Come, all you who are thirsty, come to the waters!"[1] What a summons by the prophet! And Jesus gave a like invitation: "If anyone is thirsty, let him come to me and drink."[2]

Life-giving water—physical and spiritual!

Over the centuries the Ormas have learned how to manage their lives and their herds by moving from one area of their arid tribal territory to another, the patterns being dictated largely by water supply. We admired them greatly. But was there some way that we could assist them so that the local water reserves would be less marginal, so that there would be adequate pure water for the people's health needs as well as enough watering centers for the herds to keep to a minimum the tensions over such rights?

Remembering lessons learned by development agencies in the Sahel region of Africa regarding population growth around permanent water sources, and the subsequent ecological destruction of such areas, Bob again sought advice from the specialists: hydrologist Ralph Borgeson and water expert, Doc Propst. Because the water project at Alale four years earlier was so successful, Food for the Hungry/Canada was willing to fund this scheme also. It would be wells this time.

A plan to drill several wells in Orma country was put into action with the engagement of a Kenya drilling company. This became a major undertaking. The logistics of bringing the drilling rig and all the necessary paraphernalia through miles and miles of African bush was a tremendous test of endurance.

Wells number one and two at Titila produced water suitable for bathing and laundering, but not for drinking. It was too full of minerals and tasted exceedingly salty.

[1] Isaiah 55:1, New International Version.
[2] John 7:37, New International Version.

Well number three at Waldena was of better quality, but did not produce an amount adequate for the local populace. But well number four at Kofisa and number five at Saware, both farther west and away from the influence of the Indian Ocean, produced good and adequate water, albeit from three hundred feet down in the earth! What would be the best way to raise it?

The Ormas knew about diesel-powered pumps. That would be so simple. But who would pay for the fuel and maintenance? The tribe would be forever dependent on outside assistance.

Neither did a modern hand pump, manufactured in the Netherlands and advertised as capable of pumping water from such a depth, prove to be a practical solution. It required too much physical energy to produce a small amount of water.

Then the Lord provided the answer: a group of churches in England had initiated a program of supplying windmills, manufactured in Kenya, to needy areas of the country. Ormaland was chosen as one of those areas. The first one was installed at Saware, complete with a cement watering trough. The wind accomplished easily what man's arm could not do.

Two more windmills were erected eventually: one at Kofisa and another in a second location at Waldena.

The Ormas thus saw an actual demonstration of Christian love in action, a concern that their needs be met. And if any asked, "Why?" the answer simply was to show the love of Christ for all people, the Christ who called himself Living Water.

The Leemkuils had moved to Titila. The Scheenstras would be arriving in early 1986. And Dick and Donna Swart had been appointed in 1985 to the Orma work.

Donna had earned her associate degree in nursing at East Tennessee University a few years before. After they were married in June 1979 and were living in Newton, Kansas, Dick worked at nearby Hesston College as the director of maintenance for their flying program. At the same time, he attended Bethel College to earn his degree in industrial arts. Now they were ready to put their training to good use overseas.

But first Dick would need a year of study at Western Theological Seminary, followed by an orientation course for both of them at Selly Oak Colleges in England. It would be a year and a half before they arrived in Kenya.

With the promise of more RCA personnel, we began to plan seriously for more substantial housing at Waldena. Who would replace us at the "mother" base had yet to be decided. Nor had a third site for an outreach post been designated. So future assignments still were uncertain. But it seemed right to move ahead with the erection of a simple dwelling at Waldena.

To expedite this project, a group from our most consistent source of volunteers, First Reformed Church of DeMotte, Indiana, came out in the fall of 1985. The house was to be built well back from the Galole at the new campsite a quarter-mile upriver. We would be moving there ourselves shortly.

Bob and Paul had laid the foundation, so all was ready for the volunteers to weld the frame and start putting up the walls. How grateful we were for the help they all gave and for the good fellowship we enjoyed!

Christmas that year was a memorable celebration. Jack and Deb and their two boys, and John and Caryl Busman (on their way home after a special fact-finding assignment for the RCA) joined us at Waldena. And the Leemkuils came from Titila for the festivities.

Deb and Marcia worked out a Christmas pageant to be presented as part of the tea we were hosting on Christmas Eve for the Christian community. Children were to play the parts: Justin and Craig Swart, Tamar and Nathan Leemkuil, and the six youngsters of Mary and Obed, the police corporal.

The pageant was scheduled to take place before the tea, but in Africa one has to be flexible since promptness is not always a virtue. It is often considered downright discourteous to be on time, especially where food is concerned, lest punctuality be misconstrued as a sign of greed! So Mary and her children—Timothy, Douglas, Juliana, Eunice, Philip, and Priscilla— didn't appear until the tea party was nearly over.

The older children weren't quite sure about taking part in the pageant, but they were good sports and listened to instructions and allowed themselves to be costumed. While Deb Swart and Joshua Chelanga read Scripture portions, the children came in on cue to portray the traditional tableau of the manger scene.

An ordinary basket served as the manger. Never mind that Tamar, as Mary, threw the "child" onto the hay. The doll landed in an appropriate position, so on with the pageant! Timothy Obed was Joseph, Justin and Craig were shepherds, and the others were wise men and angels. The sun, lowering in the west, became a natural spotlight, adding a dramatic aura to the closing scene.

This little drama helped us all to focus again on the glory of Christmas and the significance of God's gift to all people.

Pastor Amos and the Chelangas were our guests the next day for our Christmas feast. After dishes were done, we sang carols in English and Swahili. We were all full of gladness, but also much aware of the Orma people who are blind to the Truth and would have nothing to do with Christianity—yet! An incident involving the Chelangas pointed up this fact. Hauwo Wari was a lovely young Orma girl. Every day she came to the Chelanga home to help Leah with her household chores. Leah was expecting their first child and welcomed some assistance. As they had time together, Leah witnessed to Hauwo about Jesus, his power, and his love. She taught her a few Christian songs that Hauwo loved to sing. She seemed near to the kingdom.

One Sunday morning the Chelangas and Hauwo walked with us on the path to the church. As we passed through the shop area, I expected Hauwo to leave our group, but she continued on and entered the church with us. She stayed for the whole service. I was afraid for her. Did her parents know where she was? What would happen when they found out?

When Hauwo reached home later in the morning, she found the people of her village extremely angry because she had dared to go to the Christian church. They shouted at her, reminding her that Christians are infidels, that their religion is false, that Isa is not the Son of God, and that Allah alone is to be worshiped—not the three gods of the Christians. They told her she'd be punished severely if she ever went to the church again. Nor was she permitted to go to the Chelangas' home for a long time.

The Muslim spiritual leader at Waldena, Mohammed Boru, was especially harsh in his denunciation. Hauwo was so frightened by all the threats of impending evil that she became ill for several days. It was apparent that she had not expected such a horrified and irate reaction from her people.

Joshua and Leah were able to make peace with Hauwo's family. But the whole incident was clearly a setback for any casual witness in the Chelanga home or elsewhere.

We can only pray that the truths she heard and the songs she learned to sing were enough to convince her of the true identity of Islam's Isa.

In 1986 we prepared to travel to Nairobi to meet Roger and Susan Scheenstra, newlyweds of eight months.

Susan Eisinga was raised in Friesland, Wisconsin, the ninth and youngest child of Newton and Cora Mae. They were active members of the Christian Reformed Church. But Sue's best friend was Jennifer Haga, the daughter of the Reformed Church pastor, the Rev. Henry Haga.

When the girls were in high school, the Hagas moved to Chino, California. In the course of time, Sue also relocated to California to pursue a career in nursing. She lived with the Hagas.

Roger grew up in Ontario, California, and was involved at Lincoln Avenue Reformed Church in Pomona. By the time Sue moved to California, he was also a good friend of the Haga family. Inevitably, Roger and Sue met. In fact, they dated during their first year of college—at the end of which Sue informed Roger that he was not the one for her. But they remained good friends over the next five years.

Roger's interest in missions began through his friendship with the Hagas and as a result of attending mission conferences at Urbana, Illinois. All through college he was clearly focused on preparing for service overseas. Sue described his keenness this way:

> His enthusiasm spilled over into his friendships and our whole Bible study group. So I went along to many AIM prayer meetings, and I was part of his support in prayer and finances for his two summer volunteer mission experiences [in southwestern Kenya]. He exposed me to a lot dealing with missions. I thought that maybe "someday" I'd do a short term mission in nursing.
>
> Roger returned from Reformed Bible College at Christmas 1984. In January he asked me if I'd consider "pursuing our relationship." He was planning to leave in May to work among the Ormas, so that was a loaded question. Rog didn't ask for an immediate answer. He said, "Take all the time you need to make your decision, but I leave in three and a half months for Kenya!"
>
> Over the next two months, I spent much time in thought and prayer about our relationship and what it would mean to marry Rog. I felt it was important that I not only love Rog, but also that I have a real call to a career as a missionary. I had never felt that before. But I finally realized that God was using Roger to extend that call and opportunity to me, and that God had done much to prepare, equip, and enable me to serve him. So I said "Yes!" to Rog's proposal and God's call in the same breath.
>
> That it was the right decision was confirmed for me beautifully in the next letter I received from my mother. She wrote me that back when she and Dad just began their family, she had gone to

some missionary meetings and had been led to pray that someday one of her children would serve the Lord as a full-time missionary. She said she had nearly forgotten the prayer, but now God was answering it through me. That meant so much to me, and still does![3]

Now we were about to welcome Roger and Sue to Kenya, the second of a trio of couples we hoped would carry on the Orma work. They arrived on January 24, 1986.

First on the Scheenstras' agenda was language study. It is important in Kenya, no matter where one is posted, to acquire a working knowledge of Swahili.

It was expected that Sue would also be required to have some nursing orientation in a Kenya hospital before she could be licensed to practice in the country. She thought her interview on February 4 went well—and she was right. She was accepted as an enrolled nurse and needed no orientation. We could almost hear Sue shout, "Wahoo!"

As an enrolled nurse meant that she would have to work under the supervision of a registered-in-Kenya nurse, who in Sue's case would be Marcia Leemkuil.

This happy and unexpected outcome meant that Rog and Sue would be able to come to Waldena much sooner than we had thought, and we all rejoiced.

The Scheenstras made a fine adjustment, whether in the sprawling city of Nairobi or out in the bush at Waldena. Once in Orma country, they lost no time in making their little kitchen and bedroom *rondavels* into a comfortable home where they lived for a year while they soaked up Orma culture and applied themselves to the laborious task of learning the unwritten Orma vernacular.

"Bonding" had become a new concept in missionary orientation in the mid-1980s. New personnel were advised actually to live in the home of a willing national family, to become a part of that family as far as possible. It was a great method of becoming immersed in the local mores and in the language.

---

[3] Susan Scheenstra, from a letter to the author, October 1, 1995. Joint Archives of Holland, Hope College.

While our newcomers didn't carry out this idea fully, they did spend hours every day in the villages, learning about Orma ways and speech, absorbing it all more quickly and accurately than we ever did merely by the "informant" method that characterized our study in the early years.

We admired our young colleagues for their discipline in this basic learning experience. It wasn't always easy. Sue wrote to me about a particularly difficult time she had about four months into their Orma language study.

> I remember that it was the first time you and Bob went to Nairobi since our arrival, and we were left on our own at Waldena. I knew my family [was] together in Wisconsin for a big reunion. It was Jennifer Haga's birthday and I ached for a heart-to-heart talk with her.
>
> As I went out to practice Orma one morning, I suddenly felt as if all I could do was scratch the surface of communicating with the people. There were still no deep relationships. On top of that, I got scolded in a tea shop by Hauwo Wari's father because [while I engaged her in conversation in order to practice what I was learning] he said I was taking her away from her work.
>
> I felt as if I didn't know what was the right thing to do in the Orma culture. I'd probably never fit in and have close friendships or Christian sisters, or even feel at home among them. I guess it was my time for culture shock! I went home in tears and had a good long cry.
>
> At that time, too, it was such a comfort to me to remember that God had called me and he was right there with me. I wasn't there just because it was exciting or fun or nice, but because it was where God wanted me to be. By the time you got back from Nairobi, I was fine again.[4]

There were the rewarding times, too.

Through her language practice, Sue did find a good friend. Zahara was the attractive wife of none other than Mohammed Boru, Waldena's spiritual leader. Zahara and Mohammed had been married about seven years and they were still childless. Among Africans, this is a real tragedy. A woman's sole value lies in childbearing; it's her reason for being.

4 Ibid.

As their friendship developed, Zahara shared her sorrow with Sue. Sue's immediate response was this promise: "My friends and I will pray for you in Jesus' name that you may have a child. When you conceive, you will know that Jesus has power and that he is the Son of God."

Months went by. Mohammed took a second wife. Our prayers continued. Two years later, Zahara conceived. On May 10, 1989, she gave birth to a son whom they named Abdullahi. As far as we know, there was no outward acknowledgment of the power of Jesus in this wondrous event, but we believe God will have his way with Zahara and her son.

In February 1986, another team of volunteers came to our aid, this time from Addisville Reformed Church of Richboro, Pennsylvania. The group included the pastor, the Rev. Bob Hoeksema, and his wife, Lucille. They were all a tremendous help in putting up a *rondavel* for an AIC pastor at Wayu, our district center some miles east of Titila, and in finishing the guest house at Titila. They also worked on the roof of the permanent house at Waldena. In April we moved to the newest Waldena site that already was looking quite well populated. We had delayed moving because the subsequent flows of the previous year had done no further damage to the bank at the second site, so it seemed reasonable to remain there for the dry season. Now, with the Scheenstras' living quarters already in place at the new location, as well as a workshop and the still unfinished cement block house—and always the possibility of another raging river—it seemed the better part of wisdom to delay no longer. This was the best site of all, with good shade and proximity to an abundant water source beneath the surface of the sandy Galole River.

One Sunday morning during the sermon, an Orma named Omari entered the side door of the church. He sat down on a front bench. He seemed uneasy, glancing nervously left and right and back over his shoulder. Why had he come? Was he looking to see if Hauwo or any other Orma were there? But he stayed to the end, whatever his purpose. He even dropped a shilling in the offering basket and at the close of the service, shook hands all around with a big smile. We never learned why he came, but we prayed that he had heard and would heed some spiritual truth as the pastor spoke about being free in Christ.

On another day, Mohammed Boru asked Joshua, "Is it true that Jesus will come again?"

Joshua replied, "Yes, it is! Let's read about it in the Bible."

They did.

"You have a Swahili Bible," Joshua reminded Mohammed. "You should read it for yourself."

On still another day, Bocha and his friend Yusuf, both high school students in one of the Tana River towns, came to Bob with a request: "We are taking a course in Christianity at our school in Garsen. We are studying the book of Luke. Do you have a Bible you can give us?"

Bob gladly gave them a New Testament in Swahili.

"But we'd like one in English," they said.

So Bob also gave them a New Testament in English with a prayer that God's truth would speak mightily to these young men.

During the next monthlong school holiday, Bocha was a great help to the Scheenstras in language study. And Bocha in return asked them if they would help him to understand the Bible.

That July Joshua and Leah became the parents of a son. Hosea Chelanga was born by C-section at the mission hospital at Kijabe. Hosea was a joy to us all.

A Kenyan plasterer finished the walls and flooring of the house at Waldena. Now only the windows, doors, and screening were needed to make it ready for occupancy.

This same plasterer had the contract for building the new mosque at Waldena. In August the completion of the building was celebrated. We were invited, and while we were of course not welcomed into the "inner sanctum," we were most cordially treated. We were glad to be included in the day's festivities.

Bob and Rog sat with the men around the shops, while Sue and I joined the women who were sitting on the ground in groups near the roasting meat and boiling rice. Soon Bocha came and conducted the four of us to a small room in Gobu's house. A table and four chairs were set up in there. It was our private dining room!

Bocha brought us our share of the meat: roasted goat—a whole bowl of it which we picked out and ate with our fingers. We stayed there while the Ormas went to the mosque for prayers.

Bocha soon came for us again. Sue and I returned to the women's area while the men went into the outer yard of the mosque. They sat outside on the porch along with several Ormas and Somalis, mostly younger men. All the older ones were inside listening to the keynote speaker of the day.

Then Bocha took us back to Gobu's house where we were served a great platter of delightfully seasoned rice with beef.

It had been a most interesting afternoon, and being included in the celebration, even though in a limited way, made us feel that we had been accepted as part of the community.

In August our first volunteer teacher arrived. Marcia Leemkuil was becoming somewhat overwhelmed with running their home and the clinic besides teaching Tamar and Nathan. It was obvious that she needed help. Teresa Wyant came to the rescue!

The school was one of a kind. Paul had erected a sturdy, four-posted, twenty-foot high water tower in their front yard at Titila. Halfway up, he fashioned a screened-in room that served admirably as a classroom. It was accessible only by ladder. Predictably, it was named the Water Tower Academy—which led to the equally predictable family saying: "It graduates only drips!"

But Tamar and Nathan were far from being drips, and under Teresa's tutelage, they made good progress.

But sadly, the Water Tower Academy was short-lived.

Paul had been experiencing strange sensations in his chest. When he went for a check-up at the Kijabe Medical Center, he was advised that he would need a pacemaker and was referred to a specialist in Nairobi. The specialist reported that it was a benign condition; no surgery was needed.

But when the doctor at Kijabe disagreed with the specialist, the Leemkuils decided to go to the United States immediately and get the matter taken care of right away. They planned to be gone three months. It was hard to see them go. One question was in all of our minds: would they return?

RCA secretary for Africa Warren Henseler and his wife, Barbara, arrived in Nairobi in September. Their intention was to acquire a deeper knowledge of Africa than the usual brief visits provided. They planned to stay for three months. Jack and his family had gone to the United States for a few weeks, so their apartment was available for the Henselers.

Bob and I welcomed Warren and Barbara at Nairobi's airport and stayed to help them get settled and to become a bit familiar with the city. During their sojourn, the Henselers would also be flying to Zambia to visit Arlene Schuiteman and to Ethiopia to see the Doorenboses, as well as traveling around to RCA areas of interest in Kenya. It was doubtful that they would be granted visas to Sudan to see the Fords and Barbara Kapenga. But in

October the second Gathering would convene at Lake Naivasha, and it was hoped that all RCA personnel would be able to be there at that time.

On October 17, we were delighted to roll out the welcome mat for the Henselers at Waldena. Verne Sikkema flew them in from Nairobi. And with them were Arlene Schuiteman and Dr. Edwin and Luella Mulder! They had come to Kenya for the Gathering. Ed, who was general secretary of the RCA, would be our worship leader. We were honored to have all these dear friends with us now.

One evening, the moon was full. It was beautiful having our supper outside with that marvelous chandelier as our only illumination. About nine o'clock, I looked up and made a surprising discovery: the lower edge of the moon was in shadow; an eclipse was in progress! We all watched as more and more of the moon was covered. We were so excited at seeing this phenomenon. The moon gradually became a burnt orange color, and soon a silver glow appeared. It was an awesome spectacle!

In a voice of mock wonder, Ed exclaimed, "Well, Bob, you think of everything!" How we laughed. But truly, it was a worshipful experience for each one of us. How great and wonderful a Creator is ours, and we can call him Father!

Then it was time to converge on Lake Naivasha. There were about forty of us. Again we were refreshed. Ed Mulder led us superbly in our devotional studies. We missed the Leemkuils. Jack and Deb had returned to Kenya in time to join us.

It was decided at this Gathering that Jack and Deb (who were in transit to an interim assignment in southern Sudan) would first spend a few weeks at Titila to carry on there as best they could, hoping for the Leemkuils' return early in the new year. Teresa Wyant could teach Justin in Water Tower Academy.

We traveled back to Waldena in convoy. John and Caryl Busman (who couldn't seem to get Africa out of their systems, and we understand why) were also with us. Bob hoped that John would be able to give advice concerning the ability of the Dutch pumps to raise water from the well at Saware. He came up with partial answers: steel pipe instead of plastic, and a longer pump handle to increase leverage. These two changes improved matters. But it wasn't until the windmills were installed that adequate water became readily available.

The third location for the AIC/RCA outreach among the Ormas was decided upon at last; it would be in an area called Daba about midway between Titila and Wayu, east of Waldena and situated on the Galole River. The Scheenstras were enthusiastic about opening the work there after they had completed a year of Orma language study at Waldena. Warren Henseler, still in Kenya at the time, was in on the specific site decision and in meeting with the local leaders to obtain their approval, which was given without hesitancy.

About this time, we suddenly found ourselves with a new AIC pastor at Waldena. Pastor Stephen and his family, who had been assigned to serve at Wayu, were extremely lonely without other Christian fellowship. They found the cultural differences between their Kamba people and the Ormas to be more than they could cope with alone. So it was determined that Pastors Stephen and Amos would "exchange pulpits." We were so sorry to lose our Pastor Amos, but comforted that he would still be with us in the Orma work.

Another Christmas rolled around, another memorable celebration. The year before, we had hosted a tea for the Christian community. This year we gave an open invitation. We had no idea how many would come.

Deb, Sue, and I had baked dozens of cookies and brewed gallons of sweet ginger tea. All was ready when people began to arrive. We ended up having a tea party for thirty-five. How glad we were to be able to show hospitality to some of our neighbors in this way.

Platters and teapots soon were empty. As the special time came to a close, Bob introduced Pastor Stephen. He said, "Christmas is our celebration of Jesus' birth. Pastor Stephen will read the story of that birth from the Bible. As you may or may not know, that story is also told in your holy book, the Koran. Morrie and I read it just this morning in Sura nineteen."

This fact obviously was news to many of our Muslim friends and primed them to listen attentively and with respect as Pastor Stephen read the glorious passage. Afterward, everyone was friendly and seemed in no hurry to leave. We know God was there, enabling this witness to take place that Christmas Eve.

Pastor Stephen was with us about a year. He found Waldena more palatable than Wayu, but eventually he moved his family back to their tribal area contiguous to the Orma toward the west.

As for Pastor Amos, he ministered at Wayu for a time and then became very ill with malaria. He went home, was hospitalized in Hola, but his body did not respond to treatment. All who loved him and were blessed by his ministry were shocked to hear of his death. He had been a dear friend and colleague. "Precious in the sight of the Lord is the death of his saints."[5]

January 1987 brought news that the Leemkuils would not return; it was imperative that Paul live where he could receive medical help quickly. It was a relief in a way to have this definitive word and to know that Paul was where he needed to be. But it was a blow, nonetheless, for us personally and for the whole Orma program. The Leemkuils were good friends, and tireless, innovative workers. Yet we were confident that God would bring blessing out of this apparent setback. Another couple would have to be recruited in order to make up the full complement of personnel for the Orma work. We prayed earnestly and often.

Jack and Deb were not in a position to remain at Titila indefinitely. They were eager to pursue their urgent hope of getting back to currently peaceful Juba in southern Sudan to record for Wycliffe's Summer Institute of Linguistics (SIL) all Scripture that their teams in Sudan had finished translating. They had been seeking someone to do just that when Jack "fell into their lap."

They returned to Nairobi, and on February 6 flew on SIL's Sudan Branch plane to Juba where they settled into the community there once again.

Teacher Teresa Wyant returned to the United States.

More volunteers came to us that winter. John and Connie Vanden Brand and Bill and Carolyn Overway from Grace Reformed Church in Holland, Michigan, spent a month at Waldena helping with the myriad details of establishing this mission center. At the same time, Hope College student John Dunham, son of retired Oman missionaries James and Joyce Dunham, spent three months at Waldena as part of an international studies course taught by Dr. Neal Sobania.

John was quiet and unassuming with a droll sense of humor. We all loved him, volunteers and staff alike, and he ate with gusto and appreciation everything I served—a prime qualification in my book for a perfect guest!

On February 27, a day imprinted in our memories forever, Dick and Donna Swart with their three children arrived in Nairobi. They had been delayed several weeks because Donna had taken ill while they were at Selly Oak Colleges in England and the family had to return to the United States. But by God's mercy and grace, and the prayers of many people, she was healed. We traveled together to Waldena on March 10. The family settled

5 Psalm 116:15, New International Version.

into the mostly completed cement-block house, and thus began an especially happy year when three generations of Swarts shared life together at Waldena.

We were full of thanksgiving. Two-thirds of the proposed Orma team was now on site. And the Scheenstras, with nearly a year of language study behind them, were more than ready to move to Daba. The move was accomplished in April. Comfortably nestled in the shade of acacia trees, their oval bedroom and round kitchen *rondavels*, with a cleared and swept courtyard for their dining and living room, made an attractive campsite. From this small oasis of Light and Truth, Rog and Sue launched their daily ministry to the Ormas in Daba.

One of the highlights of each year, besides the all-mission conference at Kijabe in December, was the Women's Prayer Conference in May. Missionary women and nationals gathered at Brackenhurst, the Baptist Conference Center in Limuru, for a weekend of fellowship and inspiration.

To my great joy and amazement, I was asked to be the Sunday morning speaker that year. The conference theme was "The Lord Is King." Others would speak on the sub-themes: "The Redeeming King" and "The Reigning King." The subject assigned to me was "The Returning King."

The whole experience—preparation and presentation—was thrilling and uplifting as we contemplated again the sure hope of Christ's Second Coming. As an added joy, Bob had been asked to preside over the service and to conduct the Last Supper remembrance—the sacrament that Jesus had told his disciples to observe until he returned. It was all so beautiful and meaningful, and the entire assembly was blessed by a real sense of his presence among us. Having had Donna Swart and Sue Scheenstra as my roommates that weekend was another blessing.

The whole time, I kept pushing to the back of my mind the thought that this was the last prayer conference before our retirement.

Retirement was looming more visibly on our horizon with each passing day. We knew by this time that when the hour came, our Orma team would be complete.

Del and Debbie Braaksma had been appointed to the Orma field. This was a gracious answer to our prayers.

Delvin Braaksma and Debra Williams grew up on farms in Wisconsin— the Braaksmas were active members of First Reformed Church in Friesland, while the Williams family participated in the life of the first Presbyterian Church in Cambria.

Del earned a degree in animal science from the University of Wisconsin. Debbie received a degree in social work from the University of Minnesota. After their marriage in 1977, they bought the Braaksma family dairy farm, and for several years Del managed and operated this successful business.

But in the deep recesses of their hearts, Del's and Debbie's interest in missions kept nudging them. This interest had been kindled in their early years and was fortified through Inter-Varsity Christian Fellowship. Missionaries on home leave spoke at their home church in Friesland. These contacts, along with books on missions and the Bible itself, honed their desire to serve overseas until they no longer could ignore the pricks and prods.

Finally, to the astonishment of their families and community, they sold the farm and applied for missionary service. They were appointed by the RCA in September 1986 for service in Africa.

After a year of study at Western Theological Seminary, Del and Debbie were assigned specifically to the Orma work. They were commissioned in July 1987 at the Furloughing Missionary Conference in Madison, Wisconsin.

By this time they had two sons, Stephen Thomas and Michael John, and a tiny daughter, Bethany Ellyn. We eagerly awaited their coming in August.

The waiting period did not drag.

Our daughter Gayle visited us again that summer. She was so elated to be back in Africa. Her husband had left her seven years earlier, and life had been rugged. But God had been her strength and she had coped. We were so proud of her. Now we would have her with us for some weeks.

In honor of her fortieth birthday, we had planned a partial family reunion at Turtle Bay Lodge near Malindi on the Indian Ocean. We would all convene there on August 4: Dick's family, Gayle, and Bob and I from Waldena; Chloe and Mark Young and family from Saudi Arabia; Jack and family from Nairobi; and Dr. Richard Smith, former pediatric colleague of Mark in Arabia and recently widowed.

(To our great disappointment, and theirs, Jack and family were not able to join us. Jack's eyesight was deteriorating badly. He had come to Nairobi from Juba in July for an examination. It was discovered that he had a detached retina and was advised to proceed to the United States immediately. Deb and the boys were able to fly to Nairobi in time and they all flew home together, still hoping to be back for the reunion. But it was not to be.)

After a week at the coast and another at Waldena, it was obvious that romance was in the air and a relentless courtship had begun. The principals: Gayle and Richard! (They were married in June 1988 with Bob and Gayle's pastor officiating.)

Jack and his family had returned by the time we arrived in Nairobi. The surgery had been successful and he was thankful for somewhat improved eyesight. They left for Juba on September 4 to take up again the recording of Scripture for SIL.

August 25 was an exciting, significant day. KLM brought the Braaksma family from Wisconsin, the Fieldhouse family from DeMotte, Indiana, and Kristen Vanderbilt from East Williamson, New York—all bound for Orma country!

The Braaksmas would study Swahili for the next few months in Nairobi. Dave and Connie Fieldhouse and their three children would live at Titila for six months, especially to supervise the building of a school, to honor a commitment Paul Leemkuil had made to that community. And Kristen would be the Swart children's first teacher at Waldena.

Along with our AIC colleagues, we had a treasure-trove of personnel to carry on the program in Orma country. It was all the Lord's doing.

XXVIII
Nairobi Ministries:
Daystar and a New
PRMI Outreach

While God was calling together personnel and program in Orma country, he was also directing other new ministries in which RCA missionaries had a vital interest.

Ken Shingledecker was a Mission Kid. Born in Burundi, the allure and enchantment of Africa would always be a part of him. When Ken went to the United States to continue his education at Georgia Tech, he knew he would be preparing himself to return to Africa, perhaps to be involved in development or engineering in Burundi. God did call him back to Africa, but in a quite different role.

After graduating with a degree in civil engineering in 1974, Ken moved to East Lansing, Michigan, where he held two part-time jobs: one with a construction company; the other with Inter-Varsity Christian Fellowship (IVCF) at Michigan State University. Two years later, he joined IVCF full-time and moved to its national office in Madison, Wisconsin. His particular responsibility took Ken where one would expect to find him: in the missions department where he was asked to develop mission training programs for students, as well as to assist in the coordination of the Urbana Student Missions Convention held every three years in Urbana, Illinois. It was in this context that he became aware that he was being called to Christian ministry in Africa.

With Inter-Varsity, he traveled across Africa the summer of 1979 to visit his "student missionaries" and to seek out new opportunities for students in the future. On this trip he visited Kenya and became acquainted with Daystar Communications in Nairobi.

Daystar was then a small communications training and research institute run by an independent American missionary. About thirty students were enrolled in a two-year diploma program, and the staff, mostly Americans, numbered less than ten.

It was not easy for Ken to leave Madison for this summer assignment, due in large part to his interest in a young teacher named Connie Cato.

Connie grew up in a Christian home in Duluth, Minnesota. She graduated from the University of Minnesota-Duluth with a degree in elementary education. After teaching for two years in rural Minnesota, she moved to Madison where she taught for two more years just outside the city. It was during this time, in 1978, that Ken and Connie met.

Connie was reticent at first about committing herself to a life in Africa. Understandably, she was not in a position to share fully in Ken's enthusiasm for the continent he called home. They considered marriage seriously only after Connie had become open to the possibility of serving in Kenya. While she had no strong sense of call in that direction at this point, she did feel called to marry Ken, and as his wife, would work with him and support him in whatever God led them to do.

To give further foundation both to the prospective marriage and to the probability of a career overseas, an Inter-Varsity friend made it possible for Connie to join Ken for two weeks in Nairobi. They met Daystar personnel, learned more about the school's program, and thus were able to evaluate the prospect of their serving with this quite new and promising institution. In a conversation with Dr. Don Smith, the executive director, he told them about a two-year internship program Daystar had developed for people who were interested in learning about Africa and cross-cultural communications, while also being involved in the school's ongoing research and training ministry.

It was a valuable two weeks. Ken and Connie probed the possibilities together, and they were both ready for whatever the future might hold. They were married that September.

After a yearlong dialogue with Dr. Smith, the Shingledeckers made the decision in 1980 to give themselves for a two-year term of service with Daystar. An application to go out as RCA missionaries at that time was denied. So Inter-Varsity seconded them to Daystar for those two years.

Ken and Connie arrived in Nairobi in January 1981. They spent the first six weeks living in a dormitory room on the Daystar campus. They ate African food in the cafeteria—a diet new to Connie—and within a couple of weeks, she began to feel ill and suspected she had fallen prey to some African parasites. They went to the Seventh Day Adventist clinic where they were informed, after an examination, that parasites were not to blame. Connie was pregnant.

That was good news. But her illness plagued her all those weeks in the dormitory. Having only a communal bathroom at the end of the hall exacerbated her misery. To this day, cafeteria and dorm life at Daystar are unpleasant memories for Connie.

Finally they were able to move into their own home, and life became much more tolerable.

In July they participated in a six-week Foundation of Christian Communications course at Daystar, and Ken began an ambitious research project: identifying the unreached peoples of Kenya and documenting the extent of Christian outreach within each tribal group. The project was sponsored by the National Christian Council of Kenya and funded by World Vision.

Besides yielding much statistical data, this study also gave Ken a few insights as to the unique value of such schools as Daystar. For example, on one coastal trip he was accompanied by a Kenyan about his own age who had recently returned from ten years of higher education in the United States. When they arrived at the church guest house in Malindi, the Kenyan began to complain about the bad conditions of the room and refused to eat the food that was prepared for them. Ken himself actually found the state of affairs to be quite acceptable.

Experiences like this led Ken to develop his commitment to education for Africans within the African setting in order to avoid removing them from their culture and so rendering many of them unable to live and communicate with their own people upon their return.

In less than two years of research, Ken produced thirteen volumes of data. A summary report of the research findings was published in 1983 under the title, "Unreached Peoples of Kenya."

During his first three years with Daystar, Ken was almost entirely involved in research, though he found time as well to coordinate several monthlong communications courses for church leaders, and to take a few graduate level courses himself. He also helped to develop a short-term missionary training program for the Africa Inland Mission and launched an annual summer missions training program for Inter-Varsity.

Brian Shingledecker was born in September 1981, but motherhood did not deter Connie from becoming involved at Daystar with student accounts. Both Ken and Connie also served that year with a small English-speaking congregation of the Africa Inland Church. It was a group of about fifty people who met in a carport in Nairobi West.

By the fall of 1983, their two-year term having been extended by several months, the Shingledeckers felt it was time to return to the United States. Daystar had been handed over to an African director in late 1979; the American founder had left in 1981; and by 1983, the institution had become a fully African-run facility. Ken was now ready to move on to something besides research and writing up reports. Also, they were expecting their second child and wanted the baby to be born in the United States. They left Nairobi in October 1983.

Ken had hoped to return to his former position with Inter-Varsity, but IVCF had changed management and there was now no place for him on the staff. So he and Connie made a quick decision to apply to Wheaton graduate school.

A second son, Jason, was born in Duluth in early December 1983, and soon the family moved to Wheaton in time for the January semester. Ken earned his master of arts in intercultural studies in May 1985. By that time, the Shingledeckers knew that God was leading them back to Nairobi and Daystar, but first they needed to make an inquiry and mend a relationship.

When Ken and Connie made the decision to leave Daystar in 1983, it was not only a matter of timing; there was also some frustration over the new administration, and the new executive director had wanted to know in detail what the problems were. Over lunch the three discussed the situation. It was a frank confrontation.

Now Ken was faced with the humbling task of writing to Dr. Talitwala to ask him if he would be willing to let them return. There was no response by mail. But when the executive director made a trip to the United States, they were able to get together, again over a meal. They discussed their differences of 1983 and, in Ken's words, apologized to one another for the things done and said, "and he graciously agreed to have me come back and join the staff at Daystar."

But Dr. Talitwala at that time made it abundantly clear to Ken that there would be no role for him in administration since all those positions were now held by Kenyans.

The Shingledeckers again sought backing from the RCA, but were advised that Daystar's ministries did not fall under the priorities of the RCA mission in Kenya. So Ken and Connie resigned from Inter-Varsity and joined Daystar as Daystar missionaries. After spending a few months raising their support, they left for Kenya, arriving in late November 1985.

In 1984, Daystar's name had been changed to Daystar University College (DUC). It had become a Christian liberal arts college offering a bachelor of arts degree in cooperation with Messiah College of Pennsylvania. It still offered the short courses program, however, under the Institute for Christian Ministries and Training (ICMT), an adjunct of DUC.

Ken joined the staff of ICMT where he served as coordinator of communications courses until an incident in the accounting department drew him once again into administration. An accountant had stolen a large sum of the school's money, and Ken was called on to take over the accounts department until a new finance manager could be hired. Connie was still serving as the student accountant.

Ken spent a full year in administration before returning to ICMT as director of extension training in January 1987. Over the next four years, he helped to design and implement a major restructuring of Daystar's short courses program and the research department. He also became coordinator of the communications and media department, besides teaching communications and strategy in the short courses.

During this six-year term, Ken and Connie continued their involvement in the Africa Inland Church that had moved from Nairobi West to a new Nairobi suburb called Plainsview. Ken was elected an elder and served as church treasurer, while Connie taught Sunday school and junior church. The membership grew to more than five hundred during this period. So the people decided to begin construction of a new church building. Ken was a member of the building committee.

The Shingledeckers' relationship with their African brothers and sisters was a special joy to them. Ken remembers a particular elders' meeting when the casual chitchat preceding the meeting was going on in the Kamba language.

One of the elders turned to me and asked me a question in Kikamba. After a long pause and no answer, another elder volunteered the information that I didn't know Kikamba. Everyone had a good laugh, and then the elder who had asked the question said, "But you are so African that I forgot you didn't speak our language."

At other times when Connie and I would be enjoying the fellowship in our small group Bible study or at a married couples gathering, our Kenyan friends would tell us how unlike other Americans we were. They would take our hands and hold them as they talked and they would say we are just like them, except for the color of our skin. We even learned to come late for social events instead of being the first to show up!

We took these incidents as a real compliment and an indication that our effort to identify with the Kenyans had been successful.[1]

In October 1987, Stacie Mwende was born. (Mwende is a Kamba name meaning "beloved one.") Connie now discontinued her work at Daystar. She had begun attending Bible Study Fellowship and had helped to start a weekly mothers' fellowship group. These two programs, along with raising three children and caring for the needs of her husband, were enough to keep her more than busy.

When Brian and Jason were old enough, they attended a Kenyan nursery school, and later, Rusinga School, which was Christian in orientation and run by Kenyans.

1987 held another event that made a difference in their lives: Warren Henseler wrote to them asking if they would like to become RCA missionaries. He had met Ken and Connie at the previous Africa Gathering. At his recommendation, they had been included as new missionaries in the 1988 missions program budget.

The Shingledeckers hardly could believe that this had happened ispecially in light of two earlier unsuccessful bids for this much desired relationship. Now the RCA had come to them with this proposal!

Having come this far in their ministry with another support base, it took Ken and Connie a few months to make a decision. But eventually they

---

[1] Ken Shingledecker, from a letter to the author, November 18, 1996. Joint Archives of Holland, Hope College.

accepted the offer because it would provide more solid backing in terms of both finances and supervision, and it would also put them into the mainstream of the RCA mission effort, toward which they felt very positive.

So in 1988 the Shingledeckers became official RCA missionaries. From September to December, they took a short leave in order to visit many RCA churches in the Midwest. They returned to Nairobi in January 1989, heartened by RCA support and inspired to get on with their multifaceted mission.

By summer 1991, the family prepared for their scheduled one-year home assignment. They spent that year in Pasadena, California, where Ken enrolled in graduate school at Fuller Theological Seminary. Then they moved to Holland, Michigan, to share themselves and their story with many of the Midwestern churches and to encourage further support. They returned to Nairobi in January 1993.

Daystar University College now had an enrollment of eight hundred fifty students in the B.A. and M.A. programs, and had begun construction of a new, three-hundred-acre campus in Athi River thirty miles southeast of Nairobi.

During this period Ken wore many hats. As assistant to Dr. Talitwala, who was now Daystar's principal, he was also his management advisor, liaison with the Daystar U.S. office, and responsible for administration of student scholarships, housing, and orientation of new expatriate staff, and coordination of the institution's forty-plus computers. Ken held this position for two years.

In September 1994, the school again was upgraded to become Daystar University. It was granted a charter as a private university by the government of Kenya, the first Christian university to be granted this honor.

Dr. Talitwala became the vice-chancellor of the new university, and Ken became the assistant to the vice-chancellor with the same responsibilities as before. Ken continued in this capacity for two more years, meaning that for four years he had been involved entirely in administration.

On May 20, 1995, the university held its first graduation ceremony. A Presbyterian brochure carried the following description of the occasion:

> What a joy it was to watch as the students processed down from the terraces up onto the platform to receive their diplomas. Those who came from rural areas were clearly the pride of their villages. As the students stood at the announcement of their names, the mothers

came dancing out of the crowd, hollering and clapping, and swept their prodigy forward for their moment of glory.

With the flags of the nations flapping overhead, one was confronted by the political dynamics of the student body drawn from places such as Rwanda, Sudan, Somalia, Ethiopia, Burundi, Zaire, and Liberia.

There were some tensions, some reconciliations, and some meaningful embraces. This only added to the wonder of the day and the sense that there is indeed hope for this continent, despite what the media portray. These are the people who will usher forward that hope: servants of Christ in the marketplace, schools, churches, and other Christian ministries.[2]

By 1996 student enrollment had risen to over twelve hundred in the degree programs, with the entire B.A. curriculum now located at the new Athi River campus. More than twelve new buildings had been completed, including seven student dormitories and a new administration-classroom building.

Amid all their Daystar activity, the Shingledeckers did not neglect their commitment to the Africa Inland Church in Plainsview. The new church building was now a reality. Funds for the roof had been provided for the grateful congregation by the Reformed Church in America. The new AIC facility seats over one thousand worshipers.

All three children by this time were attending Rosslyn Academy a few miles outside of Nairobi. The American curriculum and association with other American children were positive experiences for them and surely would prove to be a good orientation for the next step in the life of the Shingledecker family.

Ken and Connie were feeling very much that God was leading them once again away from Nairobi and Daystar and back to the United States. They arrived in July 1996. Visiting churches and reporting on their last three years of ministry occupied much of their first year at home. But they also had their spiritual antennae extended to be alert to where the Lord wanted them to be next. Ken expressed their situation in these words:

We all are quite sure we want to be in the USA for some time and would love to locate in Michigan. But what kind of employment we

[2] Marta D. Bennett, "New Dawn at Daystar," May 1995. Joint Archives of Holland, Hope College.

may be able to find that is both financially adequate and ultimately fulfilling is yet to be discovered. We have talked of many things, but do not have any clear leading from the Lord—only that it is time to get up and move. We feel a lot like Abraham who was told to go and he went, not knowing where God would lead him.[3]

In the Summer 1996 Daystar bulletin, this brief item appeared: "Ken and Connie Shingledecker (U.S. liaison) who are seconded to Daystar by the Reformed Church in America, will be leaving Daystar to return to the U.S. and pursue other ministry opportunities."[4]

Clearly Connie, who sensed no personal call to Africa before she and Ken ventured out together, was greatly persuaded by the Spirit through all their years in Kenya that this was indeed where she belonged, working beside her husband and launching out as well into her own special ministries—even editing for some years the special keep-in-touch news sheet for RCA personnel in Africa, "RCA Update."

Ken and Connie faithfully represented the RCA in Africa. Through them, our church has played a significant role in helping to build up the national church of Kenya, and indeed the church in many other African nations, through discipling and leadership training.

After the dedication of Portable Recording Ministry's Nairobi studio in September 1984, preparation to record Scripture went full steam ahead. Jack Swart began by enlisting the Bible societies to find out into which languages the Bible, or Bible portions, had been translated. He then searched for a qualified reader for each of the language groups, one who could read smoothly and distinctly.

Once a reader was recruited and oriented, he sat before the microphone in a small room in the studio. Jack was at the controls in an adjoining room, separated from the reader by a glass window.

Scripture in many tribal languages was recorded for use by pastors and evangelists. This recording was not done only for Kenyans. One of the

---

[3] Shingledecker, from a letter to the author, March 10, 1996. Archives.
[4] *Daystar U.S.*, "Missionary Movements," Summer 1996. Joint Archives of Holland, Hope College.

Jack recording at the PRM studio in Nairobi

readers was none other than the Murle, John Kajach, son of songmaker Ngachor of Pibor, Sudan. John's voice, reading Murle Scripture, doubtless has been heard wherever Murles have fled as a result of the relentless civil war in that country. Hearing Scripture in their own language surely has been a major factor in the growth of the Murle church these many years.

Recording was a challenging and satisfying task. To know what God's Word in many vernaculars could and would accomplish for Christ's kingdom spurred on Jack and the readers day after day.

Jack began to realize, though, that if this was to be an ongoing ministry, an African must be trained to take his place in the future. A Kenyan named Boaz was that person. He and Jack worked together almost from the start.

While all this was going on in the studio, Deb Swart also found satisfying activities. The Cannatas (with whom they had lived at Pibor) were now based in Nairobi. Deb and Ginny met together every week for an intense course called "Master Life." Through this discipling, Deb was led to disciple

Jack Swart with his wife Deb and two sons,
Justin (right) and Craig, in Nairobi

several Kenyan women. She was also asked to take part in the pilot program for Bible Study Fellowship that was just opening its ministry in East Africa.

So both Jack and Deb were fruitfully and joyfully employed in God's work, and the boys were happy in excellent schools.

But after two years, with Boaz fully capable of carrying on the work of recordist, Jack felt a strong pull to return to Juba, which was enjoying a relatively peaceful interlude. It was of the Lord. As mentioned in the last chapter, SIL had been praying for a recordist to come and also needed a manager for the Wycliffe Center—a position it wanted Jack to assume as well. Deb agreed to be the hostess for the Center's guest house.

So, with jobs awaiting both of them, and having been given the RCA's approval for this change in direction, the Swart family flew to Juba in February 1987.

Even young Justin was excited about returning to Juba. He told Craig all he could remember about the town. And now he was sure that they would be able to go to Pibor again, and he, as Craig's big brother, would show him all the special places. Deb added, "It was a hope, a dream, and a prayer we all kept in our hearts always."

But that dream was never realized.

In Juba Jack had a shipping container for a recording studio. He took care of his managerial duties in the morning and did the recording in the cooler hours of the afternoon and evening. It was heart-lifting to record the New Testament in Juba Arabic as well as many portions of Scripture in other languages in which the translators were working.

Soon came the emergency flight to the United States for Jack's eye surgery for a detached retina. Though the operation was successful and his sight was considerably improved, they were told that cataracts were developing in both eyes and a disease was destroying the retinal cones. Jack might someday find himself living in a black and white world. But for the time being, Deb said he could "still hit a mean tennis ball and get a great golf score and read to his sons every night."

The family was able to serve in Juba only a few more months. The situation in the South was again rapidly deteriorating. The sights and sounds of war were coming closer to the town every week. In February 1988, the Swarts flew to Kenya for a two-week vacation from the mounting tensions. At the airport in Nairobi, Justin and Craig were on the lookout for army men and guns. Stress for the whole family was palpable.

After a few days at the Mennonite guest house and a short time on the coast at Mombasa, they felt refreshed enough to go back to Juba. But word came through the SIL office in Nairobi that the situation was worsening. Whether they should return was up to them.

It was such a difficult decision, the hardest they had ever been asked to make. They prayed for the Lord's direction and sought counsel from parents, the RCA, friends, their pastor—whoever would listen to them. It finally became clear that they were not to go back to Juba. But what was the alternative?

The family moved into an apartment. Deb taught the boys at home. Jack visited the SIL and PRMI (Portable Recording Ministries International) offices almost daily, wondering about the next step. Did this idleness mean that they were to leave Africa? Perish the thought!

Then the answer came. On one of his visits to his old haunt at PRMI, he noticed several New Testament cassette tapes on the shelves, some of them in the very same place in which he had put them a year before. He had a meeting with Tesfahun Agidew, the director, to discuss the matter of those dust-gathering tapes. Something must be done! Would the RCA consider seconding Jack once again to PRMI?

After some negotiations, the approval was given and Jack was able to move into the familiar PRMI Nairobi headquarters. Now he was in a position to dream dreams and get on with the business of moving the cassettes off the shelves into some productive ministry. But what would be the strategy?

Only a few days later, inspiration burned. Local Church Cassette Libraries would be the vehicle. Making cassette libraries available to churches scattered around the countryside would be a viable means of equipping them for further teaching and outreach ministries. In the hands of pastors and other church leaders, the possibilities for productive use were unlimited.

Director Tesfahun approved the plan and Jack went to work. He designed and produced a library box that would hold a cassette player, a solar panel, an album of New Testament tapes, and whatever other teaching or music tapes were on hand and appropriate for various church groups.

The first step in implementing this new program was to inform the churches that it existed. Jack therefore made survey trips for this purpose. He traveled to many areas of northern and northwestern Kenya to demonstrate how the libraries could be used in evangelism as well as in discipling. While the churches would be expected to defray some of the costs of the units, PRMI would provide a subsidy. Gifts from friends also would help to cover the expense.

Following a survey trip, it was up to the pastor to write a letter indicating a desire to have a library. After a further exchange of letters and the receipt of the church's share of the cost, a training seminar then was organized to be held in that particular church. Church leaders from the surrounding area were invited to attend.

Each seminar and workshop took a long day. At the close of the session, the library was dedicated to the glory of God amid much singing and praise.

From the beginning, the response was beyond expectation. Churches welcomed this new tool with alacrity. Jack's own enthusiasm was contagious, and interest spread far and wide, not only in the originally targeted areas of rural Kenya, but eventually also in Tanzania, Uganda, Sudan, Ethiopia, and even on the islands of Lake Victoria. Jack had contact with pastors in all these countries.

The mounting interest kept him busy producing the custom-built libraries with the help of his able assistant, Julius Kamau. Jack was eminently happy in his work. God's Word was going forth, churches were being strengthened for their own ministries, and the Lord was adding to his church many who were responding to his message of life and hope.

Kenyan women excited about the cassette ministry

XXIX
Our Final Months in Kenya

The Scheenstras were settled at Daba, the farthest east of the three mission posts in Orma country. Language study continued, but they were also able to begin their ministry in that community. Sue had clinic hours in the shade of a tree a short distance from their living area, and they both had countless opportunities to make friends with their new neighbors, ever alert to openings to speak a gentle word about Jesus Christ or to pray in his name—and always to live his life among the people. Rog and Sue found much joy and satisfaction in this pioneer situation and rose to the challenge courageously day by day.

The volunteer Fieldhouse family was comfortably at home in Titila. The Ormas there had raised money for the building of a school, according to a previous agreement, and Dave Fieldhouse was making good progress in its construction. All materials had been gathered ahead of time: cement, stone, steel, and roofing. So he could get on with making the cement blocks for the walls and with putting up the frame. The Titila Ormas were so proud of "their school." It was theirs because they had paid for it; it wasn't a government building or a mission building. It was all theirs; they had done what they could to make it possible. Now, with someone with know-how on the job, their dream was being realized.

This was Dave's fourth trip to Kenya as a volunteer, and Connie's second. They were becoming old hands at this kind of mission activity, and we appreciated their assistance and admired their abilities and adaptability.

446

Dick and Donna Swart and their busy family had transformed the cement block house at Waldena into an attractive house. Dick made cupboards, counters, and a dining table in the kitchen, and he rigged up lights powered by the sun. Donna has a flair for decorating and in no time, each room was a pleasant, homey place.

Language study was at the top of their daily agenda, but they always had time for their children and their Orma friends who came to visit. Close relationships with Africans came easily and naturally for Dick and Donna. Eventually Donna had an Orma house built right in their yard so that the frequent visitors would feel comfortable and at home over cups of tea.

After all the years of separation from our children by continents and oceans, to have both of our sons within reach meant more to us than words can express. And having one of those sons and his family on the same acre of ground with us for a whole year was a remarkable gift.

Besides the mutual gratification of being able to work together that year and to share frequent meals, Grandma Swart took special pleasure in hosting grandchildren for morning cocoa and peanuts each day. It was at those times that I kept my ears wide open for unusual and memorable remarks.

On one occasion Caleb said, "Grandma, you're bilious!" Well, that set me back on my heels while at the same time being hard put to contain my laughter. After some questioning, it came out that he thought bilious meant "funny." Donna thought he might have meant "hilarious."

Another time Leah asked, "Grandma, who is older, you or Grandma Giles?"

Because my hair is white and Grandma Giles' hair is dark, I asked her, "Can't you tell just by looking at us?"

"No, 'cause you're both all wrinkled up!" she replied very seriously.

It was a wonderful year.

Kristen Vanderbilt was now living in the *rondavels* formerly occupied by the Scheenstras. And the little round house in which John Dunham had lived had been moved to a shady spot nearer Kristen's quarters. It was now the school house. A "blackboard" had been painted on two of the metal wall panels. Pictures and other educational helps gave the room an exciting aura.

Every day Kristen and Leah went happily to school. Caleb joined them three days a week for two hours. And even three-year-old Shelah had her hour each week in the classroom. It was a cheerful learning situation. Kristen was a born teacher, and it was obvious that she loved children.

Del and Debbie Braaksma finished their Swahili study in Nairobi and moved to Waldena before Christmas. In preparation for their coming, we had moved our tent across the road to a small grove of trees between the new house and the workshop. Twin *rondavels* had replaced our tent. With these little houses for their bedrooms, and the kitchen which we had left in place, the Braaksmas were comfortably set up and sheltered for the few months of language study they would engage in before moving to Titila. And Stephen and Michael joined the Swart children in Kristen's schoolroom.

A Kenyan nurse named Gideon had been appointed to run the clinic at Titila. He was of much the same caliber as Joshua Chelanga, and we welcomed him heartily to the Orma team. Gideon, like Joshua, also enjoyed preaching. Besides that, he played the guitar and liked to teach us new songs in Swahili. We were all blessed with our national staff.

Bob and I attended our last AIM conference at Kijabe at the end of November. It was excellent as always.

The evening of December 3, Dick and Donna took us to the Silver Springs Hotel in Nairobi for dinner. We were thrilled to be having this special time with our son and his wife. They conducted us down a long hallway to a poorly-lit dining room. It seemed so strange. And then the lights were switched on! There before us was the whole RCA crowd as well as Paul and Erma Lehman, hosts at the Mennonite guest house; Robb and Megs McLaughlin, old friends from Sudan days; and John and Karen (Sikkema) Loudon. What a joyful surprise! Our letter of thanks appeared in the fourth issue of the "RCA Update" edited by Connie Shingledecker:

> It was all so perfectly done, the secret so perfectly kept, the meal so delicious, the program so delightful and hilarious, the gift so very appropriate, the fellowship of the evening so precious, and the surprise so complete—it was overwhelmingly wonderful.
>
> Thank you, thank you for all the lovely arrangements you made for that memorable evening, Ken and Connie.... Roger Scheenstra certainly did a great job of planning the program. How we enjoyed the music of Del and Debbie Braaksma with the clever paraphrase of "Country Roads" and the lovely "Friends"; the skits by Larry and Linda McAuley and Molly Beaver brought back so many memories; the poem read and written by Sue Scheenstra and Connie Shingledecker—so well done; the heartwarming "remembering"

talks given by Robb McLaughlin, Paul Lehman, Verne and Lorraine Sikkema, Karen Loudon, and Ken Shingledecker; the sweet surprise within the surprise: the voices of Jack and Deb, Justin and Craig on tape sent from Juba [at least two months before the war in the South heated up]; and Dick's much-loved remarks preceding the presentation of the gift from all the folks with an accompanying poem beautifully written by Donna.

The gift was a water color of a camel and two Somalis—a typical scene in Orma country. It was painted by Sue Stolberger who spent weeks out of the last two years down our way among the Somalis and their camel herds observing, sketching, drinking camel's milk—really immersing herself in the Somali lifestyle. It is a pleasure and a dream come true to have one of her paintings. Thank you again, all of you, whose names were on the card with the lovely poem.[1]

On December 18 we headed back to Waldena, leading the way for the Braaksmas and Donna's sister Deni and her family who were new appointees for work at AIM's Rift Valley Academy at Kijabe. Tom and Deni Dainty and their three children would spend Christmas with us all at Waldena—our last Christmas in Africa.

It was another wonderful celebration. With twenty-eight of us gathered there, the little church on the outskirts of Waldena "town" rang with Noel praises. Bob presided over the service. There were many musical numbers. Gideon gave the meditation. A gift exchange, a turkey dinner, and a simple Christmas pageant led by Debbie Braaksma all made the day one of joy and wonder.

All of a sudden it was 1988—forty years since that January in 1948 when we set sail with the McClure family and Wilma Kats on the Italian troopship Saturnia. It was a time for remembering, and a time for tying up loose ends.

At the top of our list was Alale. We needed to make a return visit there before leaving Africa. And we did just that at the end of January.

---

[1] Morrie Swart, *RCA Update*, February 1988. Joint Archives of Holland, Hope College.

What changes had occurred in the five years since we had left that fascinating border post. Larry and Linda McAuley now lived in a cement block house with Luke and yet another son, Matthew, who was born in August 1985. (And in 1989, a daughter whom they named Miriam blessed their home. God had given the increase!) Thanks to Larry's vision and implementation, fine school buildings, funded by Worldwide Christian Schools, had been constructed. Under Linda's able leadership and the services of qualified Kenyan teachers, Pokot children were being educated, not only in the basic curricula, but also in Christian truths.

Pastor Ronald Chomom and his family were no longer at Alale. Pastor Alfred Maiyo had replaced him and the church was growing, in numbers and in faith.

Across the long, grassy airstrip was the mission medical center with Molly Beaver as the nurse-in-charge.

Molly was born in Orange, California, but when she was a senior in high school, she and her family moved to Sioux Center, Iowa. She became a member of the Central Reformed Church. In 1981 she graduated from Augustana College in Sioux Falls, South Dakota, with a degree in nursing. Later she received her master's degree from the University of Iowa.

Molly served as a staff nurse at the University of Iowa Hospital where she worked in the school-age and adolescent unit. Much as she enjoyed what she was doing, Molly had a strong premonition that God was about to call her to some other place of service. She prayed that God would open the necessary doors and show her his direction for her life. The door God opened pointed her to Africa, and in September 1984, she left for Kenya.

Before beginning the inevitable three months of Swahili study, Molly was able to fly up to Alale with Dr. William and Helen Brownson for a two-day preview of the place where she would eventually live and work. She remembers sleeping in her yet unfinished house.

Six months of orientation at Kijabe Medical Center followed language study. At last, in July 1985 she arrived at Alale with her newly acquired Kenya Registered Nurse license in hand. The Alale staff welcomed her joyfully, and her work began immediately and overwhelmingly.

Within the very first week, three seriously ill patients came for help: a man with a bowel obstruction, a boy with a gangrenous arm, and a woman suffering in delayed labor. Each one needed hospital care. This meant three tortuous trips to Kapenguria four hours away. Larry drove, but Molly was beginning to wonder if she could endure the responsibility, pace, and severity of the medical demands at Alale.

She endured—by God's grace!

That same month, she initiated mobile clinics to take medical help to more distant villages. And in September, using the services of Helimission, Molly was able to schedule regular visits by helicopter to otherwise inaccessible mountainside settlements.

The coming of Rosemary Chumo in February 1986 was a great boon to Molly. Rosemary was a Kenyan nurse of the finest order, and she and Molly worked together happily for several years. When Rosemary went to Canada to study, Susan Tuliapong, another Kenyan nurse, took her place. Molly described both of these nurses as wonderful, godly women who were an asset to the medical care in Alale.

(These happy relationships, together with Pastor Alfred's faithfulness in ministry, are more fine examples of the success of the AIC/RCA Joint Projects concept and a confirmation of God's blessing upon our cooperative mission.)

A few paragraphs from Molly's letters will help you to know her.

> Last Wednesday through Sunday I spent up on a mountain called Kalapata. It's a three-hour walk away. They've been asking for a long time if we'd be able to have a clinic up there. There's an empty tin house I could stay in.
>
> I learned many things. The first one is that I'm not as tough as I thought I was. The Pokot have a very rough life, and for me to live even a bit like them for those few days was "interesting"!
>
> The house had a dirt floor. That saves a lot of sweeping time! To get to water you go down one hill, up another, around behind the mountain, and then down again. The amount of water you get is the amount you can carry. And of course, since getting there was two hills down and one hill up, to come back with the water is two UPS and one down! It's hard work.
>
> Cooking over a fire is another experience I thought wouldn't be so hard. [But] I didn't have hot boiling coffee one single time up there unless someone else cooked it for me! I haven't yet caught the hang of how they keep that fire going!

It WAS good exercise, hiking on all those mountains and visiting people. And people are slowly learning about the Lord. They sing in "church" (under a tree) with joy, and they listen to the sermon better than they used to.

Now I'm back at Alale and wondering when I'll be able to go again. My fingernails are FILTHY, my legs are stiff, my stomach hurts from all the corn and beans that people gave me to eat. BUT, I walked home carrying a live chicken, someone else carried a live rooster; we had several ears of corn, some beans—all gifts for us. It shows that people are receptive to us and to the gospel! Pretty exciting![2]

The nine volunteers who have been here for these two weeks have been wonderful. I can't explain the feeling when you see one thing after another getting done—and so QUICKLY! Every day you go and look and it's different. That just doesn't happen here! I feel like we've had our tongues hanging out in amazement the entire time. They've been awesome, and we're all a bit sad to see them packing up to go. The Lord has blessed and taught us through them.[3]

The longer I live in Kenya the more I realize that in almost every situation it doesn't matter what you know, but whom you know. The best thing to do is ask—always. Even if the thing you're looking for doesn't relate at all to a particular shop, the shopkeepers are likely to know where you can get it.

If you want eggs in Kitale (the town where we shop), where do you go? You go to the petrol [gas] station. If you want to leave your film to be developed, where do you leave it? At the petrol station.

Where can you get the freshest and most crispy potato chips? You get them at the jewelry store. You can get beef at the butcher, but they don't sell pork because [of their religion]. Pork is at the grocery store.

---

[2] Molly Beaver, from her newsletter, November 7, 1991. Joint Archives of Holland, Hope College.
[3] Ibid. March 9, 1993. Archives.

You can buy fabric from a lady who will invite you into her car, and while you sit inside, she will show you her material.

Popcorn comes from a neighbor lady who bought it from the farmer who grows it.

At the petrol station you can also get gunny sacks, gas cylinders (for our stoves), kerosene, glasses, and soap. You can probably get anything else you want, provided you ask! But if diesel or gasoline is in short supply, where do you go? To the hardware store, of course.

The key word is "ask."

It's like Christianity. For Christians, it's not what you know, but whom you know. We can ask, and Jesus will come inside and be our Savior, giving us eternal life! That's the good news we have to share. Please pray that I may take opportunities to share, whether I'm shopping in Kitale or working with the Pokot in Alale.[4]

There is a place called Tukumon. I go there every Tuesday for a mobile clinic. The Pokot there have a young church which only women and children regularly attend, and there are two young men who lead it.

The Christian women in Tukumon recently began a ladies' group. When I go for the weekly clinic, one of the Pokot women from Alale goes with me to lead the meeting. They'll talk about how to live with an unbelieving husband, and about kids, sickness, mothers-in-law, personal temptations, and standing firm against sacrifices.

One woman gave this testimony last week. Her child had a fever, and her mother-in-law and husband decided that they should kill a goat as a sacrifice so the child would be well. The woman did not want them to do it, but in this culture, she cannot stand against the two of them.

She took the baby outside and began to pray. After everyone had fallen asleep, the woman came back inside. She was very quiet, not wanting to awaken the others. She put the baby down beside her

---

4 Beaver, "A Missionary Letter," July 5, 1993. Joint Archives of Holland, Hope College.

*Molly Beaver and Rosemary Chumo made regular visits
by helicopter to visit remote mountain settlements*

and continued to pray. Most of the night, trying not to fall asleep, she tended the fire, prayed, and felt the baby's forehead to see how hot he was. In the morning, the baby was fine, and the perfectly healthy goat that had been brought into the hut for the sacrifice was dead. No one knows how it died. She called to her husband saying, "Come and take this goat away. Satan has been defeated."[5]

In between volunteers, birthdays, Christmas, and climbing Mount Kenya, I HAVE done a bit of work! We continue with our mobile clinics by car and by helicopter. Then there are the bookkeeping, the school needs, and the million other little things that make the days seem to fly by. The Lord is good. His mercies are new every morning, and he makes us able to go on. Great is his faithfulness![6]

[5] Ibid. August 20, 1993. Archives.
[6] Beaver, from her newsletter, March 9, 1993. Archives.

Bob and I were elated to be back at Alale to see the McAuleys and Molly and to observe what great strides in ministry had been made in the short five and a half years since we had left. Not only were the school and clinic making a tremendous impact on the community, but the church also had become a vibrant body of believers. We were thrilled to gather in the long, narrow meeting house with scores of Christians who made the rafters ring with their joyful singing and moved us all with their remarkable testimonies. How we praised God for what he was doing through his servants as they relied on his power to work through them. The church had come into being and the Bread of Life was nourishing people's spiritual lives.

And as the Living Water was flowing through the body of Christ there, we saw, too, how the pipeline was still carrying water from the spring on Mount Lorsuk down to the mission and on to the community, bringing pure, life-giving water to hundreds of people.

The many-faceted mission program at Alale—including Larry's experimental plots and grinding mill; Linda's and Molly's work with the women in sewing and Bible studies; and evangelism carried out by each member of the staff—was all being used by the Lord to improve and change lives in the name of Jesus. Our hearts truly rejoiced!

> There they stood as we remembered,
> Lorsuk and Kachegaleu:
> Mountain twins, sparsely timbered,
> Standing tall, looking down,
>
> Looking down on Alale.
> What change the years have brought!
> Life enriched, empowered—Say!
> See what God hath wrought!
>
> School, dispensary, experiment plots,
> Sewing and knitting, too;
> Carpentry skills, and grinding lots
> Of maize for Pokot stew.
>
> The name of Jesus lifted high
> In word and life and deed,

Drawing men in sweet supply,
As fruit from planted seed.

And Mount Lorsuk and Kachegaleu
In all have played a part;
For water giving life below
Flows from Lorsuk's heart.

As the moon rose full above their slope,
Imparting heavenly glory—
"God bless Alale with peace and hope
As his people tell the Story."

—MFS

Our retirement preceded Arlene Schuiteman's by one year. She had long hoped that we would be able to visit her in Zambia, and we were eager to do so before we left the continent. It was arranged that we would make the trip the last week in February. Much to our delight, Molly Beaver planned to travel with us.

Tickets and reservations were all in order. We were in Nairobi at Mayfield, AIM's guest house, when Bob became ill with a very potent virus that developed into pleurisy and pneumonia. There was no way that he could travel to Zambia, but he insisted that Molly and I go anyway. A mission doctor was caring for him, and with the Scheenstras in from Daba for several days, and Jack and family in from Juba, I knew he'd be in capable, caring hands. Regretfully I canceled his reservation, and Molly and I proceeded with our plans.

Jack took us to the airport, and soon we were on our way. Though my pleasure in this excursion had diminished and my heart was burdened with concern and disappointment, the sense of adventure returned as we flew southward, thrilled again to see the snowy heights of Mount Kilimanjaro above the clouds just over the Tanzanian border, and excited over the prospect of a week in Zambia.

Arlene had come to Lusaka from Macha to meet us. What a happy reunion! After a night in the Southern Baptist guest house, we drove south to the Zimbabwe border, going through immigration and customs on both sides, and arrived at the Rainbow Hotel before dark.

The next day, wearing raincoats and carrying umbrellas, we walked and walked and viewed Victoria Falls in all its magnificence. What a sight! The wonder of Niagara pales in contrast.

We crossed back to the Zambian side the following day and saw the eastern end of the falls. It was a lovely sunshiny day and the spray was bright with numerous rainbows. Arlene was giving us glimpses of beauty that we would never forget.

The next three days at Macha were unforgettable, too: seeing where Arlene lived and worked, and meeting her Zambian and Brethren in Christ friends and colleagues. It was such a privilege to be there. And it was obvious that our hostess was a much-loved and respected member of that mission.

The week passed so quickly; Arlene was taking us back to Lusaka almost before we knew it.

Verne and Lorraine Sikkema met us in Nairobi and whisked us to Mayfield. I found Bob feeling much better, but it would be a few days before he could make the trip back to Waldena. Dick and Donna were planning a community farewell for us on March 12. We wanted to be there!

The doctor finally said we could leave for Waldena on the tenth if we would take two days to get there—which we did.

The farewell feast was a delightful occasion. A bull had been slaughtered, cut up, and roasted; kilos and kilos of rice were cooked; and gallons of sweet ginger tea were boiled. Many Ormas were there as well as our mission family.

The feasting was followed by speeches, and we were each given gifts by Sub-Chief Gobu. Bob prizes especially his fine Orma knife. We were grateful to Dick and Donna for such a grand finale to our Waldena years.

A last safari to one of Kenya's game parks brought our overseas career to a close. With our two sons and their families we drove southeast from Nairobi to spend a couple of days at Amboseli Game Reserve, which borders Tanzania and boasts wonderful views of 19,000-foot Mount Kilimanjaro.

Kenya's game animals seemed intent on making our final safari a memorable one. Elephant and rhino, giraffe and zebra, and many varieties of antelope were all within easy access. And on our last early morning drive, a pride of lions slowly crossed the track within a few yards of our vehicle. That big cat display capped the climax of our tour. The days on Africa's plains with Jack and Dick and their dear families seemed to us a fitting and satisfying closure to our forty years.

The day of our departure was March 23. As our plane lifted off, we glanced out the plane's west window. I said, "Oh, look! The Ngong Hills!" All of a sudden, the familiar scene of those "knuckles" on the horizon jolted us out of a kind of numbness. We weren't going on leave; we were LEAVING! And for a half hour, we said not a word; we just let the tears flow.

In April we received a letter from the Rev. Julian Jackson, personnel coordinator of the Africa Inland Church. It warmed our hearts, particularly as it had to do with the fine young people whom the Lord had called out of the RCA to work in Kenya.

> Dear Bob and Morrell,
>
> Greetings in the precious name of our Lord Jesus Christ.
>
> The Bishop and Staffing Board of the Africa Inland Church wish to send a heartfelt thank you for all of your service to the AIC, first in the Alale area and subsequently in Orma country. All concerned have tremendously appreciated your willingness to start and develop the work and ministry at Alale and then willingly go to Orma to begin once more.
>
> I have also been requested to share with you the church's thankfulness for the excellent team which you brought, developed, and left behind you in Orma.
>
> The Bishop and Staffing Board send a prayer for God's richest blessings on your retirement from the Kenya field but not from the Lord's service.
>
> Personally I so much enjoyed sharing in the Lord's work here with both of you and have appreciated and been so grateful for all your life and testimony which has been a blessing to so many.
>
> Yours in Him,
> Julian

XXX
"All the Days Ordained for Me"

In summer 1989 Jack and Deb Swart received two attractive invitations. One was from Deb's sister Darla, who was to be married November 25. She wanted the whole family to take part in her wedding.

The second invitation came from the board of the Africa Inland Church Missionary College in Eldoret, Kenya. They were asking Jack to bring greetings at the school's first graduation ceremony on November 19 and, with AIC Bishop Ezekiel Birech, to cut the ribbons at the dedication of the school's new library.

After much discussion, Jack and Deb decided regretfully that they could not afford to go as a family to the wedding. And after much more discussion, it seemed right that they all plan to attend the commencement and dedication in Eldoret. In Jack's letter of acceptance, however, he suggested that Verne Sikkema of MAF or Larry McAuley of Alale might be better choices. But the board's original choice prevailed.

An RCA missionary was asked to take part in this special occasion for two reasons.

In January 1989 five women from Reformed Church Women's Ministries (RCWM) traveled to Kenya on a multipurpose mission: to visit students and facilities where scholarship recipients were studying; to travel to mission stations in order to see first hand what the women missionaries were doing and to offer them personal encouragement; and to assess the need for education and training within the Africa Inland Church.

RCWM representatives visited the missionary college that had been established in recent years with AIM/AIC missionary Jonathan Hildebrandt as its first principal. The women were impressed with the school and its curriculum. As a result, they recommended that RCWM make available a substantial gift for the building of a conference center. (The Robert and Morrell Swart Conference Center was dedicated on April 14, 1991, with Linda McAuley assisting AIC Bishop Ezekiel Birech in doing the honors.)

The second reason had to do with the school's library. Tom Iverson and his wife, members of the RCA, had volunteered for a time in Eldoret. They too were much impressed with the missionary college, so much so that when the family cabin in Montana was sold, the money was given to the college for the library. It was a gift from the Iverson family in memory of their father Andrew.

These then are the two links between the RCA and AIC Missionary College.

One day in late September Jack came home for lunch. He laid an envelope on the table.

"What's this?" Deb asked.

"It's for you," Jack replied.

Deb slowly picked up the envelope, absolutely in the dark as to what was inside. Just as slowly she opened the envelope and found, to her great joy and surprise, a round-trip airline ticket to Sioux Falls, South Dakota, about forty miles from Deb's hometown, Edgerton, Minnesota.

Deb was overwhelmed by this happy turn of affairs. She could now go to her sister's wedding. It was Jack's love gift to her.

So Deb flew to the United States in the second week of November. Her "three men" were on their own. The boys went to Rosslyn Academy every day, and Jack continued with the Local Church Cassette Libraries ministry with PRMI. Forty one libraries were already in use and requests for eighty-two more were in hand. This outreach program had mushroomed beyond early expectations.

Jack had also been asked to speak at a Wycliffe Bible Translators conference at the Baptist Conference Center in Limuru. This was held during the week before the college festivities. The theme of the conference was "I Press Toward the Goal." Jack spoke about his work and witnessed to the power of God in his life. He shared with the group that his eyesight was deteriorating and he was facing the very real possibility of becoming blind. He assured his listeners that God was preparing him for that eventuality, and that in the meantime he was pressing on to accomplish all that God had called him to do.

The weekend came. Jack and his boys drove the four-hour stretch to Eldoret on Saturday. They stayed with Jonathan Hildebrandt and his wife Dottie.

The graduation service began at 10:15 Sunday morning with over one thousand people in attendance. In the course of the program, special visitors brought greetings. Jack brought greetings from the RCA. In a letter to us, Jonathan Hildebrandt quoted him as saying:

I bring you greetings from "Bishop" Wilbur Washington [who was president of General Synod that year] and all the members of the Reformed Church in America. "Bishop" Washington is in bed right now, but when morning comes in America, his thoughts will be with us here.

I am pleased and encouraged by what I see here today. Tomorrow I am going to call the Rev. Warren Henseler at the Reformed Church in America headquarters to tell him about this wonderful meeting and what God is doing. I can assure you that the Reformed Church in America will continue to support this missionary college in its ministry.[1]

Dr. Titus Kivunzi, principal of Scott Theological College in Machakos, was the speaker. Then the Rev. Justus Nzau of the Africa Inland Church Mission Board offered the prayer of dedication for the graduates and Bishop Ezekiel Birech gave the charge. The presentation of diplomas and a closing prayer ended the service.

The people were then asked to gather around the Andrew Iverson Library for the dedication. Jonathan Hildebrandt introduced Jack who read a biography of Andrew Iverson. He went on to tell about the women who had

[1]Jonathan Hildebrandt, from a letter to the Swart family, November 21, 1989. Joint Archives of Holland, Hope College.

Jack brought greetings from the RCA

come to the campus the previous January and their desire to assist in the training of church leaders. He said, "They decided to give 200,000 Kenya shillings [about $30,000 at that time] to complete the building which the Iversons had begun. They also gave 400,000 Kenya shillings [about $70,000] to build a conference center where seminars could be held for pastors and missionaries."[2]

In a letter written to us on November 21, Jonathan described the rest of the ceremony:

> Jack then officially presented the library to Bishop Birech on behalf of the Iverson family and Reformed Church Women's Ministries. Bishop Birech then expressed the appreciation of the Africa Inland Church for the lovely building, and then gave his prayer of dedication.
>
> Next, Jack cut the first ribbon and Bishop Birech cut the lower ribbon. We walked into the building where Jack unveiled the

[2] From a cassette tape, November 21, 1989.

donors' plaque. Then Jack, the bishop, and the church leaders inspected the building. When they reached the other end, the bishop unveiled the plaque saying that he and Jack had opened the building on November 19, 1989.

After that, we went outside and people began streaming into the building. Jack said a quick good-bye and left about 2:30.

Truly it had been a lovely weekend. Dottie and I had really enjoyed Jack and the boys.[3]

In the United States that same weekend, Bob was finishing up a three-week speaking tour in the Midwest. On Saturday I drove from our home in Canon City, Colorado, to Colorado Springs to attend some special functions at Springs Community Church (RCA) and to stay with Bob's cousins, Cy and Jo Hanko, to await Bob's return by plane on Monday.

I was resting Sunday afternoon when there was a gentle knock on the bedroom door. It slowly opened, and there was Pastor Steve Brooks and his wife Linda.

"Mind if I sit down?" Steve asked as he made a place beside me. "We have bad news. Al Pruis [pastor of Deb's home church] called to ask us to let you know that Jack and the boys were killed about an hour out of Eldoret as they were on their way home."

Incredible! Oh, Deb!

Deb had received the word from her friend Sharon Bateman in Nairobi. I called our daughter Valerie in Michigan. She tried to get in touch with her dad, but it was the RCA's Roger DeYoung who gave him the news. Bob in turn called daughters Merry in Oregon, Gayle in New Jersey, and Chloe in Saudi Arabia.

Dick heard about his brother's death when MAF made a special flight to Waldena. The government had closed all mission airstrips, so the pilot had no other option but to drop a weighted note onto the strip.

The note was worded in such a way that Dick thought that Jack alone had been killed. So the family packed up immediately to go to Nairobi to care for Justin and Craig. It was doubly devastating to learn that the boys had died, too. Caleb for a time was inconsolable over the death of his cousins.

Jack's and Dick's families had planned to spend Christmas together at Waldena and to plan ways in which the cassette library ministry could

3 Hildebrandt, from a letter to the Swart family, November 21, 1989. Archives.

enhance the work among the Ormas. To realize that this would not take place added to the terrible sense of loss.

Without going into the logistics involved, but acknowledging God's direction in it all, Deb, her parents, Jerold and Sophie Schoolmeester, and Bob and I met at Chicago's O'Hare International Airport that Monday evening, November 20. Miraculously, all travel documents were in hand, and we flew to Nairobi.

Dick and Donna were there to meet us, as well as PRMI's Kenya director, Tesfahun Agidew, and two Kenya couples from Parklands Baptist Church that Jack's family had attended. Such tough, tender moments!

We stayed at Deb's maisonette. Friends poured in, the phone rang incessantly, meals were brought in, and through it all, Deb responded graciously, giving assurance of the inner peace she was experiencing in the midst of her unfathomable sorrow because she knew that her husband and her sons were with their Savior and hers, Jesus Christ.

On the U.S. Thanksgiving Day, we viewed the wounded bodies of our beloved ones. It was only too obvious that their injuries had been severe.

After our arrival in Kenya, we had learned with a kind of relief that the accident had nothing to do with Jack's vision. He had left the celebration in Eldoret early so that he would be driving home to Nairobi in the brightness of daylight when he could see clearly. But on the way down the escarpment into the Great Rift Valley, a runaway double semi, loaded with tons of coffee beans from Uganda, overtook them and crushed their small vehicle.

Being in that room with the remains of our son and his little boys was a solemn occasion, heart-rending but precious. It was a moment suspended in time when we bade our final farewell. Yet there was a poignant, positive sense that the three were really not there.

Later in the morning Bob and I went to the airport to meet Chloe, who flew in from Dhahran, Saudi Arabia. There was only a thirteen-month difference in Chloe's and Jack's ages; they had been very close. It was a comfort to us all to have her with us, and to her to be there.

The funeral was held the next day at Parklands Baptist Church. The three wooden caskets lay on supports at the front of the auditorium, flower-bedecked, but stark in their simplicity. Hundreds of Parklands Church members were in attendance, as well as children from Justin's and Craig's classes at Rosslyn Academy.

As part of the service, several people recalled memorable times with Jack. His father was the first to speak, pride in his son shining through his grief.

Jon Arensen, a colleague years before at Pibor who had talked with Jack as recently as Saturday evening at Eldoret, remembered him as a good friend. He told of some amusing incidents which made us chuckle in spite of ourselves. Dr. Kivunzi, the speaker at the graduation ceremony on Sunday, told of his anguish when he heard the news. And Tesfahun Agidew gave thanks for Jack's ministry with PRMI.

Pastor Tope's message was wonderfully appropriate. I took particular comfort from his word picture describing the scene at that roadside: "And Jesus came down and received the three souls to himself." There is no doubt in my mind that he was there and escorted them to their heavenly home.

At the Langata Cemetery on the outskirts of Nairobi, even as the pallbearers (brother Dick, Tesfahun, Keith Bateman, Paul Lehman, Arnie Newman of PRMI, and Kenyan friends) made ready to lower the caskets, there was an air of victory among us all. Deb had thanked everyone for being there and had praised God for giving her peace of heart and fortitude to speak. Life was being lived on a higher plane. Burial was taking place, but Jack and Justin and Craig were alive with Christ forevermore. Our hearts lifted at the thought.

Dick had skillfully and lovingly crafted three markers in the shape of crosses with the three names carved on them. These were placed at the head of each grave. (Deb has since replaced the wooden crosses with simple white head stones inscribed with appropriate Scripture.)

Jonathan and Dottie Hildebrandt had come from Eldoret for the funeral. The accident had been such a shock for them.

> When we got the phone call at 9:30 that night from Titus Kivunzi, it was as if the beauty had turned to ashes. Were we to blame? What if the meeting had ended thirty minutes, or even five minutes, earlier? They might not have met that truck at that fateful spot.
>
> We could hardly sleep that night. Our only comfort was that God is still in control, and although we cannot understand, we can accept his peace and his comfort at this time.[4]

That very night God had given me a message of inestimable comfort and insight into his sovereignty. I was reading from the Psalms when this verse, so familiar yet until now so obscure, glowed before my eyes with a holy light:

[4] Ibid.

Dick places the crosses with the assistance of Jerold Schoolmeester;
Caleb, Sophie, and Deb look on

"All the days ordained for me were written in your book before one of them came to be."[5]

Jack at thirty-seven, Justin at ten, and Craig at six, in the inscrutable purposes of God, had lived out the full measure of their days. And Jack could see perfectly now. Was his first clear vision that of the face of his Savior?

Back in the United States, we were overwhelmed at the outpouring of love as we attended two memorial services. The first one was at First Reformed Church in Edgerton, Minnesota. A week later, we flew to Michigan for the second service held at Dimnent Memorial Chapel on Hope College's campus. Both occasions had been thoughtfully planned and beautifully carried out, to give honor to the Lord and to the memory of our dear ones. We were amazed and humbled by the numbers who came out on those cold, snowy evenings to pay tribute to those who had gone on before us. We were deeply comforted and touched beyond words.

5 Psalm 139:16, New International Version.

Deb had remained behind in Kenya. She alone spent Christmas with the Swart family at Waldena, and then faced an unknown future. With courage and grace, and with the comforting, helpful counseling of Harry and Pat Miersma who were based in Nairobi with SIL, Deb carried on the work of the Local Church Cassette Libraries for some months.

Later she joined Jon and Barb Arensen on the SIL team that was finishing the translation of the Murle New Testament. She learned how to use a computer that had been modified for typing and printing the distinctive orthography of the Murle language. And in 1996, when the book containing Genesis and the whole New Testament was dedicated among many Murle refugees in Khartoum, Sudan, Deb was one of the honored guests. It was a thrilling occasion for her, the Arensens, and the Murle church!

Deb remarried. In February 1995 she became the wife of Boniface Muriithi, whose parental home is on the slopes of Mount Kenya. Together they are engaged in a ministry to the deaf in Nairobi, working under United World Mission, but also under the direct supervision of him who healed the deaf and caused them to hear the glorious news of his kingdom—and is still doing that today.

XXXI
New Approach in Orma Outreach

We had been in the United States for a year and a half. News from Orma country was both encouraging and disquieting.

The Scheenstras at Daba, the Braaksmas at Titila, and the Swarts at Waldena all were digging more deeply into the intricacies of the Orma tongue and at the same time were building close and valuable relationships with the Ormas themselves. The latter is of course a prerequisite to earning the right to present the gospel to any people.

There was a growing awareness in each location that there were a few who were becoming more open to hearing the good news. Alertness to opportunities, discernment in recognizing God's timing, and the gift of patience were characteristic of their ministries.

On the other hand, a change in the social makeup of the area, which actually had begun before we left in 1988, was becoming more and more of a threat to stability in Orma territory. Harsh conditions in neighboring Somalia were forcing its people to wander westward into Kenya. They did not come alone, but, like their forebears through the centuries, they brought their source of livelihood and nutrition: camels, hundreds and hundreds of them.

The arrival of all these newcomers to a community already living on the edge made for tensions, especially where water supply was concerned. A herd of camels can drink a water hole dry in a short time, and then the hole must be dug deeper. Even so, the amount of water in the sandy riverbed was not limitless.

Added to this cause for anxiety were the *shifta* who accompanied the wanderers. These marauding bands attacked villages, stole livestock, and sometimes murdered their hapless victims. The Ormas were becoming understandably nervous, and the missionaries began to wonder how long it would be before they were targeted.

They didn't have to wonder long. As early as February 1990, all missionary staff felt it advisable to pull out of the area for a time. In fact, between 1989 and 1992 the team had to evacuate four times. The *shifta* had begun to assault the mission sites. Joshua Chelanga and his wife were beaten at Waldena. On one occasion Dick Swart was shot at while driving his Toyota pickup. And the Braaksma family suffered through two terrifying personal attacks. Del described those moments:

> The first time [February 1990] the bandits grabbed Debbie and then robbed us at gunpoint. They made us sit outside while our four children were inside, and they raided our home with guns and hatchets.
>
> In July 1992 just as Debbie went into our outhouse one day, five to seven bandits shot into our house until volunteer [Orma] police came. Our house became the backdrop for a gun battle. The shooting went on for forty-five minutes while the children and I were inside the house. I felt that Debbie couldn't possibly be alive. But the Lord spared all our lives; he did shelter us with his wings as he promised!
>
> Early on God showed us that he was going to use this situation for good: as a result of our evacuation, an Orma friend came out with us and accepted Christ in a Nairobi church service.[1]

Truly it was only by the grace and protection of God that all Orma personnel emerged alive and whole.

Between evacuations the staff members in each location carried on their varied work with diligence, becoming more and more aware that their time in Ormaland could be very short.

---

[1] Del and Debbie Braaksma, "To Keep You in All Your Ways," AIM International, Fall 1995: 4, 5. Joint Archives of Holland, Hope College.

One practical project that Dick was able to accomplish in September 1991 was the erection of a Kijito windmill like the ones already in place at Saware and Kofisa. He put up the mill at a strategic spot along the Galole, easily accessible to the people but out of reach of the wild caprices of the river in spate. This was a solid demonstration of love and concern in action.

At Daba one Christmas celebration was marked by witness and challenge. The whole village had been invited to the feast.

> Before the meat and rice were served on large plates for six to ten people, we shared the story of the angel Gabriel's coming to Mary with the news that God had chosen her to bear the Christ child. Mary's question, "How can this be?" brought nods of wonder from our Orma friends. We told the whole Christmas story as well as God's purpose for sending Jesus.
>
> After the story [Sue] went back to the cooking area to help serve the food. Meanwhile one man stood and decided to challenge the story and to give the Muslim view of the matter. For his conclusion, he yelled out, "Jesus didn't die! Jesus didn't die! Jesus didn't die![2]

Only the Holy Spirit will be able to persuade a Muslim otherwise.

After the second attack on the Braaksmas, it was evident that the *shifta* situation had become too perilous to risk staying on at any of the posts, especially with the number of children involved. Besides Stephen, Michael, and Bethany, Del and Debbie had another son named Daniel who was born in October 1989. Roger and Sue Scheenstra were now parents of Sarah, who was born in August 1988, and Joshua, who joined the family in October 1990. Dick and Donna still had Leah, Caleb, and Shelah at home. It was essential that these youngsters not be subjected to the trauma of continual threat of violence.

Waiting in Nairobi for peace to return to the Galole area proved to be an endurance test. The three families longed to get back to their homes and ministry. But frequent forays by the men into Orma country brought the repeated, consistent consensus of the Ormas themselves: they wanted them to come back, but the situation was still very dangerous. Wait!

Early home assignments (a more accurate term than "furlough") were a partial answer. However, as time dragged on, alternate, temporary relocation

---

[2] Roger and Sue Scheenstra, "A Missionary Letter," November 29, 1992. Joint Archives of Holland, Hope College.

became a sensible option. The Scheenstras moved to Kalacha in the Northern Frontier District of Kenya to work with AIM's Herbert and Ruth Andersen among the Gabbra people, whose language is similar to that of the Orma.

The Braaksmas were granted a yearlong study leave in Edinburgh, Scotland (where they attended a church served by the Rev. Willis Jones, an RCA pastor). Del earned a master's degree in tropical animal health from the Centre for Tropical Veterinary Medicine, University of Edinburgh, while Debbie finished with a master's degree in theology from the same university.

The Swarts spent one year at Kijabe, the home of three of AIM's fine institutions: Rift Valley Academy (RVA), the Medical Centre, and Moffat Bible College. Dick was asked to fill a need as head of the station's maintenance crew. He also taught industrial arts at RVA. Donna became the nurse at RVA's infirmary. After the year in Kijabe, and in consultation with the RCA, AIC, and AIM, the Swarts moved to Ethiopia on what they considered to be a temporary basis. Donna's parents, the Rev. Ray and Effie Giles, of the Christian Missionary Fellowship, had come back to Ethiopia after an absence of several years and were reopening their work in the Ethiopian highlands. Dick and Donna were enthusiastically available to assist them.

This move was a tremendous blessing to all concerned and proved to be a guidepost for our son and his wife in quite another direction. They had gone to Ethiopia without a shred of suspicion that a return to the Ormas was not God's purpose for them.

During this waiting period Roger Scheenstra and various small teams made flights with AIM-Air to assess the Orma situation and file monthly reports. According to the final summary, three AIC officials—the Revs. David Mbuvi, Peter Maru, and Jonathan Hildebrandt—joined pilot Ron Shaw and Roger Scheenstra for a concluding fact-finding trip. It was to consist of three meetings to determine if the time was right for missionary staff to return. The first was held in Hola with the district commissioner of Tana River District. The district commissioner assured the group that the situation throughout Orma country had changed considerably for the better. He saw no reason why the missionaries should not come back.

The second meeting was a full-blown *baraza*. People from all of Wayu Location gathered at Daba, settling themselves in the shade of thorn trees near the shops. The three AIC leaders all spoke in turn. In response to their questions, the Orma delegates gave this answer:

> Yes! The people want the missionaries back right away, tomorrow if possible. The situation has changed. In Wayu Location we are forcing outsiders to stay out of our area. The missionaries are one with us. We cannot guarantee that something bad would never happen but we will do our best to protect them.[3]

The third meeting was held at Waldena. It, too, was a well-attended *baraza*.

> After landing at Waldena, we were met on the path by Chief Odo, Sub-Chief Gobu, the KANU (political party) chairman, the headman, and a few others who escorted us to a place in town that was set up under a tree for the *baraza*. We felt the people of Waldena treated us as honored guests.
>
> The *baraza* started with prayers, welcomes, and introductions. Pastor Maru spoke, then Pastor Mbuvi, and finally Jonathan Hildebrandt.[4]

In answer to the questions put to them, they responded in much the same way as those at Wayu Location:

> We do want the missionaries to return. We need them very badly. There have been some problems with our enemies, the Somalis, but things have changed. Satan works in people's lives and that is not good. There are a few people who still like to be influenced by Satan, but as for us, we will be on the side of the missionaries. If we live, we live together. If we die, we die together. But we are together!
>
> Afterwards Jonathan expressed appreciation for all that was said, and added, "There is a saying in English: 'Talk is cheap.' What one says has to be backed up by action."
>
> After the talks were finished, we were treated to a feast of goat, *chapatis*, and *chai*. The people outdid themselves to show us that we were welcome.[5]

[3] Roger Scheenstra, "Report of Orma Trip," June 15–17, 1995. Joint Archives of Holland, Hope College.
[4] Ibid.
[5] Ibid.

That final fact-finding trip into Orma country was a turning point; from that time, the Scheenstras were quite sure that God was at last leading them back home to Daba. They had experienced a valuable interim at Kalacha and were thankful to have been able to spend the waiting period so profitably. (Among their blessings during that time was the sweet gift of daughter Rachel Sue who was born in August 1993.) Now it seemed that their hearts' desire was about to be realized. What rejoicing on the day they received this welcome message over Kalacha's radio: "The staffing board met yesterday and you are officially reassigned to Daba. You are to make preparations to move from Kalacha and return to Daba as soon as you can."6

By that fall (1995) Roger and Sue and their three children were once more getting settled at Daba. There was a great deal of repair work to do as a result of *shifta* activity. Two years before, they attacked all three mission posts, destroying everything they could not carry away. Houses, workshops, and clinics were ransacked; doors and windows were smashed.

But gradually the camp at Daba was made comfortably habitable again. The Ormas were glad to have their friends back, and Rog and Sue found an unaccustomed openness among them. The week before Christmas, several groups of men asked Rog if they could hear the Bible-teaching tapes that the Braaksmas had prepared in the Orma language. And at the Christmas feast, there were no heated challenges, only quiet listening as the reason for the celebration was shared among the small clusters of Orma guests.

But along with the newly awakened hunger and thirst for the Truth came the enemy's opposition. Reports of renewed *shifta* movements in the area made everyone uneasy. The Scheenstras spent a few nights with friends in the village.

In January 1996 they wrote to their supporters:

> We're trying to be cautious, but we don't want to run away from the opportunity for sharing so openly. We recognize this as direct spiritual warfare. We're doing all we can to maintain the whole of God's spiritual armor.7

Their fourth child, Samuel Edward, was born that same January at the mission hospital at Kijabe. When the family returned to Daba, Bill and

---

6 Roger and Sue Scheenstra, "A Missionary Letter," August 20, 1995. Archives.
7 Ibid. January 1996. Archives.

Carolyn Overway from Holland, Michigan, traveled with them. The Overways had been with the Scheenstras at Kalacha—Bill as a general assistant and Carolyn as Sarah's teacher. They would have the same roles at Daba. But Carolyn's school would have double the enrollment now; Sarah's brother Joshua was ready to begin his education.

A major building project was Bill's newest challenge. It was time for the comparatively flimsy metal *rondavels* to give way to sturdier dwelling places. So Bill and Rog were starting on the construction of a more permanent house for the Scheenstras, with plans to build one also for a Kenyan nurse who would come in God's time. To give further assistance in this undertaking, Al and Wink Tillema from First Reformed Church in Randolph, Wisconsin, arrived that March to stay for several months. The mission at Daba was astir with activity.

Into the midst of all this came the new RCA secretary for Africa, the Rev. Gene Meerdink, and his wife Arlene. The Meerdinks had come to meet some of the mission personnel in their African settings as well as to encourage and refresh them as they all assembled for another of the popular Gatherings. These opportunities for retreat as an RCA group were so beneficial and so much appreciated by all the participants.

Some weeks after the Gathering, and before the building project was finished, it was time for the Scheenstras' scheduled ten-month home assignment. Further construction would have to wait until their return in June 1997.

In their absence Orma friends guarded the campsite. The news they received from local sources was worrisome. Besides the perennial concern over prolonged dry seasons and the resultant lack of water, it was learned that because of serious raids in the northern frontier, home guards throughout the country were disarmed.

The establishment of armed home guards in Orma villages was a major part of the solution to the *shifta* problem. Without this deterrent, security along the Galole was in danger of deteriorating rapidly.

During their year of study in Edinburgh, and with news from Orma country that was less than encouraging, Del and Debbie Braaksma wrote up an alternate proposal for their continued involvement in Orma outreach. They proposed to live in one of the coastal towns where they would develop a literacy program among Orma townspeople and carry on low-profile evangelism. Del would go out from the town on regularly scheduled safaris to work on animal husbandry projects and friendship evangelism among Orma pastoralists.

The proposal was accepted at the RCA and AIM/AIC offices. So it was with joy and thanksgiving that the Braaksmas returned once again to Kenya in 1994 to serve the Ormas in Christ's name. Their home base was in Mombasa on the Indian Ocean.

The lack of road security, linked to the shifta presence, had been a problem for some time. But it wasn't long after the Braaksma family moved to Mombasa that the situation improved and Del was given permission to make survey trips into eastern Orma territory. His subsequent two-week-per-month safaris into strategic areas were well received, and he was able to develop viable programs to assist the Ormas in the care of their herds.

At home in Mombasa, Debbie wondered if being in the city might cut her off from contact with Ormas. She need not have been concerned.

> It surely seems as though the people have found our place! There wasn't a night last month in which we didn't have an Orma overnight guest as well as countless Orma folks here for meals. We find that we have opportunities to do Bible study and to share the Jesus film with these Muslim folks several times each week in the privacy of our home. Amazingly, several of them have joined us for worship.[8]

Debbie soon became heavily involved in initiating and expanding a literacy program. As early as February 1995, with a representative from Literacy and Evangelism Fellowship to lead them, she arranged for a workshop to be held in Mombasa for the purpose of constructing the first reading primer in the Orma language.

> The purpose of the program is two-fold: to introduce the Orma to the gospel by including stories in the curriculum and by giving them the tools to read Scripture and other Christian literature

---

8 Del and Debbie Braaksma, "A Missionary Letter," April 5, 1995. Joint Archives of Holland, Hope College.

which we are developing; and to assist the Orma in community development by providing them with the skills to read materials on animal and community health and by giving them the ability to make their voices heard by those making policies which affect them....

...We rejoice that we are able to move ahead with this program, yet there are many "tricky" dynamics involved as well. One concerns the people we are inviting. We are delighted that one of the Orma chiefs (a Muslim who has also attended an Africa Inland Mission school) has consented to be involved. We have also invited a local Muslim teacher (who has told us he reads the Bible and the Koran daily and has had much Christian input) and two Orma Christians who speak English.

We have decided that all biblical content will be from the Old Testament since introducing New Testament material at this point would mean that this literacy program would not be accepted by the communities....We are also convinced that once people comprehend the message of the Old Testament, they will understand their need for a Savior. We believe that these materials will serve as an effective springboard for evangelism.[9]

The workshop, which was attended also by Rog and Sue Scheenstra, was a huge success because God's hand was upon it. Without it, the workshop could have been a total disaster.

We had several technical questions to resolve before we could get to work, i.e. how to denote "whispered vowels." But even bigger challenges were in the spiritual realm. Even though we had done our homework and had explained to all participants that we would be using Old Testament Bible stories in the second reading book, they were scared when they actually started working on them.

We Christians spent time praying. We talked it through with the Orma and showed them the specific stories we would be using. Then we saw the Lord's hand at work; they cooperated beautifully in including the Old Testament stories in the reader, despite the

---

9 Ibid. December 19, 1994. Archives.

fact that the divisional education officer (a Pokomo) was against their inclusion.

> I wish you could have seen us as we were working with the Orma on these stories as the education officer sat with his Koran at the end of the table comparing what we were writing with his holy book. It truly was a miracle that God allowed us to put together such reading texts in this 99.9 percent Muslim context. There were many good opportunities for verbal witness as well during the week, for which we praise God. One night two of the Orma men came to our home to watch the Jesus film. They were very touched.[10]

Besides the literacy primer, the Braaksmas were able to prepare with Orma help scores of audio-taped Bible lessons. These were great helps in both urban and bush ministries and certainly caused many an Orma to ponder and inquire after the Truth.

On occasion, during school breaks, the whole family accompanied Del out to the villages. Their first family safari was made in August 1995. How satisfying it was to get away from the crowded, bustling, coastal city and out among the rural Ormas!

The trip wasn't easy. It had rained and the track had become next to impassable. The truck bogged down in the mud more than once. But they slogged through, the passengers sometimes having to tramp through the muck to lighten the vehicle's load. It was all part of the adventure.

The Braaksmas spent two weeks out in the villages.

> Sometimes we slept in our tent, and other times on stick and cowskin beds right in the grass huts. But we basically lived with an Orma family, eating all of our meals of traditional Orma food together.
>
> Our boys spent most of their time out trapping birds with the Orma boys.... Bethany and her Orma girlfriends had fun making a small Orma playhouse. In the evening Orma kids lie around on cow skins telling folk stories (it is a very strongly oral culture), so our older kids entered into all of that and enjoyed it immensely.

---

[10] Del and Debbie Braaksma, from a letter to the author, n.d. Joint Archives of Holland, Hope College.

Del and I spent our time discipling Orma converts, visiting in their homes, sharing the new Bible tapes with inquirers, and meeting with the community elders regarding plans for literacy and animal health projects. Del was also involved in treating sick animals.

We had a wonderful time with the Orma people. Their hospitality is unbelievable! Living with these special folks really cements strong bonds of friendship between us. It's good to really be able to step into their world with the message of the good news without so many of the trappings of our Western culture.

Did we miss some of those [trappings]? Yes, of course! It was awfully good to be able to sit on a chair again (it's only three-inch-high stools there) and to take a real shower or bath (in the village it's a bucket and cup). But we realize that we would have missed much more if we had stayed at home.[11]

In order to multiply his effectiveness in the veterinary program, Del started a training course which he called Community Animal Health Volunteer (CAHV). The trainees were taught how to treat diseased livestock and how to give advice about animal husbandry. This was done in cooperation with the district veterinary office.

Del gave the course high marks in success. Twenty Ormas were trained to be CAHVs. They had participated with enthusiasm and really seemed to grasp the content of the lessons. They could now augment Del's services by spreading themselves simultaneously among the different villages. (The CAHV program has now been duplicated by the government's veterinary department.)

In addition to the course material, Del took the opportunity to teach spiritual truths as well. Each morning began with prayer and Bible study from the Old Testament using passages relevant to herdsmen. He wondered how such studies would be received. The Lord honored Del's witness. The Ormas' response was affirming. Several trainees even ventured to make favorable comments about these daily devotional periods.

God indeed has put his seal on this new approach for reaching the Ormas. There have been the inevitable obstacles along the way, such as the bowing out of the man who had been such a help to them in translation and in

---

11 Braaksma, "A Missionary Letter," October 18, 1995. Archives.

supervising literacy classes. He not only withdrew from his position; he seemed to be renouncing his Christian faith, even to the extent of trying to hamper the Christian witness.

On the other hand, an Orma Christian retreat held in 1996 was a time of joy and blessing for all who attended. One of the highlights was hearing the group of twenty Ormas singing Christian songs in their own tongue, songs that a Christian named Hussein had helped the Braaksmas to put together. These were not translations of Western hymns; rather, they were Orma words put to genuine Orma tunes. Debbie said they sang those songs "with gusto."

There was also encouraging response during the Bible study and discussion sessions and to the viewing of the Jesus film. And the testimonies of new believers were amazing.

Hussein told how his family disowned him when he became a Christian six years ago. They tried to poison him and refused to pay his school fees. With God's help, Hussein and his family are reconciled to the point where he is welcome in the family home, and his brother (who is downstairs as I write watching the Jesus film) has made a substantial contribution toward his expenses to attend Hope College this fall.[12]

The CAHV training program out in the countryside continued to flourish under Del's leadership. He found the Orma volunteers conscientiously on the job assisting with livestock health and management. More encouragement came from an unexpected source.

In Oda we have seen a real openness to the gospel. This village is known for its Muslim fundamentalists, and initially we were wary of working there. However, we have received a warm welcome, and now Nuri, a man from the most prominent family in Oda, has been living with us for the past two months [in Mombasa] as he takes a driving course [in town] and literacy lessons from Debbie. Nuri joins us every morning for a time of Bible study and prayer, and his brother is interested as well.

When we recall how skeptical we were about getting involved in Oda (and did so only at the chief's continued requests), we realize how little faith we sometimes have.[13]

12 Ibid. July 10, 1996. Archives.
13 Ibid.

The literacy program went into a slump for a while, much to the Braaksmas' dismay. But according to a later letter, Debbie was about to begin reading classes with a group of about sixty Ormas who live on the outskirts of Mombasa.[14]

Later news was encouraging:

> Some very exciting things are happening in Denyenye! Ormas are learning to read! The first several lessons were extremely difficult....But [they] are now actually able to read simple stories.
>
> There have also been opportunities to share our faith as part of the literacy program. I open each class with a simple prayer....The Muslims freely participate in typical Orma style, lifting up their hands and saying "amin" after every phrase....Earlier this week one of our class members returned after a long battle with tuberculosis. One of his classmates said, "Remember how Hagale (Debbie) prayed for him in literacy class? God answered that prayer!" And just this morning Adan, who is struggling desperately to read, said, "It would be good for you to pray for God to help me." We stopped right then and did just that.
>
> We are also delighted to see the upsurge of national (Kenyan) missionaries who are working with the Orma. When the Orma team evacuated [the Galole area] in 1992, we knew of no other missionaries who were reaching out to the Orma. Now there are sixteen!...We praise God for his faithfulness![15]

So it is that through many avenues of Spirit-led ministries, the Lord is bringing Ormas to himself, whether in the city or in the bush.

Those in Mombasa, liberated to a degree from the restraints of tribal mores, are freer to make their own decisions, freer to avail themselves of the myriad opportunities that city life affords—whether for good or for ill. But should they be wooed into Christian programs by a desire to learn to read, or to discover firsthand what Christianity is all about, or just to accept the wholehearted hospitality of a Christian home, they have then stepped into a circle of influence dominated by the love of Christ. Within that circle, miracles happen.

14 Ibid. October 11, 1996. Archives.
15 Ibid. March 25, 1997. Archives.

Out in Oda or in Daba in the very heart of Orma country, the Spirit can move with equal effectiveness through Christian concern for the physical well-being of the people and their herds, through the use of carefully crafted literacy material, and through simple, direct evangelism carried on among good friends.

God is at work among the Ormas in southeastern Kenya, calling out those who are to be added to his church. To help accomplish his purposes, he empowered two RCA couples to live the abundant life among these likable people who need desperately to know that their Isa is Jesus Christ, Son of God, and their Savior who really did die that they might truly live.

XXXII
Mission in Malawi

It took Rowland Van Es Jr. and Jane Vander Haar several years to wake up to the possibility that their repeated "chance" meetings might be a clue to God's grand design for them.

Rowland and Jane met when they were students at Hope College. Their paths paralleled again when Jane went to Sierra Leone in west Africa as a Peace Corps volunteer and Rowland was working in the same country as a community developer with the Christian Reformed World Relief Committee (CRWRC).

But it wasn't until they met again at Michigan State University, where they were pursuing master's degrees, that they realized this was no mere coincidence; their lives were meant to mesh. They were married on July 7, 1990.

Both Rowland and Jane come from staunch Reformed Church backgrounds. Rowland's grandparents, the Rev. Peter and Henrietta Van Es, were RCA missionaries for many years among the Mescalero Apaches in Mescalero, New Mexico. His parents, the Rev. Rowland and Judy Van Es, were RCA missionaries serving in Taiwan and later the Philippines.

Jane's maternal grandparents, the Rev. and Mrs. Herman Maassen, served many RCA pastorates. Her father, the Rev. Delbert Vander Haar, also was a pastor. Her mother, Trudy, was active through the years in leadership roles of denominational women's organizations.

So it was most fitting that these two young people were united to serve the Lord together. They went back to Africa in 1990 at the request of the Nkhoma Synod of the Church of Central Africa Presbyterian (CCAP), which needed help in establishing an effective development project that would raise many of the Malawians out of abject poverty. The CRWRC was their sponsor.

In 1993, the Van Eses, in cooperation with the CRWRC, were appointed as RCA world mission associates. Under these two organizations and also in partnership with the Southern Africa Alliance of Reformed Churches, this couple served with dedication and compassion. Their program and goals were daunting.

The twin plagues of drought and famine long have tormented many parts of Africa. In a 1995 letter, Jane described the all too familiar scene, reminiscent of similar hardship in Sudan, Ethiopia, Kenya, Somalia, and Zambia.

> It is extremely dry here....The river from which we get our water has stopped flowing and the water in the dam is getting lower every day. Water is being rationed, so we have water for only a few hours each evening. The hospital here is dealing with emergency cases only, and one of the boarding schools closed to reduce water demand. In the nearby villages people are walking several miles for water.[1]

Addressing such overwhelming need in the name of Christ was a large part of the Van Eses' mission. Rowland's position as program manager of this relief effort gave him responsibilities for projects in agriculture, income generation, health care, and community development.

Jane worked with the Women in Development program of the Nkhoma Synod. Together with her African counterparts, she assisted in working out and implementing community and church plans for church fundraising, home economics, poultry raising, and agricultural projects. Jane said about her African colleagues: "It is a joy to see my coworkers reaching out to the poor in a way that maintains their dignity and helps them to recognize that they are all God's children."[2]

[1] Rowland and Jane Van Es, "A Missionary Letter," November 19, 1995. Joint Archives of Holland, Hope College.
[2] RCA, "Profile in Mission," (Jane and Rowland Van Es Jr.), December 1993. Joint Archives of Holland, Hope College.

Such relief and development efforts demanded the best in teamwork, discipline, and accountability. Regular reports were made so that the parent agency was kept informed continually about the progress of various projects. Indicative of the scope of their ministry, the following outline report was sent in 1994:

Overview/Summary: Work was on target overall in Malawi. We are working with just over 1,000 individuals or families in our agriculture, income generation, health, literacy, and Women in Development programs. In addition we have diaconal development and institutional development goals and objectives. Rowland and Jane Van Es are the CRWRC staff in Malawi (1.5 positions).

Agriculture
Objectives:
1. To increase maize crop yield by 25 percent for 150 poor families in 2 areas
2. To increase agricultural income by 25 percent and improve nutrition for 20 families by increasing food availability and variety in 2 areas
3. To increase fuel wood availability and conserve the soil in 3 areas
Results:
1. Assisted 70 families in 1 area with soya bean and common bean seed. Also taught composting. Still awaiting harvest data but rains were poor this year in that area.
2. Assisted 11 families with pilot poultry cross-breeding project in 1 area. Also assisted 4 families with pilot goat cross-breeding.
3. Established church tree nurseries which raised 30,000 tree seedlings, and assisted one community with seeds that produced some 50,000 seedlings for 120 families.
Highlights/Analysis: Work going well at Njati village with 70 families despite poor rains which have affected yields. Goat pilot project is with Nkhoma hospital's nutritional rehabilitation unit. Community forestry project went very well.

Income Generation
Objectives:
1. To help 100 needy rural people in one new area
2. Continue to help 89 needy people in four villages [which were] helped in 1993
Results:
1. Have identified 70 people for assistance in one new area.
2. Have continued to assist the 89 participants and have begun collecting on old loans from 4 villages.
Highlights and Analysis: Slow repayment of old loans and consequent slow start to work in new area. Have done work on program details and policies as well as loan application procedures.

Health (PHC)
Objectives:
1. Reduce malnutrition of 200 children at 3 sites
2. Increase outreach of Nkhoma Primary Health Care committee
Results:
1. Assisted 24 old groups with loans for fertilizer for 1 acre each.
2. Assisted 13 new groups with loans for seeds and fertilizer.
3. Loans will be collected from 37 groups in August.
Highlights/Analysis: Loans distributed on time and a better effort to be made this year in gathering yield and income data from the groups at time of repayment. Poor rains may affect recovery rate....[3]

The principle of providing loans rather than outright gifts has proved to be effective in development work. It is not only a method for renewal of funds for further projects, but also a means of building up a recipient's sense of self-worth. It encourages a recipient to move out of the trap of poverty into a more abundant life.

Rowland and Jane expressed their gratitude for fine African friends and coworkers during those years in Malawi. Rowland speaks with particular

[3] Rowland Van Es Jr., "End of Year Report for Malawi," 1993–1994. Joint Archives of Holland, Hope College.

appreciated the Rev. Gande, whose father died when he was very young. He was raised by his blind mother, and an uncle saw to it that he was educated. He first became a teacher, then a minister. He married and had fourteen children, although half of them died. As a pastor he served several congregations, usually being paid in food or labor.

Later, as a colleague with those in development projects, he served faithfully and efficiently, an example to his fellow countrymen in both industry and selflessness. While the Van Eses were on leave one summer, Gande led a workshop for pastors in one of the presbyteries. He also had the delicate responsibility of collecting the agricultural loans that had been given to congregations to help support the pastors as well as women's programs.

Rowland said of his friend:

> [He is typical of] many in Africa who completely humble me. Most Africans will not even have a cup of tea without first praying and thanking God for it. They who have lost so many children, who have so few material possessions, who often go hungry, who are often sick, they are the first to thank and praise God even, and especially, for life's simple pleasures....
>
> The Rev. Gande...has had more sorrow, yet more joy; has been made weak, yet has more strength; has suffered more wars, yet has more peace; has been a victim of more hate, yet returns more love than most of us have ever given in the first place. He has seen extraordinary death, but he is more aware of ordinary life. For him all of life is sacred and holy.[4]

Rowland also expressed admiration for three women who worked hard to improve their lot, one through literacy and the others through a poultry project.

> Mrs. Bande was illiterate but faithfully attended the adult literacy class of Nkhoma Synod's Relief and Development Department for eight months. She passed and got her certificate. After finishing the course, she volunteered to teach a literacy class of her own and after just two weeks of training was leading two classes with thirty

---

[4] Van Es, from a letter to the author, November 26, 1996. Joint Archives of Holland, Hope College.

women in each. The classes meet four days a week for eight months. She is now in her second year of this voluntary work. Then there is Mrs. Phiri. This hardworking mother joined the Nkhoma women's group and wanted a way to provide more for her children. She asked for a loan of ten young chickens. She faithfully took care of them until they could lay eggs. Because they were an improved variety, she didn't sell the eggs but raised the chicks. And after just two years, she had a flock of seventy improved chickens. From the initial loan worth about five dollars, she now had a flock worth almost two hundred dollars. In addition she has the daily income of the eggs which she can sell for about ten cents each!

Another woman raised ten chickens and was eventually able to buy a goat with the profit. In Africa, if you have a cow, you are upper class; if you have a goat, you are middle class; if you have chickens, you are lower class. And if you don't have even chickens, you are the poorest of the poor. This woman had moved in just one year from being poorest of the poor to middle class. Now that's upward mobility![5]

In the midst of the myriad details of relief and development work, Rowland also found time for preaching on occasion. He and Jane also discovered what parenting is about. Jennifer was born in April 1993 and Michelle joined the family in January 1996.

Rowland enrolled at Western Theological Seminary in Holland, Michigan, but anticipated the day when their missionary career could be resumed:

> As I look forward to returning to Africa again after graduation, I hope I will be better at keeping my life in balance. I hope I will live more for others and less for myself. At the same time, I need to keep what I can do in perspective. I can help reduce suffering, but I will never eliminate it. I need to know my place. I need to let go and let God be God. I am not in control, he is. Maybe I need to do less and be more for God and for other people.[6]

Rowland and Jane Van Es, through their Christlike demeanor and farming expertise, made an impact upon the lives of the Africans they served

---

5 Ibid.
6 Ibid.

in Malawi. The African Christians in turn greatly impressed them with the depth of their spiritual understanding and with their gracious acceptance of whatever life dealt them, whether of joy or sorrow, adversity or blessing.

This kind of interaction is the stuff of which deep friendships are made. Such is the true missionary experience.

XXXIII
Volunteers for Jesus

There is an old hymn we used to sing in Dr. Albertus Pieters' college Sunday school class in Third Reformed Church, Holland, Michigan. We students would sing it with perhaps more gusto than consecration, but who can tell how many young people took these words to heart and gave themselves willingly to the Lord's service?

> A call for loyal soldiers
> Comes to one and all;
> Soldiers for the conflict,
> Will you heed the call?
> Will you answer quickly
> With a ready cheer,
> Will you be enlisted
> As a volunteer?

A volunteer for Jesus...

In recent decades, we have known scores of volunteers for Jesus who heeded the call in response to specific needs. Time and again we marveled at how the Lord provided volunteers with just the right aptitudes for the tasks at hand.

489

Throughout this book we have touched upon several volunteers by name or by church groups. However, we have not mentioned one group that went to Alale, Kenya, in February 1991. Morningside Reformed Church in Sioux City, Iowa, sent its pastor, the Rev. Louis Lotz, and seven members of the congregation for two weeks of volunteer service.

There were nurses who assisted Molly Beaver in her mobile clinic work, especially in inoculating children against measles and tuberculosis. Men with carpentry skills had come to make tables for the school and to help Larry McAuley build a garage that would house his tractors and tools.

It was a fortnight for which they had prepared well, and when it was over, they viewed their experiences and their accomplishments with satisfaction.

Verne Sikkema flew one of the MAF planes that went to Alale to fly the team back to Nairobi. Once airborne, Lotz looked down.

> ...there's the tin-roof garage and the picnic tables we made. They look very small. Verne turns south[east] and we fly out over the Rift Valley, the great African trough that extends like a long gash from the Dead Sea all the way across East Africa to Mozambique. Looking down at the endless hills, I think about the work we did at Alale. It seems small, insignificant. I didn't change Africa much. But Africa changed me.[1]

That has been the testimony of most volunteers: Africa changed them. And in many instances volunteers brought new life into church outreach programs as they shared their varied experiences.

Volunteers have gone to Africa from Reformed churches all over the United States:

Calvary, Ripon, California
Springs Community, Colorado Springs, Colorado
First, Denver, Colorado
Bayshore Gardens, Bradenton, Florida
Calvary, Orland Park, Illinois
First, DeMotte, Indiana
Adventure Life, Altoona, Iowa
First, Rock Valley, Iowa

[1] Louis Lotz, "Small Changes in Africa." Reprinted from the *Church Herald*, June 1991: 44, 45.

Zion, Sheffield, Iowa
First, Sioux Center, Iowa
Morningside, Sioux City, Iowa
First, Grand Haven, Michigan
Hope, Grand Rapids, Michigan
Remembrance, Grand Rapids, Michigan
Grace, Holland, Michigan
North Holland, Holland, Michigan
Trinity, Holland, Michigan
Fair Haven, Jenison, Michigan
Haven, Kalamazoo, Michigan
North Park, Kalamazoo, Michigan
Grace, Wyoming, Michigan
Pultneyville, Williamson, New York
Addisville, Richboro, Pennsylvania
Faith, Lynden, Washington
Calvary, New Berlin, Wisconsin
First, Randolph, Wisconsin

This is as complete a roster as research and memory could muster. There may have been others. Be assured that our gratitude to each one is without measure. All had a part in this great twentieth-century phenomenon called volunteerism.

Thank you to teachers who gave themselves for several months, or even for a year or two, to home-school our Missionary Kids (M.K.). Teresa Wyant already has received some notoriety by having been the schoolmistress of Water Tower Academy. Rosie Siver and Ardith Vande Berg taught the Braaksma children with dedication and courage at Titila during the unsettled years of *shifta* activity.

Kristen Vanderbilt, the Swart children's first teacher at Waldena, set a high standard for those who followed her. Kimberly Fenske and Lauri Glass met the challenge commendably. All of these young women were immensely popular with their students and furthered their education with distinction. Colleen Case also taught the Swart M.K.s for a short time.

Glen DuBois spent two years at Alale. He was a great favorite with the children there and did a good job of teaching. Susie Neevel, accompanied by her husband Jeff, and Leah Wissink both played significant roles in the

Alale children's schooling, as did Micki Vande Kamp, Barb Hubers, and Jay Haarsevoort.

To teach M.K.s, whether in the bush or at a boarding school such as Rift Valley Academy in Kijabe, Kenya, is a calling of the highest order. Not only do these volunteer teachers free parents for persevering in their daily mission activities, but they also can have a profound influence on the spiritual lives of their students, complementing and strengthening parental guidance. M.K.s are a mission field in themselves. Every missionary parent will agree.

Our deep thanks go to all those who gave so generously of time and talent to the task of promoting the education of our mission children!

Volunteer couples also made long-term contributions to the mission cause. The trend started with Frank and Gladys Kieft who went to Ethiopia again and again to put their faith in action. Larry and Betty Zudweg spent two years with the building program at Godare. Dave and Connie Fieldhouse also belong in this category, as well as Steve and Pam Kragt.

In 1977, while we were waiting to go to Kenya, we met a young man at Camp Geneva in Holland, Michigan. He responded to our challenge to volunteer in mission service by spending some weeks with us in 1979 at Ileret in northern Kenya.

Twelve years later Steve volunteered again. This time he came with a family: his wife Pam, who is a nurse, and four children. They all were committed to staying for two years, assisting in the work at Alale.

Everyone there was glad they had come. Molly Beaver described Steve and Pam as "a wonderful couple and we've all thanked the Lord many times for their being here! They help out so much and are flexible and willing to do whatever."

Their talents were put to good use. Steve's first major job was the building of a new classroom for the school. He also was asked to rebuild the school kitchens at Alale and at Kauriong down the road a few miles.

In between the major projects were the important minor ones of maintaining mission vehicles and machinery and, as time permitted, working on their Alale home to make it more comfortable for all seasons. Steve was what Swahili-speaking people call a *fundi* (skilled craftsman).

Pam was equally helpful. Molly especially appreciated her readiness to help in the clinic. One night, for example, a boy who had been shot in the chest walked to the clinic. Molly called Pam because she was "the only one who can ever get intravenous infusions in. It took a few tries (no blood pressure) but she did it."

One Sunday morning after Molly had gone off with a patient to the hospital in Kapenguria, Pam found herself presiding over two women about to give birth simultaneously. "It's never dull here," she remarked.

Besides using her nursing skill, Pam was also a great help to Linda McAuley when it was time to cut out and stitch together school uniforms for Pokot students. She was right there to assist in Linda's sewing class for women, too.

There is no gift, coupled with a willing heart and consecrated by the Lord, that cannot be used to his glory anywhere in the world, and perhaps most of all on the mission field.

So in skills, attitudes, and Christianity at work, God has favored Alale, and all our mission posts, with outstanding volunteers to give encouragement and support to each staff member.

The first time we met Marvin and Shirley Brandt was in 1982. They, along with Harold and Hank Stauble from Bradenton Reformed Church in Florida, had come to Alale to help lay the water pipeline. For the Brandts, this was the beginning of a career in volunteering.

The following year they returned to Alale for five months when the McAuleys were on home assignment. They "sat the station," but they didn't just sit. Working together they saw to it that the mission program continued to function smoothly. And when Larry and Linda returned, they found that all the interior finish work on the houses and clinic had been completed.

In May 1988 it was discovered that Shirley had ovarian cancer; she endured chemotherapy for a year. Earlier they had agreed to tend the Alale mission again in 1989 when the McAuleys were on leave. How could they honor that commitment? Close family members filled in for them.

Marvin's brother, the Rev. Julius Brandt (an RCA pastor) and his wife, Willie, from Lynden, Washington, gave themselves for five months of pinch-hitting service in the shadow of Kachegaleu and Lorsuk.

Toward the end of that period, Shirley was feeling well enough to accompany Marvin to Kenya to spend a few weeks with "Juke" and Willie at Alale and to go on safari with them before returning home to the United States. The next years of the Brandts' volunteering was a sacrifice of praise to the Lord for Shirley's healing.

In 1990 they spent six months at Kitale with the Church of Christ to build a children's home. For another six months over the following winter, they lived in Karen, a suburb of Nairobi, working again with the Church of Christ to build the Kimbalio guest house.

The Brandts went back to Alale for six months in 1993–94 in order to build two classrooms and a boys' dormitory. Another six months the next year was spent in Nairobi in behalf of an organization connected with the Church of Christ: Good News Productions, International in Joplin, Missouri. For this group they built a media center for a visual tape ministry.

This project led them back to Nairobi in 1995–96 to do a similar piece of work for PRMI: the construction of a new building for sound rooms and guest quarters for nationals who are recruited to read Scripture for recording. They also put a two-story addition on the already existing facility.

In looking back over the years and assessing the richness of their experiences, Marvin and Shirley Brandt conclude that:

> We have been very blessed as we do these assists to the missions and are glad to continue as long as the Lord keeps bringing us more opportunities to serve him. Before we began to do this, we had no idea that we had any qualifications or value on the mission field. It has given us a greater zeal for missions and we try to impart this to others also.
>
> The Lord led us to the mobile home park business [in Tavares, Florida] which has enabled us to maintain an income even as we are working overseas. We thank and praise God for these many blessings and the spiritual growth we have found as he uses us in his service.[2]

Many people and programs have benefited from Marvin and Shirley Brandt's dedication to volunteer service. May their tribe increase, even until the Great Day of the Lord's return!

Bill and Carolyn Overway were another intrepid volunteer couple. We touched on their debut at Waldena in January 1987. When they came out again a few years later, Carolyn played quite a different role: as the Scheenstra children's teacher; and as such, she belongs on the roll with the others who have furthered the education of our M.K.s, building solid foundations for future learning. At Kalacha Carolyn was Sarah Scheenstra's teacher. When the family moved back to Daba, her class enrollment

---

[2] Shirley Brandt, from a letter to the author, March 1, 1997.

doubled; Joshua had become of school age and joined his older sister in the classroom. Our sincere gratitude to this choice educator, too!

At both Kalacha and at Daba, Bill again had numerous opportunities to put his gifts to work. Bill is another *fundi* who has abilities as a jack-of-all-trades and master of them all. Such a person is an invaluable asset wherever the Lord sends him.

Bill and Carolyn volunteered again in 1996–97 at Alale while the McAuleys were on home assignment. They arrived shortly before Larry and Linda left for the United States in July 1996. They were amazed to find a couple there who had lived near them in Michigan for many years. But in order to meet, they had to travel all the way to a remote border post in western Kenya!

Emery and Sharon Blanksma went to Alale as volunteers in 1990. Molly Beaver was on home assignment that year. Sharon, a nurse practitioner, had been appointed to take charge of the clinic in Molly's absence, while Emery was available for any job awaiting his expertise. Alale was rich with two *fundis* on staff.

Another monthlong visit to Alale in 1993 further whetted their interest in the Pokot people and in missions. So when they heard a short time later that Molly would be terminating after ten years of vigorous, selfless service, the Blanksmas sensed that the Lord was gently but surely urging them to go beyond volunteering to become full-fledged missionaries.

It wasn't easy to come to a decision. Emery and Sharon both had good positions at Hope College. An even greater consideration was the family they would be leaving behind: three grown children and four grandchildren.

But the divine nudging continued. After much prayer, God's will for the Blanksmas was clear. They were appointed in April 1994 and were soon on their way to Alale to become ongoing members of the staff.

One of the first projects Emery was involved with was that of helping the Pokot Christians build a new church. Later, after the Overways arrived, he and Bill worked together in trying to improve the water system. The dry season was severe and more and more people were moving to the Alale area where water was available. The water supply from the spring on Lorsuk's slope was being overtaxed. With two *fundis* on the job, the problem was dealt with as far as possible.

The clinic was shorthanded; one of the nurses had left for another position, and Sharon needed help. So she was thankful when Jonah Kipkiyeny came and joined the clinic staff. He was a fine Christian and had had training as a male midwife. He was well accepted as a medical worker among the Alale people and gave Sharon the assistance she needed. They had plans for developing a community health program.

Into this happy situation came near tragedy. Jonah went into the dispensary one day in August 1996 to check the temperature of the vaccine. At that very moment one of the propane gas cylinders exploded. Jonah suffered second degree burns. He ran to the Blanksmas' house.

> I assessed him and told Carolyn to call for a Helimission helicopter from Kitale. Our phones had not been working for weeks, but Carolyn got through right away. Tom, our pilot, arrived within the hour. We flew through a rainstorm and were able to find the airport only because a mechanic who works with Tom had put his car on the runway with its headlights flashing to show us the way.

> Jonah was admitted to a hospital in Kitale for the night. The next morning we boarded the helicopter again and flew Jonah to Kijabe Medical Center, once more flying around rain and fog to get there safely. When we arrived at Kijabe, guess what God had waiting for us! A plastic surgeon who was there as a short-term volunteer!

> This experience has caused a great outpouring of prayer and concern from the Pokot.... In the midst of what could have been a tragedy, we have seen what God can do, and we praise him for it.[3]

In Sharon's January 1997 letter, she included a note from Jonah to all those who prayed for him:

> Greetings to all the Reformed Church brothers and sisters in America. Like you already know, I was burned in a gas explosion about four months ago. I sustained second and third degree burns. I underwent treatment at Kijabe Medical Hospital and was discharged after six weeks. I am well now, though I have some patches on my hands that are still white. I thank God that every day I am seeing improvement.

3 Emery and Sharon Blanksma, "A Missionary Letter," August 25, 1996. Joint Archives of Holland, Hope College.

I would like to thank you all for your prayers and support. I believe that God worked through you. May God enrich you with his love and blessing. May he grant you grace in all you do.

May God bless you,

Jonah Kipkiyeny[4]

We all join the Blanksmas, Overways, McAuleys, Jonah, and all the Alale Pokot in praising God for sparing Jonah's life and for all those who played such vital roles in his recovery.

Kudos to a special order of ordinary—and at the same time extraordinary—people who allow the comfortable routine of their lives to be interrupted, at whatever cost, in response to needs for help in far away places for Jesus' sake. What a great company they are!

Are there other volunteers waiting in the wings? Let them be alert for their cues. God will sound the call.

[4] Ibid. January 1997. Archives

XXXIV
The Journey Back to Omo

Dick and Donna Swart would have been content to remain in mission at Waldena for the rest of their years. They had won the confidence of their Orma neighbors and had several close friends among them. Waldena had become their home village. Knowing that they were there as God's messengers according to his design, they were at peace.

Even when the roving *shifta* bands posed chronic threats to the populace, and the post at Titila was in fact under attack on two occasions, temporary interim assignments were just that: temporary and interim. They prayed and fully expected to return to Orma country. But the Master was about to make his next move on the mission chessboard.

Who can tell when the journey back to Omo actually began? Certainly the potential was born when Mengistu Haile Mariam and his communist henchmen fled from Ethiopia in 1991. Was the germ of such an idea planted in the Swarts' minds when they responded to Donna's parents' need for assistance in reopening their work in the Ethiopian highlands? It wasn't until the fall of 1993, however, that two events took place that caused the idea to take root.

Word came to them through Roger Scheenstra that the three Orma mission posts had been thoroughly looted and vandalized in early November. That news sent their hopes plummeting, though they were still open to the possibility of returning if future bulletins were more favorable.

Then in December the Swarts made a family safari down to the Omo River a few days before Christmas. December was a vacation month, so the whole family was together. "Pa" and Grandma Giles traveled with them. Dick was eager to revisit and share his memories of the place where he and Jack had spent their vacations from 1965 to 1973, and where later he had spent over a year helping his dad with the Food From Wind project. On the third day out of Addis Ababa, they arrived on the east bank of the Omo.

It had been deemed advisable for us thirty years before to take the route that would bring us to the west bank, the same side as the police posts at Kalam and Namuraputh. Tortuous though it was, it was considered at that time to be less hazardous than the eastern track.

The North Koreans changed all that. With communists in power, the Koreans made an all-weather road down to the Omo in order to expedite the development of an irrigation project along the river. They had planned to grow cotton for export.

The project was a complete failure, but the improved road made for much easier access to the remote southwestern corner of Ethiopia. As a result the police post at Kalam and the nearby government center at Raati moved to the east side of the river. The new settlement is known Omo Raati. It was here that the Swart-Giles party arrived on that December day.

Turning south they made their way as best they could, generally following the river, but having to skirt defunct irrigation ditches, alternately losing the track and finding it again. They noticed in the villages along the way that something new had been added to the Daasanach huts: shiny pieces of aluminum had been tied on among the coverings of goatskins and mats. Continuing southward Dick kept peering across the river hoping to see the old mission buildings at Nyememeri.

Suddenly I spotted something that looked like some small buildings. I was sure we weren't at Nyememeri yet, but there it was! Standing out against the skyline was the skeleton of one of the domes of the house, and then the skeletons of the rest of the buildings began coming into view as we searched the opposite shore.

It was unbelievable! Nobody was living there! What I had thought were buildings were just parts of the inner walls of the volunteer house and Thompson's house [our Nuer advanced dresser from 1969 to 1976].[1]

[1] Dick Swart, from a letter to his family, December 1993. Joint Archives of Holland, Hope College.

Having made this discovery, Dick now wanted to find our old friend Achew. He was told that he lived in one of the villages they had passed on the way. So they drove back.

> What excitement and what an emotional time that was! All the ladies and kids crowded around first of all with their *hwaba ih*, an [idiom] of surprise. Then along came Achew with this expression of disbelief on his face. We just hugged American style. He looks exactly the same, just a little older. He and his wife wouldn't let go of my hands. It's hard to put this experience into words![2]

Achew rehearsed again what had happened at Omo River Post after we had left in 1977. The police took over, making the former mission post their base of operations for the next decade until the improved road was put in and the town was moved to the east side of the river.

At that time Omo River Post was plundered of all fencing and building material that would be useful in the new town. When the townspeople had all the spoils they wanted, the Daasanach stripped the place to its skeletal remains. That explained the presence of the aluminum on the outside of the huts in the villages.

Dick's and Achew's conversation turned to our family and events of recent years.

> Get a load of this! Can you believe that news of Jack's and the boys' deaths had gotten all the way to Nyememeri? They had heard that one of "Boh's" sons and his two sons had died in an accident and they knew that they had been in a small car and a truck had run into them. News travels, doesn't it? My telling them of it just confirmed it for them and everyone was saddened.[3]

Dick was intent on crossing the river for a closer look at the old mission site. There were two hindrances: the midday wind, which made the wide river too rough to risk such a venture; and the lack of a reliable dugout. A man named Toko had a leaky version that he said he would mend, but by late afternoon when the wind had abated somewhat, the wooden canoe was still in disrepair. So Dick helped Toko nail a piece of tin over another patch on

2 Ibid.
3 Ibid.

the rotten wood and then covered that with clay. Even so the dugout had several inches of water in it by the time they reached the far bank.

They made two such trips, viewing the ruins, the derelict vehicles, and doing considerable possibility thinking. The time to leave came all too soon.

While the others broke camp and got things all packed in the car, I sat and talked with Achew and others who came along. We talked about a lot of things, mostly what had happened in the past sixteen years since Mom and Dad left, the church and what had happened to it and all the believers. A number have clung to their faith through the years, while others have gone back to their traditional ways.

We discussed the matter of the mission coming back and bringing more teaching about the *girich Wakiet* (the path of God). They have a great desire to hear more and want very much for the mission to return.

It was hard to see our time coming to an end and I almost had to be dragged to the car....I wanted to gather even more information that might be helpful with regard to the mission returning there to work....I left them with the assurance that I would come again and also that the mission would be coming again, [either I myself] or somebody else. I had tears in my eyes as we drove off toward Omo Raati and the mountains beyond.[4]

With no encouraging news from Orma country, and the Swarts' year of assisting Donna's parents coming to an end in June 1994, the reopening of Omo River Post became more and more the focal point of their future hopes. As early as March 30, Dick made a flying, daylong survey trip to Omo. He was accompanied by two persons from the Society of International Ministries (SIM) and one from the *Kale Heywet* Church (KHC), the outgrowth of SIM's mission.

There had been some debate about whose "umbrella" should cover prospective mission work on the Omo. Two Ethiopian churches felt they had legitimate claims on the area: the Lutheran-oriented Ethiopian Evangelical Church *Mekane Yesus* (EECMY) with whom the Presbyterian Bethel Church had merged sometime in the 1970s; and the *Kale Heywet* Church.

4 Ibid.

Though Bob and I were seconded members of the American (Presbyterian) Mission during the years we served at Omo River Post, it had been determined at high mission levels not to tie the emerging Daasanach church to any indigenous church; rather, it would be up to the local church body to make that eventual decision. For obvious reasons the time for such a decision had not yet come. Dick and Donna, for their own good reasons, chose to be associated with SIM and KHC.

In June 1994 the SIM council met and gave their approval for the Swarts to pursue the reopening of Omo River Post. Dick attended another SIM meeting a few days later at which they discussed secondment matters and certain conditions that must be met. There were four conditions:

1. The project must have *Kale Heywet*'s full endorsement.

2. *Kale Heywet* must be committed to supply evangelists.

3. A partnership agreement must be worked out between SIM International and the RCA.

4. The secondment must be agreed upon by SIM USA, SIM Ethiopia, the RCA, and the Swarts.[5]

SIM Ethiopia would be responsible for working out the first two conditions. The RCA's Eugene Heideman would be involved in implementing the third and fourth.

We're more and more excited as the process continues to move forward. The groundwork won't begin until we get back [from our upcoming home leave, but] SIM felt it very important that I be involved from the beginning since I know the area, the people, some language, etc. It will take a few months after we get back, but that's what we were counting on anyway.[6]

That home leave was spent with us in Canon City, Colorado. Our daughter Merry, her son Jeff, and her daughter Sarah had just been with us for a year while husband and father, Dr. Don Hill, was on duty at Incirlik Air Force Base in Turkey. Dick's and Merry's families overlapped just long enough to help celebrate our golden wedding anniversary in August. (The actual date

---

5 Dick Swart, from a letter to his parents, June 12, 1994. Joint Archives of Holland, Hope College.
6 Ibid.

Our children came during the summer of 1994
to celebrate our 50th wedding anniversary.
Back row (from left): Bob, Morrie
Front row: Chloe, Dick, Merry, Gayle, Valerie

was June 21.) Valerie and her family from Michigan, Gayle and Richard from Massachusetts, and—big surprise!—Chloe from Dhahran, Saudi Arabia, all were with us as well. And Deb, graciously representing Jack and their sons, made our family gathering seem quite complete.

Bob and I gave thanks for all the marvelous years that brought us to that significant milestone, and for the strong and fruitful branches that were added to our family tree during that half century. We take pleasure in its comeliness and rest happily, as it were, in its shade.

We felt rich beyond measure in having two of those "branches" occupying our downstairs apartment in quick succession for a year and a half. Children going off to school, piano lessons, meals together—we love to remember.

In October Dick and Donna went to Charlotte, North Carolina, for a three-week orientation course at SIM USA headquarters. Their experience there was positive and affirming; they knew they had become members of a fine organization that would help them stay on course toward their objective, however long it would take.

They returned to Ethiopia right after Christmas.

The way back to Omo took much longer than anyone had expected. Opposition on the part of one group within EECMY brought dismay and certainly played a part in causing the lengthy delay. But interchurch negotiations, church to government talks, and project discussion all took time—so much in fact that SIM finally suggested an interim assignment. The SIM missionaries among the Mursi people at Makki were scheduled for home leave. Without other personnel to relieve them and the Swarts being available, it was a logical, as well as a mutually beneficial, move to make. It would also make it possible for the nurse at Makki to remain there.

Makki is located in the South Omo area, though considerably north of the Daasanach. Living there for six months would prepare Dick and Donna once again, as nothing else could, for a life in the bush they had not experienced for three years. They also would be in a position to become acquainted with government and church offices in Jinka—which they would be relating to once they were established at Omo. It seemed to be an ideal appointment. They gladly accepted it.

A month before the move, Dick, along with SIM Ethiopia Area Director Tim Fellows and Dr. Abby from the Ministry of Health in Jinka, made another survey trip, this time by helicopter. At close range they flew over the vast plains inhabited by the Daasanach.

> Upon landing in Nyememeri we met and greeted the many people who came out to see what the helicopter was all about. The history of the previous mission and what happened to it…was explained to Dr. Abby. In response to Dr. Abby's many questions, the local people spoke very highly of the previous mission work and would like very much for missionaries to return there.…
>
> From Nyememeri we flew south along the Omo River…to get an idea of the population density and to seek out other village settlements. There were several settlements along that stretch of the river with by far the largest one being adjacent to the border [police] post of Namuraputh. The Namuraputh community I would estimate at around three thousand. The latter occupied both sides of the right fork of the river delta.[7]

---

[7] Dick Swart, "Daasanach Survey," May 15–16, 1995. Joint Archives of Holland, Hope College.

Once the survey had been completed they returned to Jinka, leaving Dr. Abby there and picking up Barbara Hartwig (nurse at Makki) and another person from the Ministry of Health (MOH). They then flew to Makki where they spent the night. While the MOH representative inspected the clinic, Dick was given the "grand tour" of Makki. He appreciated this opportunity to preview the place and to learn what was expected of them while they were in residence there.

[Back in Jinka] Tim was able to meet with church leaders, and then later in the morning we met with Dr. Abby to discuss the previous day's survey. Dr. Abby expressed an interest in any help he can get for the South Omo region. He said the government had no immediate plans for any new work in the area....He mentioned that *Mekane Yesus* had submitted a proposal for working in the Daasanach area but that there had been no final agreement as yet. He suggested that we meet and discuss with them how both organizations might work together to meet the needs of the Daasanach in South Omo....He suggested submitting a proposal and he would bring it before the [Ministry of Agriculture Committee, an Ethiopian board]. From his perspective he is willing to negotiate with both organizations but doesn't want any overlap....

Later in Arba Minch [capital of Gamo Gofu Province] Tim Fellows and I had some discussion about the previous day and our morning meeting with Dr. Abby....We questioned whether it was through medical work that we should be pursuing [an opening for ministry] among the Daasanach. We can't begin to compete with *Mekane Yesus* when it comes to money, project size, and capital investment.

Perhaps we should look at different avenues such as church planter, church facilitator, or church activities coordinator for Daasanach work. These avenues would not be tied to any government program and would allow for much more freedom to [serve] the church. But it also contains a certain amount of risk.

Say we were to be granted a work permit as one of the above; the risk would come at the time of renewal. The committee may feel that we are not doing anything or enough for the good of Ethiopia and deny the renewal....

[In any case it was decided] in Jinka that the *Kale Heywet* Church would meet with the *Mekane Yesus* Church in Arba Minch to discuss [how both churches could work] in the Omo River valley among the Daasanach people.

Respectfully submitted by:
Dick Swart[8]

Concerning the role designation, whatever it was, which would appear on his work permit, Dick had some philosophical thoughts:

> I think we need to be straightforward in why we are here. We don't fool anybody by presenting some wonderful, costly project with [the implied inducement]: "Look what we are going to do for your country." We ought to begin with our main purpose of working with the church in the spread of the gospel, and if we can help in other ways, we will see what we can do.[9]

Before they started out for Makki, Dick's work permit was approved. He was granted the title of station manager. In this capacity he was at liberty to engage in his top priorities and also carry out subsidiary projects for the benefit of the Daasanach.

The Swarts arrived at Makki the last week in June 1995. They were glad to be away from Addis Ababa and the raucous throngs of the city. Now they enjoyed watching the Mursis dance in the moonlight, hearing the many birdcalls, the bark of baboons, and the rolling, frog-like croak of colobus monkey troops in the tops of trees at dawn. Their eyes feasted upon the varied terrain of mountains, grasslands, and jungle through which the Makki River flowed. Mursi country was so much greener and luxuriant than the lower reaches of the Omo; they needed to store up images of lushness for future mental viewing. Yet, as they would discover, Omo was not without its own kinds of beauty.

On August 11, 1995, there was a meeting at the *Kale Heywet* Church Central Office in Addis Ababa with the Ethiopian Evangelical Church *Mekane Yesus*. There were eight mission and church representatives who attend the meeting:

---

[8] Ibid.
[9] Dick Swart, from a letter to his parents, May 25, 1995. Archives.

Dr. Mulatu Baffa: KHC general secretary (chairman)
Rev. Iteffa Gobena: EECMY gospel ministry director
Ato Yema Babeno: EECMY SWS president
Ato Bikela Nykalse: EECMY evangelist in Omorate [sic]
Ato Degu Deklabo: KHC representative from Southern Omo
Mr. Tim Fellows: SIM Ethiopia area director
Mr. Bill Harding: SIM Ethiopia outreach ministry administrator
Mr. Dick Swart: SIM Ethiopia missionary in Southern Omo[10]

The discussion of the day swirled and eddied around the issue of the two churches' desire to minister among the Daasanach. Though the talks at times were heated as misunderstandings and disagreements were aired, the tone for the most part was conciliatory. They honored the Swarts' vision for mission among the Daasanach and recognized the advantage of Dick's knowledge of the area and the tribal language. There was a general consensus that both churches could be involved. The group came to these conclusions:

1. Those who are directly impacted by the decision should be the ones who determine how KHC and will relate in the outreach to the Daasanach. It is the role of the central offices of KHC and EECMY to assist where needed and give their blessing to those implementing the outreach. Ato Degu and Ato Yema and other necessary local church leaders will discuss this issue and come to a mutually agreeable plan which will limit future disagreements. They will decide how to reach the Daasanach and ways that they can both work in Southern Omo and yet avoid duplication.

2. What to do with the Nyememeri property is left up those who have the clearest understanding of the situation. The KHC and EECMY leaders at the local will decide if the property should stay with EECMY or be given to KHC for their use.[11]

The months at Makki were busy and happy ones. Donna assisted Barbara Hartwig at the clinic. Dick had a full-time job just in keeping the jungle from

---

[10] Minutes on Meeting Between Ethiopian Evangelical Church *Mekane Yesus* and *Kale Heywet* Church Concerning the Daasanach Ministry, August 11, 1995. Joint Archives of Holland, Hope College.
[11] Ibid.

encroaching on the mission. Rank growth had already taken over the airstrip, so clearing that vital link to the outside world was among the first orders of business. Other jobs he had been asked to do included the plastering of the health assistant's house, finishing the installation of a new well, and continuing with the agriculture projects. He was also advisor to the KHC evangelists who ministered among the Mursis. The months passed swiftly.

In January 1996 it was time for the Makki personnel—the Carlsons and the Geddes—to return to Ethiopia. However, because the Geddes were delayed with visa problems, only the Carlsons arrived back on schedule. With the Omo negotiations still dragging on, the Swarts gladly accepted the Carlsons' invitation to stay on at Makki for a few more weeks. Besides, with an overland survey trip at Omo planned for mid-March, Makki would be a more convenient launching point than distant Addis Ababa.

The survey was carried out on March 11–15. Dick and his son Caleb and Ato Degu from KHC in Jinka drove down to Omo. They took mail from Jinka to deliver along the way. At Alduba they picked up six sacks of grain for KHC evangelists at Dimeka, Turmi, and Omo Raati. (A person's means of transport in Africa is not solely for his personal use; it's a service vehicle for the good of everyone along the route.)

It was a thrill for Dick and Caleb to see the Omo River again. Caleb called it "the most beautiful body of water I will ever see." Those are true Swart sentiments!

The rest of the party were flown to Omo Raati on an MAF plane piloted by another Vern: Vern Bell. They arrived the following morning. Bill Harding, SIM outreach coordinator; Stan Tuck, South Omo District ministries coordinator; Ato Samuel, KHC Arba Minch regional director; and James Korie, a Daasanach and presently a Bible school student from Kenya were on that flight.

The purpose of this overland survey was "to take a look at the greater Daasanach area, to get an idea of the felt needs of the people, and to seek out the most strategic location for work and reaching out with the gospel."[12]

After receiving permission from the local Mikr Bet (government office), the team visited several population centers to the east and south, far back

---

[12] Dick Swart, "Daasanach Overland Survey," March 11–15, 1996. Joint Archives of Holland, Hope College.

from the Omo. One of these centers, called Anyiriech, and considered to be the very heart of that area, was located along a dry riverbed.

There is a year-round water supply about two meters deep in the riverbed. There would be a potential for water development and perhaps some small-scale irrigation. Further testing would determine the amount of water available. We spent the night there fighting the hunting spiders that were drawn to our light. [According to Caleb's written report, there were "tons of hunting spiders."]

Wednesday morning we met with the people. Their desires were for the Word of God to be taught and for assistance with water for irrigation. It was a good visit.[13]

Another day they drove south along the river, going as far as they could below where the Omo forks and the delta begins. At Lotobolo the extent of their fact-finding was limited to the people's word that they had refused to permit the MYC (shortened form of EECMY) "to set up a health post there because that would mean fencing off an area, and they wanted to keep the entire area for their cattle." So the group didn't pursue matters further; they didn't want to raise fears or unwarranted suspicions.

On the last day they headed for Nyememeri....

...feeling the need to get there in the morning to be assured that there would be a dugout canoe available for our use. We made arrangements with a canoe owner for the use of his craft....We spent the better part of the day in Nyememeri looking at the old site and meeting with the people.

"Yes, we know 'Boh' and the old station belongs to him and any of his descendants," [they declared].

We then went back from the river to the village and were met by the Kebele (government division) leader who was irate and unreasonable for a time until the others there were able to calm him. He finally understood who we were and what we had come for. He then became polite and very supportive and invited us to come any time. We left on very good terms.

We returned to Omo Raati in the late afternoon so as to have a service with the KHC people there. It was a very significant event

13 Ibid.

for the church there to have so many visitors; it was a great
encouragement to them. They encouraged us to pray for the
Daasanach people and the future work among them.[14]

Before leaving, the survey team called in again at the Mikr Bet.
They asked the official to write a letter that would indicate local
government support for KHC to minister among the Daasanach.
The plane came for the four team members. Dick and the others
left shortly after. Acting as taxi and ambulance along the way, they
made fair progress and reached Makki at 8:30 in the evening "tired,
but greatly encouraged."

In Dick's report he stated the group's conclusions:

> ...the general consensus of our survey team was that Nyememeri
> is a vital and strategic location for our work. Some reasons for this
> would be: the past history and family ties there (which seemed very
> important to the Daasanach); the people's desire for us to be there;
> the size of the village and its "permanence"; the Kebele leader's
> invitation; the Mikr Bet's support; and the ministry possibilities.
> There seems to be a hunger for the Word throughout the Daasanach
> area which is exciting. Other areas of need mentioned were
> medical and agricultural.[15]

There was only one indication of opposition. It came from MYC personnel
at Omo Raati. If on this survey trip the team had found a suitable mission
site far to the east, they would have experienced no resistance from MYC.
But the team's findings confirmed those of earlier surveys made over thirty
years before: that Nyememeri offered opportunities for the most effectual
and diverse means of serving the Daasanach. Dick concluded his report with
these words:

> I am sorry for this difficulty [the opposition] but as a result of this
> survey trip, I feel ready to go on to the next steps of pursuing a
> proposal to begin a ministry among the Daasanach people of South
> Omo.[16]

---

[14] Ibid.
[15] Ibid.
[16] Ibid.

*The Swarts' temporary home at Omo which Dick
designed and prefabricated in Addis Ababa*

Dick moved ahead in drafting his project proposal. But it would still be months before the waiting for documents and approvals was over. These months, however, were not spent idly.

The drawing board was in constant use. Dick drew up plans for a small temporary house and a larger permanent house and prefabricated them. He designed a new type of windmill with pump for irrigation projects along the Omo. And he constructed an eight-by-thirteen-foot raft for hauling goods across the Omo. (The old Swart Craft, which had been designed and assembled by the Christian action group at Trinity Reformed Church in Holland, Michigan, and was used for ferrying vehicles and all kinds of freight across the river in the "old days," had been rescued from the communists by our friends of the Swedish mission and was now way upriver near their area of work.)

It was therapy during the waiting period to be preparing for the eventual move.

One week in May Dick and Donna knew that many prayers had been answered as they were given signs that the opposition had crumbled.

Donna and Caleb were shopping at a grocery store in Addis Ababa. The nurse who personified the MYC antagonism at Omo Raati had come to town and was also shopping there. Donna wondered if this meeting would lead to further confrontation. Quite to the contrary! She was most cordial, reminding Caleb that "thanks to your grandfather we have mangos down there" and assuring Donna that "there will be a warm welcome waiting for you when you come."[17]

That very afternoon Bill Harding had a long meeting with the head of the Norwegian Lutheran Mission, part of MYC. Among other things they discussed was the Daasanach issue.

His attitude was amazingly in favor of our working there and cooperating with them. He seemed to realize the tremendous task of reaching the Daasanach and that they couldn't do it alone. He also spoke of the tremendous significance to the Daasanach of my returning to work with them. He even said to Bill, "You need to ask for that land back"—meaning the old mission station. He said they have no plans to use it and neither does MYC. "For that place to be occupied and productive again would be very significant to the Daasanach, too," he said....

So it's really been a good week of encouragement and we feel many prayers are being answered. We have a sense of there being some progress made and that has really lifted us up.... Let's not stop praying about it, though.[18]

More months went by. In August the Swarts were told that their papers all seemed to be in order and the signing of the agreement was awaiting only a supporting letter from Jinka—a letter, that is, approving Dick's project proposal.

By the end of August it was time for Leah and Caleb, after a month's vacation, to fly off to Rift Valley Academy at Kijabe, Kenya, to be gone for three months. Caleb had hoped fervently that he could be involved in the move to Omo. It was not easy for him to go off to school with that desire unfulfilled.

In October they were still waiting for the letter from Jinka. They did however receive a supporting letter from Omo Raati, well written and including an invitation to come.

[17] Swart, from a letter to his parents, May 24, 1996. Archives.
[18] Ibid.

That was a real boost. We're not discouraged. The time has not been wasted. I keep making preparations for going, getting a lot of things done here that I would have had to do on site if we had gone before now. It has probably been easier to do them here.[19]

On November 20 it happened: the final agreement had been signed and was in hand. What rejoicing and thanksgiving! And that wasn't all. On November 28 Leah and Caleb arrived home from school (having flown to Addis Ababa on the same flight as returning survivors of the Ethiopian Airlines hijacking over the Indian Ocean).

By December 3 the family was all packed and on its way to Omo. Some stops had to be made along the way, but on Caleb's fourteenth birthday, December 9, they reached the Omo River. Could there have been a more perfect birthday gift for a lad who had been so eager to be in on all the initial adventures of arrival: hauling gear and household effects across the river on the raft (powered by an outboard motor), and setting up camp under the neem tree at the old mission site? The Lord did a remarkable thing in making it possible for the whole family to be together for those earliest days of reopening Omo River Post.

On the very day they arrived, Donna wrote us a letter. Among other things she said:

> One of the church leaders [at Omo Raati] was saying that the talk of the town among the Daasanach is that "Boh's" son Diggi has come and that they are all rejoicing. The church leaders said too that only God could bring this to pass. Isn't that the truth![20]

Amen and amen! When Bob and I left Omo twenty years before, the communists were well entrenched throughout Ethiopia after only three years of rule. The Derg was in full control at the top, and every village had its Kebele leader (a vestige of which remained at Nyememeri) who wielded absolute power in his bailiwick. We had no expectation that the country in our lifetime would be open to the unhindered spread of the gospel.

But again God proved himself to be the Sovereign Lord. Seventeen years after communism was imposed upon the Ethiopians, it was vanquished by rebel forces within the country, and Ethiopia began anew to welcome Christian missionaries inside its borders.

---

19 Ibid. October 6, 1996. Archives.
20 Donna Swart, from a letter to her parents-in-law, December 9, 1996. Joint Archives of Holland, Hope College.

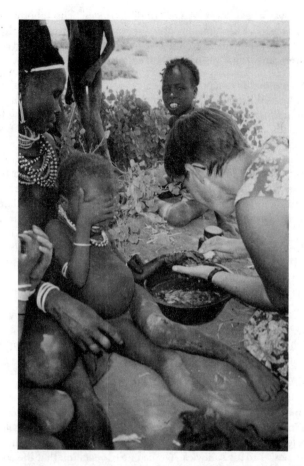

Donna treats a Daasanach child afflicted with a badly burned hand

Ironically it was church politics that delayed the Swarts in their journey
back to Omo. But lengthy though the process was, God was working out his
purposes in giving Dick time to complete the prefabrication of two dwellings
and the building of an essential river raft; in healing relationships between
EECMY and KHC before Omo River Post was actually occupied; and in
allowing the whole family to take that momentous journey together.

Dick's and Donna's unfaltering faith and unflagging perseverance under the unfailing direction of Almighty God had led them at last to their longelusive but now-realized destination.

It is awesome—and I mean awesome in the true sense of the word—to consider how God has moved in behalf of those who dwell in the Omo River valley. More than fifty-five years ago, our good friend, Captain Richard E. Lyth (who was the district commissioner for Pibor District in the AngloEgyptian Sudan), entered the British foreign service. During the Italian occupation of Ethiopia, when it was feared that such aggression might spill over into Sudan, Captain Lyth was posted in southeastern Sudan at the Ethiopian border. He and his troops were untiring in patrolling that highland area. From those high places they could look down over southwestern Ethiopia and the Omo River valley. The captain kept a journal.

On March 3, 1996, Dick Lyth's wife, Nora, wrote us a letter from their home in England. She expressed their pleasure in hearing of the Swarts' intent to move on to Omo and added: "I just read in the journal of Dick's walking over the Ethiopian highlands in 1941 looking down on the mighty Omo River valley and claiming it for the Lord in faith."

God has answered that prayer. Since then many hitherto unreached tribes in that valley have been blessed by the gospel; many have come to faith in Christ. And Dick Lyth's prayer is continuing to be answered today as his namesake, our son Dick Swart, and his wife Donna valiantly take up the ministry among the Daasanach in the lower Omo River valley to challenge them once more for Jesus Christ.

On this joyful note we bring to a close this anthology of selected stories and events in the lives of missionaries of the Reformed Church in America whom God called to serve him in African countries up the Nile and beyond.

A half-century has passed since the first contingent set sail in January 1948 for that great continent. Scores of "sent ones" have followed, and God has been building up his church through the variety of their spiritual gifts and services, anointed and empowered by the Holy Spirit.

The third millennium is nearly upon us. Until that great Day of the Lord when Christ shall come again, God will continue to sound the call to missionary endeavor. He will keep on calling the Reformed Church to remain faithful in responding to the world's need for the gospel. He will keep on calling individuals and families to go in his name for the sake of the risen Savior.

Should he call you, what will be your answer?

Epilogue

In December 1997, Bob and I, with Gayle and Richard, made a nostalgic journey back to Africa. We spent three incredibly happy weeks with Dick and Donna Swart and their children on the Omo River in Ethiopia. We were amazed at what they had accomplished in just one year. The compound had been reestablished, rising proud amid the ruin of the former mission post. The windmill project was off to a good start, with one mill of Dick's own design and fabrication already operational. And two evangelists from the indigenous church, Kale Heywet, were expected to join the team soon.

It was a pleasure, too, to meet again our old Daasanach friend, Achew. Now a graying elder and a grandfather several times over, he was the same quiet, dependable person we had known—and as loyal a friend to Dick's family as he had been to ours. Best of all, he remained a believer and respected spiritual leader of his community.

The joy of those days at the Omo was deja vu of the highest order. We were blessed beyond measure.

Next stop: Nairobi. We were scheduled to spend nearly three weeks in Kenya. One day we flew in an AIM-Air Cessna to Daba in Orma country to visit Roger and Susan Scheenstra and their four children. The older children's teacher, Kara Vander Kamp from Midland, Michigan, also was there.

516

It was heartening to see firsthand that the ministry at Daba was moving forward after many years of insecurity in the region due to shifta activity. In Nairobi itself, we had several contacts with Boniface and Deb (Swart) Muriithi, who head up an effective work among the deaf in Nairobi; with Harry and Pat Miersma, who serve as counselors with the summer Institute of Linguistics; with Karen Hoffman from DeMotte, Indiana, engaged in orientation for a two-year stint of medical work in Daba; and with Julius Kamau, at one time a fellow worker with Jack Swart at Portable Recording Ministries. ("Jack was my brother. I will never forget him. He changed my life," Julius said.)

In Nairobi, to my surprise and delight, I "found" Dr. Marilyn J. Scudder when we were all dinner guests at the home of the Miersmas. (Marilyn was in the Nairobi area for a medical conference, which also was attended by the Miersmas and Dr. Harvey Doorenbos of Aira, Ethiopia.) Though her name and address were in the RCA directory under World Mission Associates, my attempts to contact her for inclusion in this work had proved fruitless. This was so disappointing, because she remains eminently qualified for inclusion. Furthermore, a chapter title such as "A Scudder in Tanzania" surely would have interested those for whom the name of Scudder conjures up scenes and tales of India and the Middle East. Yet Marilyn Scudder has worked for twenty-eight years as an ophthalmologist in Tanzania, Africa.

To put her in genealogical perspective, Marilyn is the daughter of the Rev. Lewis and Dorothy Scudder of the Arabian mission; sister of Lew, a missionary to Cypress with his wife, Nancy; cousin of Dr. Ida Scudder of Vellore, India; and therefore related to the whole family of missionary Scudders. She followed in their train but found her calling on another continent.

In January 1970, Marilyn went to Tanzania in a *locum tenens* capacity at Mvumi Hospital under the London-based Royal Commonwealth Society for the Blind (later known as Sight Savers). Her nine-month commitment extended to sixteen.

In 1972, Christ Church of Oak Brook, Illinois—with ties to the Reformed Church in America—became her enthusiastic supporter.

From February 1973 to September 1993, Dr. Scudder served as a teacher at the Kilimanjaro Christian Medical Center (KCMC) at Moshi, a school run by the Christoffel Blinden Mission (CBM). In 1993, still under the auspices of CBM, she returned to Mvumi with the specific assignment of building up the eye department. Her superior, Dr. B. Isseme, was a student of hers at KCMC.

In retrospect, Marilyn Scudder sees her career in Tanzania as God's answer to a multifaceted petition she had prayed many years ago.

In essence, this was her prayer: "Lord, if it's your will for me, I'd like to be in mission somewhere overseas—in a place where my knowledge of Arabic would be an asset. I'd like to be near mountains, and at the same time, not far from the sea. And Lord, if my job would call for some traveling around, I'd really like that, too, but I do want to be in your will!"

Marilyn found her heart's desire in Tanzania, and as the years unfolded she began to realize that God had answered that long-ago prayer fully. Tanzania's official language, Swahili, and Arabic are closely related. At Moshi she lived close to Mount Kilimanjaro, the highest mountain in Africa. Always she was near enough to the coast to satisfy her longing for the sea. And her skills as an ophthalmologist took her on frequent "eye safaris." Thus, her hope to be on the move also was granted.

I regret that this brief sketch of Dr. Marilyn Scudder has had to be tacked on in the epilogue rather than appearing in the body of this book. Opportunities for lengthier interviews and correspondence surely would have yielded a wealth of fascinating facts and anecdotes that could have filled a chapter and more.

Our Africa safari in Kenya was over on schedule, but our sojourn was extended by another month. The night before we were to have left for home, Bob was admitted to Nairobi Hospital. Two CT scans and an MRI later, he submitted to a craniotomy to remove a large hematoma. The surgery was successful, giving us confidence that, by God's grace and the power of prayer, Bob's recovery will include full restoration of his faculties and former vitality to the glory of our Savior Jesus Christ. To him be all the praise!

Maps

Ethiopia

Kenya

Ileret

Lake
Turkana

Lodwar

Kalacha

Gotab

Alale

Kapenguria

Kitale

Elderet

Nakuru

Kijabe

Tana River

Nairobi

Mulango

Machakos

Galole River

Hola

Daba

Garsen

Waldena

Titila

Malindi

Mombasa

Malawi

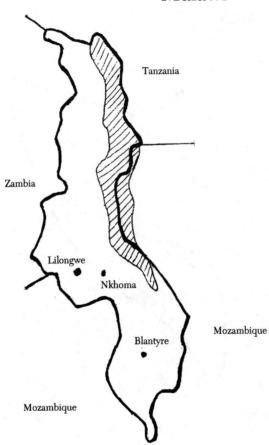

Somalia

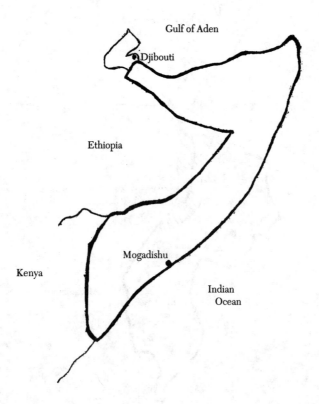

Sudan

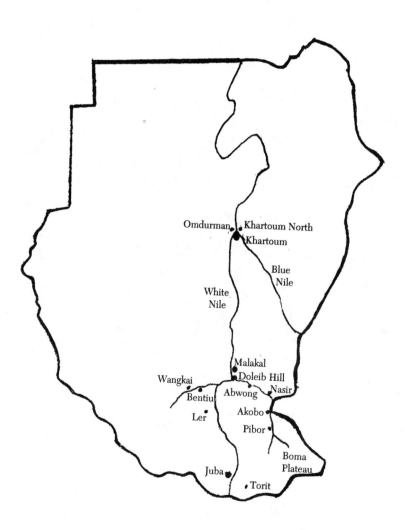

Zambia

Glossary

Aalany: Low bush with round, succulent green leaves.

Aba: Full black robe worn by Arab women.

Amin: Amen.

Astamari: Teacher.

Ato: Mister.

Balokole: Members of the revived church in Uganda.

Baraza: A meeting.

Bulgur, or burgul: Cracked wheat.

Chai: Tea boiled with milk and sugar.

Chapati: Flat, fried bread.

Chilikook: A bird of the barbet family.

Dari: Witch doctor.

Debe: Five-gallon kerosene tin.

Demoi, or dimoi: String of beads used for a bride price.

Demoriya: Unbleached muslin.

Derg: Ruling committee in communist Ethiopia.

Doleib: A palm tree.

Duka: Shop; store.

Dulab: Wardrobe; clothes closet.

Durra: Sorghum; milo.

Eendracht: Unity.

Felucca: Sailing vessel on the Nile.

Ferenji: Foreigner.

Fil Wuha: Boiling or bubbling water; hot springs.

Fundi: Skilled craftsman; handyman.

Gahwa: Coffee.

Gallinya: Language of the Galla people.

Gamoosa: Water buffalo.

Girich Wakiet: Path of God.

Goola: Small clay water container.

Haboob: Sandstorm.

Hakim: Doctor.

Harambee: Cooperation; working, pulling together.

Heglig: Thorny tree with sticky, bitter fruit.

Huko: Over there somewhere.

Hwaba ih: Daasanach expression of surprise.

Injera: Flat, spongy Ethiopia bread.

Ishi: Yes; OK.

Jebel: Hill.

Jellabiya: Long, flowing garment worn by Arab men.

Jiko: Small charcoal-burning stove.

Kaal: Enclosed yard.

Kale Heywet: Word of Life.

Kapenta: Tiny dried fish.

Kebele: Local government division under communism.

Keis: Priest; pastor.

Khor: Inlet that fills when a river is in spate.

Kwacha: Zambian money.

Lubia: Green, leafy ground cover.

Maalish: Never mind.

Manyatta: Village.

Matungtoch: Tamarind tree.

Mawn: To plaster.

Mekane Yesus: House of Jesus.

Mikr Bet: Government office.

Minfudlik: Please; if you please.

Mosi-oa-Tunya: Smoke the thunders.

Mwende: Beloved one.

Mye'de: Tree with sweet, sticky, orange berries.

Mzee: Old man (a title of respect).

Neem: Tree imported from India.

Nemoliya: A screened food safe.

Nsima: Thick, stiff cornmeal mush (Zambia).

Nug, or nugi: A nut from which oil is made.

Nyayo: Footsteps.

Nyijobi: Child of a buffalo.

Nyingu: Child of a lion.

Nyiray: Child of a hippopotamus.

Orominya: Language of the Oromo people.

Oromiya: Oromo homeland.

Pole sana: Very sorry.

Quelea: Small birds that gather in vast flocks.

Rais: Captain of a river steamer.

Rondavel: Metal prefabricated building.

Safari: Trip; journey.

Shaddoof: Irrigation mechanism.

Shifta: Armed bandit.

Sufuria: Tin cooking pot.

Suq: Market made up of many small shops.

Tef: Fine grain used in making injera.

Tukl: Round, mud-walled thatched house.

Ugali: Thick, stiff cornmeal mush (Kenya).

Ujamaa: Principle of socialism.

Wat: Hot pepper stew eaten with injera.

Wazee: Old men (plural of Mzee).

Wuha: Water.

Yeheywet Birhan: Light of Life.

Yu hai: He lives.

Zeer: Large clay water filter.

Index